The Road From Rome

1896
Apostolicae Curae (Anglican orders declared invalid)

1915
Christian Unity Octave—prayers for "return" of separated Christians

The road from action
(Life and Work)

1928
Mortalium Animos (warning against involvement in pan-Christian activities)

1925
Stockholm: "The Church's responsibility for the total life of mankind"

1935
Abbé Couturier suggests new form for Unity octave prayers

1938
Una Sancta Brotherhood for ecumenical conversation

1937
Oxford: "Church, Community and State"—proposal to merge with Faith and Order

1945
Unitas, ecumenical center established in Rome

1948
(no observers at Amsterdam)

1949
Instruction of the Holy Office, increasing ecumenical possibilities

1952
observers at Lund

1954
(no observers at Evanston)

1959
Pope John announces Vatican Council II

1961
observers at New Delhi

1962
Vatican Council II opens (non-Catholic observers present)

1963
observers at Montreal

1964
Vatican Council II decree *On Ecumenism*

1965
The Joint Consultation Committee established by the W.C.C. and the Vatican Secretariat for Christian Unity

1965
conclusion of Vatican Council II

1966
observers at Geneva

THE ECUMENICAL REVOLUTION

Books by Robert McAfee Brown

OBSERVER IN ROME

AN AMERICAN DIALOGUE (with Gustave Weigel, s.j.)

THE COLLECTED WRITINGS OF ST. HERETICUS

THE SPIRIT OF PROTESTANTISM

THE SIGNIFICANCE OF THE CHURCH

THE BIBLE SPEAKS TO YOU

P.T. FORSYTH: PROPHET FOR TODAY

The ECUMENICAL REVOLUTION

An Interpretation of the
Catholic-Protestant Dialogue
by *Robert McAfee Brown*

BASED ON THE
WILLIAM BELDEN NOBLE LECTURES
FOR 1964–65

GARDEN CITY, NEW YORK
DOUBLEDAY & COMPANY, INC.
1967

Grateful acknowledgment is made to the following for copyrighted material:

ASSOCIATION PRESS & WORLD COUNCIL OF CHURCHES: Excerpts from *The Fourth World Conference on Faith and Order*, edited by Rodger and Vischer. Reprinted by permission.

ASSOCIATION PRESS AND SCM PRESS LTD.: Excerpts from *The New Delhi Report*, edited by Visser 't Hooft. Reprinted by permission.

GUILD PRESS, INC.: Excerpts from pp. 369–70 of *Documents*, by Samuel McCrea Cavert, and excerpts from p. 673 of *Documents*, by John Courtney Murray, S.J., are included with excerpts from the Constitutions, Declarations, and Decrees of the Ecumenical Council in *The Documents of Vatican II*, edited by Abbott, published by Guild Press, America Press, Association Press, and Herder and Herder, and copyrighted 1966 by The America Press. Reprinted by permission.

HERDER AND HERDER: Excerpts from *How the Reformation Came*, by Joseph Lortz. Reprinted by permission.

JOHN KNOX PRESS: Excerpts from *Unitive Protestantism*, by J. T. McNeill. Reprinted by permission.

OXFORD UNIVERSITY PRESS: Excerpts from *Documents on Christian Unity*, by Bell. Reprinted by permission.

PAULIST PRESS: Excerpts from *Do We Know the Others?* edited by Küng; *Council Speeches of Vatican II*, edited by Küng, Congar, O'Hanlon, and article by O'Hanlon, "Grass Roots Ecumenism" in *The Catholic World*, April 1964. Reprinted by permission.

UNION SEMINARY QUARTERLY REVIEW: Excerpts from "No Religion Is an Island," by Abraham Joshua Heschel, in Vol. XXI, No. 2, Part I (January 1966) of the *Union Seminary Quarterly Review*. Reprinted by permission.

WORLD COUNCIL OF CHURCHES, INC.: Excerpts from *The Third World Conference on Faith and Order*, edited by Tomkins; *The Evanston Report*, edited by Visser 't Hooft, and *A Documentary History of the Faith and Order Movement*, edited by Lukas Vischer. Reprinted by permission.

To
Lex and Gus
fratres seiuncti super terram
sed
coniuncti in aeternitate

Alexander Miller 1908–1960
Gustave Weigel, s.j. 1906–1964

CONTENTS

PART TWO

From Contention to Contrition; or, The Reform
of the Church

PART FIVE

From Irritation to Illumination; or, The Differences
We Share

INTRODUCTION

In 1960, at the instigation of Will Herberg, Fr. Gustave Weigel, s.j., and I published a book entitled *An American Dialogue: A Protestant Looks at Catholicism and A Catholic Looks at Protestantism* (Doubleday). In those days, it was relatively unusual for Protestants and Catholics to comment about one another within the covers of a single volume, and one might have expected the book to have a reasonably long life.

So rapidly did things move, however, that within three years both of us felt that *An American Dialogue* had become "dated." We were at the second session of Vatican II together, and toward the end of it we discussed the possibility of a follow-up volume when the council had concluded. This "seemed good to us," and also, we hoped, "to the Holy Spirit." We even considered the possibility of initial chapters entitled *Retractiones*, indicating where our thought had undergone real change within three short years because of the ecumenical encounter. And it should be clearly stated for the record that by 1963 Fr. Weigel was thoroughly dissatisfied with what he had written in 1960, as all of us listening to his comments to the observers at the Vatican Council were well aware.

Although, as I say, it seemed good to us, in the inscrutable dealings of providence it apparently did not seem good to the Holy Spirit, that we should collaborate a second time, for less than a month later Fr. Weigel was dead—a martyr to the ecumenical cause to which he had given himself so unstintingly that one January afternoon his heart simply stopped beating.

The present volume is therefore dedicated to Fr. Weigel, and to another ecumenical pioneer, a friend of his and mine,

Dr. Alexander Miller, my predecessor both as Professor of Religion at Stanford and as William Belden Noble Lecturer at Harvard, who was sponsoring ecumenical dialogue in his living room long before the idea was either popular or safe.

I have not sought a counterpart to Fr. Weigel in the present volume, chiefly for two reasons: (a) there is now so much to be said that an inordinately long and expensive book would have been necessary, and high prices are an unseemly way to promote the ecumenical spirit; but, more important, (b) because we are now at the stage where a Protestant or a Catholic can survey the entire ecumenical scene without the one-sidedness that would have been almost inevitable even half a decade ago. While I do not expect the following pages to earn a *Nihil obstat* or an *Imprimatur*, I hope that Catholic readers will not feel themselves the objects of a Protestant brainwashing job. The difference between what was possible five years ago and what is possible now can be expressed as follows: previously, a criticism of Roman Catholicism by a non-Roman Catholic drew Catholics of whatever stripe into a collective defense of their beleaguered institution; whereas, today, a non-Roman Catholic criticism of the Roman Catholic Church is liable to draw the rejoinder from Catholics that it is too mild and good-mannered. The manly art of self-criticism has found refuge in a realm that formerly brooked no entrance.

Originally, this book was to be an updating of my half of *An American Dialogue*. Such a project soon had to be abandoned. Too much has happened in the interval. The atmosphere of the earlier book is no longer the atmosphere of the present. The main reason for the new atmosphere is, of course, the fact of Vatican Council II. The present volume is dominated by the council, and I make no apologies for the fact but simply underscore it. Our period of the ecumenical revolution is the period of the council, and any contemporary report that did not reflect the fact would be, to that degree, false. Consequently, with the exception of the (updated) section on "ground rules for the dialogue," and a few isolated passages from the earlier text, this is a new book.

One glaring omission must be accounted for. This is the paucity of references to Eastern Orthodoxy. The de-emphasis is not due to any feeling that Orthodoxy is unimportant on the ecumenical scene, but precisely because Orthodoxy is so important that it deserves full-length rather than tangential treatment. The issues of Orthodox-Roman Catholic and Orthodox-Protestant dialogue are distinctive issues and deserve independent treatment as such. The present volume therefore limits itself, as the subtitle indicates, to those dimensions of the total dialogue that most immediately concern Roman Catholics and Protestants. Nothing is more justifiably irritating to the Orthodox than to be presented as a kind of subheading under "Protestant" or "Catholic," and that error will not, I hope, be repeated here.

Most books on ecumenism have dealt either with the Protestant story or the Catholic story. I have tried to interweave both stories, and I have done so at the price of "covering the waterfront" in breadth rather than depth. I can only plead to the ecumenical experts that I am not writing for them, although I have relied heavily upon them. I am writing for the person who would like a map of the over-all ecumenical terrain, and could profit by occasional suggestions about where the more detailed section drawings can be located.

I have called our situation an ecumenical revolution. Part of the first chapter will define the adjective; it remains to justify the noun. To some it will sound strident to talk about an ecumenical revolution. An ecumenical awareness, perhaps, or even an ecumenical reformation, but surely not an ecumenical revolution. . . . Even Hans Küng, with whom I will be agreeing many times in the following pages, steers clear of the word:

"The actual reason for [Catholicism's] rejecting Luther was this: For all that it included genuine reforms, and despite his conservatism, often stressed today, Luther's Reformation was essentially a revolution."[1]

Küng feels that Luther chopped away so much in trying to lay bare the root of the tree that he endangered its very life.

But revolution can mean more than a dismantling or dismembering of what came before. When the history of the church in our era is written, the era will surely be described as a revolutionary era, in which changes took place beyond what anyone could have anticipated. In 1960 one of the most prominent men on the Protestant scene could write: "Pope John XXIII has shown engaging originality; it is doubtful whether he could possibly reverse, even if he wished to do so, the direction that has dominated the Church's thought for most of the past century." How confidently and serenely that was said in 1960; how utterly dated and wrong it is to say it now.

The definition of revolution that most appeals to me is one of Webster's: "the rotation of a celestial body on its axis." If one could only assume that the *corpus Christianum* were a celestial body, the image would be nearly perfect—the church rotating on its axis, the axis remaining sure and steady, but moved in new directions by the winds of change, possibly blowing in the windows Pope John opened to let in some fresh air.

Another definition goes: "A total or radical change, as, a revolution in thought." While few churchmen will lunge eagerly toward the notion of "total or radical change," the imagery conjured up by a "revolution in thought" is appealing. For although revolutions in thought do not occur overnight, they can be fundamental, deep-seated, and radical— radical in the sense of striking at the root (*radix*) of something. The pace may be so slow that the revolutionary quality is not readily apparent to human discernment, but change

[1] Küng, *The Council, Reform and Reunion*, Sheed and Ward, New York, 1961, p. 74.

there is, and of a revolutionary sort. One of the most astute observers of the ecumenical scene, Professor George Lindbeck, supports the notion:

"An ecclesiological revolution is now taking place in the Roman Catholic Church. The revolutionaries, to be sure, are transformists and gradualists, not despisers of tradition, nor rebels against authority. Nevertheless, their vision of the church is profoundly different from the one that has been dominant in the post-Tridentine period, and this leads them to press for radical reforms."[2]

A revolutionary time is an exciting time to be alive. It would be shattering to wake up some morning and discover that a revolution had taken place without our even knowing it. We must be alert for its signs, for even though it may be a quiet revolution, it is proceeding with creative and relentless energy. My hope in the following pages is to decipher certain indications of its presence.

As one who has written his fair share of words about ecumenism, I believe we are approaching the time when such words will no longer be necessary. Instead of writing about being ecumenical, we will simply write ecumenically; instead of pleading for ecumenical activity, we will simply act ecumenically. Until that time comes, however, there will be need for reflection about the new ecumenical fact. I could have no greater hope than that this book might make the fact more apparent to those presently unaware of it, thus making the book itself superfluous. To bring about its own expendability is therefore the greatest contribution to which this volume could aspire.

*   *   *

The immediate occasion for the compiling of this material was an invitation to give the William Belden Noble Lectures at Harvard University in the week after Easter in 1965,

[2] In Marty and Peerman, eds., *New Theology No. 2*, Macmillan, New York, 1965, p. 183.

coupled with the concurrence of those responsible for the invitation that a treatment of the ecumenical movement was appropriate to the concern of the founder of the William Belden Noble Lectureship:

"The Founder has in view the presentation of the personality of Jesus, as given in the New Testament, or unfolded in the history of the Christian Church, or illustrated in the inward experience of His followers, or as the inspiration to Christian Missions for the conversion of the world."

The four Noble Lectures formed the basic outline of the book, though they have since grown to seventeen chapters. (The titles of the original lectures are reflected in the titles of Parts I, II, IV, and V.)

I am grateful to the President and Fellows of Harvard University, and to the Preacher to the University, the Rev. Dr. Charles P. Price, for their many courtesies to me during the week when, as a representative of the Harvard of the West, I visited the Stanford of the East. I am equally grateful for the comments and reactions that were offered in a series of ecumenical discussions after each lecture, an appreciation I extend also to members of the Christian Leadership Conference at Naramata, British Columbia, who heard much of the same material the following summer.

The book has profited from the reactions of Stanford students who heard earlier drafts of some of the chapters in Religion 195 ("The Ecumenical Movement," MTWTh 11), given jointly with my colleague, Professor Michael Novak, whose comments on those and subsequent occasions have helped me immeasurably in understanding the Catholic dimensions of the ecumenical revolution. One of my students, Miss Carolyn Shaffer, has given unstinting help with typescript and galleys.

I have learned much more than is directly indicated in the pages below from an ecumenical brotherhood including a Frank, a Bob, a Paul, a Ted, a Dan, a John—all of whom have "s.s.'s" or "s.j.'s" after their names, but with whom in that context no titles are necessary—and from a host of priests in Rome and elsewhere whose hospitality in the wee small hours has been a more significant introduction to the ecumenical revolution than all the speeches of the council put together.

Finally, I am grateful to the Rev. Daniel O'Hanlon, s.j., and to my son Peter, for reading the manuscript from their various perspectives. While neither Father nor son bears responsibility for what now appears in print, both helped me avoid bearing responsibility for a number of statements that thanks to them do not appear in print.

It is my hope that readers will call my attention to remaining errors or omissions—in the event that, as the wistful phrase has it, there should be occasion for a second printing.

ROBERT MCAFEE BROWN

Heath, Massachusetts
September 1966

PART ONE

From Diatribe to Dialogue

or

The View from Noah's Ark

So then, like Noah, I look forth from the window of my ark and salute your book as another clear omen that the flood tide of those days when Catholic and Protestant theologians would talk only against one another polemically or with one another in a spirit of noncommittal pacifism, but preferably not at all—that flood tide is, if not entirely abated, at least definitely receding.

Karl Barth to Hans Küng, in a prefatory
letter to Küng's *Justification*, p. xxi.

CHAPTER 1

THE CHANGE IN CLIMATE

eć-u-mān-iac, n. One who loves all branches of Christendom more than his own.

Webster's Dictionary (revised)

Ecumenical dialogue should begin with an acknowledgment of one's indebtedness. Let it be recorded, therefore, that the subtitle for Part I is (as the quotation on the previous page makes clear) a steal from Karl Barth, a Swiss Reformed theologian, while the title proper, just to keep things ecumenically balanced, is a steal from the Most Rev. John Carmel Heenan, the cardinal archbishop of Westminster. Our first task, standing alongside Barth and Noah, is to observe some of the high points on the pleasantly alliterative path from diatribe to dialogue that Cardinal Heenan has described for us.

The distance we have traversed, and the rapidity with which we have traversed it, can be illustrated by an incident in the author's life that took place back in the ecumenical Dark Ages, which is to say, shortly before 1959.

Along with Will Herberg, a Jew, and Fr. Gustave Weigel, a Jesuit, I was invited to share the platform at a meeting in St. Peter's College in Jersey City, arranged by Fr. Thomas Aquinas Wassmer, s.j. Herberg and I arrived together at the entrance of the rather imposing building. I felt a bit like Dorothy in *The Wizard of Oz* entering the Land of the Munchkins, for this was my initial venture into The Mysterious Land of the Jesuits. Herberg and I walked in the front entrance of the building, and the door was firmly closed behind us, thus sealing off all access to the free world outside.

We proceeded through another door, likewise closed behind us, and as we walked down an interminably long and dimly lighted corridor, black-robed Jesuits seemed to converge upon us, silently, from all directions. Thus heavily, if not indeed oppressively, escorted, we were ushered into the outer office of the Father Rector, where once again the door was closed behind us. When we were finally in the inner office of the Father Rector, and another door had been firmly closed, a voice was heard to say to Herberg and myself, "I think we'll just line you up against the wall and shoot you right here."

This voice, I am happy to report, was the voice of a photographer.

The latter's *double-entendre* produced two dozen laughing Jesuits, a laughing Jew, and a laughing Calvinist (if the latter does not seem a contradiction in terms). But it is not so long ago that the comment would hardly have served as an icebreaker. There was a time when a Jesuit, similarly ensconced in the lair of certain of my Presbyterian forebears, would have felt equally apprehensive. And while it is true that we have not subjected one another to the firing squad in recent times, it is also true that we did not, in the interval, exactly participate in love feasts. Due to the gentility of the secularists who governed our lands with greater tolerance than we would have been able to muster, oral ammunition was all we had left, and we became experts at the telling verbal blow, the clever polemical thrust, the withering and annihilating aside. Sometimes it was subtle, sometimes direct. But whatever it was, it was diatribe, which the dictionary defines as "bitter and abusive harangue."

Deliverance from diatribe

We are in process of being delivered from diatribe, but it is well to be reminded, in the new era of ecumenical euphoria, how recent have been the beginnings of that deliverance, lest we be accused of claiming victories too cheaply won. For many centuries scorn was in the air; in some circles it still is in the air, and a few recent examples of that diatribe can underline how great is the contrast in the air we are now beginning to breathe.

Here, for example, is a series of adjectives taken from a Protestant account of Roman Catholic practices, published in 1952 by a former editor of the *Christian Century:* "odious . . . dangerous . . . distasteful . . . shabby . . . odious and ominous . . . odious and absurd . . . semi-idolatrous . . . objectionable. . . . prodigious and preposterous. . . ."[1]

To drive home the point, it need only be commented that the repeated references to olfactory stimulation are not in the context of describing the use of incense.

As late as 1960, after the arrival of Pope John but before the actual beginning of the Vatican Council, the "monolith" image of Roman Catholicism was so firmly stamped upon the Protestant mentality that it seemed inconceivable to many highly placed Protestants that new voices in the Roman Catholic Church could have significant impact upon its future, with the result that such possibilities were discounted in advance:

"So far as can be discovered, 'liberal' Catholics exert little if any influence upon the official and binding 'line' of the Catholic hierarchy, either in America or at Rome: indeed that 'line' appears pointed in a steadily more reactionary rather than liberal direction."[2]

In 1962, as "reform and renewal" were beginning to make themselves felt in Roman Catholicism, recourse was had to the device of seeing Catholicism at its worst, in order to be warned about its "real" nature. Here is a Presbyterian description:

[1] This and other examples are cited in my essay in Scharper, ed., *American Catholics: A Protestant-Jewish View*, Sheed and Ward, New York, 1959, pp. 59–124.

[2] Cf. Cowan, ed., *Facing Protestant-Roman Catholic Tensions*, Association Press, New York, 1960, p. 81.

"In order to see clearly what Roman Catholicism really is we must see it as it was during the Middle Ages, or as it has continued to be in certain countries such as Spain, Portugal, Italy, France, Southern Ireland and Latin America. . . . [There] we see the true fruits of the system in the lives of the people, with all of their poverty, ignorance, superstition and low moral standards."[3]

A leading Protestant journal sees Roman Catholicism as unwilling to listen to criticism of itself:

"The Roman Catholic Church, whatever may be its other faults, is never lacking in shrewdness or in good strategies. . . . The Jesuits have urged the Catholic Church in America to label every criticism of the Roman Catholic Church as 'bigotry.'"[4]

A heavy concentration on loaded and emotionally charged words is the customary tool of diatribe. The following phrases, taken from a Protestant description of the third session of the Vatican Council, are typical of a certain Protestant mind set:

" . . . totalitarian rule . . . the same old feudal operation . . . the same old dictator . . . firm 16th century mentality, but more tyrannical . . . his bachelor theologians at Rome . . . his hackers [i.e., his bishops] . . . his Italian cronies . . . the man in the saddle at the Vatican . . . these machinations . . . out of obsequious deference to a medieval theology of the kind which damned Galileo . . . the Roman Church attempts everywhere to fence off its people from the world about them."[5]

Even after the conclusion of Vatican II, grudging Protestant concessions that the council had effected some changes had to be put in the context of asserting (a) that the Prot-

[3] Boettner, *Roman Catholicism*, The Presbyterian and Reformed Publishing Company, Philadelphia, 1962, pp. 3–4.

[4] *Christianity Today*, as cited in Boettner, *op. cit.*, p. 422.

[5] From *Church and State*, January 1965, as cited in the *Christian Century*, March 3, 1965, p. 287. It must be acknowledged that the context of the above remarks is the disappointing and disturbing ending of the third session of the Council, but it is the tone and choice of words that are significant.

estants made such changes long ago, and (b) that within Roman Catholicism the changes do not represent significant gains since they were so long overdue:

"It was a significant move when U. S. Catholic officials a few months ago shifted the mass from Latin to English in many Catholic congregations across the country. But the Reformers switched to the vernacular of the people in the Sixteenth Century!

"And while we can be encouraged that in many quarters the Catholic Church now encourages her people to read the Scriptures for themselves, John Wycliffe and others of his kind had the Scriptures in the hands of the People more than a century before the Reformation itself!

"Other recent moves of the Roman Catholic church are in reality long over-due; her declaration on religious liberty (she now acknowledges there can be salvation outside the Catholic Church), her new attitude toward Catholic-Protestant marriages and her encyclical in December no longer requiring her people to abstain from meat on Fridays.

"The very fact that the Roman Catholic church had to shift her position on such long-cherished tenets reflects not so much progressiveness as her archaicness in holding on for so long to the medieval trappings and traditions of men."[6]

The above is only a brief, and on the whole a genteel, sampling of recent diatribe. A culling of sectarian pamphlets would make for livelier and, indeed, sexier reading (for in them references to Rome as "the whore of Babylon" continue to abound), but the above examples illustrate that within many quarters the reality of diatribe has been deepseated. While responses of this sort to Roman Catholicism are clearly still with us, at least in the outlying precincts, it is also clear that they are no longer typical samples of Protestant writings about "things Roman."[7]

[6] *Moody Monthly*, Vol. 66, No. 8, p. 19.
[7] Following the dictum of Hans Küng in *Structures of the Church* (p. 394) that one of our ecumenical responsibilities is to see the other side in the most

One can get a significant index of the new climate even from the last decade of American political life. It is hardly possible to recall how bitter were the comments in 1960 about the possibility of "a Catholic in the White House." No Catholic, we were told, could possibly be a reliable enough citizen to be entrusted with the highest office in the land. It was a foregone conclusion that all the Cabinet members would be Catholics, and probably Boston Irish Catholics in the bargain. The hot line from the White House would not be to Moscow but to Rome. Public schools would die out as federal funds were increasingly poured into parochial schools. The Catholic Church, we would learn too late, was engaged in a diabolical plot to close down Protestant churches, and getting John F. Kennedy into the White House was only one step of a skillfully devised maneuver in which every American bishop was involved right up to his miter.[8]

It is surely a measure of how far we have come that by the summer of 1964 the Republican Party felt it a political asset, rather than a liability, to have a Roman Catholic as its vice-presidential nominee, and chose as running mate to Barry Goldwater a man whose ecclesiastical affiliation appeared to be his chief qualification, while there were those within the Democratic Party who felt that it might be a grave tactical error not to balance their ticket with a Roman Catholic as number-two man. That both the Republican hope and the Democratic fear failed to materialize indicates that we can now safely write off the "Roman Catholic menace" theory of domestic politics.

---

creative terms possible, and to make our biggest critique in terms of our own position—and recalling as well some comments of Jesus about motes and beams—I have offered examples of diatribe only from the Protestant side. It would not be difficult to collect parallel examples of Roman Catholic diatribe. Some examples, however, are offered in the first half of Ch. 5 below.

[8] For a well-documented account of the impact of the "religious issue" on the 1960 presidential campaign, cf. Patricia Barrett, *Religious Liberty and the American Presidency*, Herder and Herder, New York, 1963, 166 pp.

The New Testament evidence

In order to see how the climate has changed, and why it is now characterized by dialogue rather than diatribe, some perspective is needed. Part of that perspective, at least, can be furnished by contrasting the spirit of division and discord that diatribe represents with the spirit of the New Testament and its concern for the unity, rather than the division, of all of Christ's people.

If we ask ourselves why Christians of almost all stripes and denominations are beginning to converge toward one another and effect what we have called an ecumenical revolution, surely the basic answer to that question—the answer that underlies all other answers and must be accepted as axiomatic —is that Christians are at long last coming to see that, in the light of the New Testament, diatribe and division are not only unfortunate, but a scandal and a sin as well. By no stretch of the imagination can we find in the New Testament a justification for our present denominations and competing Christian groups. The impulse there is not an impulse toward divisiveness but toward unity. The notion of denominations, let alone huge *blocs* of Christians severed from full unity with each other, is foreign to its pages.

"There is one body and one Spirit, just as you were called to the one hope of your calling: one Lord, one faith, one baptism." (Eph. 4:4–5)

Paul's word to the Galatians is that

"As many of you as were baptized into Christ have put on Christ. There is neither Jew nor Greek, there is neither slave nor free, there is neither male nor female; for you are all one in Christ Jesus." (Gal. 3:27–28)

To the Corinthians he writes in consternation:

"Each of you says, I belong to Paul, or I belong to Cephas, or I belong to Christ. [After which comes the rhetorical question:] Is Christ divided?" (1 Cor. 1:12–13)

The *locus classicus* of all ecumenical discussion is, of

course, Jesus' high-priestly prayer in the upper room as recorded in the fourth Gospel:

"I do not pray for these only, but also for those who are to
believe in me through their word, that they may all be one;
even as thou, Father, art in me, and I in thee, that they may
also be in us, so that the world may believe that thou hast
sent me."⁹ (Jn. 17:20–21)

The Vatican Council decree *On Ecumenism,* citing the
above and other New Testament passages in Chapter One,
"Catholic Principles of Ecumenism," stresses the further
New Testament note that unity is the gift of the Holy Spirit:

"It is the Holy Spirit, dwelling in those who believe, pervading and ruling over the entire Church, who brings about
that marvelous communion of the faithful and joins them
together so intimately in Christ that He is the principle of
the Church's unity."¹⁰

As soon as one has given even this brief a list of New
Testament citations, he must make quite clear that there is a
great deal of romantic nonsense written and spoken about the
presumed unity of spirit and structure in the early church.
An honest report must acknowledge that all was emphatically
not sweetness and light. There was dissension, division, and
often sheer chaos, as even a quick perusal of Paul's letters to
the church at Corinth makes abundantly clear. (Paul even
had to chastise the Corinthians for getting drunk on the
communion wine.) But in the face of these existential
realities the fact shines through with even more compelling
force that the will of Christ, as the New Testament under-

---

⁹ I have endeavored to draw out the ecumenical implications of this verse
in a sermon contained in Anderson, ed., *Sermons to Men of Other Faiths and
Traditions,* Abingdon, Nashville, 1966, pp. 129–39.

¹⁰ *On Ecumenism,* Article 2, cited in Abbott, ed., *The Documents of Vatican II,* Guild Press, American Press, Association Press, New York, 1966, p.
344. (All subsequent citations of Vatican Council documents, unless otherwise noted, will be from this edition.) For further references to the New Testament situation, cf. also Rouse and Neill, eds., *A History of the Ecumenical
Movement 1517–1948,* S.P.C.K., London, 1954, pp. 1–7.

stands it, is not to divide men but to unite them. And today, in the name of Christ, men are divided rather than united. And that is wrong. The statement of the problem is as simple as that.

This does not mean (as subsequent chapters will try to illustrate) that the cure for division is unity in an oppressive and monolithic uniformity, in which every vestige of diversity and differentiation between Christians has been obliterated. Within any notion of a reunited Christendom there must be room for a variety of ways of expressing the nature of a faith that cannot be exhaustively contained within any single mode of expression. It is one of the virtues of various plans for reunion among Protestant groups that this fact is always safeguarded.[11] There will always be an important difference between unity and uniformity, and it is an ecumenical task of paramount importance to keep that difference alive. No thinking Christian really wants uniformity. No Christian, whether thinking or not, has the right to stop short of unity.

In the lives of sinful men, the unity proclaimed by the New Testament has proved a thing thus far impossible to maintain. Even the most cursory inspection of the history of the subsequent nineteen centuries makes plain how much of the life of the church has been devoted to problems entailed by division. In the early centuries there were various groups called *heretics*, those within the church who were held to have departed from orthodoxy, or right belief, by overemphasizing

[11] Cf. for example, the Preamble to "Principles of Church Union," as developed by the Consultation on Church Union, seeking to bring together eight American denominations:

"(d) *Maximum protection must be given to existing diversities and liberties.* We seek not to diminish freedom under the gospel but to enhance it. The costs of a wider unity will doubtless require sacrifices on the part of all, including the acceptance of new limitations for the common good. Structures of authority are necessary; but these structures should leave open every appropriate channel of responsible freedom in decision-making under Christ's lordship." (*Principles of Church Union,* Forward Movement Publications, Cincinnati, 1966, p. 16).

one aspect of the truth, who sometimes left the church or were forced to leave, and others called *schismatics*, those who actually did break away over issues of faith and established rival churches. The two most serious breaches in unity, of course, were "the Great Schism" of 1054 A.D., dividing the eastern and western church, a division that persists to the present day between Eastern Orthodoxy and the churches of the West, and the Reformation of the sixteenth century, at which time Roman Catholicism and Protestantism became divided from one another, and Protestants among themselves engaged in centuries of further proliferation. That the momentum of these centuries of divisiveness is now not only being arrested but reversed constitutes one of the central facts of the ecumenical revolution.

Earlier meanings of oikoumene

Anyone who employs the English varieties of the word ecumenical can legitimately be asked to define his terms, for there are few words in the English language more loosely employed at the present time.[12]

All of the English derivatives, such as ecumenical, ecumenicity, ecumenics, and ecumenism, are simply transliterations from the Greek *oikoumene*. (For this reason, British theologians, linguistically purer than their North American barbarian cousins, frequently refer to oecumenicity, the oecumenical movement, and so forth.) The first thing to say about this word is that the original Greek word, as used by Herodotus, was innocent of any theological overtones. In its turn it derives from *oikos*, meaning house or dwelling (and, by

[12] The material in the following paragraphs can be expanded by reference to Appendix I (by Visser 't Hooft) in Rouse and Neill, eds., *op. cit.*, pp. 735–40; the brief essay by 't Hooft in Halverson and Cohen, eds., A *Handbook of Christian Theology*, Meridian, New York, 1958, pp. 90–96; Mackay, *Ecumenics: The Science of the Church Universal*, Prentice-Hall, Englewood Cliffs, 1964, esp. Ch. I; and Stirnimann, " 'Catholic' and 'Ecumenical,' " *The Ecumenical Review*, July 1966, pp. 293–309.

extension, household or family), and from this comes the verb *oikeo,* to live or dwell. From the present passive participle of the verb comes *oikoumene,* which means the land where people live or dwell, and comes in time to describe "the inhabited earth." For the Greeks, the word describes the Greek world; for the Romans, the term was equated with the Roman Empire.

The word is used sparingly in the New Testament—only fifteen times in all, eight of these being in Luke-Acts—and is again a descriptive rather than a theologically crucial word. One can distinguish three meanings from the various New Testament contexts:

a. Two usages clearly refer to *the Roman Empire* itself. Luke begins his account of the birth of Jesus with the words, "A decree went out from Caesar Augustus that all the *oikoumene* should be taxed." (Luke 2:1) And a later description of the early Christians makes clear that they were felt to be a threat to the Roman Empire: "These men who have turned the *oikoumene* upside down have come here also." (Acts 17:6)

b. On one occasion the reference seems to be to *the entire universe,* the transformed cosmos that will be under the direct rule of Christ: "For it was not to angels [but to Christ] that God subjected the *oikoumene* to come. . . ." (Heb. 2:5)

c. The other dozen references simply refer to *"the inhabited world"* conceived in the broadest terms:

"This gospel of the kingdom will be preached throughout the whole *oikoumene* as a testimony to all nations." (Matt. 24:14)

"And the devil took him up, and showed him all the kingdoms of the *oikoumene* in a moment of time." (Luke 4:5, the account of Jesus' temptation)

". . . men fainting with fear and with foreboding of what is coming on the *oikoumene.*" (Luke 21:26)

"Agabus stood up and foretold by the Spirit that there

would be a great famine over all the *oikoumene*." (Acts 11:28)

"He has fixed a day on which he will judge the *oikoumene*." (Acts 17:31)

"[Artemus is the goddess] whom all Asia and the *oikoumene* worship." (Acts 19:27)

"We have found this man a pestilent fellow, an agitator among all the Jews throughout the *oikoumene*." (Acts 24:5, Tertullus making the case against Paul)

"Their voice has gone out to all the earth, and their words to the ends of the *oikoumene*." (Rom. 10:18, Paul's only use of the word, in which he is merely translating Psalm 19:4)

". . . when he brings the first-born into the *oikoumene* . . ." (Heb. 1:6, describing God's action in the Incarnation)

"Because you have kept my word of patient endurance, I will keep you from the hour of trial which is coming on the whole *oikoumene*. . . ." (Rev. 3:10, in the letter to the church at Philadelphia)

"The great dragon is the deceiver of the whole *oikoumene*." (Rev. 12:9)

"They are devil spirits, performing signs, who go abroad to the kings of the whole *oikoumene*. . . ." (Rev. 16:14)

The theologically neutral word, however, begins to have theological, or at least ecclesiastical, overtones in the early centuries of the church. It is used to describe, for example, something *pertaining to the whole of the church*, i.e., to the church wherever it is in "the inhabited world." Polycarp prays for the community of the *oikoumene*, meaning the universal church, and Irenaeus writes of "the church extended over the *oikoumene* to the extremities of the earth."[13]

Soon it becomes customary to speak of the ecumenical councils as those councils at which the church had representa-

[13] Cf. further, Stirnimann, *op. cit.*, p. 296.

tion from all parts of the inhabited world. Even by 381 A.D. the Council of Constantinople could refer to Nicaea as an ecumenical synod. Eastern Orthodoxy today calls ecumenical only those seven church councils occurring before the great schism of 1054 A.D. Roman Catholics, believing that the fullness of the means of salvation can be obtained only by those in communion with the See of Rome, call subsequent councils, such as Trent and Vatican I, at which the Catholic Church was represented, ecumenical councils. (It is thus consistent with Roman Catholic usage to refer to Vatican II as an ecumenical council, though neither Orthodox nor Protestant would feel the term descriptively accurate since, from their perspective, the whole church was not present.)

The word has also been used to describe that which has *universal ecclesiastical validity*. The Lutheran Formula of Concord of the sixteenth century, for example, describes the Apostles', Nicene, and Athanasian Creeds as "the three catholic and ecumenical creeds," since they are creeds universally accepted as valid by all churches.

Contemporary meanings of oikoumene

1. After the Reformation, however, the word slipped into relative oblivion, and it is only within recent decades that it has returned to popular usage. That usage has come to center more and more on *a concern among divided Christians for unity*. The Oxford Conference on the Life and Work of the Church (1937), attended by both Protestant and Orthodox theologians, stated in its report that "[The churches] are ecumenical in so far as they attempt to realize the *Una Sancta*, the fellowship of Christians who acknowledge one Lord."[14]

Henry Smith Leiper, a delegate to the conference, stated in the preface to the conference report:

[14] Cf. Oldham, ed., *Foundations of Ecumenical Social Thought*, Fortress Press, Philadelphia, 1966, p. 109.

"Oxford was *ecumenical*. That old word from the Greek was reborn and brought back into circulation, along with the fundamental idea for which it stood in the early Christian centuries . . . the idea of the whole household of faith."[15]

Since Oxford, the word has become increasingly common, and during the years of travail of World War II, when the World Council of Churches was only "in process of formation," the word ecumenical came to be more and more frequently used to describe the yearning of Christians to recover the unity they had obscured by their divisions. Oliver Tomkins, long active in the World Council, has stated that "the word 'ecumenical' is used to denote *interest in Christian unity and church union*."[16]

This is the basic meaning the word has acquired in contemporary Roman Catholic usage. On two occasions, the Vatican Council decree *On Ecumenism* defines the word, and in each instance it is the concern for unity that predominates:

"There increases from day to day a movement, fostered by the grace of the Holy Spirit, for the restoration of unity among all Christians. Taking part in this movement, which is called ecumenical, are those who invoke the Triune God and confess Jesus as Lord and Savior."[17]

"The 'ecumenical movement' means those activities and enterprises which, according to various needs of the Church and opportune occasions, are started and organized for the fostering of unity among Christians."[18]

2. Protestants and Catholics agree, then, on a basic contemporary meaning of the word ecumenism. It means "the fostering of unity among Christians." But Protestant use of

---

[15] Cited in Mackay, *op. cit.*, p. 7.

[16] Tomkins, *The Church in the Purpose of God*, p. 8.

[17] Article 1, cited in Abbott, ed., *op. cit.*, p. 342. It is to be noted that the second sentence is consciously modeled on the basis of membership of the World Council of Churches, as expanded in New Delhi in 1961. Cf. Ch. 2 below.

[18] Article 4, cited in *ibid.*, p. 347.

the word has entailed a second meaning as well, and this too must be kept in mind in all subsequent use of the word. For, in recent Protestant history, ecumenical activity has dealt not only with the unity of the church but also with *its world-wide mission*. If, in terms of the earlier definition, we must be concerned that the church throughout the *oikoumene* be one, we must also, in terms of this latter definition, be concerned that the one church go forth in mission to the whole *oikoumene*. "Mission," derived from *missio* (to send forth), denotes the responsibility of the church to go into all the inhabited world, to witness to its faith in Jesus Christ. Thus "missionary activity" is likewise an expression of ecumenical concern.

Indeed, as we will see in the next chapter, it was precisely as a result of Protestant missionary activity in the nineteenth century that concern for unity first began to be focused; the first major "ecumenical" gathering of the twentieth century was a conference at Edinburgh in 1910, at which Protestant mission groups began to grapple with the scandalous fact that they were exporting their western divisions into the as yet un-Christianized portions of the world. It was justifiably disconcerting to ask a native of Hong Kong what his religion was, and be told, "I am Canadian Baptist."

In the current era, when the emphasis of the word has been so extensively concentrated on *unity*, it is important not to lose the complementary and necessary emphasis on *mission*. As far back as 1951, only three years after the formation of the World Council of Churches, members of the Central Committee of that organization recognized the dangers of an imbalance and submitted a report on "The Calling of the Church to Mission and to Unity."

"We would especially draw attention to the recent confusion in the use of the word 'ecumenical.' It is important to insist that this word, which comes from the Greek word for the whole inhabited earth, is properly used to describe everything that relates to the whole task of the whole Church to bring the Gospel to the whole world. *It therefore covers equally the missionary movement and the movement toward unity*, and must not be used to describe the latter in contradistinction to the former. We believe that a real service will be rendered to true thinking on these subjects in the Churches if we so use this word that it covers both Unity and Mission in the context of the whole world."[19]

The report continues in even more uncompromising terms, after having discussed the Biblical basis for the church's unity and apostolicity:

"Thus the obligation to take the Gospel to the whole world, and the obligation to draw all Christ's people together both rest upon Christ's whole work, and are indissolubly connected. Every attempt to separate these two tasks violates the wholeness of Christ's ministry to the world. Both of them are, in the strict sense of the word, essential to the being of the Church and the fulfillment of its function as the Body of Christ."[20]

As we shall see in the next chapter, a significant symbol of this concern that unity and mission be inextricably joined occurred at the New Delhi Conference of the World Council of Churches in 1961, just a decade after the above words were written. Until 1961 there had been two main non-Roman Catholic organs of ecumenical activity. One of these was the World Council itself, organized in 1948 with special concern for *unity*, while the other was the International Missionary Council, organized in 1921 with special concern for *mission*. It had become clearer and clearer since the formation of the World Council that there was something false about two separate ecumenical organizations, each doing only a part of the ecumenical task. The merging of the two groups thus sealed the fact that ecumenical activity includes both unity

[19] Cited in Vischer, ed., A *Documentary History of the Faith and Order Movement*, 1927–1963, The Bethany Press, St. Louis, 1963, pp. 177–78, italics added.
[20] *Ibid.*, p. 179.

and mission, both the reunion of divided Christians and the outreach of Christianity beyond the borders of the churches.

3. A final vernacular use of the word must be mentioned. Particularly since the beginning of the Vatican Council (which introduced the word ecumenism into the common parlance of the mass media), the word has also been used to indicate an attitude of good will and concern for all men. To describe someone as having "an ecumenical spirit" may not refer to that individual's concern for Christian unity and mission, but simply be a way of indicating his desire to reach out in fraternal love to all men. Although this usage departs from the technical precision the word has recently come to have in ecclesiastical circles, there is no reason, in the light of the earlier history of the word, why it could not properly become a further nuance attached to the word today.

The thrust toward dialogue

Our recovery, then, of a concern for unity and mission (as well as for fraternal good will) has made diatribe an inappropriate means of communication. As we have begun to rediscover one another, we have likewise rediscovered how much we share and how much, therefore, we have to give to and receive from each other. The appropriate means of communication in this new situation is dialogue.

But before we can appropriate the full range of what dialogue makes possible, however, we must trace in more detail the story of our mutual rediscovery, noting the highlights of this adventure, first from the Protestant and then from the Roman Catholic side.

CHAPTER 2

FROM EDINBURGH TO UPPSALA
(the development of Protestant ecumenism)

> We intend to stay together.
> Amsterdam 1948.

> We intend to grow together.
> Evanston 1954.

Few historical surveys ever stay within their appointed bounds. A description of movements in the twentieth century must devote some attention to currents at work in the nineteenth. An account of the Reformation must include an analysis of late medieval Christendom. Even Karl Barth's treatment of nineteenth-century Protestant theology has a long introductory chapter on the eighteenth century.

Similarly, an attempt to describe the development of Protestant ecumenism in the twentieth century (using the 1910 Edinburgh conference as a handy starting point) must begin "before Edinburgh." Instead, however, of jumping back only a few decades, we shall jump back four centuries. We must do this in order to controvert a widely held thesis which goes: Christian unity in the West was destroyed by the Protestant Reformers who let loose in Christendom a spirit of divisiveness that has only recently begun to be overcome.

On the face of it, the thesis seems true enough: Christian unity *was* disrupted by the Reformation, and it is only recently that concern for unity has replaced divisive tendencies on the Protestant scene. But the notion that division was endemic to the spirit of the Protestant Reformation, and that continuing division was consistent with the intention and theology of the great Protestant Reformers is far from a self-evident truth. On the contrary, as the eminent Protestant church historian, Dr. John T. McNeill, has argued with great persuasiveness, the concern of the Reformers was for unity, and contemporary Protestant concern for unity is no more than an attempt to be consistent with the real meaning of the Reformation.[1]

The Reformation concern for unity

The stereotype to be dispelled is the following: since Protestantism is an individualistic religion, it naturally leads in a divisive direction as the individualistic spirit triumphs over concern for community; formal recognition of the authority of Scripture provides no effective check on individual opinion, since each person interprets the Bible as he chooses, invoking "the right of private judgment"; thus current Protestant concern for unity is a strange, although welcome, intrusion on the Protestant scene.

But Dr. McNeill suggests that contemporary concern for church unity is "primarily to be explained as the outcropping of an element original to Protestantism, though hitherto largely frustrated."[2]

It is his contention that

"the ideal of Christian unity was a pronounced original characteristic of Protestantism, that it was by no means entirely inactive at any period, and that in the contemporary

---

[1] The theme is developed with ample documentation in J. T. McNeill, *Unitive Protestantism*, John Knox Press, Richmond, 1964, 352 pp., a re-issue of the 1930 edition, brought up to date by a new chapter written in the light of Vatican II. Paul Lehmann, paying tribute to the book in his *Ethics in a Christian Context*, accounts for its relative neglect by saying that it was "published many years ago under a title that could scarcely have been more aptly designed to deter prospective readers." Be that as it may, *Unitive Protestantism* is obligatory reading for those attempting to understand the consistency of contemporary Protestant ecumenism with its historical origins.

[2] McNeill, *op. cit.*, p. 14.

movement it has resumed vitality, and, favored by a social environment that intensely craves integration, now promises to become dominant."[3]

The argument is buttressed by means of three conceptions central to the Protestant Reformers.

1. The first of these is the Reformers' strong sense of the church as the *communio sanctorum*, the communion of saints. The Reformers emphasized "the priesthood of all believers," one of the most widely misunderstood phrases in the history of theology. Later generations have assumed that it means that "every man is his own priest," whereas the real meaning of the phrase is that "every man is priest to every other man." Rather than being individualistic, it is communal through and through. The notion is not, of course, original with Luther, but goes back to the New Testament: "You are a chosen race, a royal priesthood, a holy nation, God's own people, that you may declare the wonderful deeds of him who called you out of darkness into his marvelous light." (1 Pet. 2:9) Within this basic priesthood of all the people, the ordained clergy still have special functions, but the fundamental notion is of *all* the people, and it is thus unitive and communal, rather than divisive and individualistic.[4]

Equally important, however, is the acknowledgment by the Reformers that such a *communio sanctorum* had to have *visible* organization. The church was not spiritualized into something invisible and lacking structure. For Calvin, the task of the Reformers was to bring the lost visibility (obscured by late medieval Christendom) to light again. Indeed, the "marks" of the one, holy, catholic and apostolic church, accepted by all the Reformers, particularly stressed this visi-

[3] McNeill, *op. cit.*, p. 15.
[4] The phrase, so long a bone of ecumenical contention, is so no more. Cf. the Vatican Council constitution *On the Church*, which gives great emphasis to the notion, especially in Ch. 2, "The People of God" (Abbott, ed., *op. cit.*, pp. 24–37).

bility, e.g., the preaching and hearing of the Word, and the right administration of the sacraments. (A third mark added by Calvin, that of discipline, only underscores the point more vigorously.) Dr. McNeill concludes:

"[The Reformers] interpreted the creedal tenet of 'the Holy Catholic Church' in terms of the *communio sanctorum*, and identified the latter both with the visible communion of the saved and with the true visible church in the world which they felt themselves called to restore. Communion was for them fraught with ethical content. It involved in a high degree a corporate consciousness, a group solidarity, and the recognition of an obligation mutually to bestow religious benefits and render social services."[5]

2. The second concern of the Reformers was for *catholicity*. They understood by catholicity a concern for the wholeness, the fullness, of the church. The root meaning of *katholikos* comes from *kata* (concerning) and *holon* (the whole). They felt that this wholeness had been disrupted by the late medieval church and that the currents emanating from Rome and the papacy had become parochial and narrow, and thereby un-catholic. "Among their deepest convictions," as Dr. McNeill puts it, "was the assurance that they were the perpetuators of the catholic church of which Rome had become the betrayer."[6]

Thus the restoration of true catholicity was one of the greatest Reformation concerns. Calvin, along with Augustine, asserts that he who does not have the church for a mother does not have God for a father, and by "catholic" or "universal" he insists,

"We are taught that, as there is one head of all the faithful, so all ought to unite in one body, so that there may be one

[5] *Ibid.*, p. 56.
[6] *Ibid.*, p. 63. Roman Catholic readers who find this hard to understand are referred to the examples of recent Roman Catholic Reformation scholarship in Ch. 5 below.

church spread throughout the whole earth, and not a number of churches."[7]

For Calvin, "The church is called 'catholic' or 'universal' because there could not be two or three churches unless Christ be torn asunder—which cannot happen!"[8]

Revolt from the church, the Reformers held, was a denial of God himself. The task of the Reformation was to build up the ruins of the church.

"They did not for a moment suppose that in sharing in this movement they were separating themselves from the catholic church of Christ in its visible sense. . . . Neither Luther nor any of the Reformers thought that they were founding a new church and going forth from the visible catholic church of Christ. They refused to concede the name of Catholic to their opponents."[9]

Thus the Reformation, rather than being a denial of catholicity, was, in the intent of its proponents, a recovery of that very catholicity that the pre-Reformation church had lost.

3. As a safeguard against individualistic chaos, the Reformers appealed to *conciliarism* as a constitutional principle. Luther appealed again and again for a council, and while he stressed the difference between a "free" council and a "papal" one, he was in this concern not far from medieval exponents of conciliarism. Calvin called repeatedly for a general council to put an end to the existing divisions in Christendom. The tragedy was that when the Council of Trent was finally called by the pope it came too late, and served to deepen the cleavages between Christian bodies rather than overcome them.[10]

[7] Calvin's "Geneva Catechism," in *Calvin: Theological Treatises*, Westminster Press (Library of Christian Classics), Philadelphia, 1954, p. 103.

[8] Calvin, *Institutes*, IV, 1, 2 (p. 1014 in Library of Christian Classics edition, Westminster Press, Philadelphia, 1960).

[9] Lindsay, *Luther and the Reformation*, p. 222; cited in McNeill, *op. cit.*, p. 79.

[10] It is important to realize that the decrees of Trent are being subjected to extensive reinterpretation in contemporary Roman Catholic scholarship. Cf.

But, in the meantime, Protestant denominations developed
the conciliar principle, and their various forms of government—congregational, presbyterial, and episcopal—are all variants of, and dependent upon, the fundamental principle of
conciliarism. Dr. McNeill concludes:

"The conciliar principle took deep root in the late medieval
church, through the writings of a series of able exponents. It
was brought to momentary expression in actual government
in the early fifteenth century, but was combated with seeming
success by the papacy in the pre-Reformation period. The
widespread disruption of the monarchial church in the sixteenth century was attended by a revival of conciliarism which
became the normal principle of church government in Protestantism.

". . . the virtue of Protestantism is neither obedience nor
'private judgment' but communion. Conciliarism is the constitutional principle which gives at once order and freedom to
the exercise of the spirit of communion and the priesthood
of the people."[11]

Subsequent Reformation history illustrates the attempt to
put these principles into practice. The Marburg Colloquy, the
Wittenberg Concord, and other similar negotiations had
unity as their concern:

"They indicate that the great minds of the Reformation
really desired Christian concord and intercommunion. . . .
Whenever the Protestant theologians got together in the sixteenth century, their conferences were marked by a very large
measure of agreement. . . . We cannot exculpate the Reformers from the charge of occasionally exhibiting a schis-
matic spirit; they were sometimes unduly opinionated and
intolerant. But if they are looked at fairly, it will be seen that
they were predominantly conciliatory and zealous for peace,
concord and communion."[12]

---

the writings of such men as Hubert Jedin, Josef Geiselmann, Hans Küng, and
others.

[11] *Ibid.*, pp. 127, 129.
[12] *Ibid.*, p. 176.

The point of this historical survey is neither to justify 400 years of division nor to suggest that all virtue in the sixteenth century lay with the Reformers. It is, however, to suggest that continued division among Protestants is a violation of the ethos and spirit of the Reformation, rather than an illustration of it—an ethos and spirit that finally began to bear some cumulative fruit toward the beginning of the twentieth century.[13]

The road from mission (the International Missionary Council)

"Edinburgh 1910" stands as a symbol of the articulation of widespread Protestant dissatisfaction with existing divisions, and the concern to find a way beyond them. The nineteenth century had seen a vast expansion of foreign missions—sufficient to justify Kenneth Scott Latourette's description of it as "The Great Century"—but along with the asset of proclaiming the gospel to many millions who had never before heard it went the liability, as we have already seen, of exporting not only the good news, but also the denominational divisiveness that had come to be characteristic of European and American Protestantism.[14]

Edinburgh was a world missionary conference called to come to terms with this and similar problems. It was not a

[13] For a full account of various reunion movements between the Reformation day and our own, cf. Rouse and Neill, eds., *op. cit.*, esp. Ch. I–VI.

[14] The pages that follow do not pretend to offer a full history of early Protestant ecumenism but comment only on certain highlights relevant to the concerns of later chapters. The fullest account is Rouse and Neill, eds., *op. cit.*, which brings the story to 1948, and to which an equally full sequel is now being prepared. Among the best *resumés* are Goodall, *The Ecumenical Movement*, 2nd ed. Oxford University Press, New York, 1966, 257 pp.; Van Dusen, *One Great Ground of Hope*, Westminster, Philadelphia, 1961, 205 pp.; Tavard, *Two Centuries of Ecumenism*, Mentor-Omega, New York, 1962, 192 pp. The imagery of the "roads" is borrowed from Cavert, *On the Road to Christian Unity*, Harper, New York, 1961, 192 pp.

Readers familiar with the outlines of the story may skip over to Ch. 3.

meeting of the churches as such, but a gathering of many missionary societies, some of which were not closely identified with given denominations. It was a working conference (speeches, for example, were limited to seven minutes, an even more admirable restriction than the ten-minute limitation of Vatican II), and the conference focused on the development of a common missionary strategy for the future, attempting to avoid the overlap, duplication, and competition of the past. The chairman and secretary were John R. Mott and J. H. Oldham—two men whose impact on subsequent ecumenical development would be difficult to measure or parallel.[15]

It was clear, when Edinburgh adjourned, that a structural continuation of its concern was needed, and a continuation committee was established under the leadership of J. H. Oldham. By 1921, it was clear that more than a continuation committee was needed, and a permanent organization was established, called the International Missionary Council. For exactly forty years the International Missionary Council helped mission groups co-ordinate activities, develop corporate strategies, and, by means of various conferences, think afresh about the mission of the church in the modern world.[16]

Five such conferences were held, all of them having considerable significance for Protestant ecumenism and leading inexorably to the conclusion that concern for mission could not finally be separated, even structurally, from concern for unity.

The *Jerusalem* conference (1928) took special account of a

[15] The roster of delegates reads like a Who's Who of later ecumenical activity. Others present were Charles Brent, V. S. Azariah, William Temple, John Baillie, McLeod Campbell, Kenneth Kirk, Walter Moberly, Neville Talbot, and H. G. Wood. Cf. further on the conference Rouse and Neill, eds., *op. cit.*, Ch. 8.

[16] For convenience in following this and other "roads" growing out of Edinburgh, attention is called to the graph printed on the end papers of this volume.

growing new "religion" that was a more potent rival for man's commitment than Buddhism, Hinduism, and other traditional world religions. This was the religion of secularism. Jerusalem also underscored the point that social redemption, as well as individual conversion, is part of the missionary task —a theme coinciding with another group of conferences on "Life and Work," conferences to which we shall presently turn.

The conference at *Madras* (Tambaram) in 1938 centered on a crucial discussion of just how the Christian religion was to be related to other religions. An important book prepared for the conference by a Dutch missionary, Hendrik Kraemer, *The Christian Message to a Non-Christian World,* posed the problem. Kraemer took sharp issue with a syncretistic approach and insisted that the criterion for relating Christian faith to other faiths must not be religion-in-general but Christianity-in-particular. He saw no "point of contact" between Christianity and other religions save the missionary himself. In a summary volume of essays compiled after the conference, Kraemer stated the alternatives as follows:

"We have to choose between two positions: to start, consciously or unconsciously, from a general idea about the essence of religion and take that as our standard of reference, or derive our idea of what religion really is or ought to be from the revelation in Christ, and consistently stick to this as the sole standard of reference. To my mind, the choice of the second of these alternatives is inescapable."[17]

At the third conference, held in Canada at *Whitby* in 1947, a notable advance was registered over certain previous understandings of the task of missions. Earlier, the missionary enterprise had sometimes appeared paternalistic, with adult

[17] Kraemer, in *The Authority of the Faith,* International Missionary Council, New York, 1939, p. 21. While many rejected Kraemer's sharp antithesis, the issue raised by him has understandably remained at the center of subsequent missionary discussion. Other essays in the volume contain a representative sampling of positions.

occidentals giving something to childlike orientals. But children grow up, even though it may be hard for the parents to realize this. At least by 1947 the realization had become official, for Whitby, instead of talking about what "we" can take to "them," stressed the theme of "partners in obedience." It was acknowledged that missions should not remain indefinitely in the hands of the Westerners, and that wherever possible supervision should be turned over to "nationals." It was further realized that missionary traffic must proceed along a two-way street, with workers going from the younger to the older churches, and not simply vice-versa.

Another important ecumenical emphasis emerged at the *Willingen* conference in 1952. Edinburgh had deliberately avoided the sticky theological issue of church unity, concentrating on missionary strategy in the face of a divided Christendom. But by 1952 such issues had to be faced head on. No longer was it possible to talk about mission apart from unity, and the witness of the "younger churches," the victims of a disunity exported to them by the "older churches," was felt at Willingen with telling force. Thus the theme of Willingen was *mission in unity,* and the younger church delegates stated flatly:

"We believe that the unity of the churches is an essential condition of effective witness and advance. In the lands of the younger churches divided witness is a crippling handicap. We of the younger churches feel this very keenly. While unity may be desirable in the lands of the older churches it is *imperative* in those of the younger churches."[18]

Thus was the gauntlet laid down in the official conference

[18] Cited in Goodall, *op. cit.,* pp. 38–39. Cf. the recognition of this fact as early as 1927 in the meeting of the Faith and Order conference at Lausanne: "Our missions count that as a necessity which we are inclined to look on as a luxury. Already the mission field is impatiently revolting from the divisions of the Western Church to make bold advance for unity in its own right" (in Vischer, ed., *op. cit.,* p. 28).

report: "We can no longer be content to accept our divisions as normal."

The direction in which this concern was leading was so clear that the *Ghana* conference in 1957 recommended that the International Missionary Council (concerned with mission) merge with the World Council of Churches (concerned with unity) so that together both groups could more effectively pursue the theme of mission in unity. This union, as we have already seen, was consummated at the New Delhi conference of the World Council of Churches in 1961.

The road from action (Life and Work)

We back up once again to Edinburgh 1910 to trace a road designated as Life and Work, since it was an attempt on the part of various churches (including the Eastern Orthodox) to find methods of practical co-operation in the secular order.[19] It was felt that in addition to co-operating on the mission field, different churches could co-operate at home in practical activities designed to minister to their fellow men.

Under the impetus of Archbishop Söderblom of the Church of Sweden, a conference on Life and Work was held in 1925 at *Stockholm*. (A preliminary conference in Geneva in 1920 set the stage for this.) Just as Edinburgh had eschewed a discussion of theology and doctrine, feeling that these were too divisive, so Stockholm concentrated on "practical questions." The slogan of those involved in the Life and Work movement was *doctrine divides, service unites*. The Stockholm conference, attended by more than 600 representatives from thirty-seven countries, dealt with the church's responsibility for social issues and discussed problems of economics and industry, social and moral problems, international relations, education, and church co-operation on practical

---

[19] Cf. *inter alia*, Rouse and Neill, eds., *op. cit.*, Ch. 11-12.

matters. It thus affirmed unmistakably the church's responsibility for the *total* life of mankind.

So significant was the exchange that a second Life and Work conference was held in *Oxford* in 1937, with 300 of the 435 delegates officially appointed by their churches, and including 120 communions from forty countries. The central themes discussed at these meetings were: the church and its function in society, church and community, and church and state. Further groups dealt with education, the economic order, and the world of nations, while theological investigations basic to Life and Work were carried on under the themes of the Christian understanding of man, the Kingdom of God and history, and the Christian faith and the common life.[20]

The inclusion of the latter topics indicates an interesting development that was reflected in recommendations growing out of the conference. It had become clear that the slogan, "doctrine divides, service unites," was inadequate. It was not possible to be concerned about service to man without articulating a doctrine of man. Nor was it possible to discuss church and state relations without a doctrine of the church, let alone a doctrine of the state. Consequently, it became apparent that discussion centering exclusively on life and work was a *cul-de-sac* and must be reconceived to include discussion of the theology implicit in life and work. The outcome of the Oxford conference, therefore, was a recommendation that Life and Work be merged with an already existing movement called Faith and Order, to which we shall next turn, and that something like a "world council of churches" be created out of the two groups.

We have already noted that it was Oxford that helped to restore currency to the word ecumenical. Furthermore, with the slogan "Let the Church be the Church" (a phrase orig-

---

[20] The reports of the Oxford conference, long out of print, have been reissued as Oldham, ed., *Foundations of Ecumenical Social Thought*, Fortress Press, Philadelphia, 1966, 211 pp.

inated by John Mackay), Oxford was insisting that the church
is not just another social service agency, but has a distinctive
role and mission to perform in the world. The impact of the
German church's stand against Hitler had helped to focus
this emphasis, as had the recovery (chiefly in Europe) of a
Biblical theology stressing the sovereignty of God over the
total life of man. Thus a fresh examination of what it means
to be the church pushed Oxford further in the direction of the
need to unite Life and Work to Faith and Order.[21]

The road from doctrine (Faith and Order)

Returning once again to Edinburgh 1910, we recall that
that conference had not been a meeting of the churches, but a
meeting of various missionary societies, and that its planners
had insisted that the divisive issue of doctrine not intrude
into the proceedings. But some of the delegates were not
satisfied to ignore doctrinal issues and realized that sooner or
later they would have to be faced. A number of them, spear-
headed by Bishop Charles Brent, Anglican bishop of the
Philippines and later of Western New York, decided that
sooner was better than later. Under Brent's impetus, initiative
was taken shortly after Edinburgh adjourned to hold a conference dealing with issues of "faith and order." World War I
intervened and it was not until 1920 that a planning session
was held in Geneva to work out an agenda. Many churchmen
were apprehensive that such a conference could only end in
disaster. Nevertheless, in 1927 the first Faith and Order conference was held in *Lausanne*, Switzerland, with over 400
delegates from 108 churches, including full participation by
the Eastern Orthodox.[22]

[21] Under the auspices of the World Council of Churches, a third world
conference on Life and Work was held in Geneva in July 1966. Cf. Ch. 16
below. On the whole theme cf. Abrecht "The Development of Ecumenical
Social Ethics" in Bennett, ed. *Christian Social Ethics in a Changing World*,
Association Press, New York, 1966, pp. 153–64.

[22] An invaluable collection of Faith and Order documents is contained in

The report of the Lausanne conference is a good example of what came to be called comparative ecclesiology. At this stage in Faith and Order it was felt that differences in doctrine were so great that the most that could be done was to describe what was held in common and then note the differences. Variants of the formula, "Some of us believe . . . while others of us affirm," were common. Nevertheless, with whatever disagreements, all delegates could subscribe unanimously to the notion that

"God wills unity. Our presence in this Conference bears testimony to our desire to bend our wills to His. However we may justify the beginnings of disunion, we lament its continuance and henceforth must labour, in penitence and faith, to build up our broken walls."[23]

While the delegates could agree about the nature of the church's message to the world, there were significant differences concerning the nature of the church, the church's common confession of faith, the nature of the ministry, and the nature of the sacraments. It was important at this stage that the differences be faced fully and frankly. A reading of the report gives ample evidence that they were. (The Orthodox representatives, for example, were able to approve only Section II of the entire report.) A foundation for future ecumenical discussion had been laid.

Continuing commissions produced two significant symposia, *The Doctrine of Grace* and *The Ministry and the Sacraments*, and further study laid the foundation for a second conference on Faith and Order held in Edinburgh in

---

Vischer, ed., A *Documentary History of the Faith and Order Movement,* 1927–1963, Bethany Press, St. Louis, 1963, 246 pp. The report of the 1963 Faith and Order conference, held at Montreal, has subsequently been published as Rodger and Vischer, ed., *The Fourth World Conference on Faith and Order,* Association Press, New York, 1964, 126 pp. A useful history of the entire movement is Skoglund and Nelson, *Fifty Years of Faith and Order,* Bethany Press, St. Louis, 1964, 159 pp. A brief account (through Edinburgh 1937) is contained in Rouse and Neill, eds., *op. cit.,* Ch. 9.
[23] Vischer, ed., *op. cit.,* p. 28.

1937.[24] Representation at Edinburgh was very broad, consisting of 414 delegates from 122 Christian communions in forty-three countries. One remarkable achievement was the unanimous acceptance of a theological statement on "the grace of our Lord Jesus Christ," and the acknowledgment that on this subject there was "no ground for maintaining division between Churches." On the other subjects—the Church of Christ and the Word of God, the communion of saints, ministry and sacraments, and the church's unity in life and worship—there were both impressive agreements and significant divergences. The importance of the agreements, however, far outweighed the problems of the divergences, so that in a unanimously adopted affirmation all delegates could acknowledge:

"We are one in faith in our Lord Jesus Christ. . . . We humbly acknowledge that our divisions are contrary to the will of Christ. . . . We recognize in one another, across the barriers of our separation, a common Christian outlook and a common standard of values. We are therefore assured of a unity deeper than our divisions. . . . We desire to declare to all men everywhere our assurance that Christ is the one hope of unity for the world in face of the distractions and dissensions of this present time. We know that our witness is weakened by our divisions. Yet we are one in Christ and in the fellowship of His Spirit."[25]

One theme among many in this notable document needs to be emphasized. The delegates to Edinburgh realized that in a deep and fundamental way *they were already one.* As William Temple (who was later to become Archbishop of Canterbury) put it in his opening sermon, "The unity of the Church of God is a perpetual fact; our task is not to create it

---

[24] For the full report of the Edinburgh conference it is necessary to supplement the selections in Vischer, ed., *op. cit.*, with the materials in Bell, *Documents on Christian Unity*, Third Series, 1930–48, Oxford University Press, New York, 1948, pp. 246–86.

[25] Vischer, ed., *op. cit.*, pp. 72–74.

but to exhibit it."[26] At Edinburgh, and subsequently within the World Council of Churches, the emphasis has never been: we are divided, so let us find ways to become united. Rather it has been: we are one despite our divisions, so let us find ways to manifest more clearly the unity we already have in Christ.

The Edinburgh delegates realized from their end of the spectrum what the Oxford delegates had realized from the other end, namely that Faith and Order could not properly function without taking into account the concerns of Life and Work. If action implied doctrine (as Life and Work had discovered), so too did doctrine imply action (as Faith and Order discovered). Hence, Faith and Order, along with Life and Work, expressed approval for the formation of a world council of churches.[27]

The roads converge (the World Council of Churches)

Under mandate, therefore, from both Life and Work and Faith and Order, delegates met at Utrecht in 1938 to draft proposals for a "World Council of Churches." (The name was suggested by Samuel McCrea Cavert, a veteran American ecumenist.) Before such an organization could be formally created, World War II intervened, and it was not until 1948 that the World Council of Churches actually came into being at Amsterdam. Nevertheless, the existence of such a group "in process of formation," as its letterhead declared through the war years, was an important symbol of a unity Christians felt across national lines even during the bitterness of six years of war—a unity given tangible expression by refugee relief activities carried on during the war years and after,

[26] Cited in Skoglund and Nelson, op. cit., p. 61.
[27] Within the World Council of Churches, the concerns of Faith and Order continue under a special division with that name. Two Faith and Order conferences, Lund (1952) and Montreal (1963), have since been held under World Council auspices. Reference will be made to them below.

and by the remarkable way in which representatives of the warring nations could greet each other in Christian love and forgiveness as soon as the hostilities had ceased.[28]

What is the World Council of Churches? Almost as important a question, in the light of many misunderstandings, is the question, what is it not? The simplest answer to both questions is found in certain basic council documents. When the council formally came into existence in 1948, the report on "the nature of the Council" said, among other things:

"The World Council of Churches is composed of churches which acknowledge Jesus Christ as God and Savior. They find their unity in Him. They have not to create their unity; it is the gift of God. But they know that it is their duty to make common cause in the search for the expression of that unity in work and life.

"The Council desires to serve the churches. . . . But the Council is far from desiring to usurp any of the functions which already belong to its constituent churches, or to control them, or to legislate for them. . . .

"The Council disavows any thought of becoming a single unified church structure independent of the churches which have joined in constituting the Council."[29]

The latter point remained a source of apprehension: would not the World Council inevitably become a super-church, aggrandizing prerogatives from the member churches, and emerge as a non-Catholic counterpart of the Vatican? Within two years there was need for further clarification, and an important statement was issued by the Central Committee at Toronto in 1950. The statement first indicated what the council is not: (1) The World Council is not and must never become a super-church. (2) Its purpose is not to negotiate church unions, but to bring the churches into living contact

---

[28] Cf. Goodall, op. cit., Ch. 4, for details.

[29] Cited in Bell, Documents of Christian Unity, Fourth Series, Oxford University Press, New York, 1958, p. 206.

with each other and thus promote the cause of unity. (3) The World Council does not presuppose a single "doctrine of the church," and can include all churches who accept "Jesus Christ as God and Savior." (4) Membership does not imply that a member church feels its own doctrine of the church is merely relative. (5) Membership does not imply that a specific doctrine concerning the nature of church unity has been accepted.

More positively, the Toronto statement listed eight "assumptions underlying the World Council of Churches":

"1. The member Churches of the Council believe that conversation, cooperation and common witness of the Churches must be based on the common recognition that Christ is the Divine Head of the Body.

"2. The member Churches of the World Council believe on the basis of the New Testament that the Church of Christ is one.

"3. The member Churches recognize that the membership of the Church of Christ is more inclusive than the membership of their own church body. They seek, therefore, to enter into living contact with those outside their own ranks who confess the Lordship of Christ.

"4. The member Churches of the World Council consider the relationship of other Churches to the Holy Catholic Church which the Creeds profess as a subject for mutual consideration. Nevertheless, membership does not imply that each Church must regard the other member Churches as Churches in the true and full sense of the word.

"5. The member Churches of the World Council recognize in other Churches elements of the true Church. They consider that this mutual recognition obliges them to enter into a serious conversation with each other in the hope that these elements of truth will lead to the recognition of the full truth and to unity based on the full truth.

"6. The member Churches of the Council are willing to consult together in seeking to learn of the Lord Jesus Christ what witness He would have them bear to the world in His Name.

"7. . . . . Member Churches should recognize their solidarity with each other, render assistance to each other in case of need, and refrain from such actions as are incompatible with brotherly relationships.

"8. The member Churches enter into spiritual relationship through which they seek to learn from each other, and to give help to each other in order that the Body of Christ may be built up and that the life of the Churches may be renewed."[30]

A further clarification came at the Evanston conference in 1954, in the report of the General Secretary, W. A. Visser 't Hooft:

"The World Council of Churches is essentially an instrument at the service of the churches to assist them in their common task to manifest the true nature of the Church. It is an instrument and must therefore never be considered as an aim in itself. The important thing is not the World Council as an organization. It is therefore a sign of confused thinking to speak of the World Council itself as the World Church. And it is completely erroneous to suggest that the World Council is or has any ambition to become a Super Church, that is, a centre of administrative power."[31]

The World Council, Dr. 't Hooft went on, "can and must work to create a situation in which there is so much in common between the churches, that there is no adequate reason for them to remain separate from each other.[32]

---

[30] Cited in Bell, *op. cit.*, pp. 219–23. Each of the eight propositions receives elaboration in the full text.

[31] In 't Hooft, ed., *The Evanston Report*, SCM Press, London, 1955, p. 25.

[32] *Ibid.*, p. 26. Although the story of the World Council is the story of churches rather than individuals, it would be impossible to explain the creation, let alone the survival, of the World Council, apart from the leadership furnished by Dr. 't Hooft. A front-rank theologian who has the gifts (noticeably lacking in most theologians) of executive and administrative ability, Dr. 't Hooft has guided the World Council through its unpromising beginnings to

Such commitments were reaffirmed in 1961 at the New Delhi conference, which adopted a more fully developed "basis for membership." Critics of the World Council had insisted that uniting so many diverse groups would lead to a watering down of conviction, and to theological indifferentism. Actually, the reverse occurred, for the 1961 statement is fuller and more explicit than the original 1948 statement at Amsterdam, which said simply, "The World Council of Churches is a fellowship of churches which accept our Lord Jesus Christ as God and Saviour." New Delhi amplified this as follows:

"The World Council of Churches is a fellowship of Churches which confess the Lord Jesus Christ as God and Savior according to the Scriptures and therefore seek to fulfill together their common calling to the glory of one God, Father, Son and Holy Spirit."[33]

It will be seen that the understanding of Lordship has become more dynamic ("confess" replaces "accept"), that a Scriptural basis of belief has been acknowledged, that a trinitarian understanding of God has been formally articulated, and that a life of common service has been affirmed as inherent in the meaning of the church.[34]

Space does not permit a full discussion of the topics considered at the three assemblies of the World Council thus far held, although much use will be made of assembly materials in subsequent chapters, but some idea of their scope can be

---

make it one of the most important forces in contemporary Christendom. To the degree that any one name can be cited as responsible for the development of an organization as complex as the World Council, Visser 't Hooft's is the name.

Cf. further Mackie and West, eds., *The Sufficiency of God, Essays in Honour of W. A. Visser 't Hooft*, SCM Press, London, 1963, 240 pp., especially the opening essay by Robert Mackie, "W. A. Visser 't Hooft: An Appreciation."

[33] Cited in 't Hooft, ed., *The New Delhi Report*, Association Press, New York, 1962, p. 152.

[34] Cf. *ibid.*, pp. 152–59 for a report on the debate accompanying the changes.

gathered simply by listing the main topics considered at each conference:

Amsterdam 1948: Man's Disorder and God's Design

1. The Universal Church in God's Design
2. The Church's Witness to God's Design
3. The Church and the Disorder of Society
4. The Church and the International Disorder

Evanston 1954: Jesus Christ the Hope of the World

1. Faith and Order: Our Oneness in Christ and our Disunity as Churches
2. Evangelism: The Mission of the Church to Those Outside Her Life
3. Social Questions: The Responsible Society in a World Perspective
4. International Affairs: Christians in the Struggle for World Community
5. Intergroup Tensions: The Churches amid Racial and Ethnic Tensions
6. The Laity: The Christian in his Vocation

New Delhi 1961: Jesus Christ the Light of the World

1. Witness
2. Service
3. Unity

Plans are now being made for a fourth world assembly to be held in Uppsala in 1968.[35]

It was noted earlier that a commission on Faith and Order was part of the newly established World Council. Faith and Order has held two subsequent conferences, Lund 1952 and Montreal 1963.[36]

---

[35] Cf. the full reports on each of the above topics in the various published proceedings: *Man's Disorder and God's Design,* The Amsterdam Assembly Series, Harper, New York, 1948, 856 pp.; 't Hooft, ed., *The Evanston Report,* Harper, New York, 1955, 360 pp.; 't Hooft, ed., *The New Delhi Report,* Association Press, 1962, 448 pp.

[36] Cf. the two reports, Tomkins, ed., *The Third World Conference on Faith and Order,* SCM Press, London, 1953, 380 pp., and Rodger and Vischer, eds., *The Fourth World Conference on Faith and Order,* Association Press, New York, 1964, 126 pp.

At *Lund* the era of "comparative ecclesiology" came to an end; the delegates were convinced that no further problems would be solved by the formula, "Some of us feel . . . while others of us are convinced. . . ." Lund was discussing the most prickly ecumenical issues (intercommunion, worship, and the nature of the church) and the delegates discovered that if they started from historic confessional loyalties, it was almost impossible to move beyond them. They therefore decided that future Faith and Order studies, rather than simply comparing different traditions, must grow out of a common Christological starting point: what do the churches share in their faith in Jesus Christ, and what does that common sharing say to them about any given problem? Lund recognized, in going beyond "comparative ecclesiology," the need "to explore more deeply the resources for further ecumenical discussion to be found in that common history which we have as Christians and which we have discovered to be longer, larger and richer than any of our separate histories in our divided churches."[37]

Lund also recognized that what are sometimes called "non-theological factors" in disunity need to be taken more seriously. Much disunity is perpetuated not simply by different ecclesiologies, but by such factors as nationalism, class divisions, racial differences, institutional pride, and so forth. These social and cultural factors must be given their due weight in seeking to overcome division.[38]

As a specific step toward union, the Lund delegates earnestly requested the churches to consider "whether they should not act together in all matters except those in which

[37] Tomkins, ed., *op. cit.*, p. 27. Cf. also Outler, "A Way Forward from Lund," *The Ecumenical Review*, October 1952, pp. 59–63, for an application of this in terms of writing a history of the church from an ecumenical viewpoint.

[38] The real catalyst in this discussion was a letter by C. H. Dodd, "Non-theological factors in the making and unmaking of church union," first read at a meeting in Chichester in 1949.

deep differences of conviction compel them to act separately?"[39]

Such a challenge was too daring. At the Montreal conference eleven years later the suggestion had to be repeated,
with dismay expressed that so few congregations had taken
it seriously. Montreal has been criticized for trying to cover
too much territory, but the report nevertheless remains impressive in the searching questions it addressed to all
churches, and in the indication it gave that difficult problems
could be tackled head on, now that "comparative ecclesiology"
had been abandoned. Montreal was also notable for the more
active participation of Orthodox theologians, and for the inclusion of Roman Catholic "observers" in the discussions and
papers.

The conference's "Word to the Churches" indicates how
far there still is to go, but also suggests how far beyond
parochial denominationalism the participants have come:

"Will you join us in the attempt to submit all that our own
churches mean to us, and all that we can understand of
others, to the judgment of Christ, Lord of us all? . . .

"Will you try to understand other churches' history as
deeply as your own? . . .

"Will you recognize that Christ calls the whole Church
into his whole ministry? . . .

"Will you, as you worship God, seek to learn from other
traditions more of what true worship is meant to be? . . .

"Will you humbly recognize that many of God's gifts to his
whole Church cannot be shared by us in our local churches,
until we become the one people of God in each place, and are
prepared to realize this by new and bold ventures of living
faith?"[40]

[39] Tomkins, *op. cit.*, p. 16. Cf. further on the Lund conference the helpful
appraisal in Skoglund and Nelson, *op. cit.*, Ch. 5.

[40] Rodger and Vischer, eds., *op. cit.*, p. 40. The questions correspond to the
five sections of the conference's discussion (cf. *ibid.*, pp. 41–90):

1. The Church in the Purpose of God

If the ecumenical courtship of "Faith and Order" and "Life and Work" was consummated by marriage at Amsterdam in 1948, the ecumenical honeymoon was over by 1952 at Lund. But no divorce seemed imminent, for at Evanston in 1954 the original Amsterdam resolve ("We intend to stay together") was expanded to read, "We intend to grow together." Growing pains are the price of growth, and the member churches of the World Council appear committed to making more manifest the unity they already have but have so grievously obscured by their sin.

Roadblocks ahead

Many problems face the World Council as it continues to grow and mature. No description would be honest that did not indicate some of them.[41]

1. *The problem of membership.* With the exception of the Roman Catholics, the Southern Baptists, a few Lutheran groups, and many Pentecostal sects, the World Council of Churches now includes most of the significant bodies of world Christians. In what ways can the council minister to such diverse groups as these and also reach out to make its membership more inclusive?

That it has increasingly reached out is indicated by the fact that among new churches accepted into membership at the New Delhi conference in 1961 were both the Orthodox Church of Russia and the Pentecostal Church of Chile. Furthermore, informal contacts with "conservative evangelicals," usually suspicious of the World Council as hiding the cloven hoof of "Romanism," have been increasing.[42]

---

2. Scripture, Tradition and Traditions
3. The Redemptive Work of Christ and the Ministry of His Church
4. Worship and the Oneness of Christ's Church
5. "All in Each Place": The Process of Growing Together.
[41] On this topic cf. *inter alia*, Cavert, *op. cit.*, Ch. III–VI, and Goodall, *op. cit.*, Ch. VII.
[42] Cf. Hollenweger, "The Pentecostal Movement and the World Council of Churches," *The Ecumenical Review*, July 1966, pp. 310–20.

As far as Roman Catholic membership in the World Council is concerned, there is no reason in principle why the Roman Catholic Church could not join since, as the Toronto statement of 1950 makes clear, membership does not "prejudge the ecclesiological situation." The time may well come when this will be an appropriate move, but most Roman Catholics and Protestants feel that at present it would be unwise tactically, since Catholic membership would engulf the council, upset all balances, and make many smaller churches apprehensive that they were simply going to be "absorbed" by Rome.[43]

2. *The relationship to "world confessional groups."* The ecumenical era has led not only to ecumenical co-operation but also to a resurgence of denominationalism. On the face of it, the two concerns appear mutually exclusive: if one becomes a more active and denominationally oriented Presbyterian or Anglican, does he thereby render his ecumenical witness less effective? Many argue in this fashion.

But a case can be made on the other side as well, a case that would go somewhat as follows: Denominations do, in fact, exist, and if, at the present time, one wishes to be a Christian, he does not simply join The Church—he becomes a Presbyterian or a Baptist or an Episcopalian; these (along with about 250 others) are his options. If he wants to work for a reunited Christendom he must have some kind of base of operations within contemporary Christendom, namely, a denomination, and he must come to know what that denomination has stood for in the past.

The hopeful thing today is that whenever a denominationalist honestly surveys his own past history and that of other denominations, he discovers that the things that bind them all together are much more central and important than

---

[43] On this issue, cf. G. Thils, *Histoire Doctrinale du Mouvement Oecumenique,* Louvain, 1955, 260 pp.; Baum, *That They May Be One,* Newman Press, Westminster, 1958, pp. 102–8, and Leeming, *The Vatican Council and Christian Unity,* Harper & Row, New York, 1966, pp. 225–27.

the things that keep them apart. When the admittedly important areas of ministry and sacrament are bracketed, there are no doctrinal areas in which the major Protestant groups are irreconcilably separated from one another.

Honest denominational self-consciousness, in other words, can demonstrate that denominations are an historical phenomenon incidental to the full ordering of the Gospel, though they may at one time have been useful instruments for the furthering of that Gospel, and that as they grow in an understanding of their respective pasts, they will grow toward rather than away from one another. So long as a given denomination is not seeking to perpetuate itself but to discover what can be its distinctive offering to "the coming great church," so long as it is willing to die to its present form in order that a new church may be born, then denominational self-consciousness need not remain a curse but can become a blessing.[44]

3. *The relationship to the "younger churches."* Earlier discussion has indicated that the "younger churches" have grown up, and that previous attitudes of paternalism on the part of more venerable institutions are rightly called into question by their offspring. To take with full seriousness the theme of "partners in obedience" means increasing effort within the World Council to ensure that the western churches do not unconsciously (or consciously) assume the role of benevolent protector of the organization, or, even more crucial, let decisions within the World Council reflect the viewpoint of white Westerners. It is therefore significant that non-Westerners of the caliber of D. T. Niles, a Ceylonese Methodist, who is principal of Jaffna Central College in Ceylon, and Fr. Paul Verghese, a priest of the Syrian Orthodox Church of India, have exercised increasing influence in policy decisions of the World Council. The con-

[44] The above paragraphs draw on "The Emerging Ecumenical Complex," *Theology Today*, January 1964, pp. 528–40.

ference on Church and Society in Geneva (1966) has likewise made very clear that the voice of the non-white non-Westerner is not going to be stifled.[45]

4. *The problem of structural growth.* During its years "in process of formation," the World Council existed in a loose and free-wheeling fashion, and as it has grown and become "established," it has tended to become more and more structurally defined. This has advantages as far as efficiency of operation is concerned, but it has the liability that structures once established are hard to disestablish, that machinery for disestablishing them becomes more cumbersome, and that vested interests in their retention become more deeply entrenched. The occasional quip that World Council officials resemble a Protestant curia contains its own warning about the dangers of overcentralized structures. The World Council must always exert prophetic leadership, and it would be a tragedy if it ever became so successful that it acted as a brake rather than a beacon.

[45] Cf. Ch. 16 below.

CHAPTER 3

FROM "SCHISMATICS AND HERETICS" TO "SEPARATED BRETHREN"
(the development of Roman Catholic ecumenism)

> I should like to say that it is our separated brethren, Orthodox, Anglican and Protestant, who gave the first impulse to the modern ecumenical movement and that we have learned much from them, and can learn still more.
>
> Cardinal Bea, in *Unity in Freedom*, p. 205.

In this characteristically generous statement, the head of the Secretariat for the Promotion of Christian Unity gets Protestant authors off the hook who might otherwise sound arrogant if they suggested that Catholic ecumenism has been in large measure a response to Protestant and Orthodox initiatives of the sort sketched in the previous chapter. For it is a fact, as Fr. Gustave Weigel once said, that "Catholics are Johnny-come-latelies on the ecumenical scene."

It is not hard to realize why this should have been so. Until very recently there was no "ecumenical problem" for the Roman Catholic (save in relation to the Eastern Orthodox, to whom Catholics have always felt closer than to Protestants). The ecumenical situation was very simple: the Protestants had strayed away from the church in the sixteenth century, willfully and often perversely denying the authority of the papacy. They had established their own "sects" and were thus guilty of both schism (splitting off from and destroying Christian unity) and heresy (the teaching of wrong doctrine). They were always welcome to return to the fold of Mother Church, but since they could not be forced to return, the next move was up to them. In the meantime, Rome would be cordial in personal relations, but always make clear that the terms of reunion involved the submission of the "schismatics and heretics" to all the statements of Catholic doctrine they had forsaken in the sixteenth century, plus a few more that had been added since.

There was a further reason for Catholic aloofness from the Protestant world. So great had been the proliferation of Protestant "sects and insects," buzzing about the ecclesiastical landscape, that a Catholic could rightly conclude that until the various Protestant groups patched up their own family quarrels there was little the Catholic Church could do in relation to them. Ecumenical outreach would have been extremely complicated, involving not outreach to "Protestants" but to Northern Presbyterians, Southern Presbyterians, Cumberland Presbyterians, American Baptists, Southern Baptists, Conservative Baptists, Augustana Synod Lutherans, Missouri Synod Lutherans—and so on, 200 times over. The 200 groups, in their turn, lived in virtual isolation from one another. Even when they began to work together co-operatively, as some of them did in America in 1908 with the formation of the Federal Council of Churches, other Protestant groups not only refused to join the Federal Council but militantly attacked it as either (a) the work of the anti-Christ, or (b) incipient "Romanism," or sometimes (c) both.

Edinburgh 1910 began to change all that. Stockholm 1925 and Lausanne 1927 changed it further, for these conferences made clear that a new factor was emerging of which the Roman Catholic Church would soon have to take account— a reversal of the Protestant tendency to disunity and the beginning of a concern for unity. They soon necessitated formal evaluations and responses from the Roman Catholic side. The responses were articulated officially by the papacy, and unofficially by a handful of ecumenical pioneers who only today are beginning to be recognized for the courageous voices they were. They were courageous because while they did not challenge the "official" view, they were incarnating, often at great personal cost, a spirit rather different from that view, a spirit that was finally to bear fruit during the papacy of "good Pope John."

Growth in official ecumenical concern

A study of recent papal pronouncements on ecumenical issues uncovers a shift from an initially negative attitude to both an increasing sensitivity to the ecumenical scene and an increasing openness to Catholic participation in it.[1]

Back in 1896, Pope Leo XIII in the encyclical *Apostolicae Curae* had declared that Anglican orders were invalid, and had thus quashed hopes that reciprocity of clerical acknowledgment might develop between the Roman Catholic Church and the Church of England. At the time of the early ecumenical conferences, invitations were extended to the Vatican to send observers, but these were usually declined.

During the same period, however, the papacy issued various encyclicals and speeches dealing with Eastern Orthodoxy, and in the writings of Leo XIII and Pius XI an attitude of great esteem for the Orthodox was noted. Pius XI, for example, writes of the Orthodox: "They have faithfully preserved the greater part of divine revelation. Among them is

[1] Some use is made in the following pages of material originally gathered for Brown and Weigel, *An American Dialogue*, Doubleday, New York, 1961, esp. pp. 106–11. The best resource for papal treatment of the problem is Baum, *That They May Be One*, Newman, Westminster, 1958, 181 pp.; its main points are condensed in *The Catholic Quest for Christian Unity*, Paulist Press, Glen Rock, 1965, Ch. 2, "The Evolution of Ecumenism in Papal Pronouncements." Cf. also Leeming, *The Churches and the Church*, Newman, Westminster, 1960, esp. pp. 164–82, and Tavard, *Two Centuries of Ecumenism*, Mentor-Omega, New York, 1962, 192 pp. The latter surveys both Protestant and Catholic ecumenism and treats in fuller detail some of the movements described in Ch. 2 and 3 of the present work.

found a sincere obedience to Christ, a special love of his holy Mother, and the frequent reception of the sacraments."[2]

In another notable passage, Pius comments on the attitude that must inform approaches to the Eastern churches:

"For a reunion it is above all necessary to know and to love one another. To know one another, because if the efforts of reunion have failed so many times, this is in large measure due to mutual ignorance. If there are prejudices on both sides, these prejudices must fall. Incredible are the errors and equivocations which persist and are handed down among the separated brethren against the Catholic Church; on the other hand, Catholics also have sometimes failed in justly evaluating the truth or, on account of insufficient knowledge, in showing a fraternal spirit. Do we know all that is valuable, good, and Christian in the fragments of ancient Catholic truth? Detached fragments of a gold-bearing rock also contain the precious ore. The ancient Churches of the East have retained so true a holiness that they deserve not only our respect but also our sympathy."[3]

Such attitudes did not prevail, however, when dealing with the West, and *Mortalium Animos* (1928), issued shortly after the Lausanne conference on Faith and Order, can only be described as a dash of cold water in the face of burgeoning ecumenical hopes. For this encyclical did not talk about "detached fragments of a gold-bearing rock [containing] the precious ore," but instead about "a false Christianity quite alien to the one Church of Christ." The pope seemed to feel that the heretical movement of "modernism," condemned by papal decree in 1907, was now reappearing in Protestant guise.

[2] Cited in Baum, *The Catholic Quest for Christian Unity*, p. 41.

[3] From Pius XI's speech of January 11, 1927, cited in *Irenikon*, 3 (1927) 20, cf. Baum, *That They May Be One*, p. 110. In *An American Dialogue* I cited this quotation, minus the final sentence, and thereby gave the impression, erroneous in the context, that this was a papal response to Protestant ecumenical concern.

Consequently Catholics were warned to take no part in "pan-Christian" activities. The statement was unequivocal:

"This being so, it is clear that the Apostolic See can by no means take part in these assemblies nor is it in any way lawful for Catholics to give such enterprises their encouragement and support. If they did so, they would be giving countenance to a false Christianity quite alien to the one Church of Christ."[4]

There is, it must be added, an expression of real concern for the divided Christians, but only in the context of the dissidents returning to the forgiving but immobile mother:

"The Church embraces the brethren separated in faith with an 'unfeigned love,' and with the ardor of prayer for their return to the mother from whom God knows how many of them without personal guilt remain distant."[5]

The document indicates that the church must remain "unyielding before everything that awakens even only the appearance of a compromise," because she knows herself to be the "only one infallible, certain source of the whole truth and the fullness of grace."

In retrospect, the over-all document seems harsh, and it must therefore be judged in the context that produced it. The Protestant ecumenical movement was still in its infancy; it was propounding slogans such as "doctrine divides, service unites"; it had not yet been deeply touched by the renewal of Biblical theology that gave Catholics and Protestants so much in common during the war years; and Protestants were still in the most tentative stages of exploration among themselves, let alone reaching out with prophetic insight to Roman Catholicism. So *Mortalium Animos* today must be viewed simply as an historically interesting state-

[4] Cited in Tavard, *The Catholic Approach to Protestantism*, Harper, New York, p. 107. Unfortunately for students of the ecumenical movement, the document is not included in Denzinger, *Enchiridion Symbolorum*.

[5] Cited in Swidler, *The Ecumenical Vanguard*, Duquesne University Press, Pittsburgh, 1966, p. 211.

ment that has long since been transcended by subsequent papal statements.

During World War II, when beleaguered Catholics and Protestants in Europe found themselves in concentration camps together because they placed allegiance to Jesus Christ higher than allegiance to Adolf Hitler, they discovered that the things they shared, in the face of their common enemy, were much more important than the areas where they still differed. Pius XII recognized this in his Christmas message of 1941, in which he expressed concern not only for the well-being of Christians in communion with the Holy See but also for other Christians who "without belonging to the visible body of the Catholic Church, *are near to us through faith in Jesus Christ.*"

A further advance during this period was the increasing recognition that not only do those separated from Rome suffer loss but that Rome itself is harmed by division. Even though there is never any whisper of a suggestion that the Catholic Church lacks anything essential for the fullness of the church, it becomes clearer than before that all bodies are harmed by division and that all (the Catholic Church included) are strengthened by moves toward unity. Gregory Baum observes:

"It is only in recent times that the official documents of the Holy See have been ready to admit that the divisions of Christendom actually do harm to the Catholic Church, and that the whole Mystical Body will benefit from the perfect reconciliation of Christians. In former times the benefits of a reunion were foreseen only for the separated Churches. However, Pius XI and Pius XII are quite outspoken; they look forward also to the wholesome effects of Christian unity on the Catholic Church. 'From the full and perfect unity of all Christians the Mystical Body of Christ and all its members, one by one, are bound to obtain a great increment.' "[6]

[6] Baum, "Ecumenical Attitudes," in *Apostolic Perspectives*, December–January, 1959, p. 7.

The papal attitude, then, during the twenty-year period from *Mortalium Animos* (1928) to the Amsterdam assembly officially inaugurating the World Council of Churches (1948), is one of great caution, moving from almost outright condemnation of Protestant ecumenism to one of greater concern for Protestants and the gifts that all Christians might give to one another. Even by 1948, however, the concern was not yet sufficient for the Holy See to feel that Catholics could be present as so-called observers at the Amsterdam assembly. Consequently, although an invitation to attend was issued, a statement from the Holy Office several months before the assembly forbade Catholics to accept such an invitation. In the face of this disappointment, it was encouraging, however, that as the assembly opened, the Dutch bishops, in whose country the meetings were being held, sent a remarkable pastoral letter to their people, urging their prayers on behalf of the assembly:

"During these days, pray for all those who take part in this congress, and for the many other non-Catholic Christians, who longingly look out for unity, who truly follow Christ and live in His love and who—although they are separated from Christ's flock—yet look to the Church—be it often unconsciously—as the only haven of salvation. Especially pray for those who act as leaders of non-Catholic Christians. . . ."[7]

Just as the great ecumenical upsurge represented by Stockholm and Lausanne had brought forth an official Catholic response in the form of the encyclical *Mortalium Animos*, so the new upsurge represented by the formation of the World Council of Churches necessitated further Catholic reaction. How were Catholics to appraise the new movements, and, just as important, what was to be their own relationship to movements seeking the reunion of divided Christians? The

---

[7] Cited in Leeming, *op. cit.*, p. 292. The full text is found on pp. 290–94. It should be clear that at this stage of ecumenical life the prayers were to be offered so that the non-Catholics would finally decide to "return" to the one true church.

Catholic response to these questions was contained in the Instruction of the Holy Office, *Ecclesia Catholica*, issued on December 20, 1949.[8] For many years it served, as Fr. Charles Boyer of Unitas said, as "the great charter of Catholic ecumenism." Evaluated in the light of what has happened subsequently, the Instruction seems fairly rigid and confining, but evaluated in the wake of *Mortalium Animos*, it represents a great step forward. It is full of cautions: Catholic participation in ecumenical discussions must be firmly under the control of the bishops, Catholics must not give the impression that the Catholic Church itself is responsible for the errors of the past, Catholics must not be subjected to ecumenical activities in a way that might endanger the security of their faith. But it also registers the fact that the ecumenical movement has become one of increasing importance to Catholics, and that Catholics, rather than absenting themselves from it, must find a proper measure of involvement in it:

"The work of 'reunion' belongs above all, to the office and charge of the Church. Hence it behooves bishops, whom 'the Holy Ghost hath placed to rule the Church of God,' to bestow upon it their special attention. They should therefore not only carefully and efficaciously keep this movement under vigilant observation, but also prudently foster and guide it unto the twofold end of assisting those who are in search of the truth and the true Church, and of shielding the faithful from the perils which readily follow in the tread of the movement."[9]

While it is acknowledged that these tasks fall upon all within the church, there is a mild warning against overly active lay involvement, with the main burden being placed upon those in holy orders:

"The excellent work of 'reunion' of all Christians in the

---

[8] The full text is in Leeming, *op. cit.*, Appendix II, pp. 282–87.

[9] Cited in Todd, *Catholicism and the Ecumenical Movement*, Longmans, London, 1956, p. 27.

one true Faith and Church should daily become more inte-
grated as a distinguished portion in the universal pastoral
charge and be made an object of concern that the whole
Catholic people take to heart and recommend to God in
fervent supplications. . . . All indeed, but mainly priests and
religious, must be admonished and encouraged to seek to
fecundate and promote the work by their prayers and sacrifices."[10]

Two reactions to the Instruction are worth noting. Professor Roger Aubert, a Roman Catholic, sees two tendencies
within it:

"It cannot be disputed that while remaining, as is their
duty, unyielding on the matter of principles and very prudent
in the area of practice, the Roman authorities are here taking
a less rigid attitude than has been characteristic in the past.
Far from disavowing the activities which have been increasing in recent years, they urge the bishops to promote those
among them which seem likely to produce favorable results."[11]

From the non-Catholic side, Oliver Tomkins comments:

"The instruction *Ecclesia Catholica* aptly illustrates the
whole situation: on the one hand, the clear, persistent and
reiterated claim of the Roman Church to be the Catholic
Church and to offer no terms for reunion but submission and
return; on the other hand it gives formal and official recognition, slowly conceded as the ecumenical movement has
gradually taken shape, to the fact that fellow-Christians care
deeply for unity in the Church of Christ, and that they must
be taken seriously, in charity and prayer."[12]

As a result of this new openness, four observers from the
Roman Catholic Church were given permission to attend the
Faith and Order conference at Lund in 1952, an ecumenical

[10] Cited in *ibid.*, p. 28.
[11] Aubert, *Problèmes de l'Unité Chrétienne*, p. 17, my translation.
[12] In Rouse and Neill, eds., *op. cit.*, p. 693.

breakthrough of the highest significance. Archbishop Brilioth of the Church of Sweden took account of their presence in the following terms:

"That for the first time Roman Catholic observers have been appointed, by due authority, is an important sign that the great Church of Rome is not indifferent to what is being done in order to further a better understanding between Christians of different traditions, and that an amity of souls can exist in spite of ecclesiastical barriers that appear insurmountable."[13]

Attendance at a Faith and Order conference was one thing, but attendance at a world assembly of the World Council was still, apparently, another, for when the Evanston assembly was held two years later in 1954, it was expected, on the basis of the Lund precedent, that official Catholic observers would be present. Unaccountably, however, permission was not granted, and the second world assembly, like the first, had to be held without the benefit of Roman Catholic presence. The assembly, however, gained considerable attention in the Catholic press and many individual Catholic theologians wrote appraisals of the documents both before and after the assembly.[14]

The pattern of Catholic involvement as observers began to be stepped up, however, following Evanston. At the North America meetings of Faith and Order at Oberlin in 1957, two eminent Catholic ecumenists were present, Fr. Gustave Weigel, s.j., and Fr. John Sheerin, c.s.p., both of whom subsequently played a notable part in the fostering of American ecumenical relations. At the very important meeting of the Central Committee of the World Council of Churches, held in St. Andrews, Scotland, in the summer of 1960, in anticipation of the third assembly of the World Council to be held in New Delhi the following year, five official Roman Catholic

---

[13] In Tomkins, ed., *op. cit.*, p. 106.
[14] On the whole episode, cf. the comments of Visser 't Hooft in *The Evanston Report*, pp. 27–28.

observers were in attendance. Their presence was particularly important since one of the main items under discussion was a statement on "Christian Witness, Proselytism, and Religious Liberty," a theme that was to loom large at the Second Vatican Council, which had already been announced by Pope John.[15] But the more important breakthrough came the next year when, under the pontificate of Pope John, Roman Catholic observers were for the first time officially present at a world assembly of the World Council of Churches, being present throughout the New Delhi meetings.

Thus has the pattern been established. Such is the degree of ecumenical participation now prevalent that it is unthinkable that the World Council would hold any significant meeting without inviting Roman Catholic observers, and equally unthinkable that the invitation would not be accepted.[16]

[15] On the treatment of this theme at Vatican II, cf. Ch. 12 and 13 below.

[16] The above pages have purposely concentrated on the development of *rapport* between Roman Catholicism and movements related to the growing Protestant ecumenical consciousness. But it should also be noted that there were various centers of activity in Europe that were providing initiatives from the Catholic side for ecumenical discussion. One of these was Unitas, a center in Rome, created under the initiative of Fr. Charles Boyer, s.j., for the study of non-Catholic traditions and their place in the ecumenical movement. The Foyer Unitas became a meeting ground for Protestant-Catholic discussions, and during the last two sessions of the council became the location for the weekly meetings of the Protestant and Orthodox observers with theologians from the council.

Le Centre Istina, in France, was originally established to foster relations with Orthodoxy, but has latterly turned to a wider consideration of the ecumenical movement as a whole. Similarly, the Benedictine Priory at Chevtogne, in Belgium, was originally asked to serve as a place for the study of Eastern Orthodoxy, but has also become a center for Protestant-Catholic discussion as well.

One of the first movements in Europe was Una Sancta, founded after World War I in Germany, to enable Catholics and Protestants to meet regularly to discuss their differences. On this, cf. Swidler, *The Ecumenical Vanguard*, Duquesne University Press, Pittsburgh, 1966, 287 pp.

The impact of "good Pope John"

The above pages have described only the bare bones of the story, and the story does not begin to be complete without taking account of the unprecedented impact upon the world of Giuseppe Roncalli, by the grace of God Pope John XXIII.[17] In an entirely unexpected way, this great-hearted man captured not only the imagination, but also the affection, of the non-Catholic and even the non-Christian world. In an equally unexpected way he thrust the Catholic Church into the twentieth century, by his two main encyclicals, *Mater et Magistra* and *Pacem in Terris*, and into the center of the ecumenical movement, by calling into being the Second Vatican Council.

A good many years ago, Karl Barth remarked that one of the main difficulties Protestants had with Roman Catholicism was that they could not hear the voice of the Good Shepherd emanating from the See of Peter. This makes it even more significant that after John's pontificate it was the same Karl Barth who commented, "What if we [Protestants] should discover that the last are first and the first last, that the voice of the Good Shepherd should find a clearer echo over there than among us?"[18]

Pope John's manifest concern for Christian unity, his spontaneous outreaching to the separated brethren, indeed his manifest concern for all men and his spontaneous outreach-

---

[17] The literature about Pope John is almost as mammoth as was his person. His own *Journal of a Soul* (McGraw-Hill, New York, 1964, 453 pp.) does not lead one to expect the great things the final years of his life produced, and much of the biographical writing is already bathed in sentimentality. However, cf. E. E. Y. Hales, *Pope John and His Revolution*, Doubleday, Image Books, Garden City, 1966, 234 pp., for an account of what he taught and did, and Bianchi, *John XXIII and American Protestantism*, Corpus Books, Washington, 1967, for a description of his ecumenical impact.

[18] Barth, "Thoughts on the Second Vatican Council," *The Ecumenical Review*, July 1963, p. 364. The entire article is worth attention, pp. 357–67.

ing to the entire human family, have all created a new situation. This period in ecumenical history, when enough perspective has emerged for a history to be written, will undoubtedly be known as the Johannine era, and the impact of Pope John will be found to have made its way into the most remote and unlikely places. There is no way of knowing exactly what the cardinals were expecting when they chose Pope John. But it can confidently be stated that the cardinals did not get, in him, whatever it was they were expecting. It can almost as confidently be stated that had the cardinals known what they would be getting, a good many votes would have been cast differently. The election is a signal instance of the ability of the Holy Spirit to use the actions of men and at the same time override their intent.

There were those, when he was elected, who said that John, already an old man, was simply to be a caretaker pope, to hold the church together for a few years until an outstanding leader emerged for the next great phase of Roman Catholic history. To which, now, the only possible response is, "Caretaker pope, indeed. He took more care of the church in four years than had been taken care of it in the preceding four hundred."

The ecumenical pioneers

But we must be fair. It would not be proper to assert that Pope John singlehandedly inaugurated the ecumenical revolution, or that he initiated Roman Catholic ecumenical concern. That concern, represented by a group of Catholic ecumenical pioneers, was at least in the wings, waiting for a chance to get on stage. But it would be proper to say that Pope John *released* that ecumenical concern. Nor would it be proper to say that, until John, the papacy had not really been concerned about things ecumenical; the previous pages should bear out the point. But it would be proper to say that in him the tentative ecumenical concerns of previous popes were drawn together and articulated with a fresh urgency that had to issue in action.

Until the time of John, however, Catholic ecumenists had to tread a very wary path. Unless they were exceedingly circumspect, they found themselves warned and admonished by the Holy Office. If they were the least bit forthright, or began to propound new ecumenical ideas, they could receive more than warnings or admonitions; they could have their writings suppressed or be removed from their teaching positions. How many such ecumenical casualties there were in the decades of the thirties and forties may never be known, since the activities of the Holy Office were, in those days, shrouded in secrecy. But it is an acknowledged fact that many of the theologians whose ecumenical ideas finally found acceptance at Vatican II were among those under gravest suspicion in the years preceding the council.[19]

It was one of Pope John's greatest contributions to the ecumenical scene that he gave such men the assurance that they could speak out without fear, and the sudden rush of ecumenical activity and writing that began almost simultaneously with his pontificate is an indication of how eagerly men had been awaiting some such sign. Indeed, it is fair to say that the ecumenical pioneers may also have helped to prepare the way for a Pope John, so that there was some groundwork already laid within the Roman Catholic Church, ready to be receptive to the freshness of his message. There were many such pioneers and only a few can be cited here.

Among the first was Fr. Max Metzger, who after World War I helped to found the Una Sancta movement in Germany for ecumenical conversation among Catholics and non-

---

[19] Cf. the poignant account by Fr. Yves Congar, O.P., of his early ecumenical difficulties in the long autobiographical introduction ("The Call and the Quest 1929–1963") to his collection of ecumenical essays, *Dialogue Between Christians*, Newman, Westminster, 1966, pp. 1–51.

Catholics.[20] There was Abbé Paul Couturier, a pioneer in re-focusing the Christian Unity Octave in terms that made it possible for non-Catholics to begin to join with Catholics in what has since come to be called the Week of Prayer for Christian Unity.[21] There was Fr. Gustave Weigel, s.j., who for many years carried the load of ecumenical outreach almost singlehandedly in American Catholicism, and who literally worked himself to death for the separated brethren. There is Fr. George Tavard, an outstanding French ecumenist, who was writing in the area of ecumenical theology and history long before it was popular or even safe to do so. There is Bishop Willebrands, who was engaged in ecumenical activity in his native Holland long before there was a Secretariat for Christian Unity for him to oversee. There is, perhaps pre-eminently, Fr. Yves Congar, several of whose early books on ecumenism were withdrawn from circulation by the Holy Office, and who was for a time removed from his teaching position, but who has happily lived to see the Catholic Church catch up to where he was a quarter of a century ago. And there are others. But it was Pope John who indicated that the things these few Catholics were doing in isolation were now the kinds of things all Catholics should be doing in concert.

The ecumenical impact of the Vatican Council

Pope John did more than usher in an era of good feeling emanating from his own boisterously gentle optimism. He set in motion a series of specific events when he announced, in January 1959, that he intended to call a council of the Roman Catholic Church. It is symbolically appropriate that his decision to do so came to him during a moment of prayer

[20] For a full account of Metzger's activities, still relatively unknown on the American scene, cf. Swidler, *op. cit.*, esp. Ch. 8.

[21] Cf. further, Ch. 17 below, and more fully Villain, *L'Abbé Paul Couturier*, Casterman, Paris, 1957, 380 pp.

in the Christian Unity Octave, so that from the beginning the notion of the Vatican Council and the notion of the scandal of disunity have been inseparable. Pope John probably had no clear idea of what he was unleashing by his words, "Let us have a council," nor could he have foreseen what would happen when a church, after 400 years, was willing to open the windows, as Pope John suggested, to let in some fresh air. When the dust of four centuries is blown about, the scene gets a bit blurred, and while to many Catholics the council came as a genuine release, there are others for whom all that it represents has been a source of real insecurity and threat. But ecumenically the council was a breakthrough of unprecedented proportions and we must note, however briefly, some of the ingredients of its ecumenical impact.[22]

First of all, the very calling of the council was an event of ecumenical importance. Ever since Vatican I (1869–70), which promulgated the dogma of papal infallibility and gave the impression that henceforth all power would inhere directly and almost exclusively in the office of the bishop of Rome, Protestants had felt that there would be no more councils of the Roman Catholic Church. The pope could now make all decisions unilaterally, and even if he polled his fellow bishops informally for advice, the initiatives and the power remained with him. Thus the images of papal monarchism and a monolithic ecclesiastical structure became more firmly imbedded in Protestant understandings of Catholicism with each passing year after 1870. The fact that this explicit papal power was formally exercised in the promulgation of an infallible dogma (the Dogma of the Assumption of the Virgin into Heaven, *Munificentissimus Deus*, 1950) only strengthened the image Protestants had of the irrevocable direction upon which Roman Catholicism had set itself.

[22] Later sections of this book will analyze many of the events and documents of the council in more detail. See especially Parts III and IV below.

Needless to say, such images did not enhance, in the Protestant perspective, the likelihood that significant dialogue between Protestants and Catholics would develop in the future, let alone that any kind of significant interchange and *rapport* would grow. Rome, it seemed, had committed itself to an ever more isolated existence, increasingly out of touch with the rest of the Christian, and non-Christian, world.

Consequently, the fact that a council was called was in itself an event of considerable magnitude, for it destroyed the conventional Protestant expectations and indicated that new things could happen even within the apparently impregnable and isolated fortress that was the Vatican. That the bishop of Rome wished to consult with his fellow bishops, not simply informally, but within the context of a solemnly convened council, indicated that papal monarchism and "one-man rule," the *bête noire* of so much non-Catholic apprehension, were not irrevocably fixed. At that stage, the mere fact of the holding of the council, quite apart from what it accomplished, would have been a notable ecumenical contribution.[23]

But it soon became apparent that more could be expected than a perfunctory gathering of bishops to rubber-stamp ideas emanating from pope and curia, and that while the council was called primarily to deal with internal Catholic matters, its import would be ecumenical as well. After stating that the council's most pressing topics would be "those which concern the spread of the Catholic faith, the revival of Christian standards of morality, and the bringing of ecclesiastical discipline into closer accord with the needs and conditions of our times," Pope John continued:

"This in itself will provide an outstanding example of

[23] It is a tribute to the hopes the council raised that very soon both Catholics and non-Catholics realized that much more was possible than simply the holding of a council, and all began to expect significant achievements to grow out of its deliberations. This is an expectation that was, as later chapters will argue, in large part realized.

truth, unity and love. May those who are separated from this Apostolic See, beholding this manifestation of unity, derive the inspiration to seek out the unity which Jesus Christ prayed for so ardently from his heavenly Father."[24]

The deed that gave substance to the word was Pope John's creation of the Secretariat for the Promotion of Christian Unity. It is significant that this Secretariat was established independently of the curia—the court of officials that helps the pope with the running of the church—and that it thus had considerably greater freedom and maneuverability than would otherwise have been the case. It is also significant that, although originally established to work in conjunction with the council, it was broadly hinted that the Secretariat might remain as a permanent structure of the Roman Catholic Church once the council was over, a hint which has since become established fact. Perhaps most significant is the fact that the Secretariat provided, for the first time in Roman Catholic history, a *structure* for ecumenical activity. In the past, individual Catholic ecumenical voices had been no more than that: "individual Catholic ecumenical voices." It could never be presumed that they spoke for any beyond themselves. Now, with the formation of the Secretariat, it became clear that ecumenism had entered the church, officially and formally, and that there was a structural means for implementing ecumenical concern.

That the formation of the Secretariat was not merely a hollow and formal gesture became clear when Pope John indicated those who were to serve within it. As head of the Secretariat he appointed Augustin Cardinal Bea, s.j., a German Biblical scholar, who subsequently became one of the real leaders of the council, and who made of the Secretariat an exceedingly significant organ of ecumenical exchange as well as a very powerful force within the council itself. The

---

[24] *Ad Petri Cathedram*, cited in Baum, *The Catholic Quest for Christian Unity*, p. 51.

significance of having a Biblical scholar in this post—Fr. Jean Danielou, s.j., has correctly described Holy Scripture as "the meeting place of Christians"—was not lost on the non-Catholic world. The choice of secretary was also an inspired one. For the task of actually running the Secretariat the pope chose Msgr. (now Bishop) Jan Willebrands, a leading Dutch ecumenist with much experience in ecumenical affairs, a man whose spirit and depth of commitment have had an incalculable impact on the many non-Roman Catholics with whom he has had dealings since the formation of the Secretariat.

As the council got underway, the very existence of the Secretariat, coupled with its independence of the curia, proved important ecumenical boons, for most of the conciliar matters dealing with ecumenical affairs were included within the portfolio of the Secretariat. Thus it was the Secretariat that had the task of drafting the crucial schema *On Ecumenism;* it was the Secretariat that provided the succession of texts for the statements on Religious Liberty and on the Jews; and it was the head of the Secretariat, Cardinal Bea, who was appointed co-chairman (with Cardinal Ottaviani) of a special conciliar commission to write a new version of the ecumenically crucial document *On Revelation.* Furthermore, as the council met each succeeding fall, and ecumenical concerns became more and more predominant in the thinking of the bishops, the Secretariat provided a means of access between members of the council and non-Catholic observers present at the council.

Pope John's decision to invite Protestant and Orthodox observers to attend the council was his further contribution to the new ecumenical climate. It will be recalled that only during his pontificate were Catholic observers finally permitted to attend a world assembly of the World Council of Churches; it was Pope John who gave permission for five such observers to be present at New Delhi in 1961. The precedent of Catholic observers at a non-Catholic council having been established, the question that remained was: would the Catholic Church reciprocate? Would non-Catholic observers be invited to be present at a Catholic council?

Shortly after New Delhi, the answer came from the Vatican, and it was an affirmative answer. Consequently, when the Vatican Council convened in the fall of 1962, not only were there present in St. Peter's all the bishops and heads of religious orders of the Roman Catholic Church, but also a small group of Protestant and Orthodox observers. The latter were permitted to be present at all the working sessions, from which all others were excluded, were given the *sub secreto* documents prepared exclusively for the use of the council fathers, and were enabled to share in the unparalleled experience of frequent and frank discussion and contact with all members of the council.

As the sessions of the council unfolded, the role of the observers became more and more that of informal participants. The observers did not, of course, have either voice or vote, but as *rapport* and trust were established between the observers and the council fathers, there was an increasingly high rate of exchange of opinion. The Secretariat for the Promotion of Christian Unity arranged official weekly meetings of the observers and members of the council, at which the observers were asked to comment frankly on the documents under discussion, and—particularly when the documents dealt with ecumenical issues—the opinions of the observers were taken with real seriousness by the leaders of the council. Frequent changes in the wording or the tone of the final documents can be traced to these briefing sessions.[25]

---

[25] The point is not made to suggest that the observers were somehow "running the show" from behind the scenes, but on the contrary to indicate the high degree of trust that the council showed toward the observers, and how much more than a mere formal gesture was the decision to include them within the council's proceedings. I have indicated in more detail my own experience as one of this group in *Observer in Rome*, Doubleday, New York, 1964. For a fuller account of an observer at all four sessions, see Douglas Horton, *Vatican Diary*, 1962–65 (four volumes), United Church Press, Philadelphia, 1963–66.

While the real ecumenical fruit of the council is undoubtedly the new spirit that was engendered between the Catholic participants and the non-Catholic observers—a spirit that becomes widespread as the observers seek to interpret the meaning of their "Roman holiday"—there is also a very tangible fruit of the council in the decree *On Ecumenism,* adopted so overwhelmingly by the council at the conclusion of the third session.[26] The document makes clear how new is the attitude that has emerged. No more is there talk of "schismatics and heretics," but rather of "separated brethren."[27] No more is there an imperial demand that the dissident return in penitence to the Church who has no need of penitence; instead there is recognition that both sides are guilty of the sins of division and must reach out penitently toward one another. No more are Protestants dismissed merely as "sects" or as sociological entities alone; instead it is acknowledged that there is a measure of "ecclesial reality" to be found within their corporate life.

The way is open, as a result, for a new type of ecumenical encounter, the full import of which we can scarcely begin to measure.

[26] A detailed analysis of the document is undertaken in Ch. 11 below.

[27] The phrase has seemed to the present author a happy one, both descriptively and theologically. Paul Evdokimov, however, in *The Ecumenical Review,* April 1965, p. 98, is dissatisfied with it. "From *what* are we 'separated'?" he asks. Surely the answer must be that we are separated from one another, and that the separation is felt on both sides of the divide. In his account of the decree, Fr. Thomas Stransky, c.s.p., of the Secretariat for Christian Unity, points to the precision of the phrase used in Article 3, *fratres a nobis seiuncti,* brethren separated from us. This does not imply that Protestants are separated from one another or from Christ. ("The Decree on Ecumenism," p. 50.)

CHAPTER 4

DIALOGUE: A TIRED WORD BUT AN ENERGETIC REALITY

> We must come to understand the outlook of our sepa-
> rated brethren. . . . Of great value for this purpose are
> meetings between the two sides, especially for discussion
> of theological problems, where each can deal with the
> other on an equal footing. . . . In this way, too, we will
> better understand the attitude of our separated brethren
> and more aptly present our own belief.
>
> Vatican Council decree *On Ecumenism*, Art. 9.

The "in" word on the contemporary Protestant-Catholic
scene is the word dialogue. Among those who are *really* "in,"
however, the word, tired from overuse, tends to be spoken of
almost disparagingly as a worn cliché. This may be a good
thing, for perhaps before long Catholics and Protestants will
stop talking about dialogue and simply engage in it.

After centuries of polemics, hostility, and diatribe, Catholics and Protestants are now talking to one another and (what
is equally important) listening to one another. In the previous chapters we have seen some of the reasons for the
emergence of this new state of affairs. There has been a recognition that division is contrary to the will of Christ, and
that all who call themselves members of His Body must tear
down the walls of partition that have kept them separated
for so long. As this concern has received tangible Protestant
and Orthodox expression through the creation of the World
Council of Churches, that very fact has drawn Roman Catholicism into the ecumenical encounter, and the latter has
given to all Christians the gift of a new spirit exemplified in

Pope John and extended to all men by Vatican II. All Christians have discovered how close they are drawn to one another by their common Scriptures, their many centuries of common history, the common suffering they have endured together (most recently in Hitler's concentration camps), and the common guilt they bear for the destructive divisions they are now seeking to overcome.[1]

Such things can now be taken for granted in a way that even a few years ago was unimaginable. And what they mean, initially, is that the various partners involved can no longer live in isolation from one another. They must get reacquainted, and discover at first hand who they really are. The walls of isolation have crumbled and the era of dialogue and confrontation has begun.

Indeed, not only are Catholics and Protestants talking to one another, but other contacts, equally surprising, are being established. The reader is invited to fill in the blanks in the following description of a recently initiated dialogue:

"Father Stephen Hartdegen, professor of Sacred Scripture at Holy Name College, Washington, who is a former president of the Catholic Biblical Society of America, agreed that 'a very good start' was made creating 'dialogue' between ——————— and ———————. There was, he said, 'a spirit of sincerity and goodwill which, without any compromise, sought mutual understanding.' "[2]

One might imagine that this was the report of an initial meeting between, say, Roman Catholics and Lutherans. But the report is actually describing an exclusively Roman Catholic Mariological Congress, at which dialogue was initiated between Roman Catholic "dogmatic theologians and Scripture scholars." This is no mean achievement, as one discovers when he reads further and learns, according to one of the

---

[1] The latter theme will be developed in detail in Part II below.
[2] *Herder Correspondence*, July 1965, p. 221.

participants, that "some of the theologians didn't seem to trust the Scripture men."

Ground rules for the dialogue

So there is dialogue on all levels, between Catholic dogmaticians and Catholic Biblical scholars, Catholic and Protestant theologians, Catholic and Protestant seminarians, Catholic and Protestant parishes, official representatives of the various churches, and very unofficial representatives as well. Such talk will continue, and it is crucial that it do so. A few ground rules may therefore be useful as the dialogue spreads:[3]

1. *Each partner must believe that the other is speaking in good faith.* This is the indispensable minimum for any kind of dialogue. As long as the Catholic feels that the Protestant is trying to get the inside story on Vatican II simply so that he can discredit it as one vast political maneuver, the Catholic is going to be understandably reticent about speaking openly and frankly. As long as the Protestant feels that current Catholic talk about "religious liberty" is still only an expedient cover-up for a long-range plan to Take Over, he will preclude the possibility of any good emerging from the discussion. *Any* dialogue must assume a common devotion to truth.

But in the Catholic-Protestant dialogue there is an ingredient more significant than a common devotion to truth. There is a common devotion to the One who said, "I am the . . . Truth." The reason why, in this particular dialogue, we must believe that the other partner speaks in good faith is

[3] The following paragraphs are adapted from material appearing in *An American Dialogue*, pp. 26–34, and originally published simultaneously in the *Commonweal* and the *Christian Century* early in 1960, where they seemed to reflect a fairly widely held consensus. The ground rules themselves are as originally stated (save for the sixth), though the illustrative material has of course been updated. Specific examples of the *content* of dialogue will be offered in Ch. 15 below.

not merely because we assume that the other is a civilized man, but because we are both servants of Jesus Christ. Catholic-Protestant discussion possesses this tremendous advantage, which is not present in discussions with other world religions: both partners share a common faith in Jesus Christ.

Sharing this faith makes us "brethren," albeit "separated brethren." The phrase is both descriptively and theologically important. We are, descriptively, "separated," and the point needs no elaboration. But we are also, both descriptively and theologically, "brethren"—so denominated because we are children of the same Father, share a faith in His Son, and have been baptized in the Triune name. No amount of "separation" can irrevocably destroy the fact that we are "brethren," however much it may obscure the fact to those outside. It is fundamentally important that while the adjective may modify the noun, it can never displace it. If another era stressed the fact that we are "*separated* brethren," the current era clearly stresses the fact that we are "separated *brethren*." The nuance is of incalculable importance, and is the true basis on which the dialogue proceeds.

2. *Each partner must have a clear understanding of his own faith.* This implies both an eagerness to articulate his position, and also a willingness to have it scrutinized. The point may seem painfully obvious, but it needs to be pressed against those who feel that dialogue involves little more than an exercise of good will. But ill-informed geniality (what *Humani Generis* referred to as "false irenicism") does the ecumenical cause no good. The Catholic who tries to soft-pedal the issue of papal infallibility for diplomatic reasons, or has convinced himself that the dogma is not very important in the articulation of Catholic truth, is simply not a responsible representative of the faith he is called upon to understand and communicate. Similarly, the Protestant who doesn't know why he affirms (or denies) episcopacy will do little to clear away the fog of misunderstanding in which the

Catholic partner will flounder as he surveys the broad spectrum of Protestant opinion on the matter.

It used to be possible to affirm that the Protestant had the harder task here, since Protestantism represented such a variety of points of view and was so relatively reticent about expressing those points of view in doctrinal capsules. But the Catholic today has some problems as well. He can no longer simply turn to the Baltimore Catechism for his answers. He has to take account of the fact that certain ways of stating the truth (though not the Truth itself) are in flux, and he must be familiar with some new resources—the sixteen documents of Vatican II, for example, as well as the whole host of books that have followed in their wake. The corresponding Protestant resources, it might be suggested, are located in the kind of ecumenical consensus emerging out of the various assemblies of the World Council of Churches, always tempered by whatever denominational twist the Protestant in good conscience must give to his interpretation of World Council teaching.

3. *Each partner must strive for a clear understanding of the faith of the other.* This is both a precondition of dialogue and a result of it. It is a *precondition* in the sense that neither partner has a right to waste the other's time by starting the dialogue in total ignorance of the other's position. Both partners are required to do some serious homework in advance. There are plenty of misunderstandings that can be dispelled by a little honest reading.

However, not even honest reading will ever provide a full understanding of the faith of the other. This can only come as a *result* of dialogue. For it will only be in some kind of give-and-take, face-to-face encounter, that the most deepseated misunderstandings will be cleared up. Only as the Protestant is willing to let the Catholic explain, in relation to his own devotional life, why Mary is so important to him will the Protestant really be able to understand existentially the importance of the distinction in Catholic theology between the "worship" of God and the "veneration" of Mary, and avoid the typical Protestant error of confusing the terms.

As a result of recent ecumenical encounter, it further becomes important to note that "a clear understanding of the faith of the other" (Rule 3) is likewise a precondition for "a clear understanding of [one's] own faith" (Rule 2). So far has the dialogue now come that it is impossible any longer to understand one's own faith apart from the context of the faith of the other partner. Protestant understanding of the church must now take account of certain insights in the Vatican Council constitution *On the Church*. Catholic understanding of "religious freedom," finally clarified at Vatican II, must be seen in the context of World Council discussions of the same subject which laid part of the groundwork for the Vatican Council declaration.

There are two important corollaries to this mutual striving for a clear understanding of the faith of the other:

a. The first corollary is *a willingness to interpret the faith of the other in its best rather than its worst light.* If this sounds obvious in principle, it is far from obvious in practice. Too many Protestants still read papal encyclicals only to discover further examples of what they politely call papal dominance and less politely call thought control. Too many Catholics are still unwilling to acknowledge that there might have been some legitimate concerns at stake in the Protestant Reformation, even though Catholic scholarship (as we shall see in the following chapter) has completely revised the traditional picture of Luther as a lustful monk who couldn't accept the discipline of obedience. There are plenty of misunderstandings on both sides to be exploited. Those who want to exploit them can have a field day. They can have everything, in fact, except fruitful dialogue.

This does not mean glossing over problems or pretending that grievous sins were never committed. It does mean that the best becomes our norm rather than the worst. If Protestants want to be appraised in terms of Reinhold Niebuhr rather than Carl McIntyre, they must be willing to evaluate the papacy in terms of John XXIII rather than the Borgias.

b. Another corollary is that each partner must maintain *a continual willingness to revise his understanding of the faith of the other.* This is the hardest part of the whole enterprise. Dialogue can be a shattering experience, for it can force us to give up our most cherished caricatures. It may even mean acknowledging that there are valid reasons (and not reasons based on faulty premises) why the partner in the dialogue holds the faith he holds. Such discoveries mean acknowledging that some of the reasons one partner has had for rejecting the faith of the other are inadequate if not downright wrong. Thus the Protestant who has rest content with the notion that papal primacy means "one-man rule" is in for some rude surprises when he first encounters the notion of the "collegiality of the bishops," while the Catholic who feels that Protestantism is nothing but "the right of private judgment" will be disturbed when he learns that many Protestants live under a strong sense of the discipline imposed by their confessions and church authorities.

The process, though disturbing, is essential, since confrontation must be based on truth rather than caricature. Even if no more comes of it than this, both partners may take comfort from their contributions to the noble work of caricature assassination.

4. *Each partner must accept responsibility in humility and penitence for what his group has done, and is doing, to foster and perpetuate division.* This used to be a rather daring thing to say, since although individual confessions were not too hard to come by, institutions had a high degree of internal resistance to any kind of corporate breast-beating. But no one, reading the literature of the World Council, or the promulgations of the Vatican Council, would have to go far before finding illustration of the fact that both sides of the divide now acknowledge that guilt for division is shared, and that neither can approach the other with an attitude of moral

superiority, as though all fault lay only on one side, i.e., the other side.[4]

This means more than simply acknowledging, however penitently, the patent fact of past error. It also means the kind of amendment of life that can only properly proceed out of contrition. The Vatican Council caught the spirit of this concern. The decree *On Ecumenism* not only states, concerning sins against unity, "in humble prayer, we beg pardon of God and of our separated brethren,"[5] but also points out that change must result:

"There can be no ecumenism worthy of the name without a change of heart. For it is from newness of attitudes (cf. Eph. 4:23), from self-denial and unstinted love, that yearnings for unity take their rise and grow toward maturity. We should therefore pray to the divine Spirit for the grace to be genuinely self-denying, humble, gentle in the service of others and to have an attitude of brotherly generosity toward them."[6]

5. *Each partner must forthrightly face the issues which cause separation, as well as those which create unity.* It was important for the ecumenical dialogue to begin with a stress on the things that unite Protestants and Catholics. And after 400 years of polemics, it was encouraging to discover that the things uniting them were far more widespread than the things dividing them. This context of shared commitments is the only creative context in which to pursue the causes of our division, for it is the context of love. If only shared commitments are discussed, the sentimentality engendered will ultimately issue in disillusionment, for the differences will finally out. But if only the differences are discussed, the cynicism engendered can lead to even deeper separation. The context of shared commitments, then, must be the context in

---

[4] Documentation for these claims is provided in Ch. 6 below.

[5] *On Ecumenism*, Art. 7, Abbott, ed., *op. cit.*, p. 351.

[6] *Ibid.*, Abbott, p. 351.

which the areas of disagreement are openly and honestly faced.

Some differences, of course, seem insurmountable. There would appear to be no halfway house, for example, between believing (a) that the pope is infallible, and (b) that the pope is not infallible. No one has yet found takers for the notion of being a little bit infallible. The difference must be recognized openly and forthrightly. And yet the issue is not quite as foreclosed to fruitful discussion as we have usually felt. For both sides have been quite unclear as to what they mean by infallibility, and there are certain interpretations of it, apparently acceptable to Catholics, that dispel a considerable amount of traditional Protestant apprehension.[7]

But it must be remembered that this airing of differences may also make clear that the cleavages, in certain areas at least, are much deeper than the partners to the dialogue had previously thought. The day that most Protestants accept episcopacy (a day that will surely come) is not going to be the day that both Protestants and Catholics will have come to share belief in episcopacy, for by it they will still mean very different and seemingly irreconcilable things. The Protestant who naïvely assumes that as soon as Roman Catholics have been properly enlightened they will "give up" those beliefs the Protestant does not share is in for a depressing experience. Likewise the Catholic who is sure that Protestants can be brought back to the Catholic Church by the concession of a few "fringe benefits" (such as a married clergy or a few deletions from canon law) is going to discover that Protestant convictions run a little deeper than that.

All of which may sound depressing. If the recognition of differences is liable to accentuate them, what is the point of talking at all? The atmosphere would indeed be discouraging if there were not a final ingredient for the dialogue.

6. The final ingredient is this: *Each partner must seek to*

[7] For an elaboration of this controversial point, cf. Ch. 15 below.

make the dialogue a source of renewal in his own church.[8] The point of dialogue is not that the partners emerge from it as they were before, but precisely that they be transformed by it. No one can encounter the opposite partner in any true way without a corresponding enrichment of his own vision of the Christian faith. And it will not be enough simply that he treasure this new discovery to himself; he must use it within the life of his own community of faith to help bring about the transformation of the latter. This does not mean that anyone has a blueprint for the ecumenical future, but that the future will include the "reform and renewal" of all involved is clear, even though the details of where and in what ways that reform and renewal will proceed are known to no man. A heavy hand laid upon the dialogue to try to force it in some preconceived direction will surely betray the venture, for each new step along the way creates a brand-new situation, and this means that new possibilities may emerge that were not visible from the earlier vantage point. Each partner therefore must strive to keep his own church open to this possibility.

If we talk together, and offer our talking to God, and seek to discern what the total experience suggests for the renewal of our own church, then we can be sure that God will show us the next step, a step so hidden from us now that we can only affirm, "With men it is impossible, but with God all things are possible." This tells us why dialogue is so important: not because we know what will come of it but precisely because we do *not* know what will come of it. Apart from the fact that we believe the Holy Spirit will use our con-

---

[8] Here I gratefully accept the suggestion of Fr. Gregory Baum, in *The Catholic Quest for Christian Unity*, p. 145, that my original statement was not strong enough, and amend it as he suggested. The original statement read, "Each partner must recognize that all that can be done with the dialogue is to offer it up to God." Fr. Baum commented: "Much more can be done with the dialogue and its results than to offer them up to God. The dialogue is a spiritual thing and hence a means for self-searching and interior renewal."

versations for the renewal of the church, we have no way of predicting just what He will do with what we do.

Which means, of course, that the atmosphere of dialogue is, above all and before all and beneath all, the atmosphere of prayer. And if we are really willing to offer the dialogue to God as a source of renewal for the church—with all the shattering implications that may have for our present understandings of the church—then we can be confident that out of our stumbling declarations and our imperfect words God will forge the instruments out of which may one day come the fulfillment of the prayer of His Son, "That they all may be one."

Ecumenism and conversion

But here, right at the heart of the matter, we encounter a significant kind of resistance to dialogue.[9] To put the matter bluntly: there is a lurking fear in some Protestant quarters that the recently developed Roman Catholic ecumenical concern is a kind of trick, a "soft-sell" technique designed simply to get Protestants to "return" to the Catholic fold with less pain. A Catholic poster for the Christian Unity Octave a few years ago symbolized the stance: it showed people from the four corners of the earth flocking into St. Peter's. The question, indeed, must be soberly faced: *can* Catholicism ever really mean by ecumenism anything other than conversion to the Catholic Church? When all the new cordiality has been expended, when all the newer and friendlier words have been uttered ("separated brethren" instead of "schismatics and heretics"), when all the joint prayers (with ecclesiastical permission) have been offered—is not the

[9] The paragraphs that follow grow out of an address given to the Catholic Theological Society of America, and contained within the *Proceedings* of the Twentieth Annual Convention, pp. 95–105. In slightly different form the material appeared as "Ecumenical Qualms," *The Commonweal*, September 24, 1965, pp. 697–99.

Catholic ecumenical gesture still the beckoning invitation, "Come home?"

Where is home? When the question is once asked, the answer is self-evident: home is Rome. Can it honestly be otherwise, as long as the Roman Catholic believes that his is the only true church of Jesus Christ? Would not the Catholic be denying something very precious and vital to his own heritage if he were even to hint at anything like a parity between churches? Does not the Catholic face the ecumenical situation with (in Mark Twain's words) "the calm confidence of a Christian with four aces?"

So goes the query. It is an honest if disturbing query, and the stage has been reached in ecumenical relationships where it can be honestly and disturbingly asked. For some Catholics, of course, the posing of the query raises no problems whatsoever. It simply clarifies what is in fact the situation, and the ecumenical cause is ill served by attempting to disguise the truth. Cardinal Heenan, for example, in certain of his ecumenical utterances, makes the point without apology and without rancor. The ultimate aim of ecumenical activity is the restoration of all Christians into the one true church of Christ. And Cardinal Heenan and other Catholics know very well where that one true church of Christ is located. "It is dishonest to dissemble," he asserts. "By 'one fold' we mean the fold of Peter. The ultimate object of ecumenism is reunion of all Christians under the Vicar of Christ."[10]

Is Catholic ecumenical activity, then, no more than a muted or disguised version of the old plea to return? A case can be made for the fact that it has become something different. Not only has the imagery of "return" been abandoned (the decree On Ecumenism studiously avoids it), but the mind set that produced it is not the regnant mind set in

---

[10] Cited in America, May 29, 1965, p. 798. Cf. also his intervention at the second session of the council, printed as Appendix VI in Leeming, The Vatican Council and Christian Unity, Harper & Row, New York, 1966, pp. 294–97.

many parts of Catholicism today, however much it may linger
in certain other parts. While this does not mean that Catholics have abandoned their belief that theirs is the one true
church, it does mean that they have acknowledged a very
important fact, in the decree *On Ecumenism* and elsewhere,
namely that the one true church is *reformable,* and indeed
that it stands in need of constant reformation.[11] This means
that a new imagery is replacing the old imagery of a static
church, "without spot or wrinkle," waiting passively for the
penitent Protestants to crawl to it for shelter. The new
imagery is rather that of both groups, Catholic and Protestant, moving out toward one another, moving as far as each
can without sacrificing its integrity, but nevertheless moving
out at a certain risk—the risk of realizing that an encounter
is going to take place, and that in an encounter into which
two partners genuinely enter, neither partner emerges from
the encounter precisely as he was beforehand.

And this in turn means that in the course of the ecumenical encounter, the Catholic Church will be changed as well
as the Protestant churches. In the encounter the Catholic
Church will move toward newer understandings, deeper ap-
propriations, of those truths it already holds, and the Catholic, as he looks to what his church will be fifty years from
now, need not believe he will find there an exact replica of
what he sees today. For the church will have engaged in far-
reaching inner reform, partly as a result of the ecumenical
dialogue. It will even have gained certain things from the
best of Protestantism, just as in the interval Protestantism
will have gained from the best of Catholicism.[12]

This means, then, that no one can draw an ecumenical

[11] For elaboration and documentation of this point, cf. Ch. 6 and 7 below,
and van Beeck, "Toward an Ecumenical Understanding of the Sacraments,"
The Journal of Ecumenical Studies, Winter 1966, pp. 57–112.

[12] The Catholic or Protestant who feels that this is wishful thinking need
only look back to the Catholic Church of *five* years ago to see what startling
changes have come as a result of the new ecumenical situation.

blueprint for the future. And the old conversionist notion of "surrender" will disappear, in the sense of meaning, "Surrender to *my* notion of the church," for the notion of the church will develop and grow and deepen. If the notion of surrender survives at all, it, too, will have been transformed, so that it will come to mean, "Let both of us surrender our pride, whether individual or ecclesiastical, to Jesus Christ, and allow him to do whatever he will with our penitence and contrition, for the upbuilding of his church."

If the argument thus far seems to be based too exclusively on speculation about a future no one knows, it may be noted in addition that the Vatican Council has been quite specific in distinguishing between ecumenism and conversion:

"It is evident that the work of preparing and reconciling those individuals who wish for full Catholic communion is of its nature distinct from ecumenical action."[13]

The *relatio* for the second version of the text, delivered when it was introduced to the council, made the point even more clearly: "It would be a quite wrong view of ecumenism if it were to be regarded as a new tactic for achieving conversions more easily."[14]

Either the Protestant takes the council at its word here, or he does not. Catholic ecumenists do, in fact, increasingly press the distinction. Past Catholic apologetics tended to be aimed at the conversion of individuals, but this is not seen today by many as the way to cope with Christian division. As Fr. Baum, one of Catholicism's most creative ecumenical theologians, states,

"However important the apostolate of conversions may be in certain situations, it is not the Church's response to the divided state of Christianity. Conversion work by itself bypasses the real problems of Christian disunity, the pu-

---

[13] *On Ecumenism*, Art. 4. The paragraph goes on to add, with less than luminous clarity, "But there is no opposition between the two, since both proceed from the marvelous ways of God."

[14] Cited in Jaeger, *A Stand on Ecumenism*, Kenedy, New York, 1965, p. 92.

rification of the dissident Christian traditions, and the transformation of the Church herself toward greater catholicity."[15]

And even Cardinal Heenan, the Archbishop of Westminster, whose comment quoted earlier might seem to some non-Catholics to undermine the possibility of genuine dialogue, goes on:

"The dialogue is not intended to convert the participants. It would be idle to expect non-Catholics to enter a dialogue if its primary object were to convert them to Roman Catholicism."[16]

There is yet a further point that emerges in Catholic thinking about the matter. It is the suggestion that *ecumenism* (for the purification of the church) is the posture for Catholic-Protestant relations, whereas *conversion* (for the sake of the non-believers) is the posture for Catholic-non-Christian relations.[17] It is quite clear that for any Christian church, conversion is a part of its concern, and the one who wishes entrance into it by the path of conversion will certainly not be denied. Indeed, the church that does not actively seek to spread its good news and share its life with others surrenders the right to the name of church.

But recent developments in Catholic and Protestant understandings of the church make necessary a refinement of this point. It is now accepted by both groups that baptism incorporates one into the church of Jesus Christ. Thus the Protestant is, in Catholic eyes, already within the church,

---

[15] Baum, *The Catholic Quest for Christian Unity*, p. 205. The entire chapter, "Ecumenism and Conversion Work," is worth attention.

[16] Cited in *America*, May 29, 1965, p. 798.

[17] To those "outsiders" to whom this may sound ominous, it should be made clear that contemporary Protestant and Catholic evangelistic concerns disavow all kinds of proselytizing activity, e.g., the use of coercion, unfair means, bribery, political power, etc. All the church can do is offer something; it can never demand that the offer be accepted. Cf. further on this important point the whole of Part IV below, both in relation to religious liberty in general and the special case of the Jews in particular.

however imperfectly. He at least shares some, and indeed many, of the benefits given by Christ to those who are members of His Body.[18] Surely in this situation the main thrust of conversion work on the part of both Catholic and Protestant should be directed to those who stand in no relationship whatsoever to the Body of Christ. Once again, Fr. Baum makes the point well:

"While it is imperative that the Catholic community become more imbued with the ecumenical spirit—for the sake of its own inner renewal—it is also indispensable that the Church continue her effort to convert individuals. *There need be no conflict here.* Ecumenism makes the Church more truly Catholic, and conversion work deals with individual souls whose religious convictions are only vaguely related to traditional Christianity."[19]

The posture of Catholics and Protestants to one another, then, is not the posture of seeking to gain more converts from the other than one loses. It is not to engage in conversion work at all, though conversion may sometimes result. It is rather to come to know one another, to break down misunderstandings, and most of all through common search and endeavor to engage together in the task of purifying the church, recognizing that all parts of the church (particularly the part to which one himself belongs) stand in need of the reform and renewal that the Holy Spirit appears pleased to use ecumenism to produce.

The risks of dialogue

The word "risk" has occasionally occurred in the preceding pages, and account must be taken of it, for at no point is risk greater than in the area just discussed. There is always

---

[18] Cf. the elaboration of this point in the discussion of the decree *On Ecumenism,* in Ch. 11, and its further implication in Ch. 15 below.

[19] *Ibid.,* p. 206, italics added.

the risk that one who enters into the dialogue may, in fact, find himself persuaded of the truth of the other faith to which he has been exposed and desire to embrace it. There will be, as there has been, a certain amount of two-way traffic on this street and no one can predict when and where it may or may not happen. But there are other risks as well, risks that should openly be faced lest one enter the dialogue in naïveté.

There is the risk of discovering that what one thought his counterpart believed was only a stereotype of that belief, along with the uncomfortable readjustments that have to be made in the face of the discovery. There is the risk of discovering that one shares far more with his counterpart than he thought, along with the unsettling restructuring of the lines of division. There is the risk of learning that one has been comparing the best of his own faith with the worst of his partner's, along with the uncomfortable discovery that when the procedure is reversed (and even more when it is discarded), the faith of the other emerges as an extremely attractive option.

Diatribe is more comfortable, since it precludes the necessity either of thinking or listening, and it is a sign of the increasing maturity of both Catholics and Protestants today that they are coming to prefer dialogue.

*   *   *

We began with Noah, sailing through stormy waters of diatribe. We may end with him also, by observing that above the flood there has clearly emerged an Ararat of dialogue on which the ark can come to rest.

PART TWO

From Contention to Contrition
or
The Reform of the Church

The ecumenical task of the theology of both sides is seriously to consider the truth in the error of the others and the possible error in their own truth.
Hans Küng, Structures of the Church, p. 394.

We must fight their error with our truth. But we must also fight the error in our truth.
Reinhold Niebuhr, as reconstructed
by the Niebuhrian oral tradition.

CHAPTER 5

THE REFORMATION
OF THE INTERPRETATION
OF REFORMATION INTERPRETATION

> To us in the twentieth century Luther still addresses
> urgent questions. Can evangelical Christians be truly
> Catholic and can Catholic Christians be truly evan-
> gelical?
>
> Fr. Avery Dulles, s.J., preaching on
> "Luther's Unfinished Reformation."

For a long time, Protestants had a convenient way of distinguishing between the ethos of their own faith and that of
Roman Catholicism. The device was to suggest that Protestantism took seriously the theme *ecclesia semper reformanda*
(the church always in process of being reformed), but that
Roman Catholicism was unable to do so.

Until recently, most Protestants would have taken this line
and pressed it rather hard. And while the distinction may
not have lost all of its usefulness, its value has indeed been
impaired by recent events on the Catholic side of the divide,
so that Protestants are presently forced to acknowledge that
the theme of "ongoing reformation" characterizes contemporary Catholicism as well as contemporary Protestantism.
Indeed, Karl Barth, never one to fear unleashing his ample
theological artillery against Rome, has commented:

"How would things look if Rome (without ceasing to be
Rome) were one day simply to overtake us and place us in

ie shadows, so far as the renewing of the Church through the Word and Spirit of the Gospel is concerned?"[1]

As he surveys the ecumenical scene, the Protestant has to acknowledge that something is happening that he never thought could happen, namely that the Roman Catholic Church, which he had assumed was beyond the possibility of significant self-criticism and reform, is engaging today in precisely that activity.[2]

The interpretation of the sixteenth-century Reformation has been one area where Catholic and Protestant assessments have been most at odds. It is therefore particularly significant that the interpretation of the Reformation has been one of the points at which new assessments have been made from the Roman Catholic side. The subject provides a convenient introduction to the shift from contention to contrition.

---

[1] Barth, "Thoughts on the Second Vatican Council," *The Ecumenical Review*, July 1963, p. 364. To get the full force of this question, cf. Barth's comment to Fr. Danielou on the absence of Rome from the Amsterdam conference of the World Council of Churches in 1948:

"Your Church could simply not have sat next to us, but (visibly or invisibly) high above us somewhere on a throne. There just is no room for the rich among the poor. . . . It is asking too much that we should take your claims to superiority completely seriously and at the same time should look forward to your presence among us." (*Theologische Existenz Heute*, n. 14, pp. 19 f., cited in Küng, ed., *Do We Know the Others?* (Concilium series), Vol. 14, Paulist Press, Glen Rock, 1966, pp. 45–46.

[2] Catholic readers, to whom this development does not seem at all surprising, should recall that for many years the chief exposure Protestants had to Catholic thinking was to the language of papal encyclicals, not noted for their reticence or modesty concerning the full sufficiency, in all things, of Roman Catholic Christianity. The following quotation is merely typical:

"Certainly the loving Mother [i.e., the church] is spotless in the Sacraments, by which she gives birth to and nourishes her children; in the faith which she has always preserved inviolate; in her sacred laws imposed on all; in the evangelical counsels which she recommends; in those heavenly gifts and extraordinary graces through which, with inexhaustible fecundity, she generates hosts of martyrs, virgins and confessors. But it cannot be laid to her charge if some members fall, weak or wounded." (*Mystici Corporis*, Para. 66, N.C.W.C. translation, p. 26.)

Conventional Catholic assessments of the Reformation

It has not always been so. As a Protestant seminarian in the early 1940's, I recall hearing a then-eminent Roman Catholic radio personality (who has since achieved even greater eminence and who shall remain nameless) describe the Roman Catholic Church as being like a wire stretching from the present day back to the first century, a wire along which the power of the Holy Spirit was conducted. But in the sixteenth century, he went on, some "protesters" tried to graft a rope onto the wire, and although the rope has persisted down to the present day, it is obvious to all that electric power cannot be conducted through a rope, and that consequently Protestants have no access to the power of the Holy Spirit generated back in the first century.

At the same time that such things were being unleashed over the air waves, Protestant ministers were beginning to preach "Reformation Sunday" sermons, leaving little doubt in anyone's mind that the ills that ravaged the late medieval church in the sixteenth century were precisely the ills that continue to stalk through the halls of contemporary Romanism in the twentieth. "Reformation Sunday," rather than being an occasion to celebrate the positive principles of Luther, Calvin, and Knox, became an annual excuse for an anti-Catholic tirade.

The attitudes thus employed were similar to the famous exchange between a Roman Catholic prelate in England and a member of the Church of England. Said the Roman Catholic to the Anglican: "Where was your church before the Reformation?" Responded the Anglican to the Roman Catholic: "Where was your face before you washed it this morning?" The exchange, whether apocryphal or not, can be said to epitomize the basic polemical thrust of each group for the past 400 years.

It is not hard to understand why Roman Catholics should

have taken a dim view of the Reformation and why, until quite recent times, they should have persisted in calling it, not a reformation, but a revolt. For the conventional Catholic view has surely been that there was a unified church in the West until Luther and his cronies came along and revolted against it, setting up new and rival churches of their own devising and thus sundering western Christianity into hundreds of competing sects. (Fr. William Clancy, of the Oratory of Pittsburgh, states that his one contact with Protestantism in the course of a Catholic education was a college course entitled, "The Protestant Revolt and the Catholic Reformation."[3]) Indeed, the ease with which the term "revolting" can be shifted from verbal to adjectival form renders it peculiarly adaptable to polemical usage, as varying inflections of the phrase "the revolting Protestants" may serve to illustrate.

Jacques Maritain, in an early book called *Three Reformers*, puts Luther in the same class with Descartes and Rousseau, each of them exemplifying the revolt of the individual from the group, and representing the spirit of extreme and rampant individualism. Thus Maritain can refer to the Reformation as "an immense disaster for humanity," and Karl Adam can go on to attribute all the ills of subsequent western culture to it: "The sixteenth century revolt from the church," he writes, "led *inevitably* to the revolt from Christ in the eighteenth century, and then to the revolt from God of the nineteenth."[4]

Dom Aelred Graham, a Benedictine priest, writes:

"[The Reformation] was inexcusable. For a group of Chris-

---

[3] Clancy, "How American Protestantism Looks to a Roman Catholic," in Cowan, ed., *Facing Protestant-Roman Catholic Tensions*, Association Press, New York, 1960, p. 69.

[4] Adam, *The Spirit of Catholicism*, Macmillan, pp. 8–9, italics added. The quotation is meant to mirror an attitude, not to pillory Adam, who was one of the early participants in the Una Sancta movement in Germany, and whose later book *One and Holy* (Sheed and Ward) represented an early ecumenical breakthrough.

tians to withdraw from the community of Christendom and set up a rival altar is immeasurably more scandalous than any amount of corruption in ecclesiastical high places."[5]

As these examples indicate, the spirit of the Reformation is interpreted as a spirit of subjectivism and individualism, a series of divisive actions by individuals who set their own private hunches against the clear and collective authority of the church. The attitude is epitomized in a Catholic pamphlet on the Reformation:

"Long before a single Protestant sect saw the light of day the Catholic church was carrying on her divinely appointed mission to mankind. . . . The problem of deciding which is the true Church boils down to the question: Whom are you to believe—Martin Luther, the founder of Protestantism, or Jesus Christ, the divine founder of the Catholic Church? That is the whole problem in a nutshell."[6]

In the same pamphlet, the author deals with the Reformation under the title, "Luther's Revolt," and entitles the following chapter, "Luther's New Doctrines," dealing chiefly with the doctrine of justification by faith alone—on the presumed "newness" of which we shall shortly enlist another Catholic appraisal.

Around the turn of the century, the polemic came to rest particularly on the person of Luther, and Heinrich Denifle and Herman Grisar both published long treatments of him. Dr. Leonard Swidler, a contemporary Roman Catholic historian, describes the attitudes that prevailed:

"For Denifle, Luther was an apostate monk, married to a runaway nun, who started the Reformation in order to give

[5] Graham, *Catholicism and the World Today*, McKay, New York, 1952, p. 157.
[6] "Finding Christ's Church, With a Map to Show the Way," Ave Maria Press, Notre Dame, 1950, pp. 44, 46. In recent years the author of these words has become one of the leading spokesmen for Catholic ecumenical openness. Contrast the spirit represented in O'Brien, ed., *Steps to Christian Unity*, Doubleday, Garden City, 1964, 321 pp.

play to his lust. Luther was through and through wicked: 'Luther, there is nothing godly in you!' Grisar, who published his three-volume biography of Luther well after World War I, did not launch such a massive frontal attack against his subject as did Denifle. He was, nevertheless, out to annihilate him. For Grisar, Luther was a psychopath, out of whose diseased mind the Reformation was spun."[7]

The general impression one gathers from these conventional views of the Reformation is that the whole enterprise was engineered chiefly so that Luther, the ex-monk, could have an excuse for marrying Katharina von Bora, the ex-nun, and that anyone today who followed Luther's teachings could be doing so only for selfish, if not immoral, reasons.[8]

Contemporary Catholic reassessments of the Reformation

But a new note has entered Catholic Reformation scholarship, and four examples, out of many that could be selected, will illustrate the shift.[9]

1. A pioneer work in this field was Fr. Louis Bouyer's *The Spirit and Forms of Protestantism*.[10] While there are many

[7] Swidler, "Reappraising the Reformation," *The Commonweal*, October 30, 1964, p. 156.

[8] For further examples of such themes, cf. the chapters by Iserloh, "Luther in Contemporary Catholic Thought," and Ganoczy, "Calvin in Present-Day Catholic Thought," in Küng, ed., *op. cit.*, pp. 5–15, 34–41.

[9] For an overview from a Roman Catholic perspective, cf. Dolan, *History of the Reformation*, Desclee, New York, 1965, 417 pp.; and, more briefly, Swidler, "Catholic Reformation Scholarship in Germany," *Journal of Ecumenical Studies*, Spring 1965, pp. 189–204, also available in slightly condensed form as Ch. 2 of *The Ecumenical Vanguard*, Duquesne University Press, Pittsburgh, 1966, pp. 17–38. See also, Clebsch, "New Perspectives on the Reformation," *Religion in Life*, Autumn 1965, pp. 8–19, and Persson, "The Reformation in Recent Roman Catholic Theology," in Marty and Peerman, eds., *New Theology I*, Macmillan, New York, 1964, pp. 94–108.

[10] Newman Press, Westminster, 1956, 234 pp. The French title of the original book was *De Protestantisme à l'Église*. I have commented more fully on the volume in "A Step Forward in Catholic-Protestant Understanding," *Christianity and Crisis*, April 1, 1957, pp. 35–38.

points in Fr. Bouyer's interpretation with which the Protestant, and particularly the Protestant historian, might want to take issue, the over-all thesis of the book is noteworthy indeed. Against those who refer to the Reformers simply as theological heretics, Fr. Bouyer spends the first half of his book describing the main theological concerns of the Reformers under the heading "The Positive Principles of the Reformation." These he lists as the free gift of salvation, the sovereignty of God, the principle *Soli Deo Gloria* (glory to God alone), justification by faith, and the sovereign authority of Scripture. Against those who argue that such things as "justification by faith alone" are "new" teachings, Fr. Bouyer insists that this and the other "positive principles of the Reformation" are the very heart and center of true Catholic faith. Medieval Christendom, he avers, had either lost sight of them or grossly distorted them, so that they were in danger of being lost altogether. What the Reformers did was to bring them back into the center of Christian understanding. So, to Fr. Bouyer, the "spirit" of Protestantism was a much needed restorative for the church catholic.

Then in the second half of the book he goes on to deal with what he calls the negative elements of the Reformation, and the decay of its positive principles. He sees the Reformers as caught within medieval nominalism, from which they could not extricate themselves, so that as they attempted to apply their own positive principles they were led in increasingly negative directions. Thus although the *spirit* of Protestantism was exemplary, the *forms* of Protestantism became negative and divisive, leading to individualism and denial of authority and Protestantism could not in fact achieve its central intention, which was the re-forming of Christendom. The task today, Fr. Bouyer feels, is for all to recognize that the full flowering of the positive principles of the Reformation can only come as they are reintegrated into the Roman Catholic Church.

Fr. Bouyer found himself, understandably enough, caught

in a rather uncomfortable crossfire. Catholic critics assailed the first half of his book, with its generous interpretation of the Reformers' principles, and were mollified only by his last half, which did, after all, bring everything back into the bosom of Mother Church. Protestant critics, on the other hand, happy at his positive presentation of the Reformation in the first half (although his attribution to them of a nominalist position drew considerable criticism), felt somehow that they had been sold down the river in the second half, where they were told, in effect, to give up the struggle and return to Rome. But it is always the fate of one who breaks new ground to be thus caught, and Fr. Bouyer must be honored for his courage in attempting to occupy a terrain that was not, when the book was written, a very comfortable or densely populated location.

2. The kind of analysis that Fr. Bouyer applied to the ideas of the Reformers has been applied to the historical situation at the time of the Reformation by the German historian Fr. Joseph Lortz.[11] Lortz points out that the situation in late medieval Christendom was indeed a desperate one. Corruption in the church was a scandal, and resistance to reform was high because nobody enjoying the fruits of a corrupt situation ever wants it changed. One could buy anything in the church if he had enough money, from forgiveness of sins to a bishopric and all the avenues of income that the latter afforded. One could enter the priesthood without having to let such matters as the vow of clerical celibacy inhibit in the slightest the free expression of his sex life.

Lortz thus details, with painstaking honesty, the low estate

---

[11] Lortz has done a two-volume study of the period in German, *Die Reformation in Deutschland*, now in process of being translated. But two smaller works are already available in English, *How the Reformation Came*, Herder and Herder, N.Y., 1964, 115 pp., with an important introduction by Fr. Daniel O'Hanlon, s.j., and *The Reformation: A Problem for Today*, Newman, Westminster, 1964, 261 pp. Due apparently to some mixup on copyright agreements, about a third of the latter volume is only another translation of the text of the former.

to which the church had sunk and makes clear that it was not only inevitable that a reformer should come along—so bad was the situation—but also that it was almost as inevitable that when a reformer *did* come along, the church would resent him, resist his attempts at reformation, and drive him out. "The historian," Lortz writes, "must come to the conclusion that a revolt against the Church could hardly have been avoided any longer," and then concludes, "A 'reformation' had become a historical necessity."[12]

This then, for Lortz, poses the real tragedy of the Reformation period: the church was desperately in need of reformation, but it was *so* desperately in need of reformation that it could not bring itself to acknowledge its need. Thus pre-Reformers like Wycliffe and Tyndale and Hus were cast out, and each rebuff to reforming movements only made the need of reform more stringent. Luther, Lortz realizes, had no intention of "leaving the church," and wished only to work within it as a loyal son for its renewal. He tried all the devices: disputations, appeals for a general council, appeals to the pope, appeals from the pope ill informed to the pope better informed. But to no avail. Thus he was finally forced to carry on his reforming activities despite pope and curia, and to endure excommunication at their hand.

So much is, of course, familiar territory to all students of the sixteenth century. The significant point that Lortz introduces into his assessment—the point of crucial importance for the present chapter—is his insistence that the Roman Catholic Church must share responsibility for the divisions in Christendom that followed. Rome's resistance to reform means that Rome must share responsibility for what happened, namely the sundering of the unity of the western church.

Lortz, then, seeks to correct the conventional picture that the fault was all on one side—doubly important, when one

---

[12] Lortz, *How the Reformation Came*, p. 110.

remembers that the conventional Catholic has always had a clear understanding of which side that was.

"The Reformation is a Catholic concern in the sense of Catholic co-responsibility, and that also implies shared Catholic guilt. . . . Within the area of Christian concepts the guilt we [Roman Catholics] share calls for an unconditional *mea culpa*. . . . If we do not make this confession, then it will be impossible to arrive at an understanding at the human level or a settlement in the Christian sphere. The confession of guilt by Pope Adrian VI gives us an example."[13]

Pope Adrian VI's confession of guilt is a remarkable statement. Only freshly exhumed from the mines of scholarly research into which for several centuries it had safely been interred, it represents a note of contrition unfamiliar in most Reformation writing, for it offers a public acknowledgment of the guilt which Catholics, from priests to curia to pope, should have been ready to acknowledge, and which, apparently, only Adrian had the readiness to acknowledge. (With pardonable Teutonic pride, Lortz refers to Adrian as "the last of the Germanic popes.") What Adrian said was this:

"We freely confess: God permits this persecution of his Church [i.e., the divisions of the Reformation] on account of the sins of men, and especially of prelates and the clergy. . . . Holy Scripture declares aloud that the sins of the people are the consequence of the sins of the priesthood. . . . We know all too well that for many years things deserving of abhorrence have taken place around this Holy See. Sacred things have been misused, the commandments transgressed; in everything there has been a turn for the worse. Thus it is not surprising that the malady has spread from the head to

---

[13] Lortz, *How the Reformation Came*, pp. 112–13. The term *mea culpa* (which older Roman Catholic readers may remember from the days when they had a Latin mass) is the individual acknowledgment of guilt which Lortz here says must characterize the entire Catholic Church when it surveys the wreckage of Christian unity perpetrated in the sixteenth century.

the members, from the popes to the hierarchy. We all, prelates and clergy, have gone astray from the right path, and for long there has been none that has done good."[14]

Adrian goes on to promise (in terms that have once again become familiar in our day) that he will reform the curia. But in six months Adrian was dead, and his statement of contrition disappeared from Catholic thinking for almost 400 years (as did the notion of curia reform), replaced by the language of contention.

One of the values of the work of men like Bouyer and Lortz has been their willingness to look at the Protestant Reformers in terms of their *intentions*, and not just in terms of the consequences of their actions when viewed from the comfortable hindsight of four centuries. From the standpoint of a concern about the consequences of the Reformation, the Catholic can only view the Reformation as a baleful event, since it did, in fact, entail the division of Christendom. But viewed from a concern about the Reformers' intentions, such as the restoration of true faith and the overcoming of corruption and scandal, the Reformation must be seen in a different light. Had the church in the Reformers' day been open to reform, division might have been avoided. Thus the fact that division took place must be laid at the door not only of the Reformers but also at the door of the church that refused to be reformed. (This led a Catholic reviewer, in commenting on Catholic layman John Todd's remarkably irenic book on *Martin Luther*,[15] to wonder if, had the church in Luther's day displayed the sensitivity to such matters that it now does, we might not instead of celebrating "Reformation Sunday" be celebrating together the Feast of Blessed Martin.)

3. Another exemplar of Reformation reappraisal is the contemporary Swiss theologian Hans Küng. Küng, dean of the Roman Catholic theological faculty at the University of

[14] Cited in Lortz, *How the Reformation Came*, p. 95.
[15] Newman Press, Westminster, 1964, 290 pp.

Tübingen, writes in terms that are particularly resonant to
Protestant ears. To say this is not to render his Catholicism
suspect, but simply to note that he has a remarkable sensitivity to the kinds of questions that exercise Protestants. His
doctoral dissertation, for example, is a comparison of the
doctrine of justification in Karl Barth and the Council of
Trent.[16] Küng recognizes that the supreme theological issue
in the sixteenth century was the meaning of "justification by
faith." The Reformers' rallying cry was *sola fide*—by "faith
alone" one is saved and not by works. The Catholic response
was an insistence on a combination of faith and works as
necessary for salvation, and the latter position appeared to
have been definitively affirmed by the Council of Trent.

Küng, however, has re-opened the entire question. He has
examined Barth's *Church Dogmatics*, IV/1, to get a representative Protestant position, and has then sought to re-examine
the teaching of Trent—but to examine it free from the
polemical intent of trying to show how right Trent was
against the aberrations of the Reformers in the sixteenth
century, or their spiritual descendants (such as Karl Barth)
in the twentieth century. And Küng's amazing discovery is
that what Karl Barth says about justification is what the
Tridentine fathers were really trying to say, when understood
in their historical and polemical context. Küng does not insist that no differences of emphasis remain, but he does insist
that the differences are not basic enough to justify, on these
grounds alone, the continuing Protestant-Catholic division.

After reading the dissertation, Barth wrote Küng a letter
(included in the published version) in which he said to Küng
in effect: you have correctly understood my teaching on justification, but can you possibly be right about Trent? Con-
versely, Roman Catholic reviewers of the book have said in
effect: Küng has correctly understood Trent's teaching on

---

[16] Küng, *Justification: The Doctrine of Karl Barth and a Catholic Reflection*, Nelson, New York, 1964, 332 pp.

justification, but can he possibly be right about Barth? It would appear that Küng has struck pay dirt.[17]

Another remarkable book was written by Küng just prior to the beginning of Vatican II.[18] When *The Council, Reform and Reunion* first appeared, it seemed *avant garde* indeed, and one wondered, back in the pre-conciliar days, how long it would be before the author found himself in serious difficulty with the Holy Office. One re-reads it, now that the council has been completed, and realizes that most of what it contains has already been given sanction by the council fathers themselves, and that not only can one's fears about the Holy Office begin to fade away, but that so widespread has been the impact of the council that the Holy Office itself has begun to fade away, replaced by a more up-to-date structure designed not to spy on theological investigation but to foster it.

In his appraisal of the Reformation, Küng says that the council must provide for "the renewal of the Catholic Church, drawing on the resources of her own essential nature, through the meeting of all that is justified in Protestant demands and criticism." He continues:

"To whatever extent the Protestant protest is justified, it is the Catholic Church herself, against whom the protest is made, who must take it up and provide the remedy which will make the protest pointless."[19]

[17] Barth acknowledges that if Küng's interpretation of Trent is correct, he, Barth, has seriously misunderstood Trent and must take a trip to the church in Trent where the fathers held their sessions, beat his breast, and say, *Patres, peccavi*, Fathers, I have sinned. He pleads, however, that his interpretation is what later generations of Catholics had also felt Trent was saying, and then rather slyly asks whether Küng would have seen the new dimensions in the Tridentine formulations had he not also read Barth's *Church Dogmatics!*

[18] Küng, *The Council, Reform and Reunion*, Sheed and Ward, New York, 1961, 208 pp.

[19] *Ibid.*, p. 96. Fr. Maurice Villain had made the same point previously, though not of course in relation to the council, in his *Introduction à l'Oecumenisme*, Casterman, Paris, 1959, esp. Part IV, Ch. II. I have given an analysis of Villain's main points in *An American Dialogue*, pp. 116–21.

In other words, Küng says to Catholics, not only must we acknowledge (along with Pope Adrian VI) that Catholics too are responsible for the sins of division, but the Catholic Church, recognizing whatever is valid and legitimate in the Reformers' protests, must seek to meet those protests and thus neutralize them, so that there will no longer be reason for divisions to remain between us. This means, he insists, Catholic recognition of the *religious* motives of the Reformers. It means an acknowledgment that the Reformers were motivated by a true love of the church and a concern over its low estate, rather than by a perverse desire to rend Christendom asunder. It means acknowledging with the Reformers the central place that Scripture must have in the life of the church. It means recognizing that the liturgy must be the people's liturgy, in which the laity participate, rather than a clerical act in which the laity are merely spectators. It means giving a greater stress to the notion of the priesthood of all believers. It means the reform of the curia. It means an unequivocal affirmation of religious liberty for all men. It means the removal of the papacy from the realm of power politics.

Surveying the finished results of the council in the light of such proposals, one cannot fail to observe that Fr. Küng's batting average is phenomenally high.

4. In the light of these emphases in Küng's writings, and also in light of the fact that so many of these concerns were actually met by the Vatican Council, it is encouraging to see that the initiative thus gained is being pressed. A significant example is a sermon given by Fr. Avery Dulles, s.j., during the Christian Unity Octave in January 1965, entitled "Luther's Unfinished Reformation," a quotation from which is cited at the beginning of the present chapter. Fr. Dulles, a teacher at the Jesuit theologate at Woodstock, Maryland, points out that "the Lutheran Reformation has had, and continues to have, enormous positive significance for us Catholics." He notes that "Luther, by his angry protests against

the weaknesses of late medieval Catholicism, greatly strengthened the forces within the Church which were already working for reform." After citing some of Luther's valid concerns, he continues:

"The Church in the Counter-Reformation did not give sufficient value to these sound Lutheran principles. . . . Only in the present generation has Catholicism begun to be genuinely self-critical. . . . [The] new climate of humility, charity and Christian freedom, thoroughly in accord with the Gospel, has made it clear that the Church is capable of genuine self-reform."[20]

And Fr. Dulles then makes an extremely perceptive comment:

"Modern Lutheran thinkers . . . have frequently pointed out that Luther envisaged the Reformation as a corrective movement within the Catholic Church. A reformed Church he wanted indeed, but not a separate Church. The only Church which he willed to reform was the one holy Catholic Church, founded by Christ himself. . . . If all this is true, we must conclude that Luther's Reformation is still an ongoing thing. So long as there are two separate Christianities, Protestant and Catholic, his objective remains but half achieved."[21]

*   *   *

When one confronts the spectacle of a Jesuit urging Roman Catholics to bring the concerns of Martin Luther to fulfillment, then indeed it is clear that there has been a reformation of the interpretation of Reformation interpretation.

[20] "Luther's Unfinished Reformation," Graymoor Press, Peekskill, pp. 5–6. The sermon is also available in *The Catholic Mind*, XLIII (1965), pp. 32–35, with a portrait of Martin Luther on the cover.

[21] *Ibid.*, pp. 9–10. Cf. the similar emphases in the Lutheran scholar Carl Braaten, discussed in Ch. 7 below.

CHAPTER 6

"BREAKING THE HEART OF STONE"
(the development of contrition)

Blessed art Thou, God, the Father of our Lord Jesus
Christ. We have sinned against Thee; we have introduced divisions into Thy work of unity. Even in our
proclamation of Thy truth, we have often been narrow,
exclusive, and lacking in love. We have forgotten the
beam in our own eye in order to judge the speck in our
brother's eye. We have lived, ignoring them and scorn-
ing them; we have often wanted to conquer and subju-
gate them. But Thou, Lord, Father of mercy, Thou wilt
break our heart of stone and give us a heart able to repent.

Prayer of Cardinal Léger at the ecumenical
service during the Faith and Order meetings
at Montreal in 1963.

We are emerging from a period in which contention was the
controlling attitude between Protestants and Catholics. Both
sides tried to score points against each other, by piling up
evidence to show how right they were and how wrong the
opponents were. Much of the justification for this was provided by a reading of history that was partisan in the extreme,
and this makes more remarkable than ever the new disposition within Catholicism, which we have just examined, to
reassess the significance of the Protestant Reformation.

Implicit in this new disposition is a willingness to acknowledge not only that the fault back then lay on both sides, but
even more important to acknowledge that the fault for the
persistence of division today lies on both sides. The presup-

position of each side, then, in reaching out toward the other, is contrition both for past wrong and also for persistence in allowing past wrong to dominate current concern. So basic is this attitude to the ecumenical dialogue that we must indicate in some detail how it has been established.

Contrition in contemporary Catholic concern
—a glance at recent history

The new note is worth underlining in contemporary Roman Catholic life for at least two reasons: (a) because until very recently the note was almost completely lacking in official Catholic statements, and (b) because many non-Catholics, conditioned by the triumphalist tone of past Catholic statements, are not yet ready to revise their former estimates without the introduction of considerable evidence. Catholic readers may wonder why the public expression of contrition on the part of the Catholic Church should occasion such surprise in Protestant circles. For them, Fr. Maurice Villain has both stated the quandary and supplied the answer:

"It is somewhat difficult to see that these ideas, which had for a long time been accepted by professional ecumenists, were seized upon with such astonishment by outside observers; the reason is that they saw them for the first time mentioned in an *official* document of the Roman Church."[1]

The first step in the development of contrition has already been noted in the previous chapter, represented by Pope Adrian's remarkable statement of contrition for the sins of pope, curia, hierarchy, and priesthood in the sixteenth century. A second step is exemplified by such men as Fr. Lortz, who recognize that "the Reformation is a Catholic concern in the sense of Catholic co-responsibility, and that also implies shared Catholic guilt."[2]

[1] In Küng, ed., *Do We Know the Others?*, p. 124.
[2] On these points, cf. Ch. 5 above.

A third step is represented by the recognition of recent Catholic theologians that the whole so-called triumphalist imagery of the church must be called into question. Only at the eschatological consummation of all things will the church be pure and "without spot or wrinkle." Such a description does not characterize the empirical church on earth. The recognition is almost perfectly epitomized by the late Cardinal Meyer's plea, at the second session of the council, that Catholics remember that until the end of time the *church* must pray (as St. Augustine once said), "Forgive us our sins."

One of the pioneers in bringing this point to focus in contemporary Catholic thought has been Fr. Yves Congar, O.P., who for years has foreshadowed tendencies that finally came to fruition in the promulgated documents of Vatican II. His early book, *Vrai et Fausse Réforme dans l'Église*, acknowledged that "self-criticism was quite new in the church," although it had been present with remarkable robustness in early periods of church history.[3] (Dante, for example, had in *The Divine Comedy* populated Hell with popes.) Congar sees two important tendencies in modern concern for reform. One of these is "the desire for authentic actions," so that what the church *actually* does corresponds to what it *intends* to signify by what it does. The other concern is "the need for adaptation or revision of certain forms in the concrete life of the church," since many things the church now does conceal rather than reveal the Gospel with which she has been entrusted. While noting that "an imperfect but stable order is often preferable to change," Fr. Congar nevertheless summons Cyprian (*Ep.* LXXIV, ix, 2) to suggest another stance: "Custom without truth is nothing but the seniority of error."

Fr. Congar goes on to show how *integralism* has been the opponent of reform. (This term has been a key one in recent

---

[3] Portions of Fr. Congar's book, which has never been translated, have been reprinted in *Cross Currents*, Summer 1951, pp. 80–102, and Summer 1953, pp. 358–65.

Roman Catholic discussion. It suggests an attitude of rigidity, particularly in matters of doctrine, a desire to imprison the truth in modes of speech from the past and thrust them unchanged on the future. It further suggests that this rigidity is to be maintained in authoritarian fashion and that challenge to such a way of doing things is to be equated with disloyalty.) In Fr. Congar's terms, integralism becomes so concerned to maintain order and stability that openness and creativity disappear. In an effort to resist change, the church structure becomes rigidly paternalistic and the advocates of integralism "see things accomplished only from the top down, by the intervention of authority." Thus any movement for change from below is resisted by those in authority. In the face of this, Fr. Congar feels constrained to urge those in authority not to be so resistant to reform that they force those with legitimate concerns to leave the church. "It is necessary, therefore," he concludes, "that a balance be maintained between creative forces and stability, between new demands and tradition."

This might seem a modest plea from the vantage point of the historical hindsight provided by Vatican II. But it was, when written, a daring plea. For, at the time, what Fr. Congar calls "creative forces" and "new demands" were virtually at the mercy of "stability" and "tradition." Put another way, the dynamic forces within the church were almost smothered by the static forces. That this situation began, slowly, to change is due to the courage of the Fr. Congars. Their pleas for a new vitality, with the inevitable corollary that something was seriously wrong with the integralist vision, became the seed-bed for the flowering of a sense of contrition that was finally manifested at Vatican II.

The theme assumed even more robust form in the writings of Fr. Karl Rahner, s.j., another theologian responsible for shaping the atmosphere that made Vatican II possible. As early as 1947, Rahner was writing about "The Church of

Sinners."[4] He notes that Catholic theology makes much of the holiness of the church. But it is clear that this is not enough to say. How is the Christian, who believes in the holiness of the church, to understand the unholiness he discovers within it? Rahner offers two responses:

(a) *Sinners belong to the church.* This is clear enough to anyone with honest eyes, and it is a reality that can be accepted by anyone willing to take the New Testament estimate of man seriously. Both sin and rebellion clearly exist in the lives of those within the church. Such a recognition is not particularly damaging to Catholic thought since it does not touch the church *qua* church. Or does it?

Rahner presses further. It must be acknowledged, he says, that (b) *the church is sinful.*

"After what has so far been said, one can no longer in any context of faith maintain that there are sinners 'in' the Church as in an external confessional organization, but that this carries no implication about the Church herself."[5]

It is not enough to acknowledge that the church houses sinful people; the things those sinful people do as the church leave their imprint upon the church.

"It is obvious that the sin exists not only in the private life of the churchman but can enter very essentially into the concrete context of his activities as a representative of the Church as well. . . . There is no teaching according to which the inspiration of the Holy Spirit, which is always with the Church, would restrict this influence of sin in Church leaders to their private lives and not permit it to invade the area of their work in the Church."[6]

Rahner has the courage to pursue the argument to its con-

<hr>

[4] *Stimmen zer Zeit.* The essay is available in English in *Cross Currents,* Vol. I, Spring 1951, pp. 64–74.

[5] *Cross Currents,* Spring 1951, p. 68.

[6] *Ibid.,* p. 69.

clusion: "This is to admit that the Church in her activity can be sinful."[7]

This does not lead him, of course, to abandon the church, or to believe that sin in the church destroys the efficacious work the church can do; the church remains until the end of time as "the presence on earth of God and of His grace." Rahner is clear, furthermore, that the church can never become so disfigured by her sin that the power of the Spirit departs from her: "Sin in her remains a reality which contradicts her essence; whereas her sanctity is a manifestation of that essence."[8]

What are Christians to do when confronted by this picture? Contrition must engender "an impetus to the renewal of our own Christianity and through us of that of the Church."[9] It is as unthinkable that one would leave the church because of its sinfulness as that one would try to minimize or conceal such disfigurements. Christians will "carry and endure the disgrace of the Church" as their own, and this will open the possibility of seeing in a new way beyond the sins of the church to the holiness and glory of the church.

That the theme of contrition had clearly surfaced by the time Vatican II was announced can be illustrated by Hans Küng's plea, a full year before the convening of the council, that it should begin on a note of contrition:

"It would be a truly Christian act if the Pope and the Council (perhaps at the very beginning, when they are invoking the Holy Spirit) were to express this truth: Forgive us our sins! Forgive us our sins, and in particular our share in the sin of schism! Pope Adrian VI said it long ago. An honest, humble confession of this sort by the leaders of the

---

[7] *Ibid.*, p. 69. It is interesting that in 1961 Hans Küng expressed some difficulties with the notion. Cf. Küng, *The Council, Reform and Reunion*, p. 34.

[8] *Ibid.*, p. 71.

[9] *Ibid.*, p. 71.

Church today would be pleasing to our heavenly Father as few words or deeds could be; and one word of repentance would open more doors to us amongst our separated fellow-Christians than any number of pressing invitations to return."[10]

The council did not, in fact, open in this fashion, though before its convening Pope John made informal comments moving in this direction: "We do not intend to conduct a trial of the past. All we want to say is, 'Let us come together. Let us make an end of our divisions.' "[11]

The inclusion of a statement acknowledging contrition for the sins of division was discussed by the Secretariat for the Promotion of Christian Unity in early plans for the ecumenism decree. After considerable debate within the Secretariat, however, a proposed statement was withdrawn. It was feared, perhaps rightly, that such a confession was too far ahead of where the bishops were in their own thinking, and that to press too rapidly in such a direction might jeopardize the entire document.

Such a confession did, however, make its way into the promulgated document, and the steps leading to its inclusion are significant. The breakthrough was provided by Pope Paul's allocution at the beginning of the second session, a statement that may appear to later historians as monumental as Pope Adrian's statement is now beginning to appear to contemporary historians. In the course of his speech, the pope turned directly to the non-Catholic observers present in St. Peter's and said, referring to the centuries of separation,

"If we are in any way to blame for that separation, we humbly beg God's forgiveness. And we ask pardon too of our brethren who feel themselves to have been injured by us. For our part, we willingly forgive the injuries which the Catholic

---

[10] Küng, *The Council, Reform and Reunion*, p. 184.

[11] Even this statement was meat too strong for the Vatican newspaper *Osservatore Romano* to digest and report, and we owe its preservation to the German journal *Herder Korrespondenz*.

Church has suffered, and forget the grief endured during the long series of dissensions and separations."[12]

Nothing as forthright and as official had been said in 400 years. It would be hard to measure the impact these words have already had and will continue to have. As one who was privileged to be present on the occasion, I recorded the following reactions later the same day:

"I predict that this statement will become a kind of charter to characterize the atmosphere that must inform future ecumenical discussion, not only because of its source, but because it is so forthright in stating the two essential ingredients that must be present in any genuine reconciliation: (a) a plea for forgiveness for the wrongs one has inflicted, and (b) a granting of forgiveness for the wrongs one has suffered. I would hope that in comparable situations on the Protestant side, our own leaders can make statements that are as generous and gracious. As long as this attitude prevails, there are no barriers too strong to exclude the visitation of the Holy Spirit in our ecumenical endeavors."[13]

Not all reactions were as favorable. Some observers felt that the statement still hedged, and justified their complaint by pointing to the fact that the pope's declaration of Roman Catholic responsibility was conditional, "*If* we are in any way to blame for that separation . . .", implying that perhaps they were not; whereas his statement of Protestant responsibility was unequivocal, "We forgive the injuries the Catholic Church *has suffered.*" If such reactions of dissatisfaction reached the pope, he made his own mind unmistakably clear in an audience with the non-Catholic observers a few weeks later: "In Our Speech of September 29, We ventured to give the first place to Christian forgiveness, mutual if possible. 'We grant pardon and ask it in return.' "[14]

---

[12] In Küng, Congar, and O'Hanlon, eds., *Council Speeches of Vatican II*, Paulist Press, Glen Rock, 1964, pp. 146–47.

[13] Brown, *Observer in Rome*, Doubleday, New York, 1964, p. 23.

[14] Cited in *ibid.*, p. 80.

As a result of the pope's statement, the document that had originally omitted a statement of Catholic responsibility for the sins of division was criticized precisely for that omission. On the first morning of discussion, for example, Cardinal Quintero of Venezuela urged acknowledgment of the fact that many past mistakes in Catholic history are due to defects in the church, and not just to historical circumstances. The church must not resemble the Pharisee who proudly denied his own sin, but be like the publican who beat his breast in contrition. The document must therefore state explicitly that the Catholic Church asks pardon from God and from the separated brethren for its own responsibility for the divisions of Christendom.[15]

Equally strong was the intervention of Bishop Elchinger of Strasbourg, in one of the most notable ecumenical utterances of the council:

"We all certainly believe that the Church is holy, just as we believe it is one, catholic and apostolic. But we also know that God has put his holy gifts in vessels of clay (2 Cor. 4:7), that is in men who are sinners. We no longer refuse to confess our sins, as our Holy Father Pope Paul testified in his address of September 29th, and at the reception for our brothers the Observers on October 17. And this must be not merely a general confession, but must detail all the particular questions and deeds where we have fallen short in various ways, or where divinely revealed truth has been honored with warmer fervor by our separated brothers."[16]

Archbishop D'Souza of Bhopal, India, pointed out that the text of the *schema* on ecumenism must indicate that "the Catholic Church as a Church has finally learned humility." He continued:

"The Sovereign Pontiff himself humbly begged pardon of

---

[15] In Küng, Congar, and O'Hanlon, eds., *op. cit.*, pp. 149–51.
[16] *Ibid.*, p. 216. The full text is on pp. 215–21. My own reactions are contained in *Observer in Rome*, pp. 187–88.

God and of the separated brothers themselves at the beginning of this session, and the schema urges us to inner renewal and conversion of heart. . . . After the famous confession which Pope Adrian VI ordered his legate in Germany to make at the start of the Reformation, such statements were very rarely made in the succeeding centuries. It is right for the Catholic Church to say that she has received the fullness of truth and of the means of grace, but it seemed that from this the false conclusion was drawn that she was practically guiltless."[17]

As a result of these and similar requests, the promulgated document has three explicit references to Catholic responsibility for the sins of division. Each represents a different level of approach to the problem:

(a) After describing the original unity of the church, the decree acknowledges the fact of joint responsibility for the ensuing divisions:

"But in subsequent centuries more widespread disagreements appeared and quite large Communities became separated from full communion with the Catholic Church— developments for which, at times, men of both sides were to blame."[18]

(b) The document acknowledges that when the Catholic Church has strayed from the Gospel, "ongoing reformation" must ensue:

"Christ summons the Church, as she goes her pilgrim way, to that continual reformation of which she always has need,

[17] *Ibid.*, pp. 210–11. Other speeches on this theme are contained in Part III, "Reunion of All Christians," pp. 145–227. Cf. also the excerpts from the speech of Bishop Laszlo in Jaeger, *A Stand on Ecumenism*, pp. 122–23.

Forty-three bishops at the third session requested that a phrase describing non-Catholics as ones who had "separated themselves" from the Roman See be amended, so that it would not suggest that blame for the separation rested on them alone. (Cf. Jaeger, *op. cit.*, p. 128.) Note also that when "divisions" among Christians are referred to, the word *scissurae* is used in the Latin text instead of *schismata*, because of the pejorative tone of the latter.

[18] *On Ecumenism*, Art. 3, cited in Abbott, ed., *op. cit.*, p. 355.

insofar as she is an institution of men here on earth. Therefore, if the influences of events or of the times has led to deficiencies in conduct, in Church discipline, or even in the formulation of doctrine (which must be carefully distinguished from the deposit itself of faith), these should be appropriately rectified at the proper moment."[19]

It is remarkable that this statement, instead of merely mentioning deficiencies "in conduct," goes on to mention deficiencies "in Church discipline," for the latter suggests more than the failings of individual members; it suggests that the church *qua* church stands in need of reform—a stronger statement than that of the previous quotation, which merely asserts that "men of both sides" were to blame.[20]

But even more remarkable is the assertion that there could have been deficiencies "in the formulation of doctrine," though the statement is carefully qualified in the parenthesis that follows. This statement opens up a host of possibilities for reform, for it means that Pope John's distinction between the "sacred deposit" of faith and ways of expressing that faith, as well as the strictures of Pope Paul and Cardinal Léger against "theological immobilism," have been given conciliar approval.

So the precondition of reaching out to the other in true love is the putting of one's own house in order. Inner reform and renewal are essential:

[19] *On Ecumenism*, Art. 6; Abbott, p. 350.

[20] The decree, however, still manifests considerable caution on this point. The quotation cited, for example, does not rise to the heights suggested by Cardinal Quintero, since it limits deficiencies to "the influence of events or of the times." Reference is made earlier in the decree to the fact that "during its pilgrimage on earth, this People, *though still in its members liable to sin*, is growing in Christ. . . ." (Art. 3, Abbott, p. 846), the italicized words making clear that the sin is in the members rather than the institution as such. However, it should be noted that the words "in its members" were added by Pope Paul only one day before the final vote. The council fathers were clearly ready to accept the statement without the explicit qualification. On the matter of the "papal interventions," cf. Ch. 11 below.

"In ecumenical work, Catholics must assuredly be concerned for their separated brethren, praying for them, keeping them informed about the Church, making the first approaches towards them. *But their primary duty is to make an honest and careful appraisal of whatever needs to be renewed and achieved in the Catholic household itself,* in order that its life may bear witness more loyally and luminously to the teachings and ordinances which have been handed down from Christ through the apostles."[21]

(c) Having acknowledged joint responsibility for the sins of division and the consequent need for reform, the document expresses the double movement urged in Pope Paul's allocution, the need to confess one's own sin and to forgive the sin of the other:

"St. John has testified: 'If we say that we have not sinned, we make him a liar, and his word is not in us' (1 Jn. 1:10). This holds good for sins against unity. Thus, in humble prayer, we beg pardon of God and of our separated brethren, just as we forgive those who trespass against us."[22]

It is hard to see how there could have been a more clear-cut, forthright declaration than this.

The council, however, did more than merely talk about contrition. At the session on December 7, 1965, the council acted in a way that indicated the new stance of the church more clearly than even the finest statement alone could ever have done. On that occasion, a declaration was read in St. Peter's (and simultaneously in Istanbul) issued jointly by Pope Paul and Patriarch Athenagoras of the Orthodox Church of Constantinople. It dealt with the schism of 1054 A.D. between East and West, and the mutual excommunications and anathemas that followed by both pope and patriarch in the eleventh century. After pointing out the baleful effects that this ancient event had had, pope and patriarch

---

[21] *Ibid.,* Art. 4; Abbott, p. 348. Italics added.
[22] *Ibid.,* Art. 7; Abbott, p. 351.

in the twentieth century, "in common agreement," declared that:

"a. They regret the offensive words, the reproaches without foundation, and the reprehensible gestures which, on both sides, have marked or accompanied the sad events of this period.

"b. They likewise regret and remove both from memory and from the midst of the Church the sentences of excommunication which followed these events, the memory of which has influenced actions up to our day and has hindered closer relations in charity; and they commit these excommunications to oblivion.

"c. Finally, they deplore the preceding and later vexing events which, under the influence of various factors—among which, lack of understanding and mutual trust—eventually led to the effective rupture of ecclesiastical communion."[23]

The document noted that such a gesture of mutual pardon would not end all the differences between Catholicism and Orthodoxy, but it made clear where pope and patriarch desired such action to lead:

"They hope, nevertheless, that this act will be pleasing to God, who is prompt to pardon us when we pardon each other. They hope that the whole Christian world, especially the entire Roman Catholic Church and the Orthodox Church, will appreciate this gesture as an expression of a sincere desire, shared in common, for reconciliation, and as an invitation to follow out, in a spirit of trust, esteem, and mutual charity, the dialogue which, with God's help, will lead to living together again, for the greater good of souls and the coming of the kingdom of God, in that full communion of faith, fraternal accord, and sacramental life which existed among them during the first thousand years of the life of the Church."[24]

---

[23] Cited in Abbott, ed., *op. cit.*, p. 726. The text is also available in Rynne, *The Fourth Session*, Farrar, Straus and Giroux, New York, 1966, pp. 315–17.

[24] *Ibid.*, pp. 726–27.

Is it inconceivable that Catholics and Protestants might sometime in the future be able to engage in a similar act of reconciliation concerning some, at least, of the events that have divided them?

Penitence as a Protestant possibility
—a glance at recent documentation

It would be invidious to imply that the ecumenical revolution demands Catholic contrition without a corresponding need for Protestant penitence.[25] The Protestant may try to suggest that penitence is built into the life of those who embrace the Protestant slogan *ecclesia semper reformanda* (the church always in process of being reformed), and that in recent years the Catholic Church has done no more than catch up to where the Reformers were four centuries ago. But the suggestion is too facile. For if there has been Catholic triumphalism, there has been Protestant triumphalism as well, often of a particularly unlovely sort, and there is nothing more fatal to a true understanding of the church than failure to be contrite because contrition is casually claimed as part of the definition of what the church is. Even though Reformation confessions had a built-in recognition that, as the Westminster Confession put it, "Councils may err" (including, it must be assumed, the "council" that produced the Westminster Confession), it must be acknowledged that later Protestants themselves became as triumphalistic about their own confessions and traditions and denominations as they ever accused the Roman Catholic Church of being.

Protestant penitence is surely needed at many points, but perhaps most of all in a sober recognition that Protestantism not only *fostered* division but has *perpetuated* division. And

---

[25] No theological meaning is to be read into the substitution of "penitence" for "contrition." It illustrates only that the author is attracted by alliteration.

perpetuation of division is the particular sin of which Protestants have been guilty, for they have complacently come to accept division as normal, rather than as something tragically abnormal. The notion of a divided church is not only a contradiction in terms, but also a scandalous and shocking thing. The only thing more scandalous and shocking has been the complacency with which many Protestants have avoided being scandalized and shocked by it.[26]

But Protestants, like Catholics, are being jarred out of their complacency. Recognizing that Protestants have plenty about which to be penitent, it will be useful to document some of the ways in which this recognition has received expression.

In the face of the horror that Nazism represented in Europe, one of the most remarkable declarations of recent times has been the "Stuttgart Declaration" of October 1945, in which members of the Evangelical Church in Germany, in welcoming representatives of the World Council of Churches to a meeting, confessed:

"We are the more thankful for this visit in that we are not only conscious of oneness with our nation in a great community of suffering, but also in a solidarity of guilt. With great pain we say: Unending suffering has been brought by us to many peoples and countries. That which we have often witnessed to our congregations we now proclaim in the name of the whole church: We have in fact fought for long years in the name of Jesus Christ against the spirit which found its terrible expression in National Socialist government by force; but we accuse ourselves that we did not witness more courageously, pray more faithfully, believe more joyously, love more ardently."[27]

The very coming into being of the World Council of

---

[26] On this point cf. further the concluding section of Ch. 7, dealing with Professor Carl Braaten's reassessment of the Reformation.

[27] Cited in Littell, *The German Phoenix*, Doubleday, New York, 1960, Appendix C, p. 189.

Churches could only have been brought about on the basis of the penitential presupposition that the churches had been guilty of grave sin by the persistence of their divisions. At the assembly at Amsterdam, bringing the World Council into being, the note of penitence was prominent:

"Within our divided churches, there is much which we confess with penitence before the Lord of the Church, for it is in our estrangement from him that all our sin has its origin. It is because of this that the evils of the world have so deeply penetrated our church, so that amongst us too there are worldly standards of success, class division, economic rivalry, a secular mind. Even where there are no differences of theology, language, or liturgy, there exist churches segregated by race and colour, a scandal within the Body of Christ. We are in danger of being salt that has lost its savour and is fit for nothing."[28]

As the delegates at the Lund Faith and Order conference in 1952 noted, "The word penitence has often been on our lips here at Lund." They acknowledged,

"We cannot but express our deep disappointment and concern that there is not a larger measure of agreement among us. We echo the view of the preparatory Commission on Intercommunion that 'neither we nor the Churches from which we come have yet gone deeply enough into the penitence from which healing may arise.' "[29]

It was recognized at Lund that the intransigency of the churches had to be challenged, judged, and finally shattered, and that only on the far side of judgment would mercy be found:

"Those who are ever looking backward and have accumulated much precious ecclesiastical baggage will perhaps be shown that pilgrims must travel light and that, if we are to share at last in the great Supper, we must let go much that

---

28 Cited in Vischer, ed., *op. cit.*, p. 80.
29 In Tomkins, ed., *op. cit.*, p. 57.

we treasure. Churches settled and self-assured will have to hear again the Lord's heartbroken concern for the sheep without a shepherd and know that to be His Church is to share in His world-embracing mission. Churches too much at home in the world will hear themselves called out of the world. Churches too wrapped up in their own piety or their own survival will see again Him who identified Himself with the deprived and the oppressed."[30]

The Evanston assembly in 1954, after dealing with "Our Oneness in Christ," went on to deal with "Our Disunity as Churches." Acknowledging that there can be a diversity which is good, as reflecting the diversities of gifts given by the Spirit, the assembly report went on to comment, "But when diversity disrupts the manifest unity of the body, then it changes its quality and becomes sinful division."[31]

"[God] has also given to us today a fresh awareness of the sin which characterizes the divided state which we have inherited. . . . We must remember that we are culpably implicated in sin not wholly of our making and cannot disassociate ourselves from the sin of division. Confession of our oneness with Christ carries with it confession of solidarity with our brethren in sin.

"We ask each other whether we do not sin when we deny the sole lordship of Christ over the Church by claiming the vineyard for our own, by possessing our 'church' for ourselves, by regarding our theology, order, history, nationality, etc., as our own 'valued treasures,' thus involving ourselves more and more in the separation of sin. . . ."[32]

To acknowledge this corruption of the treasure bequeathed to the churches suggests that a radical remedy will be required:

"Concretely, this means that when churches, in their ac-

---

[30] In Tomkins, ed., p. 21.
[31] 't Hooft, ed., *The Evanston Report*, p. 87.
[32] *Ibid.*, p. 88.

tual historical situations, reach a point of readiness and a time of decision, then their witnessing may require obedience unto death. *They may then have to be prepared to offer up some of their accustomed, inherited forms of life in uniting with other churches,* without complete certainty as to all that will emerge from the step of faith."[33]

The New Delhi assembly in 1961 acknowledged that many of the ills of the church could be laid to structures that had become a hindrance to witness:

"We must inquire of ourselves whether our present structures do not preserve our divisions in a fossilized way, instead of enhancing the unity of the witnessing community. The scandal that renders the Gospel insignificant in the eyes of the unbelieving world and turns away genuine enquirers and potential converts is not the true scandal of the Gospel, Christ crucified, but rather the false scandals of our own practices and structures."[34]

New Delhi also strongly indicted the equivocation of the church on the race issue,[35] a theme that was powerfully restated at the Montreal conference on Faith and Order two years later:

"We are shamefully divided by racial prejudice and discrimination. This denies the dignity of man, subverts our unity in Christ, and stultifies the mission of the Church. God is judging our racially divided Christian communities through the contemporary revolutionary events in many parts of the world. In Christ there is no defense or excuse for the wilful continuation of groups, church meetings or fellowships which are racially exclusive. We therefore call upon Christians in their local churches to show the marks of Christian discipleship whatever the cost."[36]

[33] *Ibid.*, p. 88, italics added.
[34] 't Hooft, ed., *The New Delhi Report*, pp. 88–89, report on "Witness." Cf. also the Montreal Faith and Order report, p. 81.
[35] *Ibid.*, pp. 103–4.
[36] Rodger and Vischer, eds., *op. cit.*, pp. 85–86.

Moving beyond contrition

To be sure, it is one thing to issue public statements of penitence, calling for reform, and another thing actually to embody the reforms that are called for. But penitence is the precondition of reform, and perhaps enough has been said to indicate that the Protestant, as well as the Catholic, has begun to utter the *mea culpa* that Professor Lortz describes as the necessary prerequisite for health and vitality in the life of the church today. Only when this has been done can both Catholic and Protestant move on to an implementation of the principle *ecclesia semper reformanda*—the church always in process of being reformed.

CHAPTER 7

ECCLESIA SEMPER REFORMANDA
(the conditions of true reformation)

Ecclesia reformata, sed semper reformanda (the church reformed, but always in process of being reformed).
>> Rallying cry of the sixteenth-century Protestant Reformers.

Ecclesia reformata, sed semper reformanda (the church reformed, but always in process of being reformed).
>> Rallying cry of the twentieth-century Roman Catholic Reformers.

Two facts have emerged from our historical survey: (a) there is now a recognition on both sides that reformation is an ongoing activity in the life of the church, rather than something that happened in the sixteenth century—with either redemptive or baleful results, depending upon one's perspective, and (b) the precondition of ongoing reformation is active contrition and penitence coupled with a resolute desire for amendment of life, both individual and corporate.

These are important conditions for the internal life of any church, but they become even more important in the era of ecumenical revolution. We must therefore draw together some of the conditions of ongoing reformation that must obtain as Catholics and Protestants face each other in the years ahead.[1]

---

[1] The problem of combining "ongoing reformation" with a belief in "irreformability"—a major task from the Roman Catholic side of the divide—will be discussed in Ch. 15 below.

The church as the "pilgrim people of God"

One of the controlling images of the church in the documents of Vatican II is the image of the church as "the pilgrim people of God."[2]

This opens up important possibilities on the ecumenical front, for explicit in the notion of pilgrimage is the notion of a people who have not yet arrived, who are still on the march, whose "perfection," to the degree that they have it, is always a matter of something still to come in its fullness, rather than something that can be claimed as a present possession.

Some examples from the council's decree *On Ecumenism* will illustrate the presence of the theme:

"The Church, then, God's only flock, like a standard lifted high for the nations to see it, ministers the Gospel of peace to all mankind, as she makes her pilgrim way in hope toward her goal, the fatherland above."[3]

It is out of this context that the decree goes on, in the next article, to acknowledge the separations in the church, "for which, at times, men of both sides were to blame,"[4] and to speak of the fact that "during its pilgrimage on earth, this People, though still in its members liable to sin, is growing in Christ."[5] The connection between the pilgrim people and the necessity of ongoing reformation is even more clearly indicated later in the document:

"Christ summons the church, as she goes her pilgrim way,

---

[2] I emphasize the point in spite of J. C. Hoekendijk's comment that "the 'pilgrim people of God'—is in our day a superconfessional cliché" (*Christianity and Crisis*, July 25, 1966, p. 172). One man's cliché may well be another man's insight, and it will be a long time before the notion becomes as threadbare among the rank and file as it apparently already is among the experts.

[3] *On Ecumenism*, Art. 2; cf. Abbott, ed., *op. cit.*, p. 344.

[4] *Ibid.*, Art. 3; cf. Abbott, p. 345.

[5] *Ibid.*, Art. 3; cf. Abbott, p. 346.

to that continual reformation of which she always has need, insofar as she is an institution of men here on earth."[6]

This means that such images of the church as the seamless robe of Christ, without spot or wrinkle, are not images that can be applied to the present empirical church as we know it, since the church is still engaged on the pilgrim way, still striving, still failing, still needing (as we saw in an earlier chapter) to pray until the end of time, "Forgive us our sins."

In more formal theological language, this is an eschatological vision of the church, a vision of the church moving toward a consummation—a consummation to be brought about not by the muscular spirituality of its adherents but by the judgment and grace of God—and recognizing that only at the consummation will the church have become what it truly is. Thus the church here and now is always the church of the "not yet," the church that can never be complacently measured by its achievements (a rising curve of membership or proven "relevance to the social situation," for example), but must always be judgmentally measured by the fact that since it is still on pilgrimage and remains far short of its goal, its claims for itself must be more modest than they have usually been in the past, and that efforts to close the gap between what is demanded of it and what it produces must be unceasing.

If this forward-looking aspect of self-understanding can enable the church to live on earth without undue pride, it can also help the church to live without despair. Both safeguards are important. The primary sin of the church has surely been pride, the tendency to claim as a present possession those qualities which can only be a future hope. But in this sober facing of the failings of the church can come a reaction of despair, of losing heart because the pilgrimage is so long, the road so rough, and the companions on the way so apparently devoid of grace. Here the antidote is a shift of focus

[6] *Ibid.*, Art. 6; Abbott, p. 350.

from the constituent members of the church to the head of the church, and what God wills for the church. As the Dutch Missionary Council put it at Willingen:

"The focus on the future of Christ preserves [the Church] from overestimating what she achieves on earth and from the danger of losing her preaching in a social-ethical idealism. On the other hand it preserves her from despair arising from disappointments, since she is sure that her work is not in vain in the Lord."[7]

Destroyed by this imagery, then, is any notion of a static conception of the church, of a church so full of perfections and graces that all it needs to do is dispense them properly, the due forms having been followed.

At the same time, all Catholics would affirm (and surely Protestants would agree) that the church on pilgrimage is nevertheless the place to which the pilgrim goes for sustenance on his journey, and that the Holy Spirit will never so forsake the church that it becomes the unambiguous abode of Satan rather than the ambiguous abode of Christ. But gone, in this imagery, is any note of complacency about the state of the church; complacency is replaced by a note of scrutiny and concern lest the church remain guilty of betraying its high calling.

It is already apparent that the imagery of the pilgrim people of God is not a private rediscovery of Roman Catholicism, and much common ground can be shared by virtue of the fact that the imagery has been prominent in Protestant thought as well.[8]

Edmund Schlink made it a focal point at Lund by his address there,[9] and it had also been important in various conferences of the International Missionary Council, perhaps

[7] Cited in Margull, *Hope in Action*, Muhlenberg Press, Philadelphia, 1962, p. 19.

[8] In the following paragraphs I anticipate material I hope to develop more fully in *Frontiers for the Church*, Oxford University Press.

[9] Cf. "The Pilgrim People in God," in Tomkins, ed., *op. cit.*, pp. 151–61.

most notably in an address at Whitby in 1947 by John Mackay, for many years a missionary in South America, and later president of Princeton Theological Seminary.

"The whole Church must brace itself to face the frontier. That is to say, it must become a mobile missionary force ready for a wilderness life. It must be ready to march towards the places where the real issues are and where the most crucial decisions must be made. It is a time for us all to be thinking of campaign tents rather than of cathedrals."[10]

Staying with the imagery, Dr. Mackay further commented at the Ghana conference of the International Missionary Council ten years later:

"The Church must become afresh a pilgrim Church and engage in a new Abrahamic adventure . . . [a] pilgrim missionary church which subordinates everything in its heritage to the fulfillment of its mission."[11]

The theme was likewise incorporated in the report on "Witness" at the New Delhi conference in 1961, in a way that clearly shows its relationship to "ongoing reformation":

"A reappraisal of the patterns of church organization and institutions inherited by the younger churches must be attempted, so that outdated forms which belonged to an era that is rapidly passing away may be replaced by strong and relevant ways of evangelism. This is only one illustration, but an important one, of how the Church may become the Pilgrim Church, which goes forth boldly as Abraham did into the unknown future, not afraid to leave behind the securities of its conventional structure, *glad to dwell in the tent of perpetual adaptation*, looking to the city whose builder and maker is God."[12]

---

[10] In Ranson, ed., *Renewal and Advance* (the report of the Whitby conference), Edinburgh House, London, 1948, p. 203.

[11] Cited in Margull, *op. cit.*, p. 77.

[12] 't Hooft, ed., *The New Delhi Report*, p. 90, italics added.

"Protestant principle and Catholic substance"

Paul Tillich has provided a second way of dealing with the theme of ongoing reformation. His widely cited "Protestant principle" might seem at first glance a particularly unfortunate theme to introduce into ecumenical discussion, overloaded as it is with partisan implications. But as Tillich made clear, particularly in his later writings, the "Protestant principle" is to be understood in the context of "Catholic substance."

"The Protestant principle (which is a manifestation of the prophetic Spirit) is not restricted to the churches of the Reformation or to any other church; it transcends every particular church, being an expression of the Spiritual Community. It has been betrayed by every church, including the churches of the Reformation, but it is also effective in every church as the power which prevents profanization and demonization from destroying the Christian churches completely. It alone is not enough; it needs the "Catholic substance," and the concrete embodiment of the Spiritual Presence; but it is the criterion of the demonization (and profanization) of such embodiment. It is the expression of the victory of the Spirit over religion."[13]

In his earlier and classic statement of the Protestant principle, Tillich described it thus:

"[The Protestant principle] contains the divine and human protest against any absolute claim made for a relative reality, even if this claim is made by a Protestant church. The Protestant principle is the judge of every religious and cultural reality, including the religion and culture which calls

---

[13] Tillich, *Systematic Theology*, Vol. III, University of Chicago Press, Chicago, 1963, p. 245. In the preface to this volume (written during the course of Vatican II), Tillich is just as explicit about the necessary relationship of the two concepts: "Although my system is very outspoken in its emphasis on the 'Protestant principle,' it has not ignored the demand that the 'Catholic substance' be united with it. . . ." (*Ibid.*, p. 6).

itself 'Protestant.' . . . It is the guardian against all the attempts of the finite and conditioned to usurp the place of the unconditional in thinking and acting. It is the prophetic judgment against religious pride, ecclesiastical arrogance, and secular self-sufficiency and their destructive consequences."[14]

It is clear that the Protestant principle is a helpful vantage point from which to judge the idolatries of men and nations, but for our present purposes the important thing is to see the Protestant principle as the vehicle for a critical assessment of the church itself, the prophetic judgment (as Professor Tillich says) against "ecclesiastical arrogance." We can see this operating both negatively and positively.[15]

Negatively, the Protestant principle involves *the repudiation of idolatry* and corresponds in Biblical terminology to the first commandment, "You shall have no other gods before me." (Ex. 20:3) The problem is not the "absence of God," or the "death of God," but rather "the proliferation of gods." Men are not atheistic but polytheistic, giving their final allegiance to gods who are not truly God, and they thus worship man-made gods or idols. Acts of idolatry we may define with Tillich as "all the attempts of the finite and conditioned to usurp the place of the unconditional in thinking and acting." Whenever a partial object of loyalty is transformed into an ultimate object of loyalty, we have an instance of treating a man-made object as though it were divine.

This is always the ecclesiological temptation. If Protestants have sometimes felt that Catholicism exemplified this in its uncritical acceptance of certain structures of the church, Protestants have been no less guilty of absolutizing human elements of their own denominational life. Those Catholics

[14] Tillich, "The Protestant Principle and the Proletarian Situation," *The Protestant Era*, University of Chicago Press, 1948, p. 163.

[15] Here I recast some material originally developed in *The Spirit of Protestantism*, Part I, Ch. IV. The ideas seemed to me at the time to be distinctively Protestant ones, but I now believe that Roman Catholics can also in large part affirm them.

who feel that their church does not stand in need of reform and renewal, and that Vatican II is therefore an unfortunate parenthesis in the ongoing history of the indefectible church, are guilty of idolatry, just as are those Protestants who are unwilling to face up to the reforms of Vatican II for fear that their own indefectible picture of the "errors of Romanism" would be jeopardized. No church, no institution, is exempt from the temptation to idolatry.

Positively, it would seem clear that the Protestant principle involves *the affirmation of the Lordship of Christ*. To repudiate idolatry is to remove from the center of life what does not belong there so that the center can be occupied by the one who rightfully does belong there. And in both Protestant and Catholic understandings of the Gospel, the one who "rightfully does belong there" is Jesus Christ as Lord.

The earliest Christian confession was the simple declaration *Kurios Christos*, Christ is Lord, an affirmation Protestants and Catholics have always shared together. The background of the affirmation is the requirement placed on all Roman citizens in the first century annually to affirm *Kurios Caesar*, Caesar (i.e., the state) is Lord, lord being understood as the one to whom one's highest allegiance is given. Thus, in the face of this demand, the early Christian affirmation of *Kurios Christos* was not only the explicit affirmation that Christ is Lord, but also the implicit denial of Caesar as Lord.[16]

A moving contemporary illustration of the way in which the affirmation of the Lordship of Christ is at the same time the repudiation of idolatry is found in the Barmen Declaration of 1934, in which the German Confessing Church indicated how its allegiance to Jesus Christ meant repudiation of Hitler:

"Jesus Christ, as He is attested for us in Holy Scripture,

[16] Cf. further Cullmann, *The Earliest Christian Confessions*, Lutterworth Press, London, 1949, 64 pp.

is the one Word of God which we have to hear and which we have to trust and obey in life and in death.

"We reject the false doctrine as though the Church could and would have to acknowledge as a source of its proclamation, apart from and besides this one Word of God, still other events and powers, figures and truths, as God's revelation."[17]

The application of the principle to the life of the church should be clear enough. Ongoing reformation is possible to the degree that the churches and the members thereof give their allegiance to Christ as Lord, rather than to someone or something else as Lord, for it is this allegiance that provides the criterion for judging the ongoing life of the church.

Mary can be worshiped in such a way that the Lordship of Christ is diminished. So can Luther.

"The time has come for judgment to begin with the household of God." (1 Peter 4:17)[18]

There is a third way of understanding the impetus for ongoing reformation. The Biblical mandate that judgment must begin with the household of God is an indispensable ingredient of ecclesiastical integrity. The notion is a disturbing but essential one. A willingness on the part of churches to speak "prophetically" about the sins of society is often coupled with a strange reluctance to turn the same critical searchlight upon the inner life of the church itself. Willingness to appropriate this particular Biblical mandate involves risk, for judgment is

[17] Cited in Cochrane, *The Church's Confession Under Hitler*, Westminster, Philadelphia, 1962, p. 239. The book is a full account of the development of this historic declaration.

[18] The use that is made in the following paragraphs of this Biblical text goes beyond what is technically justifiable on the basis of strict exegesis, since the passage is a description of what is already beginning to happen, e.g., the church is being persecuted (cf. commentaries by Reike, Beare, Selwyn, *et al*). But cf. the way the theme is developed by Reinhold Niebuhr in a speech given at the Oxford 1937 Life and Work conference on "The Christian Church in a Secular Age," printed in *Christianity and Power Politics*, Scribner's, New York, 1940, esp. pp. 224–26.

a very shattering thing, and ecclesiastical insecurities mount in the face of the need to re-think or re-cast or re-formulate ideas and patterns of life that had been assumed to be beyond the need for such dissection.

An important ecumenical refinement of the Biblical mandate is the willingness to let the critical gaze be focused first of all *on one's own church*. It is admittedly painful to seek the ecclesiastical beam in one's own eye, rather than searching for the mote in another's eye, but this priority must be built into a true understanding of ongoing reformation, and it is an insight that the complementary statements by Hans Küng and Reinhold Niebuhr (cited on the introductory page of this section) seek to enshrine.

As a brief case study in the application of this insight, we may examine a Protestant reaction to the era of Protestant history that has been the subject of most frequent Protestant idolatry, the Reformation. Having earlier examined the Roman Catholic reappraisal of the events of the sixteenth century, we must now explore a Protestant reassessment of the same period, particularly in the light of the conviction that "judgment must begin at the house of [Protestantism]." A significant statement of such an attitude has recently been offered by the Lutheran scholar Carl Braaten.[19]

Professor Braaten argues that the concern of the Reformers was never to establish an independent church but to reform the existing church. It is tragic that the church was split. But, as Professor Braaten goes on,

---

[19] Professor Braaten's article was originally published as "The Tragedy of the Reformation and the Return to Catholicity," in *The Record*, Lutheran School of Theology, Vol. LXX, August 1965, No. 3, pp. 5–15, and in slightly abridged form as "Rome, Reformation and Reunion," in *Una Sancta*, Pentecost, Vol. 23, No. 2, pp. 3–8. A symposium of reactions to the latter version is included in *Una Sancta*, Vol. 23, No. 3, and the paragraphs that follow are adapted from my own contribution to it.

Cf. also the much fuller treatment of a similar theme by Lindbeck, "The Ecclesiology of the Roman Catholic Church," *Journal of Ecumenical Studies*, Spring 1964, pp. 243–70.

"A still greater tragedy is that what was intended to be only a temporary church has become a permanent arrangement with no end in sight. The reformation was not intended to bring about a protestant church, much less a collection of protestant churches. The reformation was a movement of protest for the sake of the one Church. The reformation was necessary, but protestants have made a virtue out of a necessity."[20]

It is a source of both difficulty and promise that Protestant and Catholic assessments of the relationship of tragedy and necessity have been undergoing some change:

"Roman Catholics have agreed that the reformation was tragic, but few of them have seen that it was necessary. Protestants have agreed that the reformation was necessary, but few have felt with deep and lasting pain its tragedy. . . . Protestants now see that the reformation was a tragedy, though it was necessary; and Roman Catholics see that it was necessary, though it was tragic."[21]

In the new situation to which the latter sentence points, the need is for what Professor Skydsgaard calls an "evangelical catholicity," which contains the possibility of both continuity and reformation. The Reformers were concerned "to become more evangelical precisely by becoming more truly catholic."[22] The two terms are not polarities in opposition to one another, but complementary truths which are both needed in the fullness of the church.

The theme is developed against the imagery of exile. In France, in the early 1940's, Pétain's Vichy government became the puppet of Hitler. The Free French were in exile, outside of France, protesting against the false government, seeking to liberate their land and longing to be reunited with their countrymen. Suppose, Professor Braaten argues, the

[20] Braaten in *Una Sancta, op. cit.*, p. 4.
[21] *Ibid.*, p. 5.
[22] *Ibid.*, p. 6.

Free French became accustomed to their situation and "began to think and act as if what was meant to be a temporary arrangement in an emergency situation had actually become for them a permanent establishment?"[23] Suppose they set up another government, called *it* France, and gave up the thought of returning to the land of their birth?

The latter situation, Braaten argues, is analogous to what happened at the Reformation. The churches of the Reformation became accustomed to separation and began to think of it as normal. The temporary government became a permanent one.

The question then is: Has the time come for the end of the government in exile? Can the separation still be justified? Does the Reformation protest still need to be heard? Braaten acknowledges that the question is increasingly difficult to answer, for "the Roman Catholic Church is not the same unreformed church she was in Luther's time."[24] Furthermore, Protestantism has not been the pure purveyor of the Gospel that some of its defenders claim it to have been, and it has been distorted in a variety of ways. In the light, then, of Rome's acts of reformation and Protestantism's acts of deformation, "is there anything which could still justify a continued protest of the protestant principle in a separate ecclesiastical order?"[25]

This is the crucial question. How one answers it signifies how deeply he is responding to the currents of renewal in our time. Braaten's answer is, "Not if the reformation call has been heard and heeded by Rome!"[26] He insists that all depends on what Rome does with the questions that the Reformation continues to address to her, and that therefore

[23] Braaten in *Una Sancta, op. cit.,* p. 3.
[24] *Ibid.,* p. 6.
[25] *Ibid.,* p. 7.
[26] *Ibid.,* p. 7.

Protestants must not be "intent on a separate existence no matter what happens."[27]

For Braaten this does not mean, as many of his critics have charged, that Protestants must "return" and surrender what the Reformation reintroduced into the church.

"If evangelical catholics harbor the hope of reunion with Roman Catholics, they certainly do not and cannot mean *return* to the Roman Catholic Church as Roman. The concept of 'return' is inadequate simply because it suggests that the Protestant party is the prodigal wanderer who has come home, while the Roman Church is like the waiting Father. There has been prodigality on both sides, and the Roman side has not been standing still. Furthermore, the concept of 'return' which grates upon Protestant nerves does not reflect Pope John's admission that responsibility is divided, and there is equal blame on both sides. The idea of a mutual advance converging upon the future fulfillment of what is valid on both sides is a better working hypothesis. It does not require either side to deny its own history, but through further historical development, it allows for a future reconciliation."[28]

If there is a difficulty with Braaten's position, it focuses on the degree to which true catholicity and continuity are the possessions of Roman Catholicism, and the degree to which these are lacking in Protestantism. Initially, it would seem clear that Roman Catholicism indeed possesses this continu-

[27] The very notion that some day the churches of the Reformation should lose their separate identity, and that a reformed Protestantism and a reformed Catholicism might one day merge, still disturbs many Protestants. An editorial on Braaten's position in the *Christian Century*, for example, was headed "Protestant Hara-Kiri," and went on to characterize it as "an absurd plea and one potentially mischievous to the ecumenical movement." The adjective "odious" was also employed. Cf. the *Christian Century*, June 22, 1966, p. 794.

[28] "The Tragedy of the Reformation and the Return to Catholicity," *The Record*, pp. 13–14. In the light of the furor over the *Una Sancta* abridgment, it is unfortunate that this crucial paragraph was not included in the latter version.

ity, going back to Christ, whereas the Protestant churches go back only to the sixteenth century. But (as we saw in Chapter 2 above) this view does not do justice to the Reformers, who saw themselves recovering the catholicity they felt the medieval church had lost. At this point, to refer to Professor Braaten's Vichy parable, the question of who is the exile and who is the inhabitant of the homeland becomes a question that is at least worth asking. Perhaps neither group fits unambiguously in either category, and the parable can be discarded in favor of the recognition that, as Professor Skydsgaard, a leading Lutheran ecumenist, has put it, "The two may at least meet in a kind of solidarity of sinfulness, and that is not always a poor place to meet, even for two churches."[29]

This is, in fact, where the road from contention to contrition has led both churches. It means that the Reformation question can no longer be approached in sixteenth-century terms, but must be approached in twentieth-century terms, taking account not only of Vatican I but also of Vatican II, not only of Protestant divisions but also of Protestant reunions. Protestants and Roman Catholics live in a new era in which both are discovering that the terrain that separates them, so familiar when viewed by the cartography of sixteenth-century mapmakers, is now entirely different from what they had imagined, and that rather than containing land mines with which they intend to destroy one another, it is now, for the first time, rich with promise and the hope of a redeeming harvest.

---

[29] Skydsgaard, *One in Christ*, Muhlenberg Press, Philadelphia, 1957, p. 43; cited in Braaten's *Una Sancta* article, p. 7. Braaten's own formula really makes much the same point: "a mutual advance converging upon the future fulfillment of what is valid on both sides."

CHAPTER 8

THE TEST OF PROTESTANT SINCERITY
(steps toward reunion)

How many churches do we have in town? Well, we used
to have two, and then they united, so now we have three.
Comment of a New Englander in answer
to a question from Dr. John Baillie.

Churches cannot unite, unless they are willing to die.
Bishop Stephen Neill, in Rouse and Neill,
eds., A *History of the Ecumenical Movement*, p. 495.

It is not enough merely to apply the principle *ecclesia semper
reformanda* to the Catholic-Protestant scene and assume that
the challenge has been met so long as Catholics and Protestants are on better terms with one another. There is a more
exacting test of Protestant sincerity than that. Not only did
the Reformation split Christendom into Protestantism and
Catholicism; it also split Protestantism into dozens, and then
scores, and finally hundreds, of denominations, so that Protestantism has become, as someone has remarked, a many-
splintered thing. We have already noted how this situation
makes a mockery of Christ's prayer "that all may be one," and
we must now note the ways in which Protestants are trying
to repair their own intramural situation.

Degrees of unity

The picture is both encouraging and discouraging. Encouraging is the fact that incredible progress has been made over

the last few decades in achieving organic reunion between formerly divided churches, a progress so great that Bishop Stephen Neill, a long-time leader of the World Council of Churches, can comment:

"The forty years between 1910 and 1950 have achieved more towards the overcoming of differences between Christians, and towards the recovery of the lost unity of the Body of Christ, than any period of equal length in the previous history of the Christian Churches."[1]

But along with the encouraging fact of progress is the discouraging fact that, as the most recent "Survey of Church Union Negotiations" in *The Ecumenical Review* notes, "Such progress is painfully slow."[2] Churches are far more willing to talk about the desirability of union in the distant future than to hammer out a specific plan of union for the immediate future.

Part of the reason for such painfully slow progress is disagreement about *how much unity* is desirable. At least four levels of response can be distinguished: (a) unity of fellowship, in which churches initiate or improve cordial relationships between each other, by meetings, conferences, joint projects, and services; (b) unity of work and action, in which churches create councils of churches (local, state, or national) to facilitate both their common tasks in society and the exploration of their similarities and differences; and (c) a deeper level of unity in which certain churches mutually recognize one another's ministries and consequently establish intercommunion with one another.

It is clear that each of these steps represents an advance

[1] In Rouse and Neill, eds., *A History of the Ecumenical Movement*, p. 446. Cf. the entire essay, "Plans of Union and Reunion, 1910–1948," pp. 443–505, as well as his *Towards Church Union, 1937–1952*, S.C.M. Press, London, 1952. A series of surveys in *The Ecumenical Review* brings the data up to date: April 1954, pp. 300 ff; October 1955, pp. 76 ff; April 1957, pp. 284 ff; January 1960, pp. 231 ff; April 1962, pp. 351 ff; July 1964, pp. 406 ff; July 1966, pp. 345 ff.

[2] *The Ecumenical Review*, July 1966, p. 385.

over the preceding one, and most churchmen would agree
with the desirability of moving through step three. Not all,
however, are concerned to move to a fourth step, (d) full
organic union, in which the participating churches surrender
their present identity so that a new and more fully united
church may result. This, as the New Delhi statement on
Unity comments,

"will involve nothing less than a death and rebirth of many
forms of church life as we have known them. We believe that
nothing less costly can finally suffice."[3]

Those who resist this fourth step often do so believing that
what is described as spiritual unity is enough, and that it need
not have visible, organic, and structural form. But to adopt
this posture is to be guilty of what Edmund Schlink, at New
Delhi, called "ecclesiastical docetism."[4]

It is one of the less happy legacies of the Reformation that
incorrect use has been made of the distinction between the
"visible" and the "invisible" church, in a way that suggests
that unity—already real in some ideal and almost platonized
invisible church—need not receive visible manifestation. But
this is to settle for a dualistic presupposition quite out of
keeping with the historical character of the Christian faith
and its insistence that spirit and matter are not two separate
entities. Christ was not just spirit, he was flesh, a creature of
time and space, manifested historically and concretely; similarly the church which is his body must manifest the unity
he desires for it historically and concretely. Nothing less than
visible, concrete unity can finally suffice as the answer to his
prayer "that all may be one."

[3] In 't Hooft, ed., *The New Delhi Report*, p. 117.
[4] *Ibid.*, p. 134. The "docetic" heresy was a denial of the full humanity of
Jesus, asserting that he only "seemed" (*dokeo*) to be fully human. To apply
this principle to church union is to assert that visible and empirical unity need
not be taken seriously.

Two descriptions of unity

Is there a way to describe this unity that the church has so sinfully distorted? Two historic documents help to provide an answer.

1. The first of these is New Delhi's carefully worked out description of "the nature of our common goal."[5] It is a single sentence, but a long sentence, and for the sake of clarity it is best divided into its component parts:

"We believe that the unity which is both God's will and his
    gift to his church
is being made visible
as all in each place
who are baptized into Jesus Christ
and confess him as Lord and Saviour
are brought by the Holy Spirit
into one fully committed fellowship,
holding the one apostolic faith,
preaching the one Gospel,
breaking the one bread,
joining in common prayer,
and having a corporate life reaching out in witness and service
    to all
and who at the same time are united with the whole Christian fellowship in all places and all ages
in such wise that ministry and members are accepted by all,
and that all can act and speak together as occasion requires
    for the tasks to which God calls his people."[6]

An entire book could be devoted to a clarification of each of

[5] In 't Hooft, ed., *The New Delhi Report*, p. 117.

[6] *Ibid.*, p. 116, para. 2 of the report on "Unity." Cf. the exegesis furnished in Nelson and Skoglund, *op. cit.*, pp. 7–19. An important forerunner is the statement in the report *One Lord, One Baptism*, Augsburg, Minneapolis, 1960, 79 pp.

these crucial phrases.[7] For the moment, what is significant is the emphasis upon the unity "being made *visible* as all in each place . . . are brought . . . into one fully committed fellowship." This is not the "spiritual" unity of the "invisible" church, but the tangible unity of the visible church. The phrase "all in each place" is used, the report reminds us, "both in its primary sense of local neighborhood and also, under modern conditions, of other areas in which Christians need to express unity in Christ."[8] The latter can mean factory or office or local congregation, and the phrase cuts across such barriers as nation, race, and class. To make the point is not to minimize other aspects of the statement—baptism, confession, common faith, sacramental life, witness and service in the world, mutually acceptable ministry and membership, for example—but to note that at New Delhi the churches pledged themselves to seek a unity that would not stop short of the most concrete and visible expression.

2. The point at which efforts toward organic unity inevitably run into trouble is that described by New Delhi as a "ministry . . . accepted by all." All churches have ministries, but not all churches accept as valid the ministries of all other churches. The dispute centers on the presence or absence of bishops as the means of validating an authentic ministry. The importance of the problem is illustrated by our second historic document, the "Appeal to All Christian People" of the Anglican bishops assembled at Lambeth in 1920.[9]

The appeal was for the union of divided Christians and it suggested four points as "essential to the restoration of unity among the divided branches of Christendom." These were

[7] The report offers its own exegesis of the key phrases. Cf. *op. cit.*, pp. 117–22.

[8] *Ibid.*, p. 118.

[9] The "Appeal" was based on the "Lambeth Quadrilateral" of 1888, which in turn had come out of Anglican meetings in Chicago two years earlier and was originally the formulation of William Reed Huntington. The text of the "Appeal" is in Bell, *Documents of Church Unity*, First Series, Oxford University Press, New York, 1924, pp. 1–5.

acceptance (a) of the Old and New Testaments as the revealed Word of God, (b) of the Nicene and Apostles' Creeds as sufficient statements of the church's faith, (c) of the two sacraments of baptism and the Lord's Supper to be used with Christ's words of institution and with the elements ordained by him, and (d) of "a ministry acknowledged by every part of the church as possessing not only the inward call of the Spirit but also the commission of Christ and the authority of the whole body."[10]

None of the first three points has posed grave difficulty for uniting Christian bodies. But when Lambeth went on to refer to "a ministry acknowledged by every part of the church," it immediately made clear what this implied: "May we not reasonably claim that the Episcopate is the one means of providing such a ministry?"[11] Lambeth did, in fact, "reasonably claim" this, as all churches with an episcopally ordained ministry continue to do. And the consequent hurdle in all church union negotiations has been the attempt *both* to secure for the united church a ministry acceptable to episcopally oriented churches, *and* to do so in a way that does not appear to impugn the previous ministries of the nonepiscopal churches.[12]

---

[10] In Bell, *op. cit.*, p. 3.

[11] *Ibid.*, p. 3.

[12] Lambeth continued, after the above question, "It is not that we call into question for a moment the spiritual reality of the ministries of those Communions which do not possess the Episcopate. On the contrary, we thankfully acknowledge that these ministries have been manifestly blessed and owned by the Holy Spirit as effective means of grace. . . . If the authorities of other Communions should so desire, we are persuaded that, in terms of union having been otherwise satisfactorily adjusted, Bishops and clergy of our Communion would willingly accept from these authorities a form of commission or recognition which would commend our ministry to their congregations, as having its place in the one family life." (Cf. *op. cit.*, pp. 3–4.) This is, in fact, what is emerging in various contemporary proposals discussed below.

From unity discussions to unity itself

Whatever the difficulties, whether posed by episcopacy or not, one of Protestantism's most pressing ecumenical tasks is to set its own house in order by eliminating the divisions that make a mockery out of the claim, "We are not divided, all one body we." Until Protestants take this mandate seriously, they have no reason to expect to be taken seriously elsewhere. As we survey the Protestant scene today, we can distinguish three types of organic union that have been consummated: intra-confessional unions, trans-confessional unions, and (what is really a refinement of the second) unions involving episcopal and non-episcopal churches.[13]

Examples of *intra-confessional unions* are not difficult to find. These occur when members of a single confessional body patch up whatever quarrels led to their earlier divisions. Thus in 1900 the Free Church of Scotland and the United Presbyterian Church became the United Free Church, which later merged with the Church of Scotland in 1929. Recently the Presbyterian Church of the U.S.A. and the United Presbyterian Church merged to form the United Presbyterian Church of the U.S.A., although efforts to reunite the century-old split between the northern and southern branches of American Presbyterianism have thus far proved abortive. The Methodists, however, have proved more adept at healing the regional breach, and in 1939 a division between the Methodist Church North and the Methodist Church South was overcome—one of the few instances in which a union was consummated without spawning a dissident splinter group. In similar fashion various American Lutheran groups have united to overcome regional and ethnic origin barriers.

Trans-confessional unions of churches coming from two or more confessional backgrounds have likewise occurred in

---

[13] Following the typology suggested by Neill in Rouse and Neill, eds., *op. cit.*, pp. 449–76.

considerable numbers. Thus in 1931 the Christian Churches and the Congregational Churches merged to form the Congregational-Christian Churches; in 1934 the Evangelical Synod of North America merged with the Reformed Church in the United States to form the Evangelical and Reformed Church; while a few years later both of these new groups merged to form what is now called the United Church of Christ. The United Church of Christ, in its turn, has already joined with seven other denominations to pursue a larger scheme of union known as the Consultation on Church Union.[14]

Perhaps the most interesting example of trans-confessional union, since it involved three separate denominations, was the creation of the United Church of Canada in 1925, composed of the Presbyterian, Methodist, and Congregational Churches of Canada, with the exception of a minority of Presbyterians who fought the union and have led an independent existence ever since. Due to Presbyterian intransigence, the union left some scars, but over the decades the United Church has grown "in wisdom and stature," and by the summer of 1965 plans were underway for a proposed union of the United Church of Canada and the Anglican Church of Canada, a merger that could conceivably take place within a decade.[15]

In none of the unions thus far accomplished have the Episcopalians been involved. The crucial test of Protestant faithfulness to the principle of organic reunion involves readiness to grapple with *trans-confessional unions between episcopal and non-episcopal churches.* There is already one striking instance of the achievement of this end, and most of the merger proposals now under consideration face the problem directly.

[14] Cf. the concluding portion of this chapter for an account of the Consultation on Church Union.

[15] Cf. the analysis of the proposal by Donald Mathers in *Bulletin* of the Department of Theology of the World Alliance of Reformed Churches, Spring 1966, Vol. 6, No. 3, pp. 1–6.

The breakthrough on this level of reunion was the establishment in 1947 of the Church of South India.[16] As early as 1919, representatives of a number of denominations in India met at Tranquebar to seek ways of overcoming the distorted witness given by the diversity of competing denominations. Through a period of over forty years, such meetings continued, and finally in 1947 four denominations—Presbyterian, Methodist, Congregationalist, and Anglican—consented to die to their previous structural existence, so that the Church of South India could be born. A few splinter groups resisted: a group of Congregationalists chose not to join though they later did so in 1950, and a group of Anglicans not only chose not to join but have ever since remained adamant in refusing to join. These were, however, minor incidents in comparison to the magnitude of the achievement of a union of both episcopal and non-episcopal churches, and a union joining all three historic types of polity—episcopal, presbyterial, and congregational. It was no exaggeration when the late Henry Sloane Coffin called it the most significant event in church history since the Reformation.

What South India provided for, on the crucial issue of episcopacy, was this: all ministries in the churches constituting the new Church of South India were accepted as fully valid ministries, whether episcopally ordained or not, but all subsequent ordinations within the new church were to be episcopal ordinations. Thus for a period of about a generation there exist (from the episcopal point of view) "irregularities" in the ministry of the new church, but within a generation the ministry will become fully episcopal, and the sense of continuity with the past, so crucial to churches practicing episcopacy, will be clearly established. These terms were not

[16] Out of the vast literature on South India, cf. particularly the following: Sundkler, *Church of South India: the Movement towards Union, 1900–1947,* Lutterworth, London, 1954, 457 pp.; Newbigin, *The Reunion of the Church,* Harper, New York, 1948, 192 pp.; Paul, *The First Decade: An Account of the Church of South India,* Lutterworth, London, 1958, 294 pp. The most recent assessment is Hollis, *The Significance of South India,* John Knox Press, Richmond, 1966, 82 pp.

fully satisfactory to the Lambeth conference of Anglican bishops, however, who, while rejoicing that such a union was being effected, remained disturbed at what would be the anomalous, not to say parlous, state of the ministry for the next several decades. (One paraphrase of the bishops' report went: "The Church of South India is clearly the work of the Holy Spirit, and it mustn't happen again.")

South India has paved the way for almost all subsequent plans for reunion, although later proposals do not incorporate a "waiting period," but propose to meet the problem of a fully accepted ministry at the time a new union is consummated. In plans for the merger of churches in Ceylon, for example, under discussion since 1934, there will be a Rite of Unification, including a statement from each minister that he is participating with the intention of receiving from God "such grace as it may be His will to bestow upon me for my ministry within the Church of Lanka as Presbyter in the Church of God."[17]

In plans for a union of churches in North India/Pakistan, "it is made clear that the *unambiguous* intent of this service is to place all the uniting ministries in the hands of God with the prayer that he will grant to all sufficient 'grace, commission and authority' to exercise their ministry in the united Church."[18] In such fashion, it will be made clear that the service is not one of "re-ordination" by the episcopal laying on of hands (thereby impugning the validity of the non-episcopal ministries), but rather a service of the "extension" of *all* ministries, episcopal or otherwise, each participant believing that he needs further grace for the new task he is about to undertake. With a certain jauntiness that still makes the point, Bishop James Pike comments on such procedures, "Each must lay hands on all, and we must leave to the Holy Spirit to sort out who has done what to whom."

Not all plans for episcopal and non-episcopal reunions have

17 Cf. *The Ecumenical Review*, July 1966, p. 356.
18 *Ibid.*, p. 358.

proceeded to a satisfactory conclusion. Plans for a union of the Episcopal Church in America and the (northern) Presbyterian Church came to naught in the early 1940s, and an elaborate proposal for a four-way merger between the Church of England (Episcopal), the Presbyterian Church of England, the Church of Scotland (Presbyterian), and the Episcopal Church in Scotland was strongly defeated by all parties save the Episcopal Church in Scotland, with the General Assembly of the Church of Scotland seeming to fear that the reintroduction of bishops would undo 400 years of Scottish history. A fresh proposal is now being explored by the four churches, but it will clearly be some time before a plan of union will find acceptance both north and south of the Tweed.[19]

The "Consultation on Church Union": a contemporary case study

The frequently cited survey in *The Ecumenical Review* describes upwards of fifty proposals for organic union now under serious discussion, and this does not include intra-confessional dialogues and conversations leading toward "federation." Not only is the number of such proposals impressive, but also the fact that many of them come from the younger churches of Asia and Africa, who have been victims of the western denominational divisions exported to them.

Rather than summarizing fifty or more proposals, it will be wiser to use one of these as a case study. Arbitrarily, the "Consultation on Church Union" has been chosen, a proposal for the merger of what are now eight American denominations: the United Presbyterian Church in the U.S.A., the Methodist Church, the United Church of Christ, the Evangelical United Brethren, the Christian Churches (Disciples of Christ), the Episcopal Church, the African Methodist

---

[19] Cf. *The Ecumenical Review*, July 1966, pp. 368–70, for a summary of the new proposals, and more fully, *The Anglican-Presbyterian Conversations*, St. Andrews Press, Edinburgh, 1966, 62 pp.

Episcopal Church, and the Presbyterian Church in the U.S.

The starting point for this proposal was a sermon preached by Dr. Eugene Carson Blake (then Stated Clerk of the United Presbyterian Church and now General Secretary of the World Council of Churches) in Grace Cathedral (Episcopal), San Francisco, on December 4, 1960. On that occasion, Dr. Blake offered "A Proposal Toward the Reunion of Christ's Church."[20] In it he called upon members of his own denomination, in conjunction with the Episcopal Church, to join with the Methodist Church and the United Church of Christ in forming "a plan of union both catholic and reformed." (Later the consulting churches extended this aim to be the search for a united church "truly catholic, truly evangelical and truly reformed.") Subsequent to the original proposal, the number of constituent bodies has grown from the original four to the eight noted above.

Reaction to the sermon was widespread, covering the whole range of comment from Bishop James Pike's immediate rejoinder that the sermon was "the most sound and inspiring proposal for the unity of the church in this country which has ever been made in its history," to that of the Rev. John Heuss, rector of Trinity Church in New York, who described it as "so unrealistic and un-Biblical that it borders on fuzzy-headed thinking." Despite a few rejoinders even sterner than the latter, and skeptical comment by such leaders as Method-

[20] The text of the sermon, along with Dr. Blake's reflections upon it two years later, is contained in Brown and Scott, eds., *The Challenge to Reunion: The Blake Proposal Under Scrutiny*, McGraw-Hill, New York, 1963, 292 pp., which also contains a series of essays evaluating the proposal. Cf. also Hunt and Crow, eds., *Where We Are in Church Union*, Association Press, New York, 1965, 126 pp. The official reports of the first four meetings of the Consultation are available in COCU, Forward Movement Publications, Cincinnati, 1966, 95 pp., and the specific plan for union that has evolved is available as *Principles of Church Union*, Forward Movement Publications, Cincinnati, 1966, 16 pp. Full reports of the annual meetings of the Consultation are available in printed form from Consultation on Church Union, Box 69, Fanwood, New Jersey. Portions of the following paragraphs are adapted from "Concord at Lexington," *The Commonweal*, June 11, 1965, pp. 380–82.

ist Bishop Gerald Kennedy, the over-all reaction was rousingly positive, and an exploratory session was held in Washington in 1962, at which time the representatives constituted themselves the "Consultation on Church Union," inevitably abbreviated by the press to the not entirely helpful acrostic "COCU." Subsequent meetings of the Consultation or COCU have been held annually at Oberlin, Princeton, Lexington, and Dallas.[21]

There have been at least five problem areas raised by Dr. Blake's initial sermon which can be mnemonically classified as: bustle, bigness, bureaucracy, belief, and bishops. The first three focus on the inordinate energy that will be required to bring such a union into being and the "ecumenical battle fatigue" that can easily result, the awesome and even cumbersome size of a church of over 25,000,000 members, and the red-tape slowdown that could easily result from the intricate structure thereof. Concern about belief focuses on the fear of reunion by theological compromise, with the result that much of the energy at the annual meetings has been devoted to arriving at conclusions that have theological integrity.[22] It is noteworthy that on many issues that had been expected to pose stumbling blocks—Scripture and tradition, for example—a surprisingly widespread consensus was rapidly achieved.

After three years of meetings, the delegates to COCU decided that the time had come for action, and rather than continuing to indulge themselves in years of theological discussion, they decided at the Lexington meeting in 1965 to proceed to a specific plan of union.[23] Since the delegates to

[21] It is worth noting that Roman Catholic observers have been present at the last three of these meetings.

[22] The booklet *Principles of Church Union*, cited above, deals with "The Faith of the Church," "The Worship of the Church," "The Sacraments of the Church," and "The Ministry of the Church."

[23] The decision is the more remarkable in light of the fact that meetings the previous year at Princeton had nearly ended in shipwreck, due particularly to a series of negative reactions by Methodist representatives.

the Lexington meeting had agreed that some form of episcopacy would be part of a united church, the task remaining was to offer a set of proposals for consideration by the entire constituencies of the participating denominations. As a result of the 1966 meetings at Dallas, the Consultation transmitted to the eight denominations a document entitled "Principles of Church Union," which,

"together with suggestions received from the participating churches, and which are in due course approved by the Consultation, shall become the basis upon which to formulate a Plan of Union."[24]

Ecclesiastical machinery being what it is, a number of years will pass before a clear picture emerges of the reaction of the eight denominations and the kinds of strings they may want to attach to their continuing participation.[25] The important point for the present discussion, however, is that the Consultation has moved beyond pleasant ecumenical talk about the future desirability of union to hardheaded ecumenical action about the present imperative of union.

How does COCU propose to deal with episcopacy? All eight denominations have indicated willingness to accept episcopacy in the united church. No single view of its meaning, however, is required:

"The united church accepts the office of bishops. Because this office is a principal symbol and means of continuity and unity of the Church, we therefore provide that bishops shall be chosen, consecrated, and governed in their ministry by the constitution of the united church. We understand that the episcopate historically came into existence without reference to any single doctrine or theory of its being or authority. We

---

24 Cf. *Principles of Church Union,* pp. 4, 9.
25 The mind boggles to contemplate how much time will have to be spent on such *minutiae* as the correlation of various pension plans, let alone the consolidation of theological education.

do not, therefore, set forward any such interpretation to the exclusion of others."[26]

The document goes on, however, to specify certain functions that have been entrusted to bishops by the church: pastoral oversight, liturgical leadership, and administrative responsibility.

Is this approach a creative breakthrough, or is it simply an evasion of deep-seated differences? The answer depends on who is talking. None of this, for example, would be satisfactory to the Roman Catholic, for not even Anglican ordinations, let alone non-episcopal ordinations, are currently held to be valid. The resultant ministries would thus still be invalid in Catholic eyes. Many Episcopalians, likewise, will be unhappy at the failure to spell out a clear understanding of episcopacy and will feel that their own gift to a united church has been compromised and gravely diluted. Many non-Episcopalians will object that the proposal is not only a subtle trick to get everybody "regularized" by Anglican standards, but also that it introduces episcopacy permanently into their church life—a dimension they have been perfectly content to live without in the past and see no reason to appropriate in the future.

But there is another side to the argument. It is patently clear that episcopacy will be one of the features of a reunited church. Those who cannot accept this as a premise will have to settle for a permanently divided Christendom and content themselves with patching up denominational family quarrels. The realistic question is not "Will a fully reunited church have bishops?" for the only possible answer is, "Yes." The realistic question is, "What does episcopacy mean?"

Here it is interesting and important that the Episcopalians themselves are by no means of one mind on this vital question. For some—to repeat the traditional distinctions—episcopacy is of the very *esse*, the very being, of the church, and

[26] *Principles of Church Union*, pp. 48–49, italics added.

without it there is no church at all. For others it is of the *plene esse*, the fullness, of the church, and without it there can be a church but it will be a defective church. For the rest, episcopacy is of the *bene esse*, the well-being, of the church, a helpful and important way of demonstrating the historic continuity of the church with its past.[27]

Two important facts emerge. One is that the third interpretation does not pose insuperable problems for most Protestants; indeed, in this sense most of them already have something very close to bishops in their present structures, even though the term is not used. The other is that all three interpretations are legitimate interpretations for the Episcopalian who approaches ordination. Therefore, if the Episcopal participants in COCU can in the future allow to other denominations the same diversity of interpretation that they presently accord their own ordinands, the barriers at this point are no longer insuperable.

The objection to this line of argument is the repetition of an earlier question: is this not reunion by compromise, by ducking the crucial issue rather than facing it? Four brief responses can be offered:

1. Granting the importance and inevitability of episcopacy in a reunited Christendom, it is better to reunite in terms of openness of definition than not to reunite at all; because,

2. Once reunited, all the churches can *grow together* into whatever further meaning episcopacy may come to have for them, confident that the Holy Spirit may be pleased to give them corporately such further understanding as has been denied to them individually.

3. It must be remembered that a mutual laying on of hands at the time of the consummation of such a union is not a trick. Traffic goes both ways. The Holy Spirit has used non-

---

[27] There is the story of a young curate who, after receiving a dressing down from his bishop, was heard to mutter, "Episcopacy may be of the *esse* of the church, but it certainly isn't of the *bene esse*."

episcopal ministries in the past, and the willingness of the Episcopal priest to kneel and receive gifts of ministry from his Congregational brother in Christ is his admission that grace does not flow in only one direction.

4. Particularly in the light of Catholic-Protestant division, it must be remembered that the meaning of episcopacy is not as precise even in Roman Catholicism as it once appeared to be. To take only one example, the relation of the power of the bishop of Rome to his fellow bishops throughout the world is now in process of redefinition, as the acceptance of the principle of "collegiality" by Vatican II has made plain.[28] This means that all Christians are going to be engaged in serious rethinking of the meaning of episcopacy, and this is a problem that can be most creatively tackled as a variety of Christians wrestle with its meaning not only for others but for themselves as well.

Is it all too slow?

The previous pages will have proved wearisome going for readers who are rendered impatient by the fact that reunion is a slow, slow, slow business, and who feel that the church should be out on the firing line involved in the affairs of men, rather than sitting in conference rooms rearranging ecclesiastical furniture. There are many who prefer to bypass the majestic slowness of denominational structures, let the ecclesiastical and episcopal chips fall where they may, and simply get on with the job. The times, they insist, do not brook evasive delays, and an impatient generation, they argue, will not long notice or involve itself in institutions so ponderously slow in overcoming the divisions they should have avoided in the first place.

But if, as the early part of this chapter argues, Christians must commit themselves to the task of visible reunion—with

[28] Cf. further on this point, Ch. 10–11, 15 below.

whatever other tasks accompanying it—then impatience is proper, but must be registered not at the goal but at the slowness of moving toward the goal. This means, further, that it is not going to be enough to talk about a "united" church, but only about a "uniting" church, a church that will move on toward the next merger when the present one has been consummated, not content to stop until the prayer "that all may be one" has been fulfilled in a visible and tangible way.

This, then, is one of Protestantism's major tasks in taking seriously the mandate to "reform and renewal." It must complete its part of the reformation of the holy catholic church by the process of organic reunion of its own divided parts. Only as it does so can it face its Catholic counterpart in full integrity, for the Catholic counterpart, due to the impetus of the Second Vatican Council, is now engaged in "reform and renewal" more vast than anything those within or without its fold had dared anticipate.

PART THREE

From Counter-Reformation to Continuing Reformation

or

The Surprises of Vatican II

We will be finished by Thanksgiving.
> Prediction of an American bishop as he left for Rome in September of 1962 for the opening of Vatican Council II.

Our work has just begun.
> Prediction of another American bishop as he left Rome in December of 1965 at the conclusion of Vatican Council II.

CHAPTER 9

THE HIGHLIGHTS OF VATICAN II:
A BRIEF CHRONICLE

> If honesty required us to call a spade a spade, it was also
> occasionally necessary to call a knave a knave.
>
> Xavier Rynne, summing up four years
> of reporting the council, in *The Fourth
> Session*, p. x.

The first Vatican Council (1869–70) ended inside St. Peter's,
during a fearful thunderstorm, in the midst of which was
promulgated the dogma of papal infallibility—the dogma that
has most separated Roman Catholicism from the rest of
Christendom.

The second Vatican Council (1962–65) ended outside St.
Peter's, on a beautifully sunny day, with the church offering
itself as the servant of the world—a theme that will increasingly unite Roman Catholicism not only with the rest of
Christendom but with all men of good will.

*Inner and outer reform: two sides
of the same coin*

Those two endings are a symbol of the distance the Roman
Catholic Church has traveled in less than a century. The
church of Vatican I was defensive and ingrown, the victim of
a fortress mentality, cutting itself off more and more from
the world outside. The church of Vatican II is best described
by the word Pope John made a part of the universal human
vocabulary, the word *aggiornamento* (bringing up to date),

a church now affirming the world rather than denying it or seeking to conquer it.

A symbol of the distance the council itself traveled is observable in the fact that it began its work with the revision of the liturgy—an internal event of concern mainly to Catholics —and ended its work with the promulgation of a document on *The Church and the World Today*, dealing with specific modern problems that concern Catholics and non-Catholics alike.

But such a symbol is in danger of being too facile, as though there were a discontinuity between internal reform and outward concern. The very fact that the liturgy was reformed, for example, meant that the full implications of the Catholic faith for *all* of life had to be faced more clearly. *Leitourgia*, after all, means "the people's work," whether done in church or out, and the movement from liturgy to concern about atomic weapons and poverty is not a disjunction but a natural and inevitable progression.

This means that another distinction made during the council is not particularly useful. It was said at first that since the council was to be concerned with the inner reform of the Catholic Church, it would therefore be of concern mainly to Catholics. But it soon became clear that every branch of inner reform had ecumenical implications, so that whatever went on in the council became a matter of concern to non-Catholics as well. Non-Catholics obviously had a stake in the updating of Catholic teaching about religious liberty; but they discovered also that they had a stake in how the council treated Mariological doctrines, or papal authority, or reforms in seminary education, since these matters would mold the Catholic Church of the future—a church with which non-Catholics would have increasing contact. What began as a Catholic family affair soon became a family affair in a much larger sense, for the family was all mankind.

The end of a beginning

The Grand Cliché of Vatican II can be stated in a number of ways. The most obvious way to state it goes: the council did not end on December 8, 1965; it only began. But since clichés, no matter how obvious they sound, usually enshrine some kind of truth, two refinements of the cliché can be offered. The first goes: the council has done some important things to the church; it remains to be seen what the church will do with the council. The second goes: Pope John opened new doors for Roman Catholicism. The council kept those doors open. It remains to be seen how far the church will walk through them.

The council must not become an event in Christian history to which people only look back, but, more importantly, an event from which they look forward. That for the next few pages we look back is only so that in later pages we can look forward.[1] Part of the reason that looking back at the council enables us to look forward is that the council itself ended with a forward-looking stance. Indeed, the whole history of the council might be summarized by the mood at the end of each session.

The first session ended indecisively.

The second session ended gloomily.

The third session ended angrily.

The fourth session ended joyfully.

During the mass on the last working day of the final session, the sun came out from behind the sullen clouds outside of St. Peter's, and a shaft of sunlight, bursting through the windows, suddenly illumined the altar and the bishops concelebrating around it. Dressed as they were in white, the celebrants were spotlighted with an almost incredible intensity. One of the things most impressive about the episode

---

[1] Ch. 15–17 below will attempt to build on council insights for future ecumenical advance.

was the timing. Had the clouds parted fifteen minutes earlier or later, the shaft of light would have missed the altar entirely. (It might even have hit the Protestant and Orthodox observers.) But, coming precisely when it did, that shaft of pure, white light was almost the equivalent of a rainbow over the barque of Peter, at the conclusion of four years of stormy travel across troubled waters.[2]

The waters were often very stormy indeed, a fact that makes even more remarkable the unanimity achieved by the end of the council. And if one seeks for a single fact to account for the stormy nature of the passage, it can be found in this reality, that throughout the council the minority had the structural power, while the majority had the votes. Thus it was difficult to get a document onto the floor for a vote (the parallel of a bill getting pigeonholed in a congressional committee is not inappropriate), but once a vote could be taken, the result was overwhelmingly one-sided. Thus the mind of the council was more unified than a report on the debates would indicate, although the mind of the council certainly grew and matured during four years; some items promulgated during the fourth session could scarcely have been discussed, let alone adopted, when the council first began.

This disparity between power and votes is explained by the fact that the planning of the council took place largely in Rome, and that the chairmen of the various pre-conciliar and conciliar commissions tended to be conservatives who had spent most of their lives in Rome, nurtured in the tight, defensive patterns emanating from Vatican I. They did not want a council in the first place. Many of the curia officials, deeply apprehensive about what might happen when bishops from all over the world assembled together, hoped to post-

[2] I was present on the occasion, standing next to a priest who commented to me, "It shows that Somebody Up There likes transubstantiation," to which I could only respond, Presbyterian to the end, "We're still in the Liturgy of the Word."

pone the opening of the council until Pope John had died, in the hope that the idea would die with him. (One of the stories in Rome was that whenever a curia cardinal asked Pope John to postpone the council another year, he moved the opening date forward another month.) As one Italian bishop remarked, "Popes and councils come and go; the curia goes on forever." The documents prepared under the supervision of this sort of mentality simply tended to repeat conventional Catholic doctrine as it had been understood for centuries.

The major turning points

With this background we can turn to some of the turning points of the council, as it moved from a "pre-Johannine" mentality toward what will subsequently be called the "post-Johannine" era.[3]

1. In the light of the assumption on the part of many bishops that the council would be no more than a rubber stamp for decisions the curia had already made, it is clear that one of the most important events of the entire council

---

[3] The material discussed in Ch. 3 above, dealing with Pope John's decision to call a council, his creation of the Secretariat for the Promotion of Christian Unity, and his decision to invite Protestant and Orthodox observers, is presupposed in what follows.

For fuller treatment of the council, and of the episodes discussed in the pages that follow, consult books about the council listed in the Bibliography, Appendix II below. Some of the material that follows is adapted from a series of three articles appearing in *Presbyterian Life* in the first three issues in 1966.

It should be understood that Vatican II was a solemn assembly of all those within the Roman Catholic Church having teaching authority. Its voting members thus included all the bishops and heads of religious orders. Present also were about 400 Catholic theologians, the experts or *periti* who assisted the council fathers, a group of Catholic lay "auditors," and the Protestant and Orthodox observers. Documents promulgated at the council become authoritative expositions of Roman Catholic teaching. Thus technically the council was exclusively a Roman Catholic council, although, as Ch. 3 has made clear, it became informally and existentially a gathering in which the comments and advice of non-Catholics were often sought.

occurred within its opening minutes. A group of cardinals realized that if the council immediately proceeded to the election of members to the commissions (the small working groups designated to handle the bulk of the council's work) the result could not help but give overwhelming power to the conservative faction that had prepared the preliminary council documents, and whose names had been distributed to the fathers as the session began. Thus, although the agenda called for immediate voting, the cardinals in question were fully aware that such action would render the council virtually powerless to act in its own behalf, and make it the prisoner of a minority already committed to resist significant reform.

As soon, therefore, as the first session was called to order, Cardinal Liénart of France moved a recess so that the council fathers could meet in national groups, discuss possible candidates, and agree on those whom they wished to represent them. Cardinal Frings of Cologne, speaking also for Cardinals Doepfner and Koenig, immediately seconded the motion, which was overwhelmingly adopted, and no sooner had the council begun than it recessed for a long weekend. Over that weekend the various national groups of bishops met, submitted their own nominations for a revised slate of commission members, and were thus able to secure representation on commissions which, even though still dominated by conservative chairmen and vice-chairmen, now had membership representing currents of opinion from all parts of the world.

Had the Liénart-Frings motion been defeated, the council fathers might indeed have been "home by Thanksgiving." But because the motion succeeded, the council was able to become a genuine council of the whole church, rather than reflecting viewpoints regnant only in the southern portion of the Italian peninsula.

2. The main work of the first session centered on the reform of the liturgy. That the reforms were far-reaching became another indication that the council might genuinely become a council of "reform and renewal." Here was the

central and apparently inviolable arena of Catholic life. There had been no significant changes in the mass for hundreds of years; the language was one the people did not understand; the laity had been reduced to the role of passive spectators; the sermon had slipped into oblivion; anachronisms and repetitions obscured the structure.

Thanks to years of quiet but significant spadework, however, particularly by the Benedictines, the time was ripe for reform, and the reform was of a sort that still leaves many Catholics gasping. The changes are significant on their own account, of course, and mean that the mass now becomes not a spectacle Catholics watch, but a drama in which they participate. But the reform of the liturgy has even more implications than its own inherent worth, for it opened up to the council fathers the possibility of reform in other areas of the church's life. If something as sacred as the use of Latin in the mass could be challenged, then in principle many other things could be challenged.

They were.

3. The most direct, and ecumenically important, challenge during the remainder of the first session was the outcome of the discussion on *De Fontibus Revelationis* (On the Sources of Revelation). The key word was *fontibus*, and the key point was its appearance in the plural. The document was a good example of the ethos of pre-conciliar preparations. It had been drafted by conservative theologians, who stated in it that Scripture and tradition were the sources of Christian revelation, truth being found partly in one, partly in the other.[4]

This view, the so-called traditional interpretation of the decrees of the Council of Trent, had been challenged by many Catholic theologians during the past two decades and was being replaced by a view giving centrality to Scripture as the primary source (*fons*) of Christian truth. The pro-

---

[4] Cf. further on this problem the discussion in Ch. 15 below.

posed council document was thus an attempt to turn back the clock of Catholic scholarship and freeze a position that was under attack in many Catholic quarters outside Rome. It is therefore significant that the proposed document was roundly attacked on the council floor, and that, when a vote came, the council rejected the document, although due to a parliamentary mixup it became necessary for Pope John to intervene and withdraw the document from circulation.[5]

Instead of sending it back to the conservative Theological Commission for revision, however, he remanded it to a special commission representing a variety of theological points of view. After three years of conciliar refinement, the new document, significantly retitled *De Revelatione* (On Revelation), with the "two sources" theory thus excised, was overwhelmingly approved by the council, giving a remarkable new freedom to Biblical scholars and offering new possibilities of *rapport* with non-Catholic scholars in an area that would have been closed off for good if the earlier draft had been approved.

4. Pope Paul's opening allocution at the second session provided a significant charter for the ensuing three sessions of the council.[6]

Following the death of Pope John after the first session, the world wondered in which direction Pope Paul would lead the council. Although later events gave rise to much speculation about where Paul's sympathies lay, his initial acts as pope were unambiguously in line with those of his predecessor, and the allocution was firmly "Johannine." History will surely point to the allocution as one of the high points

[5] Xavier Rynne identifies this as the point at which *aggiornamento* became a reality in the church. Cf. the conclusion to *The Fourth Session*, Farrar, Straus and Giroux, New York, 1966, p. 252.

[6] Cf. the earlier discussion of the allocution in Ch. 6 above. The full text is in Rynne, *The Second Session*, Farrar, Straus and Giroux, New York, 1964, pp. 347–63, and at the beginning of each of the four sections of Küng, Congar, and O'Hanlon, eds., *Council Speeches of Vatican II*.

of his pontificate. After pointing out (a) the need for the church to come to a clearer understanding of itself, Paul urged (b) the necessity for inner renewal, and then went on (c) to lay down a charter for the ecumenical task of reunion, and (d) to affirm the necessity of a dialogue with the outside world. This four-point program determined the direction of the rest of the council, and as a result of Paul's decisive speech significant breakthroughs occurred in each area, however slow the program may at times have seemed to be.

5. The most far-reaching instance of the church's coming to a clearer understanding of itself (Paul's first point) focused around the famous "five questions" propounded during session two. During the debate on "collegiality" (the matter of the degree to which the other bishops share rule in the church with the bishop of Rome), the moderator for the day, Cardinal Suenens of Belgium, announced that there would be a kind of straw vote to determine the sentiments of the council on its understanding of teaching authority in the church, so that the Theological Commission charged with revising the document On the Church could have some guidance.

For fifteen days nothing was heard of the questions, and it was apparent that a behind-the-scenes battle of mammoth proportions was being waged. When the questions finally emerged for a vote, and the vote was taken, about eighty per cent of the fathers supported an understanding of teaching authority that helped to correct the one-sided teaching of the First Vatican Council (1869–70), which had seemed to place all authority solely in the pope. By affirming "collegiality," the council made clear that teaching authority is vested in the whole college of bishops (understood as the successors of the apostles), with the bishop of Rome as its head, and that neither pope nor college is truly comprehended apart from the other. This vote ensured the victory in principle of the "open-door" bishops, even though rear-guard action by the politically powerful minority continued until the very last hours of session four.

6. By far the most dramatic moment of the second session was the Frings-Ottaviani exchange on the activities of the Holy Office, which was charged with examining heresy and suppressing wrong opinions. Cardinal Frings of Cologne stated in the course of one of the debates that the activities of the Holy Office were "a scandal to the world." This forthright statement brought applause from the bishops and an angry reply, later the same morning, from Cardinal Ottaviani, head of the Holy Office. The importance of the exchange was that it brought out into the open the need for reform at the very heart of the church. Cardinal Frings said publicly what previously was only said privately, and from that moment the problem could not be overlooked.

The sweeping reform of the Holy Office, announced by Pope Paul just before the end of the council, is surely one of the fruits of Cardinal Frings' courageous utterance. The congregation is now known as the Office of Sacred Doctrine, and its task is no longer to suppress theological investigation but to foster it. The appointment of Canon Charles Moeller of Louvain, one of the most ecumenically minded theologians in the contemporary church, to effect the changes gives good reason to hope that the reform is more than token.

7. Three other documents introduced during the second session had far-reaching ecumenical implications. These were what finally became the decree *On Ecumenism*, the declaration on *Religious Freedom*, and the declaration on *The Church and non-Christian Religions*, with special reference to the Jews.[7] Scarcely any documents have more important overtones for ecumenical encounter than these, so each is discussed elsewhere in more detail.[8]

---

[7] Originally the latter two documents were Ch. 4 and 5, respectively, of the decree *On Ecumenism*.

[8] The decree *On Ecumenism* is treated in Ch. 11, the declaration on *Religious Freedom* in Ch. 13, the statement on the Jews in Ch. 14.

8. The most important moments in session three were variations on a single theme, the theme that the Catholic Church must break out of its self-imposed ghetto and relate itself to the contemporary world. (It has been suggested that the phrase to summarize session three is, "Stop the world, we want to get on.") The discussion centered on "schema thirteen," which ultimately became the council document on *The Church and the World Today*. The document represents one of the most important new directions for Catholic thought, for in it the church comes to terms with the world in which it lives and deals with such specific contemporary issues as population, marriage, poverty, hunger, education, and atomic weapons.

Even more important than the promulgated document, which can, after all, only give suggested guidelines, is the fact that conciliar debate on the document opened many new doors for Catholic thinking. For example, Cardinals Léger, Alfrink, Suenens, and Patriarch Maximos IV asked for a rethinking of the theology of marriage. Not only did they push beyond the traditional teaching that the primary ends of marriage are procreation and education of children to a stress on the equal importance of conjugal love, but they also made clear that in the light of the centrality of conjugal love the traditional ban on contraception must at least be rethought. (So delicate was the latter issue that the pope removed it from conciliar discussion and appointed a special papal commission to advise him on the matter.) Maximos IV went so far as to warn the fathers against treating marriage from the point of view of a "bachelor psychosis." Cardinal Suenens reminded the council that the church could not afford to have another "Galileo incident." The same sort of openness was manifested in further speeches about religious liberty and anti-Semitism earlier in the session.[9]

[9] The theme of "the church and the world today," with specific reference to the council document, is discussed in Ch. 16 below.

9. Another breakthrough of a different sort occurred during session three. Minute in itself, it was large in portent. On the one day that the pope attended a working session of the council, he urged the fathers to adopt with only minor revisions the statement on missions that was to be discussed that day. After he left the session, however, bishop after bishop got up and literally tore the statement to shreds, so that, rather than being adopted, it had to be sent back to a conciliar commission for total recasting.

Some Catholics were aghast that the pope's suggestion was not immediately accepted and saw in the incident an example of the disintegration of authority they feared from the council. But others, arguing from the pope ill informed to the pope better informed, realized that there was something very important about the whole episode, namely that if the other bishops *do* share rule with the bishop of Rome (as the doctrine of collegiality declares), there has to be freedom for differences of opinion even between pope and bishops. The bishops cannot be reduced to a mere rubber stamp. As an example, therefore, of the actual, rather than theoretical, authority of the bishops in relation to their head, the incident has had particular meaning for non-Catholics, as well as for the many Catholics who are eager that their church shed an understanding of the papacy built on the pattern of a Renaissance court.

The further advantage of the episode was that the rejection of the draft enabled the missionary bishops themselves to suggest creative changes during the period of rewriting and thus ensure the emergence of a strong document for promulgation.

10. There were low moments in the council as well, though none were quite as low as the ending of the third session, which in its own way was a turning point. During the last week of session three, various events, three in particular, conspired to send the bishops home discouraged and even angry: (a) a promised vote on religious liberty was not forth-

coming; (b) nineteen papal changes were introduced into the ecumenism decree too late for the bishops to have an opportunity to debate them; and (c) the pope, in his closing speech, gave to Mary the title "Mother of the Church," even though the bishops in their earlier debate had decided that the title was inappropriate. It seemed for a while as though either the conservatives had gotten through to Paul, convinced him that the council was getting out of hand, and persuaded him to recapture control after the fashion of pre-Vatican II popes, or that Paul himself had reached a similar decision. The resulting gloom lasted many months, and there were those who, seeing this as a portent of things to come, predicted that the final session would end in disaster, with nineteenth-century papalism regnant and collegiality a dead letter. That the final session did not end in disaster is due to many factors, but it is surely arguable that one of the reasons it did not was precisely because many Catholics (and non-Catholics as well) raised their voices in warning that this was not the way to move forward creatively. Seldom has there been such open and healthy criticism in the Catholic press as after session three.

11. One of the most important ecumenical breakthroughs came during the very last week of the council. The pope suggested that at his last audience with the Protestant observers there be a service of joint prayer rather than simply an exchange of speeches. As the idea took form, it was decided to include the other bishops as well. In the brochure printed for the service, the pope was not described as presiding but simply as "participating." Protestant and Orthodox observers likewise "participated" by leading in prayer and reading Scripture, while the pope preached a sermon and the entire congregation, observers and bishops alike, sang, "Now Thank We All Our God."

Many bishops in the past have been unwilling to permit such services in the churches of their dioceses. Now that the pope himself has set the precedent, however, it will be a diehard bishop indeed who feels himself able to refuse such a request. Since the question of joint worship has been one of the most delicate in ecumenical relations, inestimable good was done by the pope's gesture.[10]

12. The final high point (merely because twelve is a more realistic point at which to stop than twenty-four or forty-eight) can be symbolized by the note on which the council ended. At the conclusion of four years of hard work, it would have been no more than natural for the fathers to end on a note of self-congratulation, turning inward with justified pride and taking stock of their achievements. But the events at the end of the council showed something quite different. They showed the church turning outward toward the world, offering itself as the servant of the world. Two of the most "outward-reaching" documents of the council—the decree on religious freedom and the pastoral constitution on *The Church and the World Today*—were among the last four to be promulgated on December 7, and each was adopted with an incredibly small number of *non placet* (negative) votes.

The outward thrust was further symbolized by the open-air session the following day. Although the service was much too long (over four hours) and had some Cecil B. De Mille touches to it—one observer privately referred to it as a *spectaculum religiosum*—it nevertheless dramatized in a vivid way the church's concern to reach outward. Various cardinals read messages to groups within "the modern world"—rulers, intellectuals, artists, women, the suffering, workers, and youth—and representatives of these groups, such as Jacques Maritain for the intellectuals and the architect Nervi for the artists, received the messages.

A council that began indoors shrouded in an antiquated notion of secrecy had ended in the open air, offering the fruits of its work to all mankind.

---

[10] Cf. further on this theme the treatment of *communicatio in sacris* in Ch. 17 below.

The role of the pope

It is clear from even this brief a chronicle that the role of the pope is crucial in understanding the dynamics of the council. Pope John had won the confidence of the whole world, even as he had earned the suspicion of the die-hard curia officials whose tidy, self-enclosed world was challenged by the council. It is impossible to tell how Pope John would have fared had he lived through the duration of the council. Some feel that his charismatic gifts would have been sufficient to lead the council to unprecedented heights. Others argue, with some plausibility, that he would have been hopelessly outmaneuvered by his own curia, as he had been, for example, on an earlier occasion when he signed the document *Veterum Sapientiae*, a wholly unrealistic demand that all seminary instruction be given in Latin—a demand that was almost universally ignored, even though appearing over the papal signature.

At all events, John was succeeded by a very different kind of man, a man who did not have the personal charisma of his predecessor, but who brought to his task the advantage of having served many years in the curia, thus knowing its ins and outs, and who, knowing its ins and outs, publicly committed himself in the first weeks of his pontificate to its reform.

It is still hard, however, to assess Pope Paul. Is he a "progressive" going slowly, or a "conservative" going fast, or something entirely different? His opening allocution, as noted above, gave nothing but joy to the progressives. Yet at the end of the third session he seemed to many to have retreated almost in panic from the implications of conciliar reform and to have become either the captive of, or the leader of, the voices of conservatism. On the eve of the fourth session he issued an encyclical on the eucharist, *Mysterium Fidei*, that seemed to most interpreters to be at best a backward-looking document and at worst a repudiation of many of the creative insights of the already-promulgated constitution *On the Sacred Liturgy.*[11]

And yet, Pope Paul emerged at the end of the fourth session as pope of the church that did, in fact, enact the major items of legislation that its critics had been fearful it would not enact. The decree on religious freedom, to take only one example, is now a fact, and one of the reasons it is a fact and not a bitter unfulfilled memory is that Pope Paul resisted conservative pressures exerted on him, to the very final hours of the council, to scuttle the document.

Perhaps the clearest clue to the course Pope Paul has decided to take is indicated by his allocution at the "open session" of the council on November 18, 1965. Paul used the occasion to survey what the council had done and to look into the future. A French journalist, in reporting the speech in *La Croix,* recalled that Paul himself had described Pope John's allocution at the very beginning of the council as "the words of a prophet," and went on to describe Paul's November 18 allocution as "the words of a statesman."

That is probably the word to use. Paul is, in the best sense of the word, a statesman. He wants to lead the whole church and not just factions of the church. He is willing to wait until tomorrow, and not accomplish everything today. When he gives something to one group within the church, he gives something to the other group as well. If, every time he steps forward, he then goes half a step backward, the net result is still half a step forward. The themes of the November 18 allocution are a case in point. There will be reforms—but they will come slowly. There will be a senate of bishops—but it will not meet for two years. Plans will proceed for the beati-

---

[11] For a fair but frank analysis of Protestant perturbation concerning this encyclical, cf. Vajta, *"Mysterium Fidei:* A Lutheran View," in Küng, ed., *We Know the Others?,* Concilium series, Vol. 14, Paulist Press, pp. 157–66. An Orthodox analysis by Metropolitan Emilianos Timiadis follows on pp. 167–76.

fication of John XXIII—but also of Pius XII. The Holy Office has rendered valiant service to the church—but it will be changed. In commemoration of the council there will be a "jubilee year"—but it will last only six months.

This kind of action emerges more and more clearly as the pattern of Paul's pontificate. When he appears to lean one way, it is safe to predict that he will soon move in another way to correct the apparent imbalance. When one reflects how great are the continuing conservative pressures on him, there is cause for much rejoicing. When one reflects how great are the needs of the world to which the church whose head he is must minister, there is cause for hoping that the progressives will exert pressures also.

CHAPTER 10

THE ACHIEVEMENTS OF VATICAN II:
A BRIEF ASSESSMENT

> Bearing in mind the necessities of the present day, above all [the council] sought to meet the pastoral needs, and nourishing the flame of charity, it has made a great effort to reach not only the Christians still separated from communion with the Holy See, but also the whole human family.
>
> Pope Paul, declaring the completion of
> Vatican II, December 8, 1965.

During the closing days of the council, newsmen had a single question for cardinals, bishops, non-Catholic observers, and fellow newsmen: "Now that the council is over, do you think it has succeeded?" The question was usually followed by a request for an answer of less than 200 words.

So posed, the question is impossible and ridiculous, and answers to it ranged from the occasional Catholic who felt compelled to describe the council as "the greatest event since Pentecost," to one Protestant who responded that the council had largely concerned itself with "inane, stupid, ridiculous issues."

Such extravagances aside, there is a sense in which the question cannot yet be asked, for as suggested in the last chapter the council, far from being over, has hardly begun. What the Catholic Church will do with the conciliar documents is barely beginning to emerge, and full implementation will take years. As the decree *On Ecumenism* is vigorously implemented in some areas, it will be virtually ignored in others, even as the decree on *Mass Communications* is ignored almost everywhere.

But there is another problem. Any assessment of the council is strongly influenced by the perspective from which one makes his assessment. If we measure the council's achievements against where the church was five years ago, the advance is phenomenal. But if we measure them against where the church must be five years hence, the surface has only been scratched. If a Protestant expected the council to produce Protestant-sounding statements, he is disappointed. But if a Protestant expected the council to produce as good Catholic-sounding statements as 2300 men could be expected to produce (even granting them a large measure of assistance by the Holy Spirit), he has certainly been amply rewarded.

When the council was first announced, probably few Protestants expected much from it; the very fact that it had been called was the significant breakthrough. But after the "secrecy curtain" had been broken (chiefly by the first article appearing in the *New Yorker* under the collective pseudonym of Xavier Rynne, the columns by Henri Fesquet in *Le Monde*, and the even fuller daily reports in the Catholic journal *La Croix*), and the world began to hear that exciting things were being said on the council floor, many people became convinced that genuine reforms and breakthroughs were possible. The question then became: can the voices *in* the council become the voice *of* the council?

To an unexpectedly high degree, they did. Recognizing that an individual speech is usually more daring than a committee report that must satisfy a variety of viewpoints, it is fair to say that the council achieved much more than most people initially expected, if not quite as much as they subsequently desired.

The important tangible gains

The tangible gains of the council are fairly easy to measure: sixteen documents were approved, almost always by overwhelming majorities, and the texts are available for study. The sixteen documents are of three sorts: "constitutions," "decrees," and "declarations."[1] Books could be written on each of these documents, and undoubtedly will be. All that can be attempted here is a brief description of each one, with fuller discussion in some cases reserved for later chapters.

a. the four constitutions

1. *The Church*. From a theological point of view, this is the most important document of Vatican II.[2] The best way to view it is to see it in the context of Vatican I, since it supplements and even begins to correct certain understandings of the church that emerged at the earlier council. It must also be seen in the light of a long evolution within the council, moving from an initially triumphalistic and static view of the church to a more dynamic one. At Vatican I almost

[1] In the early days of the council there was much discussion about the relative degree of binding authority between, say, a "constitution" and a "decree." It seemed fairly clear that a "constitution" was of higher authority, and it would be a wise rule of interpretation to say that the "constitution" *On the Church*, for example, was the context in which to understand the "decree" *On Ecumenism*, rather than vice versa. As it actually worked out, however, there seemed little reason by the end of the council why *The Church and the World Today* should be a "constitution" (albeit a "pastoral constitution") while the document on *Missionary Activity* should be a "decree" or the statement on *Religious Freedom* a "declaration." Actually, the selectivity of history will determine which documents are to be influential, far more than their actual titles.

[2] Nothing seems more foolhardy than an attempt to comment on *De Ecclesia* in a couple of pages. The document deserves, and will receive, more careful attention than any other document of the council. For a fuller critique than is possible here, cf. the excellent analysis by Skydsgaard, "The Church as Mystery and as People of God," in Lindbeck, ed., *Dialogue on the Way*, Augsburg, Minneapolis, 1965, pp. 145–74.

all of the attention was focused on the teaching authority of the bishop of Rome. Materials dealing with his relationship to the other bishops were on the agenda, but were never discussed. Consequently there was a gap in formally promulgated doctrine about teaching authority that Vatican II sought to close. From this perspective, the most important section of the document is Chapter 3, propounding the doctrine of the "collegiality of the bishops." Instead of asserting that the pope alone bears rule in the church (the impression Vatican I had conveyed), Chapter 3 asserts that the pope and the other bishops together constitute the episcopal college, and that it is the college (of which, of course, the pope is the head) that defines the nature of Catholic truth.

The measure was the most hotly debated of all issues at Vatican II, since some of the fathers felt that acknowledgment of collegiality would amount to a denial of papal supremacy, but when the "five questions" seeking to clarify the matter were finally voted upon, well over eighty per cent of the fathers, as we have already seen, affirmed their belief in collegiality. Even so, the statement is very cautiously worded, and an explanatory note, added at the last moment, makes clear that papal power is in no sense diminished. The document can therefore be read in conservative terms as well as in more open-ended fashion.

A number of other emphases in the constitution are of ecumenical significance. The document, for example, does not start with "triumphalistic" statements about the indefectibility of the empirical institution of the church, but with an account of the "mystery" of the church, a mystery no man can finally fathom. The controlling image for the church is that of the "people of God," *all* the people of God. The church is not the hierarchy plus the leftovers; it is the whole of God's people, and only when that point has been clearly established (in Chapter 2) does the document go on (in Chapter 3) to discuss the role of those who are set apart to hierarchical tasks within it. "The priesthood of all the faithful" (no longer the exclusive prerogative of the Reformation churches) is developed in the treatment of the laity in Chapter 4.

The document opens new possibilities in Catholic assessments of non-Catholic churches. Successive drafts moved from the notion that "Only the Roman Catholic Church can rightly be called a church," through a view that "This church which is both visible and spiritual *is* the Catholic Church," to the conclusion that "This church which is both visible and spiritual *subsists in* the Catholic Church." While the statement lacks precision, it clearly opens the way for a more generous view of the "ecclesial reality" of the non-Roman churches, a position developed more fully in the decree *On Ecumenism.*

Another opening to the future is the eschatological dimension of the document. While the constitution is notably reticent in any self-criticism of the church, the materials are present for the development of such a critique in the distinctions made between the "already" and the "not yet," the church as it now is, and the church as it is intended by God to become.

A further item of ecumenical importance is the inclusion within the constitution of a chapter on Mary. Originally there had been a separate conciliar document on Mary, written in the style of recent papal encyclicals. However, by a very close vote, the council decided to include the Marian material within the context of the material on the church, rather than seeming to encourage Marian theology to continue developing in isolation from the rest of Catholic thought. The resulting chapter, while still a fully "Catholic" statement, has been rewritten with the ecumenical intent of describing Mary as much as possible in Biblical terms, so that an avenue of possible ecumenical discussion may be opened up.

2. *Divine Revelation.* This document also has important theological implications for the ecumenical dialogue. It states a view of revelation that goes far beyond the traditional "two

sources" view, to a view that the Word of God, Jesus Christ, comes to us through Scripture, and that it is the ongoing task of the church to interpret the meaning of Scripture. This opens new doors of *rapport* with Protestant Biblical scholarship in an ecumenical effort to rethink the issue of the relationship of Scripture and tradition, one of the thorniest points of theological division since the sixteenth century. Another ecumenical advance is the undergirding the constitution gives to Catholic Biblical scholarship, many of whose practitioners were under attack by conservative forces at the time the council opened.[3]

3. *The Sacred Liturgy.* The first document promulgated by the council, the constitution on liturgy has been a genuine impetus to reforms, many of which have already been introduced and many more of which will be necessitated by the resultant new situation. The celebration of the mass in the vernacular (save for the canon), greater attention to Scripture and sermon, and the increasing involvement of the laity in worship are only a few of the emphases with ecumenical implications.

4. *The Church and the World Today.* The longest of the council documents, this "pastoral" constitution opens up new directions for Catholic thought and action and is addressed "not only to the sons of the Church and to all who invoke the name of Christ, but to the whole of humanity."[4] It provides a basis for common action on the part of Catholics and non-Catholics in meeting the needs of the world today in such specific areas as education, marriage, poverty, illiteracy, and economic justice.[5]

[3] A fuller treatment of the substantive issues will be found in Ch. 15 below.
[4] *The Church and the World Today*, Art. 2; in Abbott, ed., *op. cit.*, p. 200.
[5] Cf. the further discussion of these themes in Ch. 16 below.

b. the three declarations

1. *Religious Freedom.* For non-Catholics this is the most important immediate fruit of the council and provides an authoritative foundation for the extension of religious freedom to *all* men. It likewise offers a base from which deviations in Catholic practice can now be challenged.[6]

2. *The Relationship of the Church to Non-Christian Religions.* The text deals with Hinduism, Buddhism, Islam, and Judaism. The document is remarkably open *vis-à-vis* the truths found in other religions and confines itself to areas of common conviction on which a new relationship between adherents of the various world religions can be established. Some have accused the document of being too generalized and dealing with only one segment of the problem of religious differences, namely those things shared in spite of differences, but since no council has ever dealt directly with such a problem before, it can be argued that the emphasis is appropriate for the initiation of such discussion. A special Secretariat on the Non-Christian Religions has been established by the Vatican to implement the Christian-non-Christian dialogue this document seeks to initiate.[7]

3. *Christian Education.* This document deals almost exclusively with internal problems of Catholic education and does not really break any new ground. Non-Catholics may be aroused by the strong emphasis on parochial school education, and the document may reawaken concern about such controversial issues as federal aid to parochial schools and "released time" programs.

---

[6] Cf. Ch. 13 below for a fuller treatment of the declaration.

[7] Article 4 of this declaration, dealing with the Jews, will be examined in detail in Ch. 14 below.

c. the nine decrees

1. *Ecumenism.* To non-Catholics as well as Catholics this is a major resource for future ecumenical activity and opens up new possibilities of ecumenical action that would scarcely have seemed possible even half a decade ago.[8]

2. *The Instruments of Social Communication.* By common consent this decree, dealing with the use of the mass media, is the least satisfactory document of the council. Inadequately debated at the first session, it was drastically reworked between sessions and voted without discussion at the second session, receiving the largest number of negative votes of any council document. It is unlikely to play a significant role in the *aggiornamento* of the church and seems already to have been swept under the conciliar rug.

3. *The Eastern Catholic Churches.* This text clarifies the relationship of the whole church to those Catholic churches in the East (often called the Uniate churches) that do not use the Latin rite. Approval is given to the distinctive rite of these churches, honor is accorded to their patriarchs (some of whom were among the most influential spokesmen at the council), and guidelines are established concerning *communicatio in sacris* (sharing in common worship) between these churches and the Orthodox churches of the East.

4. *The Church's Missionary Activity.* This may turn out to be one of the ecumenical "sleepers" of the council. For one thing, the decree gives new liberty to Catholic missionary bishops who, before its passage, were often frustrated by the need to clear everything in advance with Rome. Since many ecumenical initiatives have come from the mission areas, it is significant that the bishops in those areas, often among the most forward-looking in the church, will have a greater measure of autonomy than before. The document is therefore an important example of the beginnings of decen-

[8] A full discussion of this document follows in the next chapter.

tralization. Furthermore, the document frequently urges closer co-operation between Roman Catholics and their "separated brethren" on the mission field, thereby developing explicitly some of the principles of ecumenical relationship that are foreshadowed in the earlier decree *On Ecumenism*. Many of the contemporary breakthroughs, such as joint translations of Scripture and the shared use of physical facilities, received their initial impetus on the mission field, and the present decree opens the way for further initiatives of a similar sort.

5. *The Apostolate of the Laity*. This document, strengthened by lay participation in the conciliar commission, provides specific direction for lay activity, building on the materials about the laity in the constitution *On the Church*. While it does not move far beyond present thinking about the laity, it does provide conciliar leverage to those areas of the church where laymen are still second-class citizens. As the church attempts to develop the full implications of "the priesthood of all the faithful," the decree will provide specific guidance.

6. *The Bishops' Pastoral Office in the Church*. Just as the decree on the laity spells out some of the implications of the doctrine of "the priesthood of all the faithful," so this decree spells out some of the implications of the doctrine of "the collegiality of the bishops." It indicates that bishops should have more voice in the life of the entire church, since a bishop is not simply bishop of his own diocese, but of the universal church. Considerable attention is given to "bishops' conferences," at which certain kinds of corporate decisions may be made for a given region without having to wait for initiative or approval from Rome. Other matters of diocesan organization are treated, including prudent suggestions to elderly bishops about retiring.

7. *The Appropriate Renewal of the Religious Life*.[9] This

---

[9] The term "religious" has a technical meaning in Catholic parlance, referring to those who have entered a religious order and taken the vows of poverty, chastity, and obedience.

document deals with the inner life of Roman Catholicism, and an inner area of that inner life at that. Many suggestions are made about the reform and updating of the religious orders, although implementation is left largely to the superiors of the various groups. For example, the habit (or garb) of religious may be adapted to modern conditions as each order decides, although such change is no more than "adaptation." True "renewal" will come from interior re-dedication to the mind of Christ and the spirit of the founders of the various orders.

Protestants often have difficulty understanding the role of religious orders, feeling that Catholicism makes withdrawal from the world a model of the highest kind of Christian calling. As the present decree makes clear, however, the life of denial is less denial *of* the world than denial *for the sake* of the world, so that there can be fuller dedication to the service of Christ. It is clear, as the constitution *On the Church* likewise emphasizes, that *all* Christians are called to "holiness," and the traditional qualitative distinction between "secular" and "religious" is thereby challenged.

8. *The Ministry and the Life of Priests.* This document, mainly descriptive, represents an updating of the function and role of the priest. Setting the ordained clergy within the framework of "the priesthood of all the faithful," the text goes on to give special attention not only to their sacerdotal functions but also to their responsibility to the full ministry of the Word. The priesthood is upgraded in the recognition that bishops "should gladly listen to their priests," while priests are reminded at the same time that they "must willingly listen to the laity."

9. *Priestly Formation.* There was much informal discussion at the council about the need for reforms in seminary education. The present document embodies some, at least, of these concerns. While it cannot be described as *avant garde*, it does give sufficient direction and latitude so that, creatively employed, it could revolutionize the future of the

Catholic Church by restructuring the education of its seminarians. It urges, for example, greater attention on Biblical studies, "a fuller understanding of the churches and ecclesial communities separated from the Apostolic Roman See," and wider acceptance and employment of the disciplines of psychology and sociology. Implicit within it is a recognition that the seminarian needs more contact with the world to which he is to minister, rather than the isolation from that world that has so frequently characterized his training in the past.

Interlude: using the texts as "pointers"

These sixteen documents are destined to be one of the main staples of ecumenical investigation for the next generation. It is therefore important to employ them as creatively as possible.[10]

At a recent conference at Notre Dame on "Theological Issues of Vatican II," it was noted that the Protestant participants tended to treat the documents almost reverentially, asking about the precise meaning of this phrase or that word, whereas the Catholic participants were remarkably freewheeling, using the documents as starting points for further exploration and displaying relatively little concern about the wording that enabled them to begin exploring.

There is a reason for this Protestant conservatism toward the documents. For many years, when Protestant theologians tried to illustrate a new theme in Catholic theology by quoting Congar or Geiselmann or Küng, they would be told that the theologian in question spoke only for himself, that his statement did not commit the church, and that there was furthermore no assurance that he would survive the next purge emanating from the Piazza del Sant' Uffizio. Protestants learned, in other words, not to count their theological

---

[10] The following paragraphs are adapted from "Using Council Documents," *The Commonweal*, May 20, 1966, pp. 254–56.

chickens before they had been magisterially hatched. In the resultant Protestant search for *official* statements to confirm new trends, any straw in the wind was eagerly clutched.

Then came Vatican II and provided not a few straws, but a whole haystack of official pronouncements. Many things that were formerly only private opinions, became official church teaching. It is a heady experience for the Protestant ecumenist in this new situation to be relieved of the necessity of saying, "We see certain indications that give us a reasonable assurance that a trend will probably develop in a moderately hopeful direction within the next decade or so." Rather than all of this circumlocution, the Protestant ecumenist can now simply cite chapter and verse of any one of sixteen conciliar documents.

But there is a built-in danger here. It is the danger of trying to understand Catholicism by the backward look rather than the forward look, of trying to justify what still remains to be done simply by reference to what has so far been done. One of the gains of the council has been the liberation of Catholic theology from a static framework, and it is important not to turn the liberation into a new kind of enslavement in which all that is said or done henceforth has to be justified by citations from what Msgr. Joseph Gallagher has estimated to be the "approximately 103,014 words" of the conciliar documents—excluding footnotes.[11] It is important, of course, to have as clear an understanding of the texts as possible, and Ph.D. theses (probably to the tune of "approximately 103,-014," including footnotes) will help in that endeavor. But preoccupation with the *texts*, at the expense of the *spirit* of the texts, could hamper the onward development of Catholic theology.

Much of the freedom with which the Catholic participants at the 1965 Notre Dame conference approached the documents sprang from the fact that many of them had been in-

[11] Cf. "Preface to the Translation," in Abbott, ed., *op. cit.*, p. ix.

volved in the conciliar development of the documents and knew full well what things had had to be omitted or toned down for the sake of consensus. They therefore saw the documents as pointers to the future, rather than summations of the past.

It has become clear, even in the short time since the council ended, that what the documents really mean is still being determined. They will become what the church makes of them; not all of them will play an equally important role, and not all portions within a given document will have equal impact. The nature of these emerging priorities is still being determined, and the response of the church to the documents will be fully as important as the documents themselves.

This is why post-conciliar Catholic theology must be more than merely a theology of the council, merely a study of what the council did. It needs to be that, of course, but it also needs to be much more than that. The documents must not be used to build fences around present activity, but to build bridges toward future activity. Only so can the doors Pope John opened be left open, and the council be seen not as the culmination of an old era, but as the beginning of a new one.

The more important intangible gains

In putting so much attention on the tangible gains of the council, there is a danger of missing the real significance of the council. For the council's impact on the coming ecumenical generation will be far wider than the mere implementation of its documents. The council's greatest contribution is surely that the church of the counter-Reformation—the defensive church, the church of anathemas and condemnations, the church living on denials—has finally been laid to rest. Put more positively, the council has enabled the Catholic Church as a whole to embrace the need for ongoing reformation, to recognize that the church is always a church of sinners (perhaps even a "sinful church"), and that until the end of time it must constantly measure its considerable achievements against the even higher demands Christ lays upon it, acknowledge that judgment begins at the house of God, and take heart finally not in its own achievements but in the forgiving and renewing grace of God.

This means that the church is now in process of becoming what Michael Novak has described as "the open church."[12] Some of the fresh air Pope John wanted to blow into the church has indeed blown in. Ideas that could only be whispered about a few years ago are now discussed openly, commented upon, and even written about, without fear. Men who felt themselves part of a tiny minority, subject to repressive measures, have discovered that they are a majority, and to their credit have not instituted repressive measures against those they are replacing. Those who formerly assumed that any directive issuing from Rome represented the mind of the pope have made the liberating discovery that the conclusion does not necessarily follow from the premise, and are determined that in the future there shall be two-way traffic: ideas will flow *toward* Rome as well as emanating *from* Rome. The church is clearly on the threshold of what could be the most exciting and creative period in its entire history.

The post-conciliar agenda

All of which means, of course, that the task is far from done. Cliché or no, the council is not an end but a beginning. There are new tasks the council thrusts upon the church as well as old tasks the council did not dispose of. To non-Catholics, for example, there is particular regret that one of the most prickly issues between Catholics and Protestants—

[12] Cf. Novak, *The Open Church*, Macmillan, New York, 1963, 370 pp., which in addition to being the fullest single description of the second session of the council provides, through the focus of its title, a way of seeing the new dynamic that has entered into the church through the council.

the matter of "mixed marriages"—was left unresolved. During the third session, the council fathers voted to turn the subject over to the pope for action, so that he could issue a separate, and presumably speedier, statement of new regulations. But nothing was issued until well after the council ended, and the resulting concessions were of such a minimal nature as to make clear that more must follow.

On a more crucial issue, the population explosion and birth control, the council did not speak clearly. The subject was removed from conciliar debate so that a specially appointed papal commission could deal with it. From one point of view, it is a victory that the council did not make a definitive statement (although it did register an important advance by making "conjugal love" co-equal with procreation in the hierarchy of the goods of marriage), for it is clear that the bishops, if forced to speak in 1965, would simply have reaffirmed the traditional Catholic teaching that is so inadequate to the theological, psychological, and demographic insights of the mid-twentieth century. That the door was not closed to further development of Catholic teaching on the matter is, in terms of the dynamics of the council, a significant victory for the open-minded bishops.

But is "not closing doors" enough help for the future church? One school of thought urges patience: "Such matters must not be forced. Catholics must wait for a consensus to emerge. The new teaching on birth control will be worked out in time." Others, however, ask: "Can we afford the luxury of so much quiet deliberation? Time is running out. The human race cannot wait indefinitely for the church to make up its mind. If there is to be a new approach to birth control, it must come now rather than a decade hence."[13]

There are some Catholics who will continue to view everything the council represents with fear if not suspicion. For

[13] The issue of birth control is only illustrative. Such pleas could be addressed to other contemporary issues touched upon by the council, such as its apparent equivocation on the morality of varying degrees of nuclear warfare.

them, the church has always stood as the one clear bulwark of truth and security in a rapidly changing and terrifying world. Now, quite suddenly, they find that the church itself is changing. Things long assumed as axiomatic are being challenged, if not discarded. It does not really matter whether the changes are at the periphery or the center, for these Catholics have never distinguished between peripheral and central truth. Hence, the logic of resistance: if Friday abstinence goes, the ban against artificial means of contraception will go next, papal infallibility will then be reinterpreted, and the whole edifice will collapse. This kind of fear is undeniably present, not only among laymen but among some bishops as well.[14]

But to another group of Catholics the council has come as a genuine liberation. Such Catholics, long worried by the anachronisms and irrelevance of much official Catholicism, have discovered that the church can indeed purge itself and enter upon a new life of greater openness and sensitivity both to what is best in Catholicism and to what is best in contemporary culture. These Catholics will press forward not only in whatever ways the council documents suggest, but also in whatever ways the council documents do not specifically forbid.[15]

The tension between these two groups—those who fear the so-called open church and those who welcome it—is bound

[14] Even the typesetters are occasionally infected by it. Item: a fascinating misprint in Stransky, ed., The Decree on Ecumenism, refers to sacred theology in contrast to historical theology as "scared theology" (p. 63).

[15] The issue is highlighted by one of the council quips circulating at the fourth session. During the previous summer there had been concern that certain Dutch theologians seemed to be teaching a view of the eucharist that challenged the traditional interpretation of the "changing" of the bread and wine into the body and blood of Christ. This, coupled with other attempts by the Dutch to move ahead into other realms of aggiornamento, brought forth the comment, "In Holland, everything changes—except bread and wine." The Dutch response, in the face of unyielding conservatism on the part of the Italians, went, "In Italy, nothing changes—except bread and wine."

to generate the most important intramural activity within Catholicism for the next decade. Non-Catholics must try to understand the fears of the first group as well as the hopes of the second, even though to them it will be clear with which group the ecumenical future lies.

CHAPTER 11

ECUMENICAL ESCALATION:
THE DECREE *ON ECUMENISM*

> This is more than the opening of a new door; new
> ground has been broken. No Catholic document has
> ever spoken of non-Catholic Christians in this way.
>
> Oscar Cullmann, Protestant observer at
> all four sessions of Vatican II, comment-
> ing on the decree On Ecumenism.

The most important ecumenical fruit of Vatican II is the
new spirit that the council has created in the Catholic
Church. However, in addition to the new spirit, we have the
bonus of the conciliar document *On Ecumenism* in which,
as Professor Cullmann points out, "new ground has been
broken."[1]

[1] Much literature is available on the subject matter of the decree *On
Ecumenism*. The following documentation is only suggestive. The text of the
decree, together with explanatory notes by Fr. Walter Abbott, s.j., is in Abbott,
ed., *Documents of Vatican II*, Guild Press, New York, 1966, pp. 336–70. Cf.
also the excellent edition edited by Fr. Thomas Stransky, c.s.p., of the Secretariat for Christian Unity, *The Decree on Ecumenism*, Paulist Press, New
York, 1965, 86 pp. Fr. Stransky was as close to the development of the decree
as any single individual and his introduction and notes are particularly useful.
The fullest accounts of the development of the text, together with commentary on it, are Jaeger, *A Stand on Ecumenism: The Council's Decree*, Kenedy,
New York, 1965, 242 pp., and Leeming, *The Vatican Council and Christian
Unity*, Harper & Row, New York, 1966, 333 pp. Jaeger's work also discusses
the congruity of the decree with the constitution *On the Church* (cf. pp.
177–213). Its one weakness is the brevity of its report on the speeches at the
council. This may be supplemented by consulting Küng, Congar, and O'Hanlon, eds., *Council Speeches of Vatican II*, Paulist Press, Glen Rock, 1964, esp.
pp. 145–227, containing the best interventions on ecumenism. Cf. also volumes on the second session as a whole, listed in the bibliography. Protestant
reactions to the debate on ecumenism are available in Horton, *Vatican Diary*

The development of the decree

How has this happened? Presupposed in our answer must be the gradual growth in ecumenical understanding previously sketched, from the negativism of *Mortalium Animos* (1928), through the tentative openness of the *Instruction of the Holy Office* (1949), to the quiet groundwork of the "ecumenical pioneers" and the impact of Pope John.[2]

The conciliar approach to ecumenism was in an inchoate state even after the council got underway. Three *schemata* containing possible material were available: (a) a draft prepared by the Commission for the Eastern Churches, centering on the relationship with Orthodoxy, (b) the eleventh chapter of an early draft of the constitution *On the Church*, and (c) materials prepared by the Secretariat for Christian Unity. Only on December 1, 1962, after the conclusion of the first session, was a decision reached to combine these materials into one document. The Secretariat for Christian Unity was charged with the preparation of a new document which was the subject of intensive debate during the second session. The date of the introduction of the document for conciliar debate, November 18, 1963, is thus an historic date in ecumenical history. In presenting the document to the council, Archbishop Martin commented, "Ecumenism is something completely new. It has never been dealt with by

---

1963, United Church Press, Philadelphia 1964, and my *Observer in Rome*, Doubleday, New York, 1964, 271 pp.

Protestant and Orthodox reactions to the decree as a whole are contained in "Comments on the Decree on Ecumenism," *The Ecumenical Review*, April 1965, pp. 93–112. Cf. also the chapter by Edmund Schlink, in Lindbeck, ed., *Dialogue on the Way*, Augsburg, Minneapolis, 1965, pp. 186–220. A Roman Catholic assessment by Fr. Maurice Villain, "The Debate on the Decree on Ecumenism," is in Küng, ed., *Do We Know the Others?*, Concilium series, Vol. 14, Paulist Press, pp. 113–33.

Because of its ecumenical significance, the text of the decree is printed below as Appendix I.

[2] For an elaboration of these themes cf. Ch. 3 above.

any previous council; even in theology it has been discussed only in recent times."[3] The speeches against the document were predictable: the text should stress more strongly that Roman Catholicism is the one true church; reunion must be understood as the return of the dissidents; ecumenical openness is likely to lead to indifferentism and will be baffling to the faithful; the church must make clearer that Catholic truth is unchangeable and that no doctrinal concessions are in the offing.

But speeches favoring the document were notable for stressing that while the document was good, it was too timid and must be made bolder. Many such concerns made their way into the revised text: there was repeated insistence that Catholic responsibility for past divisions must be incorporated into the document; that a more positive attitude must be taken toward the elements of the Gospel that non-Catholics have maintained despite their division from Rome; that non-Catholics must be seen as participating in a communal life that contains valid elements of the *ecclesia*; that recognition be given to the fact that those who today are separated from the Roman See are not calumniated by historical factors over which they had no control.[4]

As a result of the impact of these speeches, as well as the written interventions submitted to the Secretariat for Christian Unity, the document was rewritten and sent to the fathers for their reflection during the summer.[5] Since the text

[3] Cited in Jaeger, *op. cit.*, p. 16. This version, originally containing three chapters, had two additional chapters added to it, dealing with religious liberty and the Jews. The first three chapters were overwhelmingly accepted by the fathers, but a vote on Ch. 4 and 5 was postponed, allegedly due to "lack of time," although there was obviously behind-the-scenes difficulty over the latter topics. Cf. Ch. 13–14 below for details.

[4] For an excellent sampling of these speeches, cf. further Küng, Congar, and O'Hanlon, eds., *op. cit.*, Part III, pp. 145–227. My own reactions to the debate are contained in *Observer in Rome*, pp. 179–201. Cf. also Rynne, *The Second Session*, Ch. IV, pp. 216–91, and Novak, *The Open Church, passim*.

[5] At this point, the chapter on religious liberty became a separate document, and the material on the Jews, after an interval as an "appendix" to the ecumen-

had been approved in substance, the revised document was not debated during session three, but simply voted on, chapter by chapter, in the light of changes the fathers had requested.

The "papal interventions"

Before its promulgation, however, an "incident" occurred on November 19, 1964. Just one day before the vote on the document as a whole, and thus too late for any conciliar discussion, nineteen further changes were made "by higher authority," i.e., at the request of Pope Paul. Dismay at this action was based on three considerations: (a) in the light of the conciliar affirmation of collegiality, the unilateral action of the pope seemed particularly un-collegial, (b) if the pope felt that changes were necessary they should have been introduced sooner so that they could have been subject to normal conciliar reflection, and (c) while most of the changes were merely verbal, one at least was substantive and seemed to jeopardize the tone of the document as a whole.

The above reactions were strongly voiced at the time. Coupled with other events of the final week (the refusal to allow a preliminary vote on religious liberty and the unilateral papal proclamation of Mary as "Mother of the Church"), the authority of the council seemed gravely threatened. In retrospect, however, The Case of the Nineteen Interventions, while unfortunate, was not disastrous, and even the substantive change can be placed in a context that does not seriously impair the ecumenical significance of the document.

The substantive change, which at the time caused particular consternation among the non-Catholic observers, occurred in a description of the Protestant use of Scripture. The earlier text had read: "At the prompting of the Holy Spirit, they *find* God in the Holy Scriptures, who speaks to them of

---

ism decree, was finally incorporated in a separate document on the non-Christian religions.

Christ." Pope Paul changed the statement to read, "While invoking the Holy Spirit, they *seek* in these very Scriptures God, as it were, speaking to them in Christ." Protestants felt that the difference between finding and seeking was considerable, and that the change implied a denigration of the role of Scripture in their corporate lives. Some of these reactions may have been triggered by the translation cited, which helped to compound the problem, the phrase "as it were" further suggesting that Protestant expectations in the matter were illusory. The translation used for the crucial sentence in *Documents of Vatican II* avoids these implications: "Calling upon the Holy Spirit, they seek in these sacred Scriptures God as He speaks to them in Christ."[6] Taken as it stands, the latter translation (which might be described as the refined standard version) is certainly an unexceptionable statement, and may even be more accurate than the original, since it could scarcely be argued that everyone who *seeks* God in Scripture *finds* him.

Although episcopal beards were still ruffled, the decree was overwhelmingly approved the next day, by a vote of 2054 to 64, and when formal promulgation followed the day after that, the *non placets* had shrunk to 11. Ecumenism, long a dream and more recently a live hope, had become a reality.

Ecumenical strengths of the document

The decree has been the subject of much ecumenical praise, and whatever reservations have been expressed have invariably come in the wake of appreciation, not to say astonishment, that so much could have been said so well by so many. Major credit for the achievement belongs to the Secretariat for Christian Unity, which shepherded the document through its early development, withstood the opposition of the die-hards, incorporated creative suggestions made from

[6] Cf. Abbott, ed., *op. cit.*, p. 363, and the comments in Stransky, ed., *op. cit.*, p. 79.

the council floor, and generously embraced numerous suggestions made by the non-Catholic observers.

We have already indicated certain themes of the decree,[7] and, in addition to these, other significant ecumenical strengths can be noted:

1. The words by which the decree will formally be known are the first words of the Latin text, *Unitatis redintegratio*, the restoration of unity.[8] This not only tells the reader something important about the mood and concerns of Vatican II, it also tells him something about the mood and concerns of ecumenism. Ecumenism is not simply developing an atmosphere of geniality or revising one's vocabulary to eliminate the epithets. Ecumenism is concerned for "the restoration of unity." As long as Christians are divided, the ecumenical movement has not completed its work.

2. The original version of the title of Chapter 1 was "The Principles of Catholic Ecumenism." The phraseology suggested that there might be various kinds of ecumenism— Protestant, Orthodox, or whatever—and that Catholics were about to describe their own special version. But it became clear from conciliar interventions that this was theologically inappropriate, as well as linguistically dubious. ("Talking about 'Catholic ecumenism,'" Fr. Weigel grumbled, "is like talking about 'Catholic weather.'")

The title was therefore changed to "Catholic Principles of Ecumenism,"[9] as a way of making the point that there is

[7] Cf. particularly (a) the recognition of joint responsibility for the sins of division, (b) the consequent need for inner renewal as the basis for ecumenical outreach, and (c) the emphasis on "the pilgrim people of God" with its implications for ongoing reformation. These themes are discussed in Ch. 6–7 above.

[8] The full sentence reads: "The restoration of unity among all Christians is one of the principal concerns of the Second Vatican Council."

[9] Both the official Vatican Press translation of the decree and the version in Abbott, ed., *op. cit.*, cite the title as "Catholic Principles on Ecumenism." Along with Jaeger, *op. cit.*, and Leeming, *op. cit.*, I have employed what seems to me a smoother rendering.

one ecumenical movement rather than two or three, and that whatever differences the various participants in it may have to work through, they are all fundamentally engaged in a common enterprise. Archbishop Jaeger comments, "The 'ecumenical movement' in the narrow sense of the word originated about the beginning of this century outside the Catholic Church."[10] By the decree *On Ecumenism*, the Catholic Church serves notice that it now wishes to be inside, rather than outside, that movement. Catholic ecumenical concern is to be placed in the context of already existing ecumenical concern.[11]

3. Acknowledgment of the "ecclesial reality" of non-Roman Catholic churches is a major theological breakthrough of the document, and it is one that came between the first and second versions of the text.[12] In the version debated at session two, a distinction was made between the *churches* of the East, i.e., the Orthodox, and the *communities* of the sixteenth-century disruption, i.e., the Protestants. The Latin term *communitates* was employed in a purely sociological sense, and (particularly when viewed against recognition of the ecclesial character of Orthodoxy) seemed to perpetuate a view of Protestants as nothing but religious individuals upon whom, somehow, somewhere, some grace had fallen, but whose corporate life was devoid of grace.

There were some notable interventions from the council floor, urging that the "ecclesial reality" of Protestant com-

---

10 Jaeger, *op. cit.*, p. 26.

11 The point is underlined by the decree's description of the existing ecumenical situation: "Taking part in this movement, which is called ecumenical, are those who invoke the Triune God and confess Jesus as Lord and Savior." (Art. 1, cf. Abbott, p. 342.) It has already been noted that the statement is a deliberate echoing of the formal basis of membership of the World Council of Churches.

12 Some of the material in the following pages is adapted from "Ecumenical Escalation," *The Commonweal*, March 19, 1965, pp. 787–90, and "Comments on the Decree on Ecumenism," *The Ecumenical Review*, April 1965, pp. 95–97.

munal life be acknowledged, so that in the promulgated version the descriptive term "churches and ecclesial communities" is used of all non-Catholic groups.[13]

The change is a basic one. It affirms, from a Catholic standpoint, that the Holy Spirit works *through* Protestant "churches and ecclesial communities," and not just *in spite of* them. God gives his gifts to the separated brethren in their corporate ecclesial life, and not merely in their individual encounters with God:

"[The separated brethren] join in not merely as individuals but also as members of the corporate groups in which they have heard the gospel, and which each regards as his Church, and indeed, God's."[14]

It could be objected that this is only a statement of how Protestants look upon themselves, but the first chapter of the decree acknowledges that those who have been properly baptized "are brought into a certain, though imperfect, communion with the Catholic Church" and, more importantly, that many of the most significant elements that give life to the Church

"can exist outside the visible boundaries of the Catholic Church: the written Word of God; the life of grace; faith, hope and charity, along with other interior gifts of the Holy Spirit as visible elements."[15]

More than this, non-Catholic liturgical actions are described in such a way that "these actions can truly engender a life of grace, and can rightly be described as capable of providing access to the community of salvation."[16] (It is important to read this description in the light of later comments in Article 22 about baptism and "the eucharistic mys-

---

[13] One Catholic *peritus* gave thanks for the inclusion of both terms, remarking that otherwise ecumenical conversation back home would become awkward, viz: "Are you going to your ecclesial community this morning?"

[14] *On Ecumenism*, Art. 1, cf. Abbott, p. 342.

[15] *Ibid.*, Art. 3, Abbott, p. 345.

[16] *Ibid.*, Art. 3, Abbott, p. 346.

tery," since inclusion of a reference to the latter, while very guarded, is an advance over the earlier draft, which made reference only to baptism. Catholic recognition that Protestants believe that the Lord's Supper "signifies life in communion with Christ,"[17] is an important base on which to build further ecumenical reflection, as the decree itself insists.) From all of this,

"It follows that these separated Churches and Communities, though we believe they suffer from defects already mentioned, have by no means been deprived of significance and importance in the mystery of salvation. For the Spirit of Christ has not refrained from using them as a means of salvation. . . ."[18]

Movement, within the space of a year, from a position that describes Protestants only in sociological terms to a position that asserts that Christ has not refrained from using the separated churches and communities "as means of salvation" is a notable example of ecumenical escalation.

It must immediately be recorded, however, that the use of the term "churches and ecclesial communities" is equivocal, and indeed deliberately so. It is not specified which groups are "churches," which groups are "ecclesial communities," and which groups, perhaps, are still only "communities," though the Anglicans seem to be granted a slightly preferential place.[19] An intervention by Archbishop (now Cardinal) Heenan warned against reading too much theological significance into the shift, but the decision clearly suggests the beginning of a new estimate, and the end of a long-dominant attitude among Catholics that Protestantism is purely an individualistic religious phenomenon.[20] It further diminishes

[17] Ibid., Art. 22, Abbott, p. 364.
[18] Ibid., Art. 3, Abbott, p. 346.
[19] Ibid., Art. 13, Abbott, p. 356.
[20] Cf. further on this theme, Baum, "The Ecclesial Reality of the Other Churches," in Küng, ed., The Church and Ecumenism, Concilium series, Vol. 4, Paulist Press, Glen Rock, 1965, pp. 62–86.

the appeal to "return" as the goal of Catholic ecumenism, as Oscar Cullmann has made clear in his appraisal of the text:

"The aim of ecumenism is no longer our 'return.' Without reservation, non-Catholic *charisma* [gifts] are recognized as such (see especially para. 4), and the text reminds Catholics that these gifts 'may contribute to an even more perfect penetration of the mystery of Christ and of the Church.' "[21]

4. Another dimension of ecumenical importance is the introduction into Catholic thought of a "hierarchy of truths":

"When comparing doctrines with one another, [Catholic theologians] should remember that in Catholic teachings there exists an order or 'hierarchy' of truths, since they vary in their relationship to the foundation of the Christian faith."[22]

Professor Cullmann comments:

"I consider this passage the most revolutionary to be found, not only in the Schema *de oecumenismo* but in any of the schemas of the present Council."[23]

One must concur in Professor Cullmann's judgment and stress the importance of the concept in the ecumenical revolution. One of the greatest stumbling blocks in ecumenical discussion has been the impression that all Catholic truth is on the same level of importance, an impression fostered by Pius XII's 1950 bull on the Assumption of the Virgin, in which he stated that one who denies the dogma "has cut himself off entirely from the divine and Catholic faith."[24] According to the decree *On Ecumenism*, however, certain truths have greater importance than others and the ecumenical dialogue must help some priorities emerge. It will be help-

21 In *The Ecumenical Review*, April 1965, p. 93.
22 *On Ecumenism*, Art. 11, Abbott, p. 354. Cf. also the decisive speech on this subject by Archbishop Pangrazio, included in Leeming, *op. cit.*, Appendix VII, pp. 298–99.
23 *The Ecumenical Review*, April 1965, p. 94.
24 Denzinger, *The Sources of Catholic Dogma*, Herder, St. Louis, 1951, para. 2333, p. 648.

ful if Catholic thought can stress the Doctrine of the Trinity as ranking higher than, say, the Doctrine of the Immaculate Conception and indicate that the Incarnation is more fundamental in the hierarchy of truths than the Assumption of the Virgin. This does not mean that the latter doctrine in each of these illustrative pairs is about to disappear from Catholic teaching, but it does mean that in the whole of Catholic teaching some imbalances may be repaired and first things put first.[25]

5. Another ecumenical strength of the document is its concern for specifics. By the time the present volume is published, a handbook from the Secretariat for Christian Unity will have been issued, spelling out further suggestions; in anticipating that event the decree nevertheless spells out three specific directions for future ecumenical development:

(a) common dialogue:

"We must come to understand the outlook of our separated brethren. . . . Of great value for this purpose are meetings between the two sides. . . . From dialogue of this sort will emerge still more clearly what the position of the Catholic Church is. In this way, too, we will better understand the attitude of our separated brethren. . . ."[26]

(b) common action:

"Cooperation among Christians vividly expresses that bond which already unites them, and it sets in clearer relief the features of Christ the Servant. Such cooperation, which has already begun in many countries, should be ever increas-

[25] A specific example of the recognition of a hierarchy of truths was the decision of the council to incorporate the material on Mary into the *schema* on the Church, rather than make her the subject of an entirely separate council document. Such action did not "downgrade" Mary (certain anxious Mariologists to the contrary notwithstanding), but placed her in a proper *context*, by assuring that she would not receive such a high priority in the hierarchy of truths as to displace her Son—a tendency that had appeared to be making rapid headway prior to the council.

[26] *On Ecumenism*, Art. 9, Abbott, p. 353.

ingly developed, particularly in regions where a social and technical evolution is taking place."[27]

(c) common worship:

"In certain special circumstances, such as in prayer services 'for unity' and during ecumenical gatherings, it is allowable, indeed desirable, that Catholics should join in prayer with their separated brethren."[28]

6. The decree is also ecumenically significant in its avoidance of "false irenicism."

"It is, of course, essential that doctrine be clearly presented in its entirety. Nothing is so foreign to the spirit of ecumenism as a false conciliatory approach [irenicism] which harms the purity of Catholic doctrine and obscures its assured genuine meaning."[29]

Although the theme is not elaborated beyond these two sentences, it is clearly a basic theme for ecumenical confrontation. Nothing is gained by pretending either that basic differences do not exist or that they can be overcome simply by ecumenical good will. The differences do matter, or they would not have persisted for 400 years. Certain hard-core differences remain when all the misunderstandings have been swept away. While it is more useful, as was suggested in Chapter 4, to discuss the differences in the context of the agreements, rather than vice-versa, it is ecumenical romanticism to assume that doctrinal concessions ("We'll accept Mary if you'll give up infallibility. . . .") are part of the ecumenical spirit.

The document, it must be added, takes seriously its own warning against false irenicism. It leaves no doubt that the Roman Catholic Church is the one totally adequate guardian and transmitter of the grace of God, and it makes clear that

---

[27] On Ecumenism, Art. 12, Abbott, pp. 354–55.

[28] Ibid., Art. 8, Abbott, p. 352. Because of their importance for the future, each of these areas will be the subject of a separate chapter in Part V below.

[29] Ibid., Art. 11, Abbott, p. 354.

other groups, however much "ecclesial reality" they may have, do not have all that the true church needs:

"Our separated brethren, whether considered as individuals or as Communities and Churches, are not blessed with that unity which Jesus Christ wished to bestow. . . . For it is through Christ's Catholic Church alone, which is the all-embracing means of salvation, that the fullness of the means of salvation can be obtained. It was to the apostolic college alone, of which Peter is the head, that we believe that our Lord entrusted all the blessings of the New Covenant. . . ."[30]

If Protestants are upset by this forthrightness, they must be reminded that to ask the Catholic Church to deny such statements about itself as a condition of ecumenical dialogue would be equivalent to a Catholic demand that the World Council of Churches amend its basic affirmation to read: "The World Council of Churches is a body of Christian Churches that accepts the bishop of Rome as the supreme head of the church." One has no right to object to the Roman Catholic Church, in a Roman Catholic document addressed to Roman Catholics, stating clearly who it conceives itself to be. Such forthrightness will forestall the disillusioned ecumenical euphoria of those who discover, only much later, that Catholics really mean it when they assert the primacy of Peter.

7. A final contribution is the recognition that the decree is an interim document. It is not the last word on ecumenism; it is only a first word, the first official Catholic word ever spoken on the subject. Under the circumstances, those who have reservations about the document should be astonished at its openness, rather than dismayed at its timidity. The promulgated decree is bolder than the preliminary draft, and Catholic ecumenical action since the promulgation has

[30] *Ibid.*, Art. 3, Abbott, p. 346.

been bolder still. The process of ecumenical escalation is underway.[31]

The decree itself concludes in similar vein:

"This most sacred Synod urgently desires that the initiatives of the sons of the Catholic Church, joined with those of the separated brethren, go forward without obstructing the ways of divine Providence and without prejudging the future inspiration of the Holy Spirit."[32]

One could ask for nothing more open-ended than this. The decree gives no justification for building any fences around what the Holy Spirit may be pleased to do with the ecumenical future, and this recognition may be one of its most important contributions.

Remaining questions

It would be an ironic example of false irenicism were the present discussion to terminate at this point. We must "further the dialogue" by indicating some of the questions and reservations that arise out of Protestant reflection on the decree.

1. A basic query runs: is the decree internally consistent? The tension within it is most acutely described by Professor Miguez-Bonino as "a tension between a Christologically-centered and a Rome-centered ecumenism."[33] Miguez illustrates this tension in the contrast between the first two chapters and the third. The first two stress the inner renewal of the church, so that Christians may "examine their faithfulness to Christ's will with regard to the Church" (clearly a Christocentric ecumenism), while the third, although it describes non-Roman churches and ecclesial communities in

---

[31] The very tentative statements about common worship, for example, already seem descriptively remote from what is actually taking place in certain parts of the Christian world.

[32] On Ecumenism, Art. 24, Abbott, p. 365.

[33] In The Ecumenical Review, April 1965, p. 111.

open fashion, seems to evaluate them "in terms of their degree of coincidence with the Roman Catholic Church" (a Romano-centric, rather than a Christocentric, ecumenism). The criterion for the evaluation of other Christian groups is the degree to which they possess or lack the marks or characteristics of the Roman Catholic Church. The implication of this Romano-centered tendency is clear: Christocentrism and Romano-centrism are virtually identical.

But such a conviction would appear to be in tension with the other theme of the document, namely the need for ongoing reform and renewal. How deep-seated *is* the need for reform and renewal, if the present Roman Catholic Church is virtually identical with the church willed by Christ? If non-Catholic churches suffer certain defects that need correction, can the Roman Catholic Church make a similar admission *vis-à-vis* itself?[34]

The concern is widespread and should be illustrated in a variety of ways. Samuel McCrea Cavert, after stating the same tension, asks:

"These assumptions seem to indicate that the Roman Catholic understanding of ecumenism is unchangeably Rome-centered. If so, how far can the Roman Catholic Church go in ecumenical relations with those whose ecumenism has no center but Christ?"[35]

Speaking of the decree's evaluation of the non-Roman churches, Jean Bosc, a French Reformed scholar, comments:

"There is a tendency to look in the other Churches for those elements which correspond to the faith of the Roman Catholic Church. But a genuine ecumenical dialogue presupposes that each partner allows himself to be challenged by the others, that he submits himself to being queried, and this does not come out sufficiently [in the decree] so it seems

---

[34] So Hébert Roux, in *ibid.*, p. 107.

[35] In Abbott, ed., *op. cit.*, p. 369. Cf. also Schlink, in Lindbeck, ed., *op. cit.*, pp. 219–21.

to me; it reveals a tendency that is still too definitely centered on Rome."[36]

Lukas Vischer of the World Council identifies the problem with a helpful image and indicates the terms of its possible resolution:

"The results reflect the image of Janus, the god of the doorways, and show two faces. On the one hand, they open the door not only to a renewal in depth, but also to a more profound communion with the Churches separated from Rome. On the other hand, they continue the tradition specific to the Roman Catholic Church; they represent an adaptation of the old Roman Catholic position to this modern age, a transposition in a modern context. All will depend, therefore, on the way in which the texts come to be interpreted in the years to come, on that face of Janus to which the Catholic Church will attach herself."[37]

2. We have already noted the new recognition in the decree of the "ecclesial reality" of the non-Roman churches. The question this welcome advance raises, however, is: how far can the Roman Catholic Church extend this recognition without becoming false to her understanding of herself? Is it really possible to grant more than minimal "ecclesial reality" to churches outside the visible boundaries of Roman Catholicism when, as the decree itself states, "It is through Christ's Catholic Church *alone*, which is the *all-embracing* means of salvation, that the *fullness* of the means of salvation can be obtained?"[38] Dr. Cavert presses the point:

"How much is involved in the Decree's reference to Protestant bodies as 'ecclesial communities'? On the one hand, this seems to imply a modification of the traditional Catholic attitude. At least, it suggests that the corporate life of Protestants has some kind of churchly reality. But, on the

[36] Cited in Küng, ed., *Do We Know the Others?*, pp. 128–29.

[37] Cited in *ibid.*, p. 130. The comment is related to the constitution *On the Church*, as well as to the decree *On Ecumenism*.

[38] *On Ecumenism*, Art. 3, Abbott, p. 346, italics added.

other hand, the hesitation in speaking of non-Catholic bodies as Churches apparently implies a difference between 'Church' and 'ecclesial community.' What is this difference? Non-Catholics still need further light as to how far the Catholic Church goes in acknowledging the reality of the Church beyond its own borders."[39]

If there is some far-reaching sense in which the reality of "church" exists outside those bodies in full communion with the See of Rome, this has important implications for the future of ecumenism. But if such acknowledgment is barely token, this will have a different set of implications.

3. A third question has to do with the lurking fear of many Protestants that the real aim of Roman Catholicism can finally be none other than "return."[40] In 1928 this was Pius XI's view; it can be found in many of Pope John's statements; and it is clearly the view of many bishops who nevertheless voted for the ecumenism decree. As earlier noted, the decree deliberately avoids such imagery, and the stress on Catholic reform and renewal is reassuring. But the question will continue to intrude itself into ecumenical discussion: can the notion of return ever fail to be an ingredient in Catholic ecumenical thinking, particularly in the light of such statements as the following:

"All Christians will be gathered, in a common celebration of the Eucharist, into that unity of the one and only Church which Christ bestowed on His Church from the beginning. This unity, we believe, dwells in the Catholic Church as something she can never lose. . . ."[41]

This still sounds to many Protestants as though the final unity of the church were rather easily identifiable with the Church of Rome to which all will finally have returned.[42]

---

[39] In Abbott, ed., op. cit., pp. 369–70.
[40] Cf. the previous discussion of this problem in Ch. 4 above.
[41] On Ecumenism, Art. 4, Abbott, p. 348.
[42] It is encouraging, however, that Edmund Schlink, scarcely one to be accused of ecumenical euphoria, can comment: "We do not do justice to the

4. Some of these queries may find resolution in a final one: what is the relationship of the decree *On Ecumenism* to the constitution *On the Church?* It seems clear that the latter document is the most authoritative document to come out of Vatican II, and this means that the ecumenism decree must be interpreted in the light of the constitution on the church, rather than vice versa.[43] A lot therefore depends on the reading one gives of the constitution *On the Church.*

On the one hand, the latter can be ecumenically helpful in its acknowledgment, for example, that all Christians by virtue of baptism are incorporated into the *ecclesia,* however imperfectly, since this is important in assessing the "ecclesial reality" of other Christian bodies.[44] Furthermore, the constitution *On the Church* gives considerable prominence to the imagery of the pilgrim people of God, which as we saw earlier is so important to an understanding of "ongoing reformation."[45] The theme of "the priesthood of all the faithful" is likewise incorporated within it.

But the constitution *On the Church* can also raise ecu-

Decree on Ecumenism if we see in it only an invitation to return to the Roman Catholic Church, repeated here with other methods and under a different name" (in Lindbeck, ed., *op. cit.,* p. 205). Cf. also the remark of Professor Cullmann quoted under point 3 of the strengths of the document.

The openness of the word "dwells" (or "subsists") has already been noted in Ch. 10.

[43] The decree explicitly acknowledges this: "This Sacred Synod . . . has already declared its teaching on the Church, and now, moved by a desire for the restoration of unity among all the followers of Christ, it wishes to set before all Catholics certain helps, pathways, and methods, by which they too can respond to this divine summons and grace." (Art. 1, Abbott, p. 342.)

[44] Cf. the constitution *On the Church:*

"The Church recognizes that in many ways she is linked with those who, being baptized, are honored with the name of Christian, though they do not profess the faith in its entirety or do not preserve unity of communion with the successor of Peter. . . .

"Likewise we can say that in some real way they are joined with us in the Holy Spirit, for to them also He gives His gifts and graces, and is thereby operative among them with his sanctifying power. . . ." (Ch. I, Art. 15, Abbott, pp. 33-34.)

[45] Cf. Ch. 7 above.

menical problems; for example, in spite of its incorporation of the theme of collegiality, the explanatory note at the end hedges this about with so many qualifications that a traditional view of papal primacy can be extracted from the document by all who wish to find it there. Furthermore, it would not be too hard to collect a string of statements from the constitution to give reinforcement to "triumphalist" conceptions of the church that make the theme of ongoing reformation so difficult to sustain.

Conclusion: an open future

Each of these four questions is a variant on the fundamental question: which emphases of the decree are to be accepted as normative? The clear answer to the question is that the answer is not yet clear. What *On Ecumenism* comes to mean (and this is true of all the council documents) depends in large measure on what the church decides it is to mean.

The conclusion of the present writer is a hopeful one. *On Ecumenism* has introduced some *new* elements into the ecumenical situation, and has introduced them more rapidly than could have been anticipated. That older viewpoints are still present in the document is no cause for surprise. Nothing, it would appear, is ever discarded in Catholic thought, but new dimensions are introduced and tend either to absorb the old or so to recast the meaning of the old that a genuine advance is actually recorded. Thus the ecumenical future, on the basis of the ecumenism decree, is an open future. What direction the future takes depends not only on what Catholics do with the decree, but on how Protestants respond to it as well.

The escalation process has begun.

PART FOUR

From Legalism to Liberty
or
Toleration Is Not Enough

Died October 27, 1553, on the block at Champel, Michael Servetus of Villeneuve d'Aragon, born September 29, 1511. We, respectful and grateful sons of Calvin, yet condemning an error which was that of his century, and firmly devoted to the liberty of conscience according to the true principles of the Reformation and of the Gospel, have erected this expiatory monument. October 27, 1903.

Text of the monument of expiation erected at the spot where Servetus was burned for heresy by the Calvinists 350 years earlier.

CHAPTER 12

PROTESTANTISM AND
RELIGIOUS FREEDOM

I am in the right and you are in the wrong. When you
are the stronger you ought to tolerate me; for it is your
duty to tolerate truth. But when I am the stronger, I
shall persecute you; for it is my duty to persecute error.
Lord Macaulay, in an Essay on *Sir James
Macintosh*, describing what he felt to be the
position of the Roman Catholic Church.

There is a clear strand of Roman Catholic history and teaching that would seem to justify Lord Macaulay's logic. But it
will be one of the purposes of the following chapters to suggest that such an attitude is no longer truly descriptive of
Roman Catholic teaching, if indeed it ever was.

The rationale for introducing a chapter on "Protestantism
and religious freedom" with such a quotation is that there
has been a tendency on the part of Protestants to assume
that *their* record on religious freedom is unambiguously noble, and that only the record of the Roman Catholic Church
is tarnished. But the attitude Lord Macaulay describes has
had its counterpart in Protestant history as well, and many
victims of Protestant intolerance in the sixteenth and seven-
teenth centuries would have been as ready to ascribe the
above quotation to one of the sons of Luther or Calvin as to
a child of the Spanish Inquisition.

If a case needs to be made for religious freedom as a positive good, the task is not one that devolves solely upon the
Roman Catholic. It is also an obligation for the Protestant,
since Protestant history and practice have been far from con-

sistent upon this matter. Consequently, even though Protestantism (through the World Council of Churches) came to a clear articulation of the principles of religious freedom some time before the Roman Catholic Church did so, Protestants must be reminded that the struggle to reach such a position has been a long and hard one. By no stretch of the imagination can the Reformers be claimed as champions of religious freedom. Both Luther and Calvin believed in repressive measures against the unorthodox, and both on occasion practiced them.[1] When the Protestant points the finger of shame at the Inquisition, he must be reminded that Michael Servetus, in attempting to escape from the Inquisition, made the mistake of thinking that he could find sanctuary in Protestant Geneva, and that it was in Protestant Geneva rather than in Saragossa that he was burned as a heretic.[2]

Indeed, if we are to assign credit for the rise of religious freedom in European and Anglo-Saxon countries, that credit must be assigned chiefly to the left-wing sectarian groups, who, in addition to whatever principles they enunciated, also had a sociological impetus deriving from the fact that the championing of toleration was conducive to their own physical survival. It can also be argued that the development of religious freedom is less the work of religious groups than

---

[1] Cf. *inter alia*, Bainton, *The Travail of Religious Liberty*, Westminster, Philadelphia, 1951, esp. Ch. 2–3, and "Truth, Freedom and Tolerance: The View of a Protestant," in Böckle, ed., *War, Poverty, Freedom*, Concilium series, Vol. 15, Paulist Press, Glen Rock, 1966, pp. 17–29. Cf. more fully, Lecler, *Toleration and the Reformation*, Association Press, New York, 1960, 2 volumes. The fullest over-all treatment is Bates, *Religious Liberty*, Harper & Row, New York, 1945, 604 pp.

[2] Perhaps the only mitigating circumstances in this unsavory event were the "clemency" of Calvin in urging that, rather than prolonging Servetus' agony by fire, he be run through with a sword, and the erection on the site of Servetus' execution of a "monument of expiation" by a group of Calvinists 350 years later, the text of which is cited at the beginning of this part of the present volume. The latter action, while emphasizing the fact that persecution was inconsistent with the "true" principles of the Reformation, can hardly be held to have done Servetus himself much good.

of the secular forces operating in society. The latter point has been strongly put (perhaps too strongly) by Rabbi Gordis:

"Religion has made many great contributions to civilization, but freedom of religion is not among them. The ideal of religious liberty is essentially a gift we owe to the secularists. . . . While there were individual saints and sages who had found it possible to unite tolerance of diversity with a fervent attachment to their own vision of God, for most men freedom of religion was the fruit of the rise of secularism."[3]

In similar vein we can hardly ascribe to enlightened theological reasoning either the gradual relaxation of the Protestant desire to destroy heretics or the cessation of the Roman Catholic inquisitorial practice of handing heretics over to a "Catholic state" for treatment calculated to make them see the error of their ways. With the growth of diversity of religious conviction in the post-Reformation period, such practices simply became impractical and were no longer countenanced by societies based on pluralistic principles.

On both sides, in other words, theological adjustment seems to have come in the wake of, rather than in the vanguard of, social change. Neither side can gain extensive laurels from the past, and the older type of Protestant rationalization ("Your side killed more heretics than ours") is particularly inappropriate from a contemporary vantage point that denies the propriety of killing any heretics at all.

"Toleration" vs. "religious freedom"

In the past, the terms "toleration" and "religious freedom" have been used almost interchangeably.[4] The linguistic pro-

[3] In Scharper, ed., *Torah and Gospel*, Sheed and Ward, New York, 1966, pp. 99, 101. A full treatment of the theme is contained in Mueller, *Religion and Freedom in the Modern World*, University of Chicago Press, Chicago, 1963, 129 pp.

[4] Cf. the work previously referred to, Lecler, *Toleration and the Reformation*, and one of the most important pre-conciliar books from the Roman

priety of this identification is increasingly open to question, however, and two reasons may be suggested for dispensing with the former term: toleration is a notion based either on expediency or indifferentism, neither of which furnishes a sufficient basis for a positive understanding of religious freedom.

1. *Toleration based on expediency.* The notion of toleration is essentially a negative notion. Those who employ it are saying in effect to those with whom they disagree, "You have no right to believe as you do, but I, from the vantage point of the power I possess over you, will nevertheless condescend to let you continue in your error."

The attitude suggests the granting of a privilege that is not deserved, and one which consequently could be revoked at any time by the one granting it. The one with power grants a concession to the one without power, so that the continuing right of the latter remains totally dependent upon the whim of the former. Thus the granting or the not granting of toleration is reduced to a matter of *expediency*: when it is expedient to be tolerant, toleration is a good or at least a lesser evil; when it is not expedient to be tolerant, toleration becomes an evil without qualification.

This is the principle behind the famous "thesis-hypothesis" view of Roman Catholic theology.[5] The *thesis* reasons from the fact that since error does not have the same rights as truth, error should be suppressed whenever it appears; the *hypothesis* reasons that there may nevertheless be certain situations in which, since it is neither practical nor possible to suppress error, it should be tolerated, at least until such time as it is expedient once again to suppress it.

Catholic side, *Tolerance and the Catholic*, Sheed and Ward. For an account of the contents and spotty fortunes of the latter, cf. Brown and Weigel, *An American Dialogue*, pp. 70–74. The theme is also developed by Pribilla, under the suggestive title, "Dogmatic Intolerance and Civil Tolerance," in *Stimmen der Zeit*, April 1949, pp. 27–40.

[5] Cf. further discussion of this position in the next chapter.

The inadequacy of the view to the one tolerated is immediately apparent, and the fact that a good deal of past Catholic history has operated in terms of it is one reason Protestants have found it hard to relax when contemplating the numerical or political expansion of Roman Catholic power.

2. *Toleration based on indifferentism.* A second justification of toleration has been built upon the argument that since nobody has the whole truth, every point of view has an equal right to a hearing. While some points of view may strike us as better than others, no excessive or exclusive claims can be made for any of them. Thus toleration is justified on the basis of *indifferentism* to truth, and any position should be tolerated so long as its espousal does not seriously infringe on the rights of others.

The practical outworkings of this position in the body politic are often provisionally satisfactory, since no single position can claim a high enough degree of exclusive authority to enable it to persecute and suppress contradictory positions. But as the basis for the espousal of *religious* freedom, toleration-cum-indifference is most unsatisfactory, for it implies the surrender of the very thing that makes a religious claim central for an individual, namely the conviction that he has been confronted by the Truth, and must surrender his life to the Truth as it has confronted him. Ultimate Truth-claims finally conflict with one another, and the argument from indifference is thus an evasion of the problem rather than a resolution of it. G. K. Chesterton describes tolerance as "the virtue of people who don't believe anything."[6] The problem, then, cannot be solved by urging those who believe they have been confronted by ultimate Truth to persuade themselves that they have not been.

[6] Much Roman Catholic resistance to developing a theological basis for religious freedom has stemmed from a fear that such a stand could only be productive of indifferentism, syncretism, and surrender of the Catholic claim to be in unique possession of the Truth. Cf. further the following chapter.

But there is a further difficulty with the proposal that toleration as indifference provides a satisfactory basis for society. The position has no resources for coping with those whose vision of Truth entitles them, so they feel, to propagate it coercively. The Nazi could argue that by revelation he had been persuaded that all Jews must be destroyed by cremation; Europe and the whole world discovered that in the face of such claims it was not sufficient to argue, "Everybody is entitled to his own opinion, and we must be as tolerant of the Nazi as we are of the vegetarian." The point needs no further elaboration.[7]

Neither expediency nor indifferentism, then, can provide the basis for a positive view of religious freedom understood as *an intrinsic right,* which must therefore under all circumstances and in all situations be upheld and defended.

Religious freedom and the World Council of Churches

Can such a view be given an adequate foundation? Is there a more solid basis for a view of religious freedom? Concern to find a positive answer to these questions has motivated much World Council thinking, even while it was "in process of formation," just as it came to motivate much Vatican Council thinking, as soon as plans for the latter were announced.

The most authoritative utterances of the World Council are a statement on religious liberty made at the Amsterdam assembly in 1948, and a second statement affirmed at New Delhi in 1961. (The New Delhi assembly also accepted a report from the Central Committee on "Christian Witness, Proselytism and Religious Liberty," to which attention will be directed later in the chapter.)[8]

[7] Cf., however, the persuasive development of these themes by Gordis, in Scharper, ed., *op. cit.,* esp. pp. 101–3.

[8] All the relevant materials and documents are easily available in Carillo de Albornoz, *The Basis of Religious Liberty,* Association Press, New York, 1963, 182 pp. The documents themselves are contained in Appendices.

The Amsterdam Declaration on Religious Liberty established four main guidelines:

"1. Every person has the right to determine his own faith and creed.

"2. Every person has the right to express his religious beliefs in worship, teaching and practice, and to proclaim the implications of his beliefs for relationships in a social or political community.

"3. Every person has the right to associate with others and to organize with them for religious purposes.

"4. Every religious organization, formed or maintained by action in accordance with the rights of the individual person, has the right to determine its policies and practices for the accomplishment of its chosen purposes."[9]

It was at New Delhi, however, that the clearest theological rationale for these conclusions was developed, and the New Delhi statement offers a positive theological basis for religious freedom. The crucial paragraph is as follows:

"Christians see religious liberty as a consequence of God's creative work, of his redemption of man in Christ, and his calling of men into his service. God's redemptive dealing with men is not coercive. Accordingly human attempts by legal enactment or by pressure of social custom to coerce or to eliminate faith are violations of the fundamental ways of God with men. The freedom which God has given in Christ implies a free response to God's love and the responsibility to serve fellow-men at the point of deepest need."[10]

This is a remarkably concise statement of the basic point in a *theological* understanding of religious freedom. Here the appeal is neither to expediency ("We will grant religious freedom so long as it is convenient to do so") nor to indifferentism ("Since nobody has the truth, we must simply live and let live"). Rather, the basis of this affirmation is the very

---

[9] In Carillo, *op. cit.*, pp. 157–58. Each of the four theses is expanded in the full text.

[10] In 't Hooft, ed., *The New Delhi Report*, p. 159.

nature of the Christian faith itself. Since God does not deal coercively with his children, his children, made in his image, cannot deal coercively with one another. More positively, since God freely offers himself to men, and invites them to make a free response, those communicating this faith to others can do no other than freely offer God to men and invite them to make a free response. Any attempt to force a response upon others (either to accept truth or deny falsehood) is a violation of the nature of the faith Christians are called upon to share.

Put this way, religious freedom is a *necessary consequence* of Christian faith, rather than a *grudging concession* to be extracted from it. Such an assertion must be at the heart of any positive view of religious freedom: man's respect for the freedom of men toward God must be a reflection of God's respect for the freedom of men toward himself. The principle therefore remains true in *all* situations, regardless of the ratio of Protestants to Catholics, or of Christians to non-Christians.

This position has developed out of many years of World Council consultations, and a clear set of practical consequences follow from the basic principle, many of which are suggested in the body of the New Delhi statement. From a variety of World Council statements, reports, books, and conferences, the following principles emerge, representing a series of conclusions about which there would be a wide degree of consensus in World Council circles:

1. Religious liberty is a fundamental human right that should be universally recognized.

2. The state should not only recognize religious liberty but help to protect it.

3. No group, and particularly no church, can rightfully employ force or violence to propagate its point of view.

4. The right *not* to believe is also a right that must be acknowledged and safeguarded.

5. Each person not only has the right to interior conviction

and private worship, but also to public expression of that conviction.

6. Freedom to give corporate expression to one's faith in voluntary public association, and in corporate acts of witness, proclamation, and teaching, must be protected.

7. One must be free to change his religious convictions, if he so chooses, without fear of social, economic, or political reprisals.

8. The freedom one claims for himself and his group is a freedom he must likewise be willing to extend to all other individuals and groups.[11]

The problem of proselytism: a description

But the matter has not been disposed of, when positive principles have been enunciated. There is a further problem that has been a source of considerable debate, and even tension, within the constituent bodies of the World Council of Churches, and a view of religious freedom has not been fully sketched until this matter has received an airing.

It is recognized that every Christian has the obligation to give "witness" to his faith, to preach, teach, evangelize, and do all within his power to acquaint others with the nature of the good news which has constrained him. This inherent right "to give witness" must at all costs be protected for individual and church, for this is what religious freedom is all about. But sometimes witness is given in ways that are inconsistent with the nature of the Christian message, and proselytism is the pejorative term adopted by the World Council to describe "the corruption of witness." In a report on "Christian Witness, Proselytism and Religious Liberty," adopted by the Central Committee at St. Andrews in 1960 and later approved by the New Delhi assembly in 1961, the

[11] The problem of limitations on the exercise of religious freedom will be discussed in the next chapter.

World Council went on record as condemning "all attempts to force men's religious beliefs or to purchase their allegiance."[12] Where the latter happens, proselytism has replaced witness. We are guilty of proselytism, the report notes,

"when cajolery, bribery, undue pressure, or intimidation are used—subtly or openly—to bring about seeming conversion; when we put the success of our church before the honor of Christ; when we commit the dishonesty of comparing the ideal of our own church with the actual achievement of another; when we seek to advance our own cause by bearing false witness against another church; when personal or corporate self-seeking replaces love for every individual with whom we are concerned."[13]

The issue is far from theoretical. As long ago as 1920, an Encyclical from the Ecumenical Patriarchate of the Orthodox Churches asked for a cessation of proselytizing activities, and at almost every ecumenical conference for the next quarter century the matter hovered on the edge of discussion. Several recent factors have forced the discussion out into the open: (a) recent technological and sociological developments have so changed the established patterns of community that all groups are subject to, and sometimes employ, coercive means of propagating their convictions, (b) religious communities, in the light of modern mobility, are often transported beyond their historical or geographic boundaries, so that an area that had formerly been identified with a particular church finds itself confronted by new religious movements that have come in from the outside, (c) missionary activity, particularly stemming from the outreach of the nineteenth century, has led directly to the establishment of new churches in areas that were formerly felt to have been sufficiently evangelized by other Christian communities.

[12] The full report is contained in Vischer, ed., A *Documentary History of the Faith and Order Movement*, Bethany Press, St. Louis, 1963, pp. 183–96.
[13] In Vischer, ed., *op. cit.*, p. 187.

Thus member churches in the World Council have sometimes felt that other churches were encroaching on them, and thereby increasing divisiveness rather than overcoming it. Should a Methodist Church, for example, go into what has been a nominally Eastern Orthodox area and seek to draw individuals (who may now have no formal church connection) into the Methodist fellowship? The problem is intensified particularly when certain churches feel they have "territorial rights" to a given locale.

Taking for granted that "every Christian church is not only permitted but required freely and openly to bear its witness in the world,"[14] the report then states the nub of the issue:

"Should errors or abuses within a church result in the distorting or obscuring of the central truths of the Gospel and thereby jeopardize men's salvation, other churches may feel bound to come to the rescue with a faithful witness to the truth thus lost to view. Their liberty to do so must be maintained. But before they undertake to establish another church, they must humbly ask themselves whether there are not still to be found in the existing church such signs of the presence of the Holy Spirit that frank fraternal contact and cooperation with it must be sought."[15]

It is difficult enough to determine where this line is to be drawn, and when the necessity of bearing true witness entitles one to become the rival of a church already in existence. And while the report cannot supply definitive criteria for drawing a line that may have to be drawn differently in different situations, it does attempt to set down certain principles for determining when the line between witness and proselytism has been wrongly drawn. The following are representative of the conclusions reached:

[14] *Ibid.*, p. 191.
[15] *Ibid.*, p. 191.

Every Christian's first duty is to work for the renewal of that church of which he is a member.

Christians must respect the convictions of those churches whose beliefs and practices differ from their own, enter into conversation with them, join with them in worship, and seek to find concrete ways of performing acts of mutual service.

When one church in an area is weak or inadequate, the first effort of other churches must be to help the initial church toward renewal, and to offer aid through personnel and fraternal workers, rather than by establishing a competing church.

Christians must disavow church actions which exert undue pressure on an individual either to change, or refuse to change, a church affiliation.

Christians must acknowledge the right of the mature individual to change his church allegiance if the individual is convinced that it is God's will for him to do so.

When two individuals from different churches marry, the conscientious decision of the two partners as to their future church allegiance should be respected.

A child should not normally be brought into a church that is other than that of his parents or guardians unless there are exceptional reasons.

One church should not receive a member of another church who is under discipline by the latter body.

When individuals do desire to change their church membership, there should be direct consultation between the churches involved.[16]

The problem of proselytism: an ecumenical extension

The discussion of proselytism has thus far taken place almost exclusively among the member churches of the World Council. At the time of the formulation of the statement dis-

[16] For an elaboration of these suggestions, cf. Vischer, ed., *op. cit.*, pp. 184–96.

cussed above, its possible implications for the Protestant-Catholic situation were not on the agenda.

While it is clear that suggestions for coping with proselytism cannot be univocally transferred to the wider ecumenical scene, even at this stage of the discussion the prediction can be hazarded that the problem will rather rapidly become an acute one in Catholic-Protestant discussion, particularly since Vatican II has affirmed that in some sense an "ecclesial reality" is present in Protestant corporate life. A number of questions suggest themselves:

What does such acknowledgment mean for the future of Protestant-Catholic relations, particularly on the so-called foreign-mission field?

To what degree, in terms of the St. Andrews statement, should Protestants go to South America, nominally Roman Catholic, and seek to convert (nominal) Roman Catholics away from the church of their fathers?

To what degree should Roman Catholics go to the Scandinavian countries, nominally Lutheran, and seek to convert (nominal) Lutherans away from the church of their fathers?

How applicable elsewhere is the decision of the Taizé community (a French Protestant monastic order) to seek to evangelize those persons who live near Taizé, but to do so with the purpose of seeing them incorporated into the Roman Catholic Church, since that is the church in which their cultural and familial ties are deepest?

To the degree, in other words, that Protestants and Catholics do actually come to see in one another the genuine presence of the *ecclesia*, the issue of "Christian witness, proselytism, and religious liberty" will be no longer an intramural World Council issue, and will become a staple in the ongoing Protestant-Catholic dialogue. Similarly, to the degree that full freedom of religious expression is acknowledged by Roman Catholicism to be an intrinsic good, the issue will be further joined, and it is to the development of the latter conviction that we now turn.

CHAPTER 13

ROMAN CATHOLICISM
AND RELIGIOUS FREEDOM

Every man is free to embrace and profess that religion which he, led by the light of reason, thinks to be the true religion.

A proposition *condemned* by Pius IX in the *Syllabus Errorum*, 1864 (para. 15).

Every human being has the right to honor God according to the dictates of an upright conscience, and therefore the right to worship God privately and publicly.

A proposition *affirmed* by John XXIII in *Pacem in Terris*, 1963 (para. 14).

Now that the Second Vatican Council has affirmed religious freedom for all men, the news is about as routinely important, Fr. John Courtney Murray, one of the drafters of the document, recently remarked, as the news that Notre Dame has defeated Slippery Rock Teachers College in football. The real news would have been the Vatican Council's failure to affirm religious freedom, just as the real news on the sports page would have been Notre Dame's failure to defeat Slippery Rock.

In more sober vein, Fr. Murray comments:

"It can hardly be maintained that the declaration is a milestone in human history—moral, political or intellectual. . . . In all honesty, it must be admitted that the Church is late in acknowledging the validity of the principle."[1]

[1] In Abbott, ed., *op. cit.*, p. 673.

The time will come when the council's affirmation of religious freedom will be the object of no more than passing reference. But that time is not yet; not only because the victory has been so freshly won as to be part of our own ecumenical history, nor because for so long the outcome of the story was in jeopardy, but also because full implementation of the principle will take time, and because further dimensions of the problem now call for clarification.

Although many things accomplished at Vatican II will be of more long-range significance than the adoption of the declaration on religious freedom, few things are more important for the immediate ecumenical future. As Cardinal Ritter remarked during the second session, if the Catholic Church is not willing to affirm religious freedom unequivocally for all men, it cannot expect those men to pay much attention to other things the council may affirm. Pending promulgation of the council statement, non-Catholics were not sure whether the Catholic Church really believed in religious freedom, and they feared that an increase in Catholic power might trigger an increase in measures designed to deny freedom of religious expression to non-Catholics.

Religious freedom before Vatican II

Why has there been this fear on the part of non-Catholics? Why have they been unable to take at face value the statements of many individual Catholics that the church has no desire to deny religious freedom to others, and no interest in the coercion of non-Catholics? There have been at least three reasons for non-Catholic apprehension:[2]

1. The *past history* of the Roman Catholic Church contains many instances of persecution of non-Catholics, par-

[2] These points are developed in more detail in Brown and Weigel, *An American Dialogue*, pp. 58–68. In the light of the action of Vatican II, they no longer seem as important as they did then.

ticularly in situations where the church had political power. Many remain persuaded that the church's abandonment of the methods of the Inquisition represents an act of calculated expediency rather than a sincere change of heart.

Pursued on such grounds, the argument may seem more hysterical than historical, but there is another way of making the point that must be taken more seriously. There is much earlier Catholic teaching to indicate that religious freedom has not been taught by the church as a right, but only grudgingly granted as a concession, and that only when forced by outside pressures to do so has official teaching conceded religious freedom to non-Catholics. To Protestants, Catholic teaching and practice in the past have seemed to conform to the thesis-hypothesis view mentioned in the previous chapter. According to this view, the Catholic religion is the one true religion and the only one entitled to be propagated. Other religions are in error and should not, therefore, be free to spread their mistaken ideas. The "Catholic state," furthermore, has the obligation to ensure freedom for the spread of Catholic truth and to deny freedom for the spread of non-Catholic error. Only thus is the cause of Truth adequately served. So goes the *thesis*, the statement of the ideal possibility.

But since the ideal possibility is seldom attainable (particularly with the decline of the "Catholic state"), the *hypothesis* covers the contingencies of reality by stating that where the thesis cannot be realistically achieved, it is permissible temporarily, and as the lesser of two evils, to grant a measure of freedom to those who serve the cause of error.[3]

---

[3] For statements of this view and documentation of it, cf. Carillo de Albornoz, *Roman Catholicism and Religious Liberty*, World Council of Churches, Geneva, 1959, esp. pp. 5–21 and Murray, *The Problem of Religious Freedom*, Newman Press, Westminster, 1965, 112 pp. (reprinted from *Theological Studies*, December 1964), where it is described as "The First View." There is a critique of Fr. Murray's book by Carillo de Albornoz, "Religious Freedom: Intrinsic or Fortuitous?", *The Christian Century*, September 15, 1965, pp. 1122–26. Murray's essay is indispensable for understanding the background of the Vatican II debates on religious freedom.

This understanding of religious freedom provides little comfort for non-Catholics since it is (a) inconsistent with the ideal expression of Catholic faith and (b) liable to be revoked by the church at any time that outward conditions make it possible to do so.

2. In addition to past Catholic teaching and practice, there have been a sufficient number of instances of *present Catholic practice* to suggest that the church does not really believe in religious freedom, and that where it has enough power to suppress the freedom of non-Catholics it will do so. Although even the staunchest opponents of Catholicism are forced to admit that this picture is changing, there still remain enough predominantly Catholic areas (such as Spain, southern Italy, and certain parts of South America) where religious freedom for non-Catholics is hard to come by to suggest that contemporary Catholicism does not grant freedom to others where it is in the majority, even though it continues to demand freedom for itself where it is in the minority.

The conclusion some Protestants have drawn is that Catholic acceptance of religious freedom when it is in the minority would change into a denial of religious freedom if Catholics came to be the majority.[4]

3. The *lack of authoritative teaching* by the Catholic Church on religious freedom is another cause of apprehension. While there have been excellent statements by individual Roman Catholics,[5] in each case it has been possible to discount such evidence by responding, "Such statements commit no one but the speaker. If the Catholic Church really believes in religious freedom, let it say so, on the highest authority, and in the most unambiguous way."

This does not mean that there have been *no* authoritative statements suggesting that some measure of religious freedom can be compatible with Catholic faith. But it does mean

---

[4] This accounts for what may be called the "51% Syndrome" of certain American Protestants, who are always predicting the baleful things that will happen when America finally "goes Catholic."

[5] Cf. the documentation in Carillo de Albornoz, *op. cit.*

that there has been such a relative paucity of statements of this sort that their weight could be discounted when measured against official statements of a contrary point of view. It is important, however, to take account of four such statements as did exist before the council's declaration.

a. Paragraph 104 of Pius XII's *Mystici Corporis* (1943) has provided reassurance that the church will not try to coerce non-believers:

"Wherefore if any persons, not believing, are constrained to enter a church, to approach the altar and to receive sacraments, they certainly do not become true believers in Christ; because that faith without which it is impossible to please God must be the perfectly free homage of intellect and will."

While this assures non-Catholics that they will not be forced to become Catholics, it gives no assurance that they may practice their own faith.

b. A speech by Pius XII, given in December 1953 to a group of Italian jurists, makes a case for "tolerance" on the grounds that there are some situations in which it is better to tolerate error than to try to eliminate it.[6] The speech indicates papal acceptance of the reality of religious pluralism, but gives no assurance, beyond the argument based on expediency, that the church recognizes the *right* of non-Catholics to religious freedom. While it can be read as an enlightened plea for a spirit of tolerance, it can also be read as no more than a sophisticated restating of the thesis-hypothesis view. As Fr. Murray delicately says:

"The document must be regarded as one of the Pope's occasional deliberate efforts to fall short of complete lucidity. The purpose was achieved in the present case. . . ."[7]

c. If the papal evidence thus far presented seems less than

[6] The text is available in *Four Great Encyclicals of Pope Pius XII*, Paulist Press, New York, 1961, pp. 211–21.

[7] Murray, *The Problem of Religious Freedom*, Woodstock Papers, p. 71.

compelling, there are two paragraphs in Pope John's encyclical, *Pacem in Terris*, that point to an affirmation of religious freedom in positive terms.[8] The first of these states:

"Every human being has the right to honor God according to the dictates of an upright conscience, and therefore the right to worship God privately *and publicly*."[9]

The most important advance registered in this statement is indicated by the italicized words. Catholic theology has almost always acknowledged the rights of interior conscience. But matters became sticky when an individual began to give a public accounting of his interior conscience, and affirmation of the right to public expression of one's convictions was a point from which most Catholic thinkers had drawn back. In the quotation cited, Pope John drew them forward.

d. The second reference in *Pacem in Terris* states:

"Moreover, one must never confuse error and the person who errs. . . . The person who errs is always and above all a human being, and he retains in every case his dignity as a human person; and he must be always regarded and treated in accordance with that lofty dignity."[10]

The importance of this observation lies in its refutation of those who "confuse error and the person who errs." This confusion was one of the hallmarks of the older view, based on the true but sterile observation that "error has not the same rights as truth." The advance Pope John builds into Catholic teaching is the recognition that persons in error do have rights *as persons*, which on no account, not even wrongness of belief, can be denied.

Thus on the eve of Vatican II, there were two rather ambiguous statements by Pius XII, and after the council had

[8] These paragraphs were important in the subsequent conciliar deliberations, since they could be cited as papal approval of a position about which some of the fathers were apprehensive, and because their existence made imperative that the council go at least as far as Pope John had gone.

[9] *Pacem in Terris*, para. 14, italics added.

[10] *Ibid.*, para. 158.

actually gotten underway[11] two considerably less ambiguous statements by Pope John, all of which called for further elaboration.

On the other side was a long legacy of Catholic skittishness about the doctrine, nourished by its outright disavowal in earlier papal statements. Pius IX had thought religious liberty a "nightmare" to be avoided at all costs. There are men, he wrote,

"Who do not hesitate to support the erroneous notion (than which none is more fatal to the Catholic Church and the salvation of souls, and which our predecessor of happy memory Gregory XVI called a madness) to wit that freedom of conscience and worship is every man's proper right. . . . In maintaining these audacious assertions . . . they do not stop to consider that they are preaching the freedom to go to perdition."[12]

Pius had then gone on to proscribe and condemn all such "evil opinions and doctrines." And yet, less than a hundred years later, Pope John had affirmed religious freedom as the right of every man. The council was faced with two popes, within a hundred years of each other, saying diametrically opposite things. How could they be made to be saying the same thing? This (as Fr. Murray pointed out at Georgetown University after the third session of the council) is what the church has theologians for.

Religious freedom at Vatican II

The waxing and waning fortunes of the declaration on religious freedom can be dramatically, and even melodramatically, described. Melodrama must be disavowed, even though, when the full story is finally told, elements of a cloak-and-

---

[11] *Pacem in Terris* appeared after the first session of the council had concluded.

[12] Cited in *Tolerance and the Catholic*, Sheed and Ward, p. 59.

dagger atmosphere will remain, so strong were the differences of opinion within the council.

The original document was prepared by the Secretariat for Christian Unity and early in the second session was sent for clearance to the Theological Commission, presided over by Cardinals Ottaviani and Browne, both seasoned opponents of change. The statement languished for many weeks on the capacious agenda of the Theological Commission, and might be there yet, had not pressures from the fathers become too adamant to ignore. So slowly did it make its way to the Vatican printing office, and so slowly were an inordinate number of typographical errors repaired, that it was not until November 19, barely two weeks before the end of session two, that the document was introduced to the council in a stirring speech by Bishop de Smedt.[18]

During the waning hours of session two there was strong pressure for a preliminary vote on the document before it was sent back to the Secretariat for revision. No vote was forthcoming, and the session concluded inconclusively, the fate of the document still undefined.

Between the second and third sessions, the text was rewritten and was debated for three days early in the third session. Some of the "heavy artillery" spoke for its adoption, with notable speeches by members of the American hierarchy, while a small group of opponents was equally vocal. On the basis of these speeches, a third draft was prepared and released to the fathers four days before the end of session three, shortly after an abortive move by the minority to remove the document from the Secretariat for Christian Unity and have it rewritten by a special (and conservative) commission.

There was a substantive shift in emphasis between these

[18] The text was originally Ch. 5 of the schema *On Ecumenism*. After the second session, it became an independent document. Bishop de Smedt's *relatio* is printed in full in *Observer in Rome*, pp. 256–66.

two texts. The earlier text had based religious freedom on the nature of the act of faith, which must be freely made, and therefore cannot be coerced—a position comparable to that of the New Delhi statement of the World Council of Churches. In the third draft, a different approach was made. The draft started with a recognition that men today are more conscious of their dignity, that they are demanding civil liberties and a juridical limitation of government so that personal freedom will not be too narrowly defined. This means that the understanding of religious freedom in the later text is less theological and more juridical—it is a right founded on the fact of human dignity (which is increasingly recognized) rather than exclusively on the theological (and not universally recognized) nature of the act of faith. The theological emphasis remains, but in a subordinate position.[14]

Three days before the end of session three, it was announced that a preliminary vote on the new draft would be held the next day. The next day, however, Cardinal Tisserant, chairman of the council presidents, exploded a sizable bombshell in St. Peter's by announcing that, at the request of several council fathers who wanted more time to study the document, there would be no preliminary vote at all.

Reaction was immediate and angry. (The day, Thursday, November 19, became known as "Black Thursday," the *Dies Irae*, the Day of Wrath, of the council.) In a few hours a petition, signed by perhaps as many as 1400 bishops, was sent to the pope, "urgently, more urgently, most urgently" asking him to authorize a preliminary vote. The request was denied, and session three, like session two, ended with no formal

---

[14] These two emphases were represented in the council by the so-called "French school" on the one hand, and men like Fr. John Courtney Murray, s.j., on the other. The final document contains the best of both viewpoints. Tribute must be paid to the work of Fr. Murray, as the real architect of the decree, who paid the price of a heart attack, two extensive periods of hospitalization, and a severe bout with arthritis, but who nevertheless has lived to see, as part of official Catholic teaching, a point of view he was disciplined by the Holy Office for advocating as little as a decade ago.

indication of the council's viewpoint on religious freedom. The outlook appeared bleak.[15]

The Secretariat for Christian Unity, however, taking the "revised text" issued at the end of session three, produced yet another draft (known as the "re-revised text") that was promptly debated at the beginning of session four. Sixty-two speeches were given on the document. On September 21, the first formal vote was taken, hedged by an assurance that the draft would be further reworked to bring it into line with "Catholic doctrine on the true religion." This vote clearly reflected the mind of the council and was most reassuring to the outside world, the document being approved in principle by a vote of 1997 to 224. An amended text was approved in October, and the final version was promulgated on the last day of the council, at which time the opposition had dwindled to a hard core of only seventy. During the last week, Rome was rife with rumors that the text would not, after all, be promulgated, so its advocates were unable to draw fully secure breaths until the final vote of promulgation had been officially announced only moments before the close of the council.[16]

[15] Chapter 9 above places this event in the context of other disturbing events of the final week. Cf. further my "Apprehensions About the Council," *The Commonweal*, December 25, 1964, pp. 442–45, as indicative of a mood that persisted for many months. As things turned out, the delay probably made possible a better statement than would otherwise have been the case. On the case for this, cf. Murray, "This Matter of Religious Freedom," *America*, January 9, 1965, pp. 40–43.

[16] For a fuller treatment of these episodes, cf. the books on the council cited in the Bibliography, which from their different perspectives help to fill in the picture. A full treatment of the whole debate is being prepared by Thomas T. Love, to be called *Religious Liberty in the Modern World: Vatican II*. Prof. Love has also written "*De Libertate Religiosa*: An Interpretive Analysis," *Journal of Church and State*, Winter 1966, pp. 30–48. Cf. also *Herder Correspondence*, 1964, pp. 202–8, 352–55, and a summary article, 1966, pp. 81–85.

The basis of Catholic fears

Why should an affirmation of religious freedom for all men have encountered such stormy weather at the council? At least four reasons for resistance can be disentangled:

1. The greatest theological and psychological fear seems to have been the belief that a statement on religious freedom would foster an attitude of "religious indifferentism" and encourage Catholics to believe that "one religion is as good as another." If freedom is granted to all points of view, so the argument went, this must imply that all points of view are equally valid.

The answer to the argument is a simple reading of the decree. Nothing within it can validate a charge that the Catholic Church has compromised its conviction that it is the trustee of the fullness of truth.[17]

2. A number of bishops were uneasy about the jump from freedom for the interior conscience to freedom for public expression of the beliefs of interior conscience. The affirmation of the former was easy enough, but affirmation of the latter seemed to involve a condoning of the right to propagate error. How could the church, divinely ordained guardian of the truth, give overt approval to the dissemination of falsehood?[18]

[17] The point was sufficiently clear in earlier drafts, but in an effort to win over the notably dissident minority, some last-minute insertions were made in the document to the effect that the "one true religion subsists in the catholic and apostolic Church" and that men who really seek the truth will surely find it there. (Art. 1, cf. Abbott, p. 677.) It is not news that the Catholic Church believes this, and Protestants regret its gratuitous insertion into the present document. Ironically, the concession did not materially alter the size of the opposition, for the non placets dropped from 254 only to 249 after the insertion was made.

[18] In technical terms, as some bishops argued, any individual can have a *conscientia recta*, but the Catholic can also have a *conscientia vera*, a conscience rooted in objectively true norms. The non-Catholic could have a *conscientia recta sed non vera*. Such a conscience would have the right to private opinion, but not to public expression or propagation of what, from Catholic presuppositions, would be error.

The answer to this objection is found in Pope John's insistence that persons in error have rights, and that this can be affirmed simultaneously with the abstract proposition that error itself does not have the same rights as truth. The point at issue is the dignity of the person, and the rights of the human *qua* human. The very nature of man, Bishop Primeau insisted on the council floor, is such that the two must go together. One cannot separate internal and personal liberty (such as freedom of interior conscience) from external and social liberty (such as the free public and corporate exercise of religion). To argue for the former but not for the latter, Bishop Primeau insisted, "is to cut man in two."[19]

3. A third objection was the fear that the document would undermine the notion of "the Catholic state." (A Protestant, in honesty, must respond that it would seem to do just that—and high time, too.) But the declaration at this point is very cautious. It reassures the conservatives that there can be provisional justification for an established church ("If, in view of peculiar circumstances obtaining among certain peoples, special legal recognition is given in the constitutional order of society to one religious body . . ."), but immediately goes on to offer assurances to non-Catholics (". . . it is at the same time imperative that the right of all citizens and religious bodies to religious freedom should be recognized and made effective in practice").[20]

4. A final objection was basic to the conservatives and has far-reaching implications for the meaning of the council as a whole: an affirmation of religious freedom would undermine the teaching authority of the church and jeopardize the

---

[19] Cited in Anderson, ed., *Council Daybook*, Vatican II, Session 3, N.C.W.C., Washington, 1965, p. 43.

[20] *Declaration on Religious Freedom*, Art. 6, Abbott, p. 685. An earlier draft treated the established church with a simple declarative statement. The final draft represents a bending of the document in a more "liberal" direction by shifting from the declarative to the conditional: "*If,* in view of peculiar circumstances. . . ." Cf. further, *Herder Correspondence*, March 1966, p. 84.

credibility of Catholic doctrine, since the affirmation would go contrary to past Catholic teaching.

The answer to this objection—a serious problem for many Catholics in areas other than religious freedom—is a complex one that will be a major source of Catholic theological speculation in the post-conciliar era. The answer is pointed to by the phrase, popularized by Newman, "the development of doctrine." Advocates of this position hold that while "Catholic truth" does not change, nevertheless (a) ways of expressing it can change, (b) new historical situations can call for the elaboration of facets of the faith that had not been clearly developed before, and (c) the "new" teachings that emerge can be shown to have been at least latently present in past teaching. Thus doctrine "develops" to greater fullness, rather than "changing," as what was formerly implicit now becomes explicit.[21]

In his opening *relatio* Bishop de Smedt gave considerable attention to this theme. He spoke of doctrinal evolution taking place according to a two-fold law: the law of *continuity* and the law of *progress*. Catholic theology, he asserted, must obviously insist that there is continuity in its teaching, but Catholic theology must also recognize that within continuity there can be development, and that new situations call not for new truths, but for new exploration of old truths.[22]

The declaration itself states that, in taking account of the

[21] This is not, of course, a full statement of the position, but each of the three points has bearing on the declaration on religious freedom. Cf. further, Baum, "Doctrinal Renewal," *Journal of Ecumenical Studies*, Fall 1965, pp. 365–81, and Murray, "The Issue of Development of Doctrine," *Theological Studies*, XXV, pp. 503–75. We can expect treatments of all the conciliar documents in the light of this principle. Fr. Murray has already returned to the theme in a post-conciliar essay, "The Declaration on Religious Freedom," in Böckle, ed., *War, Poverty, Freedom*, Concilium series, Vol. 15, Paulist Press, Glen Rock, 1966, pp. 3–16, esp. pp. 11–16.

[22] Cf. his development of the theme in relation to papal teaching on religious freedom, cited in Brown, *Observer in Rome*, pp. 256–66.

new movements among men for a recognition of human dignity, the church

"searches into the sacred tradition and doctrine of the Church—the treasure out of which the Church continually brings forth new things that are in harmony with things that are old."[23]

It then elaborates the theme unambiguously:

"In taking up the matter of religious freedom this sacred Synod intends to develop the doctrine of recent Popes on the inviolable rights of the human person and on the constitutional order of society."[24]

Strengths of the conciliar declaration

But the fears expressed were the fears of the few. So significant were the council speeches favoring the declaration that it would be invidious to single out some for comment at the expense of others. Nevertheless, Cardinal Meyer's indication of reasons for passage of the declaration provides a useful summary:

"First, men want from the Church the promotion of religious liberty.

"Second, because it will give the Church the opportunity of giving example to governments as to how they should treat religious bodies within their borders.

"Third, it will teach Catholics that true religion consists in the free, generous and conscious acceptance of God.

"Fourth, the apostolate of the Church will be assisted by the demonstration that none can be led to the Faith by force but only by hearing, preaching, and receiving the gift of God.

[23] *Declaration on Religious Freedom*, Art. 1, Abbott, p. 676.
[24] *Ibid.*, Art. 1, Abbott, p. 677. Fr. Murray comments: "In no other conciliar document is it so explicitly stated that the intention of the Council is to 'develop' Catholic doctrine." (*Ibid.*, p. 677.) The problems that the theme raises, at least for a Protestant, are briefly touched upon in Love, *op. cit.*, the concluding paragraphs.

"Finally, it will lead to a fruitful dialogue with non-Catholics and work for the cause of Christian unity."

Cardinal Meyer conceded that he thought some changes should be made in the text, but he warned that if the declaration is not passed, nothing else enacted by the council will make much difference.[25]

Particularly in the light of the Chicago cardinal's final point, a number of ecumenical strengths in the declaration can be noted:

1. Not only is the point repeated from earlier Catholic teaching that men are not to be forced to act *contrary* to their beliefs, but a positive extension of this concern is given clear enunciation, namely that men must be free to act *on the basis of* their beliefs: "Nor is anyone to be restrained from acting in accordance with his own beliefs, whether privately or publicly. . . ."[26] This reiterates that the Catholic Church must not force people to become Catholics, but more importantly stresses that the Catholic Church must not restrain people from the expression of religious convictions that draw their inspiration elsewhere than from Catholic faith. The double emphasis is repeated later in the declaration:

"[Man] is not to be forced to act in a manner contrary to his conscience. Nor, on the other hand, is he to be restrained from acting in accordance with his conscience, especially in matters religious."[27]

2. The first of the two citations above builds on paragraph 14 of *Pacem in Terris*, affirming not only that men are to be accorded the right to act privately in accordance with their

[25] Summary in Anderson, ed., *op. cit.*, p. 36. A collection of all the interventions of the American bishops is being published by Sheed and Ward, under the editorship of Msgr. V. A. Yzermans, and will indicate the tenor of American concern. An enterprising publisher should also issue the six *relationes* of Bishop de Smedt, who each time reintroduced the next text to the council.

[26] *Declaration on Religious Freedom*, Art. 2, Abbott, p. 679.

[27] *Ibid.*, Art. 3, Abbott, p. 681.

beliefs, but publicly as well. More is granted than the right of interior belief. Granted also is the right of public expression of that belief. The principle is explicitly developed:

"The social nature of man itself requires that he should give external expression to his internal acts of religion; that he should participate with others in matters religious; that he should profess his religion in community. Injury, therefore, is done to the human person and to the very order established by God for human life, if the free exercise of religion is denied in society when the just requirements of public order do not so require."[28]

3. The matter is carried further than the external expression of religious conviction, for, as the above paragraph also shows, there is acknowledgment of the right of man to give corporate expression to his faith. Religion is not an individual but a communal affair, and the full meaning of religious freedom must include this recognition.

"The freedom or immunity from coercion in matters religious which is the endowment of persons as individuals is also to be recognized as their right when they act in community. Religious bodies are a requirement of the social nature both of man and of religion itself."[29]

A point that has been insufficiently noted in discussion of the document is its provision for freedom to deal with "the organization of society and the inspiration of the whole of human activity"—a way of insisting, as Fr. Murray puts it, that "religious freedom includes the right to point out this social relevance of religious belief."[30] The notion that "religion and politics don't mix," or that religion has to do only with "spiritual" matters, is here repudiated.

4. The provisions thus far cited are drawn from those portions of the text based on "general principles" available to all

[28] *Ibid.*, Art. 3, Abbott, p. 681.
[29] *Ibid.*, Art. 4, Abbott, pp. 681–82.
[30] In Abbott, p. 683.

men, whether Christian or not. Only after presenting this material does the document discuss "Religious Freedom in the Light of Revelation."[31] It is significant that the latter comes second rather than first, and since the document was addressed to all men and not just to Catholics, it may have been good tactics to start with material all men could accept apart from revelation.[32] This means that there is an interesting reversal of methodologies between the Vatican Council and the World Council documents. The New Delhi statement, as we have seen, begins with a theological statement and concludes by annexing to its document the United Nations Universal Declaration of Human Rights. Vatican II in effect reverses the procedure, beginning with affirmations that can be made in common by all men, and only then moving on to a theological justification.

5. Mention of the New Delhi statement suggests a point at which the two documents are closely related. New Delhi affirmed the St. Andrews statement on "Christian Witness, Proselytism, and Religious Liberty," discussed in the previous chapter. And although the word "proselytism" does not occur in the Vatican Council declaration, the latter makes a similar point:

"Religious bodies also have the right not to be hindered in their public teaching and witness to their faith, whether by the spoken or by the written word. However, in spreading religious faith and in introducing religious practices, everyone ought at all times to refrain from any manner of action which might seem to carry a hint of coercion or of a kind of persuasion that would be dishonorable or unworthy, especially when dealing with poor or uneducated people. Such

[31] Ch. II, Abbott, pp. 688–96.

[32] Surely, however, both the commentator and the responder in the Abbott volume err in stating that this is the only conciliar document addressed to the whole world (cf. Abbott, p. 688 and p. 697, and also the statement in Böckle, ed., *op. cit.*, p. 4.) The same is true of the pastoral constitution on *The Church and the World Today* (cf. Art. 2, Abbott, p. 200).

a manner of action would have to be considered an abuse of one's own right and a violation of the rights of others."[33]

6. The text affirms freedom for the church and insists upon the church's independence to pursue her tasks without interference from the state—a point of considerable importance in the light of the situation of the church behind the Iron Curtain. Those who would inhibit this freedom are dealt with unequivocally: "To act against [the church] is to act against the will of God."[34]

Two comments are in order: (a) It is not fully clear from the text that this right for "the church" extends beyond the Roman Catholic Church, and some non-Catholic critics have felt apprehensive that the section might later be invoked to claim special privileges. (b) At the same time, the passage can be interpreted (as it certainly was by Pope Paul on the closing day of the council) as a declaration of the freedom of the church to be the servant of mankind. Fr. Murray offers reassuring clarification:

"Implicit in it is the renunciation by the Church of a condition of legal privilege in society. The Church does not make, as a matter of right or of divine law, the claim that she should be established as the 'religion of the state.' Her claim is freedom, nothing more."[35]

Allied to this is an insistence that the state is incompetent to judge in the interior affairs of churches or to pass judgments about what may or may not be done in the name of religion:

"Government, therefore, ought indeed to take account of the religious life of the people and show it favor, since the

[33] Declaration on Religious Freedom, Art. 4, Abbott, p. 682.

[34] Ibid., Art. 13, Abbott, p. 693.

[35] In Abbott, p. 693. While the document deals with the freedom of the church, it makes no attempt to deal with freedom in the church, so that criticism of the document's deficiencies on the latter score are naïvely facile; the theme is not part of the document's subject matter. The issue is crucially important in the post-conciliar era, but the present document is not the place to look for guidance.

function of government is to make provision for the common welfare. However, it would clearly transgress the limits set to its power were it to presume to direct or inhibit acts that are religious."[36]

Remaining problems

Not only in terms of its intrinsic merits, but in the light of its stormy history within the council due to the repeated efforts of a powerful minority to scuttle it or emasculate it, the declaration on religious freedom emerges as a magnificent achievement and one that guarantees an ongoing ecumenical dialogue that would have been virtually impossible without it. Non-Catholics rejoice at the persistence and tenacity of the council fathers who were centrally involved in the preparation, defense, and final promulgation of a document that so signally points the way to the future, and indicates "development"—if not "change"—in previous Catholic teaching.

It must, however, "point the way to the future" and not be treated as a static articulation of final truth. This necessitates critical appraisal, and three comments may be made in conclusion:[37]

1. There has been non-Catholic criticism of the last-minute insertions to placate the minority, e.g., the elaborate protection of assurance that the "one true religion" subsists in the Catholic Church, the defense of certain church-state relationships and so on. These are at worst, however, a minor irritation. In the eyes of non-Catholics the document would have been stronger had they been omitted, but it is not substantively weakened by their inclusion.

[36] *Declaration on Religious Freedom*, Art. 3, Abbott, p. 681. Cf. also Fr. Murray's comments on Art. 6, Abbott, p. 684. For further appraisal of the document as a whole, cf. Murray, ed., *Religious Liberty: An End and a Beginning*, Macmillan, New York, 1966, 192 pp., containing Catholic, Protestant, and Jewish reactions.

[37] The fullest Protestant critique is Carillo de Albornoz, "The Ecumenical and World Significance of the Vatican Declaration on Religious Liberty," *The Ecumenical Review*, January 1966, pp. 58–84.

2. There has been disappointment that the document does not contain the type of contrition for past error so remarkably present in the decree *On Ecumenism*. There have been some terrible chapters in western history written by Roman Catholic intolerance and persecution, and yet the fact is barely acknowledged, if at all. There is only one point where the matter is discussed:

"In the life of the People of God as it has made its pilgrim way through the vicissitudes of human history, there have at times appeared ways of acting which were less in accord with the spirit of the gospel and even opposed to it."[38]

As astute and sympathetic a Protestant commentator as Prof. Thomas Love describes this passage as "masterful understatement" and remarks:

"Part of the continuing pride of Roman Catholicism is its genuine inability, or unwillingness, to take upon itself the humility of the Lord it proclaims. The minimizing, or even falsifying, of distasteful historical occurrences hardly assists the Catholic Church in speaking to men deeply involved in history."[39]

But it is also important to see the intent behind the over-cautious language, an intent that Fr. Murray describes as follows:

"The avowal is made briefly and without details. But the intention was to confess, in a penitent spirit, not only that Christian churchmen and princes have appealed to the coercive instruments of power in the supposed interests of the faith, but also that the Church herself has countenanced institutions which made a similar appeal. Whatever may be the nice historical judgment on these institutions in their own context of history, they are not to be justified, much less are they ever or in any way to be reinstated. The Declaration is a final renouncement and repudiation by the Church

---

[38] *Declaration on Religious Freedom*, Art. 12, Abbott, p. 692.
[39] Love, *op. cit.*, p. 46.

of all means and measures of coercion in matters religious."[40]

3. The one substantive point in the declaration that calls for further elaboration is a point that has been inadequately treated in World Council statements as well. This concerns the proper *limitations* of religious freedom.[41] Religious freedom must not be abused so that it becomes an excuse for license. One cannot, on the basis of a religious revelation, decide to kill all redheaded elevator operators, or (to be more realistic) all Negroes who would like to exercise their option to vote, or (to be more ecclesiastical) all individuals who do not accept the dogmatic provisions of *Munificentissimus Deus*. When, in the name of religious conviction, an individual or a group trespasses on the freedom of other individuals or groups, some criteria limiting such action must be formulated. What, then, are proper limitations to the exercise of religious freedom, and how are they to be enforced?

The draft presented at the second session suggested the criterion of "the common good." When the latter is infringed, liberty is turning into license, and safeguards must be erected. But this criterion is so broad as to be of little help. Who determines what is the common good, in more than the most general terms, and who adjudicates conflicting claims? In an authoritarian state, the government can claim that *any* exercise of religious freedom threatens the common good, particularly if such expression included the right of dissent from the common good as defined by the government in power.

Fr. Murray suggested at that time that the criterion of "public order" would be more specific and provide clearer guidelines. Indeed, the Amsterdam statement of the World Council suggested this among similar criteria of limitation: ". . . such limitations, prescribed by law, as are necessary to protect order and welfare, morals and the rights and freedoms of others. . . ." The New Delhi statement goes further and

---

[40] In Abbott, p. 693.
[41] On this point, cf. particularly Carillo, *op. cit.*, pp. 69–74.

calls upon government to see that responsible exercise of freedom is guaranteed:

"The freedom with which Christ has set us free calls forth responsibility for the rights of others. The civil freedom which we claim in the name of Christ must be freely available for all to exercise responsibly. It is the corresponding obligation of governments and of society to ensure the exercise of these civil rights without discrimination."[42]

This is the criterion that appears in the promulgated Vatican Council document: "Provided the just requirements of public order are observed, religious bodies rightfully claim freedom. . . ."[43] A later article, discussing norms for the exercise of personal and social responsibility, provides a more concrete understanding of "public order" as something government has the obligation to protect:

"These norms arise out of the need for effective safeguard of the rights of all citizens and for peaceful settlement of conflicts of rights. They flow from the need for an adequate care of genuine public peace, which comes about when men live together in good order and true justice. They come, finally, out of the need for a proper guardianship of public morality. These matters constitute the basic component of the common welfare: they are what is meant by public order."[44]

So important is the point that it will be well to turn again to the "authoritative" expositor, Fr. Murray:

"Public order is therefore constituted by these three values —juridical, political, moral. They are the basic elements in the common welfare, which is a wider concept than public order. And so necessary are these three values that the coercive force of government may be enlisted to protect and vindicate them. Together they furnish a reasonable juridical

[42] 't Hooft, ed., *The New Delhi Report,* p. 161.
[43] *Declaration on Religious Freedom,* Art. 4, Abbott, p. 682.
[44] *Ibid.,* Art. 7, Abbott, pp. 686–87.

criterion for coercive restriction of freedom. The free exercise of religion may not be inhibited unless proof is given that it entails some violation of the rights of others, or of the public peace, or of public morality. In these cases, in other words, a public action ceases to be a religious exercise and becomes a penal offense."[45]

Important guidelines have here been established. But further discussion is needed in at least two areas: (a) what specific criteria can be established to constitute the clear trespassing of religious freedom? and (b) how is the government's obligation to ensure religious freedom to be safeguarded from becoming a repressive force when the exercise of religious freedom may appear to be contrary to the best interests of the government? In modern society the two areas cannot be disengaged from one another. Further ground rules must now be developed, drawing on the accumulated experience of both the World Council and the Vatican Council, and a joint committee of members of the World Council and the Roman Catholic Church has recently been established to implement this need.

So a remarkable thing has happened. An area which formerly divided Catholics and Protestants as grievously as any single area is emerging as an area not only of shared convictions, but as one in which joint consultation in the future will enable both groups together to move beyond the insights to which they came separately in the past.

[45] In Abbott, p. 686.

CHAPTER 14

THE ENLARGEMENT
OF THE DIALOGUE:
ECUMENISM AND THE JEWS

The pages Jews have memorized have been torn from
our histories of the Christian era.

Fr. Flannery in *The Anguish of the
Jews*, p. xi.

No one likes being tolerated. There is an overtone of con-
descension in the attitude that creates rather than destroys
barriers. For centuries Christians, when they were not perse-
cuting Jews, tolerated them. If, as recent events in both the
Vatican Council and the World Council suggest, we have
moved from toleration of conflicting viewpoints to a positive
acceptance of religious freedom as an inherent right of all
men, this has important implications beyond the Christian
family itself, and in no direction is it more important to spell
out these implications than *vis-à-vis* the Jews.

But, at first hearing, the notion of "ecumenism and the
Jews" sounds mistaken. We have noted two main definitions
of ecumenism: the restoration of unity among divided Christians and concern for the extension of the Christian mission
throughout the world.[1] The first does not involve Judaism directly, the second might be a threat to it. Why, then, should
the ecumenical dialogue include the Jews?

A simple answer grows out of the third definition of ecumenism, namely the desire to foster a spirit of co-operation

---

[1] Cf. the discussion in Ch. 1 above.

and good will among all men, whatever their theological or religious presuppositions. On this level of ecumenical concern, dialogue with the Jews is a natural and indeed inevitable ingredient.

Why the Christian needs the Jew

But this answer is far from sufficient, and if it were the only or the primary answer, Jews might properly feel that they were still no more than objects of toleration.

In the early years of the ecumenical era, it was important for the Protestant-Catholic dialogue to proceed in relative isolation. Catholics and Protestants needed to come to know one another again, in an atmosphere where trust and confidence could be re-established, and the stereotypes of four centuries overcome. That provisional goal is now within reach. A new step in the dialogue is called for, in which Christians must hope that Jews will play an increasing role.

One selfish but basic reason for this hope is that *Christians cannot understand who they are apart from Judaism*. Not only do both Catholicism and Protestantism have their historical roots in Judaism, but their theological and liturgical roots as well, and they therefore stand in a different relationship to Judaism than to other world religions. Judaism is not just another world religion of which Catholics and Protestants must take account; it is that religion *par excellence* which helps to define for them who they are, with which both must come to terms, and apart from which neither can understand itself or the other.[2]

---

[2] This is why it seems unfortunate that the statement on the Jews was removed from the council decree *On Ecumenism* and placed in the declaration on the non-Christian religions. There may have been strategic reasons that dictated the shift, but the final location suggests that Judaism is only one example, if the pre-eminent one, of a non-Christian religion. Fortunately, certain portions of the text, cited below, belie this impression, even though the location reinforces it.

The more Christians know about the rabbinic world of ideas and the Judaic

The fact that Christians and Jews have an inextricably bound destiny is a fact sometimes recognized from the Jewish side as well. Rabbi Heschel, speaking to Christians, comments,

"We are all involved with one another. Spiritual betrayal on the part of one of us affects the faith of all of us. Views adopted in one community have an impact on other communities. Today religious isolationism is a myth. For all the profound differences in perspective and substance, Judaism is sooner or later affected by the intellectual, moral and spiritual events within the Christian society, and vice versa."[3]

It is for the Jew to say what, if anything, he can gain from the dialogue, but there are a number of ways in which Christians will profit directly if the dialogue widens to include the Jews:

a. Catholics and Protestants need the constant reminder that they share a common heritage not only before the sixteenth century but also before the first, and that all Christians spring from the seed of Abraham;

b. Christians need the depth of insight that Jews can bring them in a fresh attempt to understand the Scriptures of the Old Testament that all hold in common;

c. Christians need to recover many dimensions of their faith that have been distorted due to isolation from the leaven of the Judaic perspective (such as their frequent attempts to "spiritualize" or denigrate the created order);

d. Christians need the help of Jews in working out a new theology of Jewish-Christian relationship that will avoid the distorted perspective such attempts have produced in the past when carried out in isolation;

---

background of the New Testament and the early church, the better they will understand not only the meaning of the kingdom of God and of messianism for themselves, but also the deep interrelationship that exists between the two faiths.

[3] Heschel, "No Religion Is an Island," *Union Seminary Quarterly Review*, XXI, No. 2, Part I, January 1966, p. 119.

e. Christians need solidarity with Jews for a more effective common involvement in the civic order, which can have the further by-product of drawing all groups closer to one another as well;

f. Christians need the constant reminder that the mere presence of the Jew affords, of the scandalous treatment of Jew by Christian in the past. If contrition is the presupposition of ecumenical encounter, nothing should be more calculated to keep the Christian humble than the presence of the Jew.

The varieties of Jewish response

But if Christians are increasingly eager to include Jews in ecumenical dialogue, it is far from clear that Jews reciprocate the sentiment. At least four levels of response are apparent:

1. Some Jews fear the new ecumenical situation but remain discreetly silent. It should not be hard for Christians to see why. The times of Jewish persecution have been the times of Christian power. When the church was strong, it tried to force non-believers, and particularly Jews, into its fold. On the other hand, when the church is weak, it is so absorbed in its own survival, or in defending itself in turn from persecution, that it has neither the strength nor the inclination to persecute. Thus a weak, or at least a divided, Christendom enables the Jew to breathe more easily. A politically and/or ecclesiastically pluralistic culture is preferable to a culture where the state has massive power (Nazi Germany), or the church in combination with the state (counter-Reformation Spain) is in charge.

The Jew, in our day beginning to reap the benefits of a pluralistic culture, cannot but look with trepidation on moves toward Christian unity that might restore to a united church power not now available to divided churches.

2. Some Jews welcome better relations between Christianity and Judaism but doubt if the situation can be productive

of *theological* advance. Rabbi Richard Rubenstein speaks poignantly for this group. In a review of the Jewish-Catholic symposium *Torah and Gospel,* he writes:

"As one reads *Torah and Gospel,* it becomes impossible not to wonder whether, after all, the theological dialogue is really possible between Catholics and Jews. . . . Must we love each other? As a Jew I feel an acute sense of discomfort when I read that Catholics 'must love Jews—this is an imperative.' . . . There is really too much that separates us. There ought to be a realistic alternative to the either-or of love or hate. Why can't we rest content with learning to appreciate and understand each other? . . . The real tragedy of the Judaeo-Christian encounter is that it is almost impossible for Christians to see Jews simply as men rather than as actors in the divine drama involving the eternal salvation of mankind. . . . Christian scholars do us no service when they affirm 'thy mystery of Israel' and speak of an obligation to 'love' us. It would be far better were Christians and Jews to regard each other simply as persons."[4]

Rabbi Rubenstein feels furthermore that theological dialogue "is ultimately impossible between men who feel that their tradition alone is the *definitive* expression of God's way for man."[5] Christianity and Judaism confront one another as mutually exclusive alternatives. No resolution of differences can come save by the capitulation of one side to the other. And the Jew has had enough of that kind of theological relation to the Christian community in the past to be disenchanted with the prospect of renewing it in the present.

3. Other Jews forthrightly disdain the possibility of significant Jewish-Christian exchange on any level. Typical of this position is Dr. Eliezer Berkovits.[6] He argues that Christianity has been a conquering religion since the fourth cen-

---

[4] In *The Commonweal,* July 1, 1966, pp. 420–21.
[5] *Ibid.,* p. 421.
[6] Cf. "Judaism in the Post-Christian Era," *Judaism,* Winter 1966, pp. 74–84.

tury, and that its present willingness to be tolerant arises not out of any inherent humility but solely out of the fact that it no longer has the power to dominate. Christianity introduced contempt for the Jew and is ultimately responsible for what happened at Dachau and Auschwitz: "What was started at the Council of Nicaea was duly completed in the concentration camps and crematoria."[7] Jews who involve themselves in ecumenical dialogue, therefore, are "either Jews without memories or Jews for whom Judaism is exclusively a matter of public relations, or confused and spineless Jews who are unable to appreciate the meaning of confrontation in full freedom. For Jewry as a whole, an honest fraternal dialogue with Christianity is at this stage emotionally impossible."[8] Not only is it "emotionally impossible," it is "immoral because it is an attempt to whitewash a criminal past."[9] It is likewise fruitless:

"Judaism is Judaism because it rejects Christianity, and Christianity is Christianity because it rejects Judaism. What is usually referred to as the Judaeo-Christian tradition exists only in Christian or secularist fantasy. As far as Jews are concerned, Judaism is fully sufficient. There is nothing in Christianity for them. Whatever in Christian teaching is acceptable to them is borrowed from Judaism."[10]

No dialogue then for Dr. Berkovits: "All we want of Christians is that they keep their hands off us and our children!"[11]

---

7 *Judaism*, Winter 1966, p. 77.

8 *Ibid.*, p. 79.

9 *Ibid.*, p. 82.

10 *Ibid.*, p. 80.

11 *Ibid.*, p. 82. It should be noted that some Christians share a large measure of Dr. Berkovits' pessimism. A. Roy Eckardt, whose field of academic speciality has been Jewish-Christian relations, is not sanguine about immediate possibilities of dialogue. This feeling arises out of his disillusionment with the Vatican Council statement on the Jews, discussed below, the impact of Auschwitz on the Jewish-Christian situation, and the degree to which Christian crimes against the Jews for hundreds of years have been neither confessed nor

4. But there are also Jews who do sincerely want to establish fraternal relations on every level, and it is with them, manifestly, that any future Jewish-Christian dialogue will be initiated. These Jews are eager, as much as human understanding and divine mercy will allow, to overcome the rifts of misunderstanding and re-establish both a viable human *rapport* and an increasing theological exchange. A quite different spirit, therefore, is epitomized by Rabbi Abraham Heschel, who insists that "No Religion Is an Island" and believes that as Jew and Christian had a common stake in the struggle against Nazism, so they have a common stake in post-Nazi problems as well:

"Nazism has suffered a defeat, but the process of eliminating the Bible from the consciousness of the western world goes on. It is on the issue of saving the radiance of the Hebrew Bible in the minds of man that Jews and Christians are called upon to work together. *None of us can do it alone.* Both of us must realize that in our age anti-Semitism is anti-Christianity and that anti-Christianity is anti-Semitism."[12] This is partly because we share so many things:

"What unites us? A commitment to the Hebrew Bible as Holy Scripture, faith in the Creator, the God of Abraham, commitment to many of His commandments, to justice and mercy, a sense of contrition, sensitivity to the sanctity of life and to the involvement of God in history, the conviction that

---

expiated. Cf. "Can There Be a Jewish-Christian Relationship?", *Journal of Bible and Religion*, April 1965, pp. 122–30, and his forthcoming book, *The Elder and Younger Brother; Dimensions of the Jewish-Christian Encounter*, Holt, Rinehart and Winston.

[12] Heschel, *op. cit.*, p. 118. The context of the remarks is Rabbi Heschel's inauguration as Harry Emerson Fosdick Visiting Professor at Union Theological Seminary. That a Jew should occupy a chair in a Protestant seminary is not only an historic event, but an indication of how seriously Rabbi Heschel takes the need for Christian-Jewish dialogue.

It is interesting that, from a very different perspective, Sigmund Freud came to the same conclusion as Professor Heschel's concluding sentence, viz: "The hatred of Judaism is at bottom hatred for Christianity." (*Moses and Monotheism*, Knopf, New York, 1939, p. 145.)

without the holy good will be defeated, prayer that history may not end before the end of days, and much more."[13]

So inextricably tied together are Judaism and Christianity that they must increasingly take account of one another. To fail to do so would be to deny an impulse basic to each:

"Judaism is the mother of the Christian faith. It has a stake in the destiny of Christianity. Should a mother ignore her child, even a rebellious one? On the other hand, the Church should acknowledge that we Jews in loyalty to our tradition have a stake in its faith, recognize our vocation to preserve and to teach the legacy of the Hebrew Scripture, accept our aid in fighting anti-Marcionite trends as an act of love."[14]

What are to be the subjects of the Jewish-Christian dialogue? Rabbi Marc Tanenbaum, who, along with Rabbi Arthur Gilbert, has given years to creating an atmosphere conducive to dialogue, points to three in particular: (a) the need for critical commentaries on the New Testament that will remove the possibility of exploiting certain passages for anti-Semitic purposes, (b) historical studies that will set Jewish-Christian relations in clearer context and remind each of the episodes the other has forgotten, and (c) theological studies dealing with Jewish-Christian relations, to dispel the ancient canards that the Jews are a deicide people, the diaspora is a punishment for the Jew's rejection of Christ, and so forth.[15] Rabbi Gilbert further urges that we engage in joint

---

[13] Heschel, *op. cit.*, p. 122.

[14] *Ibid.*, p. 125. George A. F. Knight rejects the image of mother and child, preferring the image of "sisters, for they are both daughters of the faith that they share in common from the pages of the Old Testament." (Cf. Knight, ed., *Jews and Christians*, Westminster, Philadelphia, 1965, p. 179.)

[15] Cf. his speech in "Jewish-Christian Relations," the proceedings of an institute held at St. Mary's College, St. Mary's, Kansas, February 21–22, 1965, esp. pp. 104–14. Similar suggestions were made by Rabbi Tanenbaum at the Notre Dame conference on "Documents of Vatican II," held in March 1966. The Vatican Council statement on the Jews asks correspondingly for similar areas of ecumenical co-operation.

study of the Old Testament and acknowledges that "Christian scholars have also realized that the Jewish Bible has a meaning of its own. . . . Christianity needs the corrective and supplementary understandings of the Hebrew Scripture."[16]

In view of their past history, Christians are in no position to press the Jews into ecumenical involvement. But the invitation must be continually extended. Doors can be opened, even if they are not immediately entered. More important, hearts can be opened too, and the open heart will in time authenticate the genuineness of its openness.[17]

The World Council and the Jews

During its years "in process of formation," which were the years of Hitler's crematoria, many churches that joined the World Council were involved in helping Jews to escape from Germany and in relocating Jewish refugees. The provisional apparatus of the World Council was also active in these areas.

With the horrors of the concentration camps still deeply etched in their consciousness, delegates to the Amsterdam assembly in 1948 were unequivocal in their condemnation of anti-Semitism:

"We call upon all the churches we represent to denounce anti-Semitism, no matter what its origin, as absolutely irreconcilable with the profession and practice of the Christian faith. Anti-Semitism is sin against God and man. Only as we give convincing evidence to our Jewish neighbours that we seek for them the common rights and dignities which God wills for his children, can we come to such a meeting with

[16] Gilbert, A Jew in Christian America, Sheed and Ward, New York, 1966, p. 205.
[17] Specific suggestions for topics and procedures can be found in Swidler and Tanenbaum, Jewish-Christian Dialogues, Grass Roots Ecumenism, Washington, 1966, 26 pp., and in Herschcopf and Fine, A Guide to Interreligious Dialogue, The American Jewish Committee, New York, 1966, 24 pp.

them as would make it possible to share with them the best which God has given us in Christ."[18]

It will immediately be noted that two issues are present here. The issue of anti-Semitism is an absolutely clear-cut one, concerning which Christians have no right whatsoever to equivocate, particularly since so much of the anti-Semitism in western history has been of Christian origin. As Jules Isaac points out, there have historically been three prongs to the attack: (a) that the dispersion of the Jews was a punishment for the crucifixion, (b) that Judaism in Jesus' day was degenerate, and (c) that the Jews are a "deicide race." The first two are easily dispelled by historical evidence, although the emotional prejudice lingers on; it is the third that has been so insidious in the church throughout the centuries and is not even today clearly rooted out of Christian thinking in many parts of the world.[19]

But a second topic was also present in the Amsterdam discussions, suggested by the last lines of the above citation and in subsequent paragraphs. Amsterdam also said, "Our churches must consider the responsibility for missions to the Jews as a normal part of parish work." In response to the command of Christ to preach the Gospel to every creature, the report continues, "The fulfillment of this commission requires that we *include* the Jewish people in our evangelistic work."[20]

The issues seemed less clear to delegates at the 1954 Evanston assembly. There was spirited discussion about whether there should be reference to Israel in the treatment of the

[18] As cited in the reaffirmation of the statement in 't Hooft, ed., *The New Delhi Report*, p. 148.

[19] Cf. Isaac, *The Teaching of Contempt*, Holt, Rinehart and Winston, New York, 1964, 154 pp. On the church as purveyor of anti-Semitic attitudes, cf. Olson, *Faith and Prejudice*, Yale University Press, New Haven, 1963, 451 pp., and more recently, Glock and Stark, *Christian Beliefs and Anti-Semitism*, Harper & Row, New York, 1966, 266 pp.

[20] Cf. the discussion of these points in Knight, ed., *Jews and Christians*, Westminster Press, Philadelphia, 1965, pp. 142 ff.

main theme of the conference, "Christ, the Hope of the World." So great were the differences among the delegates as to the propriety of such inclusion that it was finally voted to delete all references to the Jews from the assembly's statement. A minority of twenty-four theologians, however, represented by Professor Joseph Sittler, took issue with the assembly's action and submitted a report over their own signatures, to be included within the minutes of the assembly, indicating their belief that

"Our hope in Christ's coming victory includes our hope for Israel in Christ, in His victory over the blindness of His own people. To expect Jesus Christ means to hope for the conversion of the Jewish people, and to love Him means to love the people of God's promise. . . . We cannot be one in Christ nor can we truly believe and witness to the promise of God if we do not recognize that it is still valid for the people of the promise made to Abraham."[21]

The *impasse* is still apparent in the report of the New Delhi assembly of 1961. Rather than pursuing the mooted point about "conversion," New Delhi delegates concentrated on the issue of anti-Semitism. After reaffirming the 1948 Amsterdam statement, cited above, the New Delhi report continued:

"The Assembly renews this plea in view of the fact that situations continue to exist in which Jews are subject to discrimination and even persecution. The Assembly urges its member churches to do all in their power to resist every form of anti-Semitism. In Christian teaching the historical events which led to the Crucifixion should not be so presented as to fasten on the Jewish people of today responsibilities which belong to our corporate humanity and not to one race or community. Jews were the first to accept Jesus and Jews are not the only ones who do not yet recognize him."[22]

---

[21] 't Hooft, ed., *The Evanston Report*, p. 327; cf. also pp. 78–79, 327–28.
[22] 't Hooft, ed., *The New Delhi Report*, p. 148.

Thus the World Council has been of one mind on the baseness of anti-Semitism and of a divided mind on the further question of the "conversion" of the Jews.[23]

The varying fortunes of the Vatican Council statement on the Jews

As early as September 18, 1960—two years before the council—Pope John talked with Cardinal Bea and gave to the Secretariat for Christian Unity the task of preparing a conciliar declaration dealing with the Jewish people.[24] When word got out that such a document had been prepared, there was strong protest from the Arab states, who saw it as a political maneuver with immediate implications in the Near East, as well as from Roman Catholic bishops in Arab lands, who feared political reprisals at home if the document were approved. There was also opposition from a minority of diehard conservatives within the council itself. Typical of the latter was Bishop Carli, one of the most articulate Italian conservatives, who offered strong opposition to the statement on the council floor and could declare in *Palestra del Clero*, in the spring of 1965:

"I consider it legitimate to affirm that the entire Jewish people at the time of Christ was responsible collectively for deicide, although only their leaders and a portion of their followers materially committed the crime. . . . Judaism since the time of Our Lord shares objectively in the responsibility

[23] For a fuller discussion of the issue of "conversion," cf. the appendix to the present chapter.

[24] For a full history of the development of the text within the council, and an interpretation of it, cf. Bea, *The Church and the Jewish People*, Harper & Row, New York, 1966, 172 pp., which also includes the speeches with which Bea introduced successive drafts on the council floor. Cf. also books on the council listed in the bibliography, and summaries in *Herder Correspondence*, January 1965, pp. 21–25, and January 1966, pp. 8–11. The articles by Herschcopf on "The Church and the Jews: The Struggle at Vatican Council II," in the *American Jewish Yearbook*, 1965 and 1966, are also important.

for deicide, in the measure in which that Judaism constitutes a free and voluntary continuation of the Judaism of that former time."

What is so shocking about this statement is not only that a bishop of the church could make it, but that he should do so after the council had explicitly declared otherwise.

Interest in the statement was further heightened by controversy centering around Hochhuth's play, *The Deputy*, appearing during the council in Europe, Britain, and America, which accused Pius XII of an immoral silence in the face of Nazi atrocities.[25]

The statement finally found a temporary conciliar home as Chapter 4 of the decree *On Ecumenism* and was presented to the second session on November 18, 1963, with a long *relatio* by Cardinal Bea. To the intense disappointment of many at the council, no preliminary vote on the document was taken during the second session, but early in the third session a revised version, much weaker than the original, was debated on September 28-30, 1964. *Herder Correspondence*, in a blunt summary of the problem posed at the beginning of the third session, reported:

"The new text, which could hardly be described as either concise or courageous, did not fare well in the debate. In the original text the charge of deicide had been clearly rejected, as well as all idea of a curse which—allegedly on that account —fell on the Jews. It had stated expressly that the death of Christ could not be held against the entire Jewish people of that time and even less against the Jews of today.

"Small wonder, then, that the revised text pleased nobody; neither the Jews, who wanted a clear condemnation of anti-Semitism and an unambiguous rejection of the charge of deicide; nor the Arabs and those opponents of the Declara-

---

[25] Cf. Hochhuth, *The Deputy*, Grove Press, New York, 1964, 352 pp. and Bentley, ed., *The Storm Over The Deputy*, Grove Press, New York, 1964, 254 pp. My own reactions to the play and the controversy raised by it are in "Postscript on 'The Deputy,'" *The Commonweal*, May 1, 1964, pp. 174-76.

tion within the Church who did not want it on any account; nor the great majority of the Fathers who wanted a more courageous statement; nor the members of the Secretariat for Christian Unity, who were not really responsible for the new version and had never indeed been called to a plenary meeting after the Co-ordinating Commission had made its objections."[26]

The result was a series of magnificent speeches from the council floor, calling for a reinsertion of the emphases that had unaccountably been deleted between the second and third sessions. Rabbi Marc Tanenbaum, present in St. Peter's for the debate, described them as "positions that have never been heard before in 1900 years of Catholic-Jewish history, positions articulated with such friendship, indeed, fraternal love, as to make clear that a profound turning point had taken place in our lifetime."[27]

Many fathers spoke directly of the need to reinsert a repudiation of the age-old deicide charge, among them such important leaders as Cardinals Cushing, Meyer, Ritter, Frings, Liénart, Lercaro, Léger, Jaeger, and Koenig, along with Bishops Elchinger, Leven, Sheper, Heenan, O'Boyle, Shehan, and Mendez Arceo. Others urged specific acknowledgment of Christian guilt for past Jewish persecution. Bishop Elchinger of Strasbourg, reminding the fathers of the Inquisition, asked, "Why should we not find in the spirit of the Gospel the courage to ask for forgiveness in the name of so many Christians for so many serious injustices?"[28] As a result of such interventions, a much improved and strengthened text was presented to the fathers for preliminary approval on November 20, receiving only ninety-nine *non placet*

[26] *Herder Correspondence*, January 1965, p. 23.

[27] In Miller, ed., *Vatican II: An Interfaith Appraisal*, University of Notre Dame Press, Notre Dame, 1966, p. 357.

[28] Cf. Rynne, *The Third Session*, *loc. cit.*, and Anderson, ed., *Council Daybook*, Vatican II, Session 3, esp. pp. 55–76, for summaries of the discussion.

votes—preliminary approval by over ninety-five per cent of the fathers.

Between the third and fourth sessions, however, there were further internal crises, and it looked for a while as though Arab pressures would be strong enough to kill the possibility of a final promulgation by the council. There was also the unfortunate incident during a 1965 Lenten mass in Italy, at which Pope Paul stated that when Christ came, the Jewish people "not only did not recognize Him, but fought Him, slandered and injured Him; and in the end, killed Him." This did not raise hopes for a strong conciliar statement. Nevertheless, a final text was presented early in the fourth session, modified at some crucial points in the hope of securing overwhelming approval, and promulgated on October 28, 1965, with a vote of 2221 *placets* and only 88 *non placets*.

This bare summary of the fortunes of the document cannot begin to suggest the sense of drama, and even melodrama, occasioned by what seemed to outsiders to be a game of Ecclesiastical Hot Potato, played by courageous members of the Secretariat for Christian Unity, hostile Arab pressures, liberal and conservative council fathers, the pope, concerned Jews, and interested bystanders. Indeed, the fate of the council almost hung with this document; if it had been shelved, or even if it had been passed with a large dissenting vote, the impression, however false, would have been that the council fathers were either anti-Semitic or subservient to political pressures from the Arab states.

The conciliar declaration and reactions to it

The statement itself is embedded in a longer declaration on non-Christian religions that is positive and praiseworthy about the values in religions other than Christianity. Article 4, dealing with the Jews, is here quoted in its entirety:

"4. As this sacred Synod searches into the mystery of the

Church, it recalls the spiritual bond linking the people of the New Covenant with Abraham's stock.

"For the Church of Christ acknowledges that, according to the mystery of God's saving design, the beginnings of her faith and her election are already found among the patriarchs, Moses, and the prophets. She professes that all who believe in Christ, Abraham's sons according to faith (cf. Gal. 3:7), are included in the same patriarch's call, and likewise that the salvation of the Church was mystically foreshadowed by the chosen people's exodus from the land of bondage.

"The Church, therefore, cannot forget that she received the revelation of the Old Testament through the people with whom God in his inexpressible mercy deigned to establish the Ancient Covenant. Nor can she forget that she draws sustenance from the root of that good olive tree onto which have been grafted the wild olive branches of the Gentiles (cf. Rom. 11:17–24). Indeed, the Church believes that by His cross Christ, our Peace, reconciled Jew and Gentile, making them both one in Himself (cf. Eph. 2:14–16).

"Also, the Church ever keeps in mind the words of the Apostle about his kinsmen, 'who have the adoption as sons, and the glory and the covenant and the legislation and the worship and the promises; who have the fathers, and from whom is Christ according to the flesh' (Rom. 9:4–5), the son of the Virgin Mary. The Church recalls too that from the Jewish people sprang the apostles, her foundation stones and pillars, as well as most of the early disciples who proclaimed Christ to the world.

"As holy Scripture testifies, Jerusalem did not recognize the time of her visitation (cf. Lk. 19:44), nor did the Jews in large numbers accept the gospel; indeed, not a few opposed the spreading of it (cf. Rom. 11:28). Nevertheless, according to the Apostles, the Jews still remain most dear to God because of their fathers, for He does not repent of the gifts He makes nor of the calls He issues (cf. Rom. 11:28–29). In company with the prophets and the same Apostle, the

Church awaits that day, known to God alone, on which all peoples will address the Lord in a single voice and 'serve him with one accord' (Soph. 3:9; cf. Is. 66:23; Ps. 65:4, Rom. 11:11–32).

"Since the spiritual patrimony common to Christians and Jews is thus so great, this sacred Synod wishes to foster and recommend the mutual understanding and respect which is the fruit above all of biblical and theological studies, and of brotherly dialogues.

"True, authorities of the Jews and those who followed their lead pressed for the death of Christ (cf. Jn. 19:6); still, what happened in His passion cannot be blamed upon all the Jews then living, without distinction, nor upon the Jews of today. Although the Church is the new people of God, the Jews should not be presented as repudiated or cursed by God, as if such views followed from the holy Scriptures. All should take pains, then, lest in catechetical instruction and in the preaching of God's Word they teach anything out of harmony with the truth of the gospel and the spirit of Christ.

"The Church repudiates [reprobat] all persecutions against any man. Moreover, mindful of her common patrimony with the Jews, and motivated by the gospel's spiritual love and by no political considerations, she deplores [deplorat] the hatred, persecutions, and displays of anti-Semitism directed against the Jews at any time and from any source.

"Besides, as the Church has always held and continues to hold, Christ in His boundless love freely underwent His passion and death because of the sins of all men, so that all might attain salvation. It is, therefore, the duty of the Church's preaching to proclaim the cross of Christ as the sign of God's all-embracing love and as the foundation from which every grace flows."[29]

Had the text sprung full-blown upon the world without knowledge of previous drafts, it would probably have been

29 In Abbott, ed., *op. cit.*, pp. 663–67.

almost universally accepted as a significant breakthrough.[30] Every phrase, clause, and nuance of the previous drafts, however, had been the subject of intense public scrutiny; the magnificent council speeches of September 28–30, 1964, had been widely reported in the world press, and expectations were very high. Furthermore, the draft antecedent to the final one was generally considered to have been a more worthy document than the one finally promulgated, and there was widespread feeling that the final document had been "watered down" in order (a) to assuage Arab feelings, and (b) to make it more palatable to certain very reactionary members of the council.[31]

Jewish disappointment in the final document centered largely on two deletions from the earlier text. (a) The 1964 draft had stated, "May the Jewish people never be presented as one rejected or guilty of deicide." Retention of the word *deicide* became a symbol for many Jews of the council's sincerity, since Christian anti-Semitism has been rooted in the charge that the Jews were "God-killers" or Christ-killers. A full repudiation of past wrongs thus meant specific repudiation of the ugly charge, to the point of employing the ugly word. The word, however, was dropped, although Cardinal Bea assured the council that its equivalent was contained in the revised statement, ". . . the Jews should not be presented as repudiated or cursed by God, as if such views followed from the holy Scriptures." The chief reasons cited for the deletion were that the word should be expunged forever from the

[30] Rabbi Tanenbaum supports such a judgment: "If the words of last year's draft version were not so widely known, men of good will would now be hailing the declaration with enthusiasm" (cited in the New York *Herald Tribune*, Oct. 17, 1965). Many people also made their initial judgments about the document not from the text itself, but from sensationalistic newspaper headlines about it.

[31] All attempts to assess such matters, however, should be measured against the series of speeches given by Cardinal Bea at the second, third, and fourth sessions of the council, conveniently gathered together as Appendix II, in Bea, *op. cit.*, pp. 154–72.

Christian vocabulary, coupled with reasons of pastoral prudence (due to misunderstandings of the word). (b) The 1964 draft had stated that "the Church deplores *and condemns* [*damnat*] the hatreds, persecutions, and displays of anti-Semitism. . . ." In the final version, the italicized words were missing. This too seemed to outsiders, and particularly to Jews, like a retreat. Was it enough simply to "deplore" the death of six million Jews? Was not this worthy of "condemnation"? Defenders of the deletion argued that retention of the word would place the council on record as repudiating discrimination against Jews more strongly than discrimination against others, and that since Vatican II was not to be a council of condemnations and anathemas, the use of *damnat* (which in ecclesiastical parlance usually refers to theological heresy) was out of place. Cardinal Bea pointed out also that the Latin *deplorat* has a much stronger meaning than is contained by such English translations as "deplores" or "decries."[32]

A different type of disappointment, felt by many Christians, was the document's lack of any direct note of contrition for the church's role in past persecution and anti-Semitism. So shocking is the history of Christian persecution of Jews that inclusion of such a recognition would have added immeasurably to the moral impact of the document.[33]

In response to this charge, defenders of the document note that it does, specifically, deplore "the hatred, persecutions, and displays of anti-Semitism directed against the Jews *at any time and from any source*" (italics added). It is permissible to include the church under the umbrella of the itali-

[32] Cf. Bea, *op. cit.*, pp. 117–18.

[33] It should be recalled that the decree *On Ecumenism* contains three explicit acknowledgments of Catholic responsibility for the sins of division. Cf. Ch. 6 above. It should be clarified that references in the present volume to "Christian persecution of Jews" are inclusive of Protestantism as well as Catholicism, and that failure to acknowledge this fact in penitence is a shortcoming of World Council as well as Vatican Council statements.

cized words, even though the church is not specifically mentioned.[34]

Many, however, continue to share the reaction of Fr. John Sheerin:

"I regret however that this 'act of contrition' is not more heart-scalding and soul-stirring, for I fear that much of the Nazi anti-Semitism was a distillation of centuries of Christian hatred of Jews."[35]

But there are strengths as well. Dr. Joseph L. Lichten, of B'nai B'rith, after surveying such problems as the above, can go on to say, "The Declaration on non-Christian Religions, whatever its shortcomings, emerges as a milestone in the history of the Church."[36] If the word "condemns" disappeared, the word "anti-Semitism" was added, the first time it has been used in a formal declaration. Where the word "deicide" was deleted, an important addition was made: ". . . the Jews should not be presented as repudiated or cursed by God, *as if such views followed from the holy Scriptures.*" It is officially declared that there is no basis in Scripture for such appraisals. Dr. Lichten approvingly quotes Fr. Abbott's clarification: "From now on, no Catholic may quote the Bible to justify calling the Jews a deicide or accursed people. Any who attempted to do so would be classed as heretics."

It is a further strength that Catholics are henceforth formally forbidden to do anything in their teaching or preaching that might lead to such false charges: "All should take pains,

[34] Interpretations vary. *Herder Correspondence* assumes that this is a clear "confession of the Christians' share in the guilt of anti-Semitism" (*Herder Correspondence,* January 1966, p. 10). A. Roy Eckardt, however, comments: "In vain does one search the declaration for the slightest positive sign of penitence. Because none is present, an opportunity of the century has been betrayed." ("End to the Christian-Jewish Dialogue," *Christian Century,* March 30, 1966, p. 394.)

[35] Sheerin, "The Story Behind Vatican II and the Jews," *Our Sunday Visitor,* May 22, 1966, p. 7.

[36] "The Council Declaration on the Jews," The *Catholic World,* August 1964, p. 362.

then, lest in catechetical instruction and in the preaching of God's Word they teach anything out of harmony with the truth of the gospel and the spirit of Christ."

Fr. Sheerin notes other strengths in the document:

"Its acknowledgement of the fact that Christianity is firmly rooted in the Jewish Scriptures, that the Jews are a people 'dear to God,' that the Jews of today can in no way be charged with responsibility for the death of Christ or represented as a people rejected or accursed by God, that the Church reprobates as un-Christian 'any discrimination against men or harassment of them because of their race, color, condition of life or religion.' "[37]

Fr. Gregory Baum further notes that the document specifically corrects certain misunderstandings that have been the basis of much anti-Jewish prejudice in past Christian preaching:

"The first tendency was to glorify the new covenant by belittling the old one. The second tendency was to present the relationship between Jesus and his people as if Jesus and his friends were on one side, while the Jewish people were on the other. The third tendency was to pretend that the Jewish people, because of the crucifixion or their unwillingness to accept Christ, were a reprobated and accursed people in the post-Biblical age. The conciliar statement corrects these false and unfounded tendencies one by one. The statement shows:

"1. The Church is the continuation of the economy of mercy revealed and established by God under the old covenant.

"2. It explains that all the Christian events of salvation took place among the Jews and that, therefore, Jesus and his disciples as well as the men who opposed him belonged to the Jewish people.

"3. The statement presents the Pauline teaching that despite the unwillingness of the Synagogue to accept Christ,

[37] Sheerin, *op. cit.*

God continues to extend his calling and grant his gifts to the people, with whose fathers he had made the covenant."[38]

The task ahead is to build on the strengths of the document and to learn whatever lessons can be learned from acknowledgment of its shortcomings. It clearly gives a basis for what it describes as "the mutual understanding and respect which is the fruit above all of biblical and theological studies, and of brotherly dialogues."[39] No one has seen the purpose of that dialogue with more luminous intensity than Rabbi Heschel:

"It is neither to flatter nor to refute one another, but to help one another; to share insights and learning, to cooperate in academic ventures on the highest scholarly level, and what is even more important to search in the wilderness for wellsprings of devotion, for treasures of stillness, for the power of love and care for man. What is urgently needed are ways of helping one another in the terrible predicament of here and now by the courage to believe that the word of the Lord endures for ever as well as here and now; to cooperate in trying to bring about a resurrection of sensitivity, a revival of conscience; to keep alive the divine sparks in our souls, to nurture openness to the spirit of the Psalms, reverence for the words of the prophets, and faithfulness to the Living God."[40]

No blunting of differences

This does not mean, as Rabbi Heschel makes clear elsewhere, that there are no differences between us. There are, and we may find the clearest statement of the fundamental difference in Martin Buber:

[38] Baum, "The Conciliar Statement on the Jews," *The Ecumenist*, January/February 1966, p. 27; cf. also *ibid.*, May/June 1965, pp. 56–59.

[39] For a fuller treatment of the strengths of the document, cf. Bea, *op. cit.*, esp. Ch. IV–IX, which contain careful exegeses of each theme of the document.

[40] Heschel, "No Religion Is an Island," *op. cit.*, p. 133.

"To the Christian the Jew is the incomprehensibly obdurate man, who declines to see what has happened; and to the Jew, the Christian is the incomprehensibly daring man, who affirms in an unredeemed world that its redemption has been accomplished. This is a gulf which no human power can bridge."[41]

We can only believe that somehow and sometime, by the power of God, the gulf will be bridged. Our task in this area of ecumenical dialogue is not to try to force God's hand, but to remove as many of the false barriers as possible. Here we can best learn from Pope John. Receiving a delegation of Jewish visitors early in his pontificate, he opened his arms to them and, using his baptismal name, greeted them with the words, "I am Joseph, your brother."

In a world where totalitarian power is on the march, and where Christians still have much of which to repent, both for their own crimes against the Jews and for the crimes of others in which Christians silently acquiesced, Christians must be prepared to go one step beyond, and be ready to say with St. Paul, "I could wish that I myself were accursed and cut off from Christ for the sake of my brethren, my kinsmen by race." (Romans 9:3) But one will scarcely be able to make such an act of identification until he has first been able to open his arms and to say, "I am Joseph, your brother."

Appendix: Christianity and the "conversion of the Jews"

When one of the earlier drafts of the council statement appeared with what seemed to be a reference to working for the conversion of the Jews, Rabbi Heschel remarked, "I had rather enter Auschwitz than be an object of conversion." The reference in the draft was later deleted, but its initial insertion indicated part of the historic Christian impulse, just as Rabbi Heschel's response indicated the historical Jewish re-

[41] Buber, *Israel and the World*, Schocken, New York, 1963, p. 40.

sponse to the Christian impulse. The ambivalence of the Vatican Council on the matter is paralleled by the ambivalence, recorded earlier in this chapter, of the World Council.

The traditional Christian attitude, of course, has been that since the Gospel is for all men, the Jews are naturally included among those who should be brought to it. As Amsterdam said, but Evanston did not repeat, we must "include the Jewish people in our evangelistic work."[42]

It will be suggested in the paragraphs that follow, however, that "conversion" is not the proper stance of the Christian toward the Jew, however proper it may be to the rest of mankind. Three reasons may be offered to support this conclusion which is at variance with so much past Christian history and practice.

1. We are talking about "ecumenism and the Jews." The same kinds of ground rules that apply between Catholics and Protestants must also apply between Christians and Jews, and one of the emerging ground rules has been a distinction between "ecumenism" and "conversion" (cf. Ch. 4 above). If the purpose of the Catholic-Protestant dialogue is not to score debaters' points or convert the other, but to establish new bases of rapport and overcome the misunderstandings and prejudices that have existed for centuries, so much more ought this to be true in the Christian-Jewish dialogue. The stereotypes Catholics and Protestants have of one another pale to insignificance compared to the stereotypes Christians and Jews have of one another. As long as Christians are guilty not only of such gross misunderstandings as that the Jews are an accursed race, guilty of "deicide," but also a host of other stereotypes, as that the Old Testament God is a God of wrath whereas the New Testament God is a God of love, or that Judaism is a religion of works whereas Chris-

---

[42] For a Protestant treatment suggesting that we must move to dialogue with the Jews but also "beyond dialogue," always making clear that Christ is for *all* men, cf. Knight, ed., *Jews and Christians*, Westminster, Philadelphia, 1965, 191 pp.

tianity is a religion of grace—so long must the ecumenical dialogue be a full-time operation simply to help overcome distortions.

There is no more cause for discouragement, because of the magnitude of the task, than there is in the Catholic-Protestant dialogue. Just as the papacy may seem an irreconcilable difference between Protestants and Catholics, so Christology seems an irreconcilable difference between Christians and Jews. But dialogue does not cease because the two groups have mutually contradictory viewpoints. The possession of mutually contradictory viewpoints provides the occasion for dialogue. "We disagree," Fr. John Courtney Murray has said, "therefore we can discuss."

2. A second reason for disavowing conversion as the object of Christian-Jewish dialogue has historical, psychological, and sociological roots. To the Jew, Christianity has been a symbol of oppression, forced conversion, persecution, torture, and death by fire or sword. To the Christian, the cross is the symbol of the divine love and mercy of Christ whereas to the Jew it is the symbol of the human hatred and bigotry of Christians, who under the sign of the cross have butchered Jews, forced them into ghettos, and—in the most recent outrages—stood silently by while SS troops herded Jews into cattle cars and took them to concentration camps to be slaughtered to the count of six million.[43]

When one looks at Christianity from the historical, psychological, and sociological perspective of the Jew, one sometimes wonders how a Jew could do anything but laugh coarsely when invited to become a part of the "Christian fellowship."[44] There is little in the history of Christendom to reassure the Jew that he would be genuinely welcomed as

[43] A brief recital is Foerster, *The Jews*, Farrar, Straus and Cudahy, New York, 1962, 157 pp.; more fully, Flannery, *The Anguish of the Jews*, Macmillan, New York, 1965, 332 pp.

[44] The following paragraphs, as well as the concluding paragraphs of the chapter proper, are adapted from my introduction to Foerster, *op. cit.*

a person, or that the Christian church has truly repented of the accumulation of wrongs that Christians have heaped upon their Jewish neighbors. When and if conversion does occur—which, being a miracle of grace, cannot be given or withheld by men—the Christian is not so much entitled to feel that his church has given to the Jew the gift of salvation, but rather that the Jew has given to the church the gift of his forgiving presence. In such "frontier crossings" (as Karl Barth has called them), Christians will be the gainers far more than the Jew.[45]

Reinhold Niebuhr, in disavowing a "mission to the Jews," asserts that

"the two faiths despite differences are sufficiently alike for the Jew to find God more easily in terms of his own religious heritage than by subjecting himself to the hazards of guilt feeling involved in a conversion to a faith, which whatever its excellences, must appear to him as a symbol of an oppressive majority culture."[46]

The latter point is probably hidden from every non-Jew who does not have (as Dr. Niebuhr has) a tremendously sympathetic imagination. Not only does the Jewish convert have the guilt feeling involved in leaving a "scapegoat" group to join a "respectable" group, but he also incurs the double onus of joining precisely the group that has been most oppressive in its persecution of his own people.

3. There are also theological reasons militating against conversion. Paul Tillich has made the point, for example, that for its own sake Christianity needs the leavening presence of Judaism as a constant check against its own preten-

[45] On the persistence of anti-Semitism within the Christian church, cf. the disturbing conclusions of Glock and Stark, op. cit. Information Service, June 18, 1966, summarizes the conclusions and presents a roundup of recent statements on anti-Semitism by Christian groups. Msgr. Paul Hanley Furfey raises some questions about the adequacy of the conclusions in a review in The Commonweal, September 2, 1966, pp. 558–59.

[46] Niebuhr, Pious and Secular America, Scribner's, New York, 1958, p. 108.

sions. The mission of the Jews until the end of history, Tillich points out, will be to bear witness against idolatry, against false gods. "You shall have no other gods before me," Yahweh thundered from Sinai, and it has been the contribution of the Jews ever since to keep the reverberations of that thunder alive. This prophetic note is always needed against the Christian religion, particularly in its institutional form, since churchmen have a peculiar propensity for creating manmade gods. It is part of Judaism's ongoing contribution to organized Christianity, then, to keep reminding it of its endemic institutional pride. Tillich asserts therefore that Christianity needs the separate prophetic existence of Judaism as a check against its own idolatry. Without Judaism, Christianity cannot be its true self.[47]

The viewpoint of a number of Catholic theologians, such as Karl Rahner and Edward Schillebeeckx, is relevant to the Jewish-Christian question. They argue that the task of the Christian in the post-Christian era is not to engage in feverish conversion work to the exclusion of all else, but simply to live the life of "Christian presence" in the world, leaving to God what he will do with this witness, and being willing to live with a certain degree of agnosticism about the coincidence of the lines of the visible church and the lines of the redeemed community. Such a posture leaves the Christian free to serve the neighbor in love, rather than to look upon the neighbor only as "conversion material."[48]

From the Jewish side, the most significant wrestling with this problem has come from Franz Rosenzweig, a Jewish thinker who at one time was on the verge of becoming a

[47] Cf. Tillich, "Jewish Influences on Contemporary Christian Theology," *Cross Currents*, Spring 1952, Vol. II, No. 3, and his chapter on Martin Buber, in *Theology of Culture*, Oxford University Press, New York, 1959, Ch. 14.

[48] Cf. *inter alia*, Rahner, *The Christian Commitment*, Sheed and Ward, New York, 1963, and Schillebeeckx, ed., *The Church and Mankind*, Concilium series, Vol. I, Paulist Press, Glen Rock, 1964, 177 pp., esp. the essay by Schillebeeckx, pp. 69–101.

Christian himself.[49] Rosenzweig came to the conclusion that Christianity was, in effect, the missionary arm of Israel. The gentile would come to faith in "the God of Abraham, Isaac and Jacob" only through the agency of Christianity. The mission to the gentiles must be accomplished through the gentiles. This did not mean that Jews should become Christians, but that Jews should remain Jews and witness to their Jewish faith, for Christianity could not remain an effective force for redemption without the presence of Israel in her midst. Israel's job, therefore, was to represent in time the eternal Kingdom of God, while Christianity's job was to bring itself and the world toward that goal.

A contemporary exponent of this position, Will Herberg, likewise sees Christianity as Judaism's apostle. "Christianity arose," he writes, "at a great crisis in Israel's history, as an outgoing movement to bring the God of Israel to the gentiles by bringing the gentiles into the covenant."[50] In Christianity, God opened up a new covenant for all mankind. This does not supplant the old covenant with the Jews, Herberg contends, but rather extends and enlarges it. The task of the Jew is to stand fast in his witness to God's dealings through the old covenant into which he entered at birth; the task of the Christian is to "go out" and bring others into the new covenant which all men can enter by adoption. One is *born* a Jew, while one *becomes* a Christian. The difference between the two, *vis-à-vis* the rest of the world, is one of vocation.[51]

Can the Christian affirm this kind of position? James R. Brown replies that "a Christian can hold such a view only if

[49] On Rosenzweig, cf. Glatzer, *Franz Rosenzweig*, Schocken Books, New York, 1961, 404 pp.; Rosenzweig, *On Jewish Learning*, Schocken Books, New York, 1955, 128 pp.; Bergman, *Faith and Reason, Modern Jewish Thought*. Schocken Books, New York, 1963, Ch. III, pp. 55–80.

[50] Herberg, *Judaism and Modern Man*, Farrar, Straus and Young, New York, 1951, p. 272.

[51] Cf. further, Herberg, "Judaism and Christianity: Their Unity and Difference," The *Journal of Bible and Religion*, April 1953.

Christology is relegated to a secondary place."[52] But this surely depends on the kind of Christology the Christian has. The Jew has no reason for offense if the Christian believes that Christ has already exercised his redeeming love toward all men—Christian, Jew, and non-believer alike. Furthermore, the Christian must believe that God's ways of working are *not* bound by theological formulae, however impressive the credentials accompanying them, and should not be shocked by the notion that God can work *through* the Jewish community to reach the Jews. Why is it not possible to believe that the tasks of Jews and Christians in the world are complementary rather than contradictory, and make our dialogue a reflection of that fact?

There remains, of course, a difficulty. The Jew and the Christian do come to the dialogue with a basic difference, namely the assessment each makes of a first-century Jew. If the Christian cannot require the Jew to affirm Christ, neither can the Jew require the Christian to deny him. There are many things about which the partners in the dialogue will talk, but there must not be an unmentionable arena in the Jewish-Christian dialogue, such as Christology, any more than there should be an unmentionable arena in Catholic-Protestant dialogue, such as Mariology. The Christian, in giving an accounting of his faith, will have to include reference to the one who is the center of his faith, and the Jew must not begrudge him this, any more than the Christian can begrudge the Jew his unwillingness to be swayed by the Christian affirmation.

This means risk to both Jew and Christian, just as the Protestant-Catholic dialogue means risk to both Catholic and Protestant. There is always the possibility that destruction of the stereotypes of the faith of the opposite partner may lead one to wish to embrace that faith for himself. Traffic runs both ways on this street, and there is no way to ensure

[52] In Knight, ed., *op. cit.*, p. 150.

that this will never happen, and no reason to insist that it must not. Otherwise, the opposite partner is being treated as an abstraction—a "Jew" or a "Methodist," rather than as a person, Jacob Shapiro or John Wesley Aldersgate. What both partners must do is to talk and listen with painstaking honesty, and let God do with the exchange whatever he will.

PART FIVE

From Irritation to Illumination
or
The Differences We Share

[Protestants and Catholics] may and must talk to one
another, but with a new approach; they should proceed
from points on which they are united to discuss what
separates them; and discuss what separates them with
an eye to what unites them.

> Karl Barth to Hans Küng, in Küng,
> *Justification*, p. xxii.

The principle that we are happy to make our own is
this: Let us stress what we have in common rather than
what divides us. This provides a good and fruitful subject for our dialogue. We are ready to carry it out wholeheartedly. . . . But we must add that it is not in our
power to compromise with the integrity of the faith or
the requirements of charity.

> Pope Paul VII, in the encyclical
> *Ecclesiam Suam.*

CHAPTER 15

THE EXTENSION OF COMMON DIALOGUE

Through . . . dialogue, everyone gains a truer knowledge and more just appreciation of the teaching and religious life of both Communions. In addition, these
Communions cooperate more closely in whatever projects a Christian conscience demands for the common
good. They also come together for common prayer,
where this is permitted.

Vatican II decree *On Ecumenism*, Art. 4.

The three-step sequence cited above—dialogue, action, worship—indicates the sequence of the concluding chapters of
this book, as we attempt to move from irritation to illumination. In the past, irritation resulted from Catholic-Protestant
attempts to talk together ("Why must you be so stubborn
about infallibility?"), irritation resulted from Catholic-
Protestant attempts to work together ("Federal aid to education should—or should not—be extended to parochial
schools"), and irritation resulted particularly from Catholic-
Protestant attempts to pray together ("Why do you insist on
worshiping so strangely?").

The ecumenical revolution is transforming areas of irritation into areas of illumination, for we are beginning to learn
from one another at precisely the points where we used to be
alienated from one another. This does not mean ignoring
differences, but rather seeing the differences in the context of
the similarities, a principle that (as the title page of this section indicates) draws together such otherwise diverse theologians as Karl Barth and Pope Paul.

Our present task is not to describe *how* we should talk,[1] but rather to indicate *what* we should talk about. Before embarking on this task, however, it will be important to make clear to those as yet innocent of the fact *that* we are already talking.

The levels of dialogue—a description

Less than a decade ago, recommendations that Protestants and Catholics engage in dialogue were met, from the Protestant side at least, with suspicion if not hostility. Wary Protestants were sure that some kind of "trick" was involved and were reluctant, to say the least, to expose themselves to their Roman Catholic counterparts. Now, however, when one attempts to describe what is happening on the dialogical frontier, he is met not by hostility but by impatience: "You think that's significant? Let me tell you what happened last week in *our* town!"

Dialogue is indeed burgeoning everywhere, and a full account of what is taking place would be a book-length venture in itself.[2] Perhaps the most far-reaching development has been the inception of hundreds of "living-room dialogue" groups, small lay-sponsored discussion groups, open to Catholics, Protestants, and Orthodox, organized on the basis of procedures suggested in an easily available paperback of the same name.[3] The book offers material for seven dialogues, dealing with such topics as worship, renewal, common Chris-

---

[1] The principles underlying common dialogue are discussed in Ch. 4 above.

[2] For a sampling, cf. *An Inventory of Ecumenical Activity*, compiled by the staff of the Commission on Ecumenical Mission and Relations of the United Presbyterian Church in the U.S.A., May 1, 1966, and "Local Ecumenism" in *Faith and Order Trends*, July 1965, pp. 1–8.

An early publication of the Bishops' Commission for Ecumenical Affairs lists ninety-nine possible types of ecumenical contact; a later edition consolidates these to fifty-nine.

[3] Greenspun and Nordgren, eds., *Living Room Dialogues*, National Council of Churches, and Paulist Press, New York, 1965, 256 pp.

tian witness, and the problem of dividedness at the Lord's Table. The book not only contains reading materials for each topic but also practical suggestions for organizing the groups, eliciting discussion, and initiating worship together. Ecumenism at 475 Riverside Drive (headquarters of the National Council of Churches) or at 150 route de Ferney (headquarters of the World Council of Churches) is important, but until ecumenism has made its way into the living room, it will be little more than a professional pastime for professionals. What living-room dialogues represent, therefore, is vital.

On a slightly more official level, dialogue is taking place between members of Catholic and Protestant parishes who gather together, with clerical participation and episcopal or denominational approval, to explore their similarities and differences. This may involve discussion about the Vatican Council (for which Hans Küng's *The Council, Reform and Reunion* has been a staple item), attempts to understand one another's corporate worship (frequently by invitations to the other group to "observe" on Sunday morning), or examination of the theological issues that brought about the Reformation. Increasingly such groups are proceeding to Bible study together, not to uncover their differences of interpretation so much as to see what light their commonly shared Scriptures shed on the problems of life today.

More inclusive dialogue takes place among all the elements of both communities on such occasions as the Week of Prayer for Christian Unity, held annually during the third week of January, at special festivals such as ecumenical hymn-sings at Pentecost or during Advent, and with increasing regularity at the ecumenical redemption of the formerly divisive Protestant celebration known as Reformation Sunday.

Beyond the parish level there has been increasing ecumenical dialogue among seminarians and clergy. Yale Divinity School and Woodstock College (the Jesuit theologate in Maryland) have had several student visitations to one another's campuses; Union Theological Seminary and Fordham University have recently established a "concordat" that allows reciprocal course enrollment, joint use of all library facilities, and the loan of professors from one institution to the other; the Graduate Theological Union at Berkeley, California, has pooled the resources of a number of Protestant seminaries and the near-by Dominican House of Studies, and the Jesuit theologate at Los Gatos, with faculty also drawn from the Roman Catholic diocesan seminary in Menlo Park; and in Dubuque, Iowa, four theological faculties drawn from a Dominican monastery, the school of religion at the State University of Iowa, and the local Presbyterian and Lutheran seminaries, have entered into arrangements for joint work toward graduate degrees.

Professional theological discussion groups, crossing Catholic-Protestant boundaries, are increasingly common. Typical of such is the Stanford-Santa Clara Ecumenical Colloquium, consisting of Catholic, Protestant, and Orthodox theologians in the San Francisco Bay area, who meet once a month for discussion of papers and twice yearly for longer sessions open to a wider group of invited guests.

Formal dialogue has been instituted between the Roman Catholic Church and a number of major denominations: Catholic and Lutheran theologians are discussing the interpretation of the creeds; Catholics and Episcopalians are exploring the meaning of the eucharist; Catholics and Presbyterians are examining the meaning of "ongoing reformation in the life of the church."

On the international level, ecumenical institutes are being organized to enable scholars from various parts of the world to meet for research, discussion, and theological collaboration. The Lutherans have already established such a center in Strasbourg, and plans are underway for other centers under interdenominational auspices in Rome, North America, and Jerusalem. The latter is a particularly interesting example of ecumenical co-operation. After the pope's visit to Jerusalem in 1964, he indicated an interest in establishing an ecumenical study center there (picking up on a suggestion made by Professor Kirsten Skydsgaard, a Lutheran observer, during the papal audience with the observers at the second session of the council). But rather than establishing the center under Roman Catholic sponsorship, and then inviting others to use it, he decided to turn its establishment over to a group of Catholic and non-Catholic scholars. Consequently, the Academic Council developing plans for the center is composed of Roman Catholics, Orthodox, Anglicans, and Protestants, with Roman Catholics actually in a minority.

Perhaps the most "high level" instance of ecumenical dialogue is a Joint Working Group, comprising eight representatives of the World Council of Churches and six representatives of the Secretariat for Christian Unity, which has already met several times since its formation in 1965.[4]

Even this brief enumeration indicates that channels of communication are open to a degree that makes puny even the most optimistic forecasts of a few years ago, and yet also indicates that the surface of future possibilities has barely been scratched.

The immediate irritants—a sampling

It would be false to suggest that ecumenical dialogue is all sweetness and light. Long-time irritants do not vanish simply because the disputants are now smiling instead of sneering. But the new factor in the situation is that the partners in the dialogue now have enough confidence in the integrity of one another so that the irritants can be discussed on their own merits—or demerits—rather than in the emotionally tinged atmosphere of mutual suspicion.

There are some immediate irritants to which brief atten-

---

[4] For an elaboration of the concerns of this important group, cf. the minutes of the first two meetings in *The Ecumenical Review*, April 1966, pp. 243–61.

tion should be called since it is now possible to discuss them creatively. The following are almost always sore points on the local ecumenical front:

1. *Mixed marriages.*[5] Catholic legislation has placed a severe strain on the non-Catholic partner to a marriage by insisting that prior to the wedding certain promises be made in writing, e.g., that the non-Catholic will do nothing to disturb the faith of the Catholic partner, whereas the Catholic will prudently work for the conversion of the non-Catholic, that all children will be baptized and raised as Catholics, that the Catholic prohibition of artificial means of birth control will be honored by both partners, that the Catholic marriage ceremony will not be followed by a non-Catholic one, and so forth.

It had been hoped that Vatican II would ease at least some of these restrictions, and there was even preliminary conciliar discussion of moves in this direction. However, the item was removed from the agenda, presumably so that the pope could more expeditiously announce revisions in keeping with the new ecumenical situation. No announcement came, however, until March 1966, when the Congregation for the Doctrine of the Faith, and not the pope, published an *Instruction on Mixed Marriages.* The *Instruction* was a keen disappointment to Protestants who had hoped for something more in keeping with the spirit of the council. The promises about the baptism and rearing of children are maintained in the *Instruction,* with the irrelevant concession that the promises can now be made verbally instead of in writing! Hopes for a more ecumenically centered wedding ceremony are only slightly encouraged; the Protestant minister can now be present, but is permitted to say a few words only when the Catholic service is completed. Furthermore, the *Instruction* makes no distinction between the marriage of a Catholic to a Protestant or to a non-Christian, and does not recognize the

[5] Cf. *inter alia,* Baum, "Mixed Marriages—An Ecumenical Issue," *The Ecumenist,* July-August 1966, pp. 73–76, and the reactions of Visser 't Hooft to the recent *Instruction on Mixed Marriages, ibid.,* pp. 85–86.

validity of mixed marriages contracted outside the Roman Catholic Church.

It is impossible to believe that the *Instruction* represents more than a temporizing, interim word. The full implications of the Vatican Council documents call for more radical rethinking. To give only one example: both the constitution *On the Church* and the decree *On Ecumenism* acknowledge that Protestants are already in some sense within the church, and even that their own "churches and ecclesial communities" are means of grace that God uses for the salvation and sanctification of souls.[6] This means that a Protestant-Catholic marriage is not, strictly speaking, a marriage between someone inside and someone outside the church, but between two people both of whom, to varying degrees, are within the church. It should therefore be possible to take more significant account of this fact in the service itself, and in the reworking of the promises, in such a way that the degree to which both partners already share much of the Christian faith is used to bind them closer to one another rather than, as the present regulations inevitably do, drive them further apart. Vatican II has made the theological resources for a new view of mixed marriages available, so that this particular area of irritation can, in time, be transformed into an area of illumination.

2. *Birth control.*[7] There are two problems here. One prob-

---

[6] Cf. further on these points Ch. 11 above.

[7] Catholic literature on this topic is so vast that one Catholic editor has gone as far as to say that what the church needs is a "pill" to inhibit the conception of more books on the problem of conception.

Out of many that could be cited, the following have been among the most influential in the new discussion: Noonan, *Contraception, A History of Its Treatment by the Catholic Theologians and Canonists*, Belknap Press, Harvard University Press, Cambridge, 1965, 561 pp., is the basic resource; cf. also Roberts, ed., *Contraception and Holiness*, Herder and Herder, New York, 1964, 256 pp., Dupre, *Contraception and Catholics*, Helicon, Baltimore, 1964, 94 pp., Pyle, ed., *The Pill and Birth Regulation*, Darton, Longman and Todd, London, 1964, 255 pp., Rock, *The Time Has Come*, Knopf, New York, 1963, 204 pp.

lem has to do simply with the internal life of Roman Catholicism, and the non-Catholic has no right to interfere in what the church demands of its own constituents. What it has demanded in the past is very clear: "artificial" means of contraception are forbidden. Roman Catholic lay people, however, do not accept this teaching with the docility they once did. Nor do the theologians. Not only is there now fully open discussion about the presumed shortcomings of the official position, but considerable sociological evidence as well to suggest that many Roman Catholic couples simply do not follow the teaching of the church on this matter.

The problem becomes an ecumenical one, however, when Catholic teaching to its own constituency determines public policy for non-Catholics, who run into difficulty when they attempt to establish birth-control clinics, for example, or include the dissemination of contraceptives in legislation to aid underdeveloped countries where over-population leads to famine. As we have seen, the teaching has also been a major problem in mixed marriages.

The non-Catholic therefore has a real stake in Catholic rethinking about the matter and sees a number of pertinent facts emerging in the discussion:

a. The traditional position was subject to modification even before Vatican II. Pius XII's decision that the "rhythm method" was licit furnished a breach in the traditional ban on "contraception" and meant that at least one method of limiting the number of births was approved. The issue was thus transformed from contraception vs. no contraception to approved *means* of contraception, since the means of limiting intercourse to periods of least likely fertility was accepted, although other means were rejected. Another step forward was the acknowledgment that the education of children as well as their procreation was an end of marriage, thus suggesting that a couple should not have more children than it could hope to educate. Both advances clearly undermine the older notion that Catholic couples should simply "trust

God" for the number of children he would give them, and furnish the couples with an arena of initiative in determining both the number and spacing of their offspring.

b. At Vatican II, an important further extension of Catholic teaching was officially promulgated. This was the recognition, in *The Church and the World Today*, that "conjugal love" is also a good in marriage, in and of itself, quite apart from whether or not procreation results from it. This means a more exalted view of the place of sex than has been evident in most marriage manuals of the past, and establishes that sex in marriage can be a good even when the intent of procreation is not present.[8]

c. In addition to these internal developments in Catholic thinking, there is the external fact of the population explosion, and the likelihood that the present policy, if rigorously adhered to, will work untold hardship on mankind within a couple of generations. Catholic teaching on the implications of "be fruitful and multiply" was worked out in an era of high infant mortality and low adult life expectancy, when many children were needed if the race was to survive. Just the opposite situation obtains now, however, and teaching designed to meet one kind of human situation must not unthinkingly be projected onto a totally different situation.

d. To those who fear that a "change" in the church's teaching would undermine faith in the church's teaching authority, it can be replied that no teaching on birth control is in the realm of infallible teaching, and that if indeed a modification is called for, further postponement will cast the teaching office into greater rather than less dubiety. The church has advanced beyond its condemnation of Galileo; the church has advanced beyond its condemnation of religious freedom;

[8] After some discussion of birth control on the council floor, the topic was removed from the agenda. Subsequently a papal commission was appointed to advise the pope about any further teaching. At the time of writing, the commission has made its report, and the pope has announced only that there will be a further delay before he makes a decision.

the church has advanced beyond its condemnation of loaning money at interest. There is precedent, in other words, for advancing beyond a condemnation of certain means of contraception to a deeper understanding of the meaning of sex and marriage, as the Vatican Council foreshadows.

e. Catholic theology has always stressed the internal right of conscience. From this premise, if a couple is convinced in good conscience that it should not, for a period of time, have another child; or it is clear that the health of the mother or the welfare of the family would be threatened by another pregnancy; or that the unrealiability of the "rhythm method" in the particular case precludes it as a real option; or that the relationship between the marriage partners would be seriously jeopardized by prolonged sexual abstinence—then the question of the method of avoiding birth surely becomes a secondary or tertiary one, and the choice of method would seem best left to the couple to work out together.

The above considerations will perhaps annoy if not anger certain Catholic readers, and yet they are all considerations that can be stated in terms of the Catholic theology emerging out of Vatican II. Rather than viewing the abandonment of "traditional" teaching on birth control as a threat to the integrity of Catholic faith, it can be argued that further development in this area will be an instance of Catholic theology moving to a more complete theology of marriage, and the goodness of sex within it, than has yet been attained.

3. *Catholic power.*[9] Certain Protestants still fear the day of the Catholic "take-over." They view the Catholic Church as a political power structure that once had worldly power and still hankers after it. They feel that Catholic expressions of approval of pluralism are only time-gaining devices until

[9] Some implications of this problem have been discussed in connection with the treatment of religious freedom in Ch. 13 above. There is a more extended treatment in Brown and Weigel, *op. cit.*, Ch. 4, which states Protestant concerns about "Catholic power" in the context of the late 1950s.

the church can regain sufficient power to enforce its views on a non-Catholic minority—or majority.

The person who holds such views today, however, can hold them only by accusing the Roman Catholic Church of living and acting in bad faith and deliberately propagating falsehoods for public consumption while cannily planning contrary strategy in private. Either one does, or does not, take at face value such statements as the following:

"The Church herself employs the things of time to the degree that her own mission demands. Still she does not lodge her hope in privileges conferred by civil authority. Indeed, *she stands ready to renounce the exercise of certain legitimately acquired rights if it becomes clear that their use raises doubt about the sincerity of her witness* or that new conditions of life demand some other arrangement."[10]

Another order of concern remains, however, when the above has been disposed of, namely the use of public funds for the promotion of the activities of the church. The issue has its highest irritation index in relation to education. The state provides public schools for which all citizens are taxed, whether they use the schools or not. Many Catholics do not use them and send their children to parochial schools instead. The state permits this, but insists that the parents continue to pay taxes supporting public schools. The Catholic feels discriminated against: (a) by having to pay public school taxes and parochial school fees he is the victim of "double taxation," forced to pay twice for the education he wants his child to have, and (b) since his children are not in public schools, the latter need not be as large or employ as many people as would otherwise be the case, and yet federal aid is withheld from parochial schools even though they are in fact educating a sizable percentage of the youth of the land.

Protestants reply to the first complaint with the observation that those who wish extra privileges must be willing to

[10] *The Church and the World Today*, Art. 76, Abbott, p. 288, italics added.

pay for them, and then start to talk about "separation of church and state," pointing out that if aid is given to the Catholic Church in this area, its universities, hospitals, building programs, and seminaries will likely claim public funds that will thereby be diverted into support for a private institution. The argument is a difficult one to maintain consistently, however, since public funds already support many Protestant enterprises as well. What is sauce for the goose must be sauce for the gander.[11]

In the past, the problem has often been attacked emotionally from both sides. The issues are not as clear-cut as they once seemed to the proponents and opponents, and one of the values of the extension of the dialogue is that it may now be possible to deal with such problems as federal aid to education, and the propriety or impropriety of including parochial schools in such aid, in a new spirit.

4. *Protestant diffuseness.* Thus far we have looked at immediate irritants that appear to the Protestant to be introduced from the Catholic side. But Catholics likewise feel certain immediate irritants, introduced from the Protestant side. One of the most vexing of these is the diffuseness of Protestantism, and the difficulty of discovering who speaks for whom. A Protestant can usually get a fair idea of Catholic thinking on a given subject—though this is not as easy as it once was—but the Catholic faces a bewildering array of claims and counter-claims the minute he seeks to determine the nature of Protestant thinking. Who speaks for Protestants on the church-state issue—P.O.A.U. or *Christianity and Crisis?* Who correctly assesses the issue of "communist infiltration" in the National Council of Churches—Carl McIntyre or Eugene Carson Blake? Who represents the Protes-

[11] Recent discussions dealing with this and allied issues are Murray, *We Hold These Truths,* Sheed and Ward, New York, 1960, 336 pp., Drinan, *Religion, The Courts, and Public Policy,* McGraw-Hill, New York, 1963, 261 pp., and, from the Protestant side, Neilsen, *God in Education,* Sheed and Ward, New York, 1966, 245 pp.

tant consensus on the race issue—the Southern Baptists or the Southern Presbyterians? Who is closer to a true understanding of the church and social justice—the National Council of Churches or the American Council of Churches?

The Catholic can be pardoned if it often seems to him that the Protestant scene is confusion worse confounded, and that there is no way for him to engage with Protestantism as such, but only with one of a hundred different varieties of Protestant faith. And he can be pardoned if his initial inclination is to withdraw from the scene until Protestants have put their own house in order, though he must be discouraged from actually doing so. For once again the sources of irritation can be transformed by dialogue into sources of illumination. The Catholic can learn, through firsthand confrontation, to discriminate between the alternatives posed in the above series of questions and work his way through to a deeper understanding of the significance of internal debate within the Protestant world. And whenever he feels sure that the problem exists only *vis-à-vis* Protestantism, he may be reminded by his Protestant counterpart that the latter has some difficulties of his own when trying to determine whether, for example, Catholic thinking about Biblical study is better represented by Cardinal Bea or Cardinal Ruffini.

Issues such as those discussed above are capable of a high degree of resolution. Some of them are well on the way to resolution, and may, by the time this appears in print, have become radically reshaped by the rapid passage of events.

The ongoing obstacles—a further sampling

But hand in hand with discussion of the immediate irritants must proceed discussion of the long-range theological issues that seriously and deeply divide Christians, for which no ready-made solutions are visible, and which therefore must be the subject of further exploration. Three of the most vexing will be described briefly.

1. *Papacy and infallibility.*[12] When all other problems have been resolved, there is one that will remain to haunt the Protestant-Catholic dialogue—the different estimates the two groups make of the powers that inhere in the office of the bishop of Rome. The Roman Catholic assessment is very clear and was stated authoritatively at Vatican I:

"The Roman Pontiff, when he speaks *ex cathedra*, that is, when carrying out the duty of the pastor and teacher of all Christians in accord with his supreme apostolic authority he explains a doctrine of faith or morals to be held by the universal Church, through the divine assistance promised him in blessed Peter, operates with that infallibility with which the divine Redeemer wished that His church be instructed in defining doctrine on faith and morals; and so such definitions of the Roman Pontiff from himself, but not from the consensus of the Church, are unalterable."[13]

In the period since the above words were promulgated, the infallibility of the pope has loomed more and more as the one apparently insurmountable barrier between Catholics and Protestants. To state the matter bluntly: for the Catholic, the doctrine of papal infallibility guarantees that the Holy Spirit will not forsake the church, while for the Protestant

[12] On the history of Vatican I and the infallibility decree, cf. C. Butler, *The Vatican Council 1869–1870*, Collins and Harvill, London, 1930, 510 pp. On the over-all problem cf. B. C. Butler, *The Church and Infallibility*, Sheed and Ward, New York, 1954, 230 pp., a reply to a Protestant attack by Salmon, *The Infallibility of the Church*, John Murray, London, 1888 (reprinted 1953), 227 pp.

The most helpful opening up of the contemporary problem by a Roman Catholic is Küng, *Structures of the Church*, Nelson, New York, 1964, 394 pp., esp. Ch. 7, "The Petrine Office," and Ch. 8, "What Does Infallibility Mean?" From the Protestant side, Lindbeck, "Reform and Infallibility, *Cross Currents*, Fall 1961, pp. 345–56, has become a minor classic.

On the relation of infallibility to the development of doctrine cf. *inter alia* Baum, "Doctrinal Renewal," *Journal of Ecumenical Studies*, Fall 1965, pp. 365–81.

[13] Denzinger, *The Sources of Catholic Dogma*, Herder, St. Louis, 1957, para. 1839, p. 457.

the doctrine suggests that the church has forsaken the Holy Spirit, seeking to control the Spirit rather than living in subjection to him. The doctrine blurs the crucial distinction between the voice of God and the voice of man by asserting that one man at least can speak in the untainted accents of the Holy Ghost. The temptation to equate the two is the awesome temptation to ecclesiastical pride, to the assertion that there is one innermost precinct where the Biblical dictum that "judgment begins at the house of God" does not operate.

Such words may sound offensive to Catholic readers. They are not meant to be so; they are meant only to state the problem as clearly as possible. The Protestant does not disavow papal infallibility in order to score debater's points, but out of fidelity to his own understanding of how God works through sinful man. He does so agonizingly, for he realizes that in so doing he accentuates the difficulties on the long, hard road to reunion. The problem remains unresolvable in any humanly foreseeable way, for, as we have earlier noted, there is no halfway house between accepting and rejecting infallibility, no such thing as "being a little bit infallible."

Yet the impasse is not as total as once appeared, for Catholics are by no means of one mind about precisely what infallibility means.[14] As one tries to understand Catholic teaching, it becomes increasingly clear that the pronouncement of a dogmatic definition is not the end of the matter, as though theological discussion were now ended; it is only the beginning of the matter, for now the theologians are turned loose to try to discern the true meaning of the definition. And within this enterprise, Catholic theology enjoys an arena of spacious maneuverability far beyond what most Protes-

[14] When I attempted to state my understanding of infallibility in *An American Dialogue* back in 1960, I received in the same mail letters from two Catholics. One of them commented, "I am amazed that a non-Catholic could have such a clear understanding of Catholic teaching on this difficult point." The other, advising me to read Karl Rahner, wrote, "If infallibility were what you claim it to be, I could not be a Catholic." Q.E.D.

tants can conceive. George Lindbeck, a Lutheran theologian, has observed that "even most moderately liberal Lutherans are likely to treat their own professedly reformable Confessions as in fact more definitive" than many Catholic theologians treat Chalcedon or Trent.[15] One must always be wary, therefore, of assuming that the "real" meaning of infallibility has been definitively stated. The Protestant, as well as the Catholic, needs to be aware that many Catholic theologians place on the dogma a "minimalist" interpretation, e.g., that it says no more than that the Holy Spirit will see to it that the church does not definitively proclaim as truth what is in fact error.

From such a perspective, it is possible for Roman Catholics to make such assertions as the following:

a. All theological statements, whether infallible or not, are time-bound products of a given historical situation and must therefore always be interpreted in their historical context; so that

b. as Catholic teaching develops, new data and insights become available that make possible an amplification of earlier theological statements;

c. no theological statement, being a human statement about a divine mystery, can ever be an exhaustive account of what it is describing; so that

d. any theological statement can always be said better than it has been said so far, with greater fullness, accuracy, and insight.

To the Protestant, who can easily assent to such statements, such an understanding comes curiously close to saying, in effect, "Irreformable statements are, in fact, reformable." The Catholic would no doubt reply that while they are reformable as to form and syntax and modes of speech that are typical of a given period of history, they are not reformable as to substantive content, and that for the

[15] Lindbeck, "Reform and Infallibility," *op. cit.*, p. 348.

sake of the visible unity of the church they are needed, in order to state the faith the visible church professes. The Protestant is still left wondering just how substantive content and ways of expressing that content are finally divisible from one another and continues to wonder what is really left of the notions of infallibility and irreformability (at least as he has understood them) that justifies their continued usage.

But the Protestant has not thereby disposed of the problem, for the Catholic can legitimately enquire if the Protestant in his turn does not have certain convictions that for him are "irreformable" in the sense that he cannot conceive of the church denying them and still being the church. Surely the Protestant would have to reply that such an affirmation as *Kurios Christos* (Christ is Lord) is not an affirmation the church will one day discard, or discover to be an error it has falsely proclaimed in the name of truth. Thus the Protestant himself has a certain version of infallibility and irreformability that brings the two faiths at least within talking distance of one another.

Vatican II has introduced a further factor into the discussion. Catholic theology subsequent to Vatican I certainly treated the infallibility decrees as meaning that all infallible authority inhered in the office of the bishop of Rome, even though the definition itself was open to wider interpretation, e.g., "the Roman Pontiff . . . operates with that infallibility with which the divine Redeemer wished that *His church* [not His vicar at Rome] be instructed. . . ." Resistance to the notion of a papal monolith soon developed; by 1875 the German bishops had received assurance from Pius IX himself that Vatican I had no intention of reducing the bishops to "the pope's men."[16] Dom Olivier Rousseau, a Benedictine, summarizes the conclusions of the document as follows:

---

[16] Cf. the important essay by Joseph Ratzinger in Rahner and Ratzinger, *The Episcopate and the Primacy*, Herder and Herder, New York, 1962, pp. 37–63. The full text of the document is included as Appendix I in Küng, *The Council, Reform and Reunion*, pp. 193–201. Cf. further on the whole prob-

"1. The pope cannot arrogate to himself the episcopal rights, nor substitute his power for that of the bishops; 2. the episcopal jurisdiction has not been absorbed in the papal jurisdiction; 3. the pope was not given the entire fullness of the bishops' powers by the decrees of the Vatican Council; 4. he has not virtually taken the place of each individual bishop; 5. he cannot put himself in the place of a bishop in each single instance, vis-à-vis governments; 6. the bishops have not become instruments of the pope; 7. they are not officials of a foreign sovereign in their relations with their own governments."[17]

This is clearly something other than "papalism" as most post-Vatican I theology, both Catholic and Protestant, understood that term. It likewise establishes that with the approach of Vatican II there was need to correct what was by that time openly called the "one-sidedness" of Vatican I, which, in exalting the teaching office of the bishop of Rome, had neglected to treat its relationship to the teaching office of the other bishops. Pope Paul himself set the stage for a doctrinal advance when in his opening allocution, speaking to the name and memory of his predecessor, he said:

"You have resumed the interrupted course of the first Vatican Council. You have banished the uneasy assumption wrongly deduced from that Council that the supreme powers conferred on the Roman Pontiff to govern the church—powers acknowledged by that Council—were sufficient without the help of ecumenical councils."[18]

Out of this concern ensued a lengthy conciliar discussion issuing in the most important single theological contribution of Vatican II, the doctrine of the collegiality of bishops. To

lem of papal power and episcopal power, Fransen, "The Authority of Councils," in Todd, ed., *Problems of Authority*, Darton, Longman and Todd, London, 1962, pp. 43–78, also available in *Cross Currents*, Fall 1961, pp. 357–74.

[17] *Irenikon*, 29, 1956, pp. 121–50, cited in Ratzinger, *op. cit.*

[18] Küng, Congar, O'Hanlon, eds., *op. cit.*, p. 16.

put the matter very simply: Vatican II has affirmed that Christ gave power not only to Peter but to Peter *and the other apostles* who together comprise the "college" through which authority in the church is exercised, and that just as Catholic teaching has always affirmed that the pope is the successor to Peter, so it now also affirms that the other bishops are the successors to the apostles. Teaching authority is henceforth to be understood as *collegial* authority—the pope as head of the college and not simply *primus inter pares,* but not fully defined save in relation to the college, and the bishops as members of the college, a college not fully defined save as the college of which the pope is head.[19]

The doctrine is carefully and tentatively worded—so that both "liberal" and "conservative" can read it and take heart— but it is clear that it contains the kernel of a doctrinal breakthrough with momentous implications, leading as it will to a kind of theological and structural decentralization of power in the Catholic Church. Certain practical implications are observable already: the pope has appointed a "senate of bishops" to meet with him from time to time to assist in the rule of the church, and the documents promulgated at Vatican II were promulgated not by the pope alone, as was true at Vatican I, but by "Paul, bishop, servant of the servants of God, together with the Fathers of the Sacred Council."

The evidence cited in the above pages does not, of course, resolve the problem of papal authority that bothers Protestants, but it does indicate that the problem cannot be conceived in static terms, and that the problem today is not the same as it was in 1961, let alone in 1870. Ongoing dialogue can hopefully transform this source of basic theological irritation into one from which increasing illumination can come.

[19] Cf. the constitution *On the Church,* esp. Ch. 3, "The Hierarchical Structure of the Church, With Special Reference to the Episcopate," Art. 18–29, Abbott, pp. 37–56, and the "Note of Explanation," Abbott, pp. 97–101.

2. *The role of Mary*.[20] Next to papacy, Mariology is the area of greatest theological division between Catholics and Protestants. The problem centers on the two most recent papal pronouncements, the dogma of the Immaculate Conception of Mary, so that she was freed from the taint of original sin, and the dogma of the Assumption of the Virgin into Heaven immediately after her death.[21]

Among many pre-Vatican II Protestant difficulties with these dogmatic affirmations, three were paramount: (a) concern that the increasing attention being focused on Mary in Catholic thought was in danger of eclipsing the centrality for faith and devotion that should be focused on her Son, (b) fear that this particular strand of "doctrinal development" was proceeding unchecked, so that it would issue in a papal definition of Mary as "co-redeemer," a doctrine that would seem to Protestants fatally to undermine the New Testament stress on her Son as the sole mediator between God and man, and (c) bafflement that these dogmas, neither of which has a clear Scriptural basis, should have become so central to Catholic faith that Pius XII could say of the latter that if anyone denies or doubts it "he has cut himself off entirely from the divine and Catholic faith."[22]

---

[20] Among the most helpful Catholic interpretations of the place of Mary are Laurentin, *The Question of Mary*, Holt, Rinehart and Winston, New York, 1964, 161 pp., Semmelroth, *Mary, Archetype of the Church*, Sheed and Ward, New York, 1963, 175 pp., and Schillebeeckx, *Mary, Mother of the Redemption*, Sheed and Ward, New York, 1964, 175 pp. (but cf. the critical review of the latter by Tavard in *The Commonweal*, March 19, 1965, pp. 792–94. A full historical study is Graef, *Mary, A History of Doctrine and Devotion*, Sheed and Ward, New York, Vol. I, 1963, 371 pp., and Vol. II, 1965, 160 pp. A report on the present theological discussion is O'Meara, *Mary in Protestant and Catholic Theology*, Sheed and Ward, New York, 1966, 376 pp., with a full bibliography.

[21] For the texts, cf. Denzinger, *op. cit.*, para. 1641, and 2331–33.

[22] Denzinger, *op. cit.*, para. 2333. A different dimension of Protestant ecumenical discouragement, related to the previous discussion of papacy, is that the dogma of the Assumption represents simultaneously the one completely unambiguous exercise of the prerogative of papal infallibility and that portion of Catholic theology that seems at the farthest remove from the New Testament.

But, once again, the question is not closed. To each of the above difficulties it can be asserted that Vatican II has made a helpful contribution, and that the ecumenical situation *vis-à-vis* Catholic and Protestant interpretations of Mary is better at the conclusion of the council than it was at the beginning.[23] (a) The decree *On Ecumenism*, in its statement of a "hierarchy of truths," offers a framework in which Catholic theology can, if it wishes, begin to see the place of Mary in such a way that the centrality for faith of the saving action of her Son need not be jeopardized.[24] (b) This concern was further underlined by speeches on the council floor, notably from South American bishops, pointing out that Marian piety was indeed exaggerated, and also by the council's action in voting against a separate document on Mary, so that the material on Mary was finally incorporated as Ch. 8 of the constitution *On the Church*. In this way, the separate and independent extension of Marian theology was effectively checked.[25] (c) When the latter chapter was rewritten, it was deliberately couched in as Biblical a framework as possible, replacing the string of papal quotations that had characterized the earlier draft, so that there might be an ecumenical meeting point with Protestants and Orthodox, both of whom affirm the authority of Biblical statements but not of papal statements.[26]

The new chapter was also formulated to try to meet certain historical Protestant and Orthodox misgivings. It points out that the cult of the Blessed Virgin "differs essentially

[23] I have dealt more fully with the issue of Mariology at the council in *Observer in Rome*, pp. 99–101, 103, 117–18, 124–26.

[24] Cf. further on this point Ch. 11 above.

[25] Cf. *On the Church*, Ch. 8, Abbott, pp. 85–96. On the other hand, the pope's action at the end of the third session, in proclaiming Mary "mother of the church," opened the door again. Cf. Ch. 9 and 10 above.

[26] The question of how far the attempt succeeded is another question, for not all Catholic teaching about Mary can be drawn directly from Biblical resources; this is a matter for the ensuing dialogue to clarify. What is important at the moment is that a deliberate ecumenical effort was made from the Catholic side.

from the cult of adoration which is offered to the Incarnate Word, as well as to the Father and the Holy Spirit."[27] And the council

"earnestly exhorts theologians and preachers of the divine word that in treating of the unique dignity of the Mother of God, they carefully and equally avoid the falsity of exaggeration on the one hand, and the excess of narrow-mindedness on the other. . . . Let them painstakingly guard against any word or deed which could lead separated brethren or anyone else into error regarding the true doctrine of the Church."[28]

To be sure, the problems of Mariology have not been dissolved by the council. But the discussion has been lifted to a new level. And since Catholics have gone a first mile in trying to re-establish theological *rapport* on this issue, Protestants have an obligation to go a second mile in opening themselves to an examination with their Catholic brethren of what the New Testament says about the place of Mary in Christian faith, and then trying to understand how Catholics can be led beyond that direct evidence to further affirmations that clearly mean so much to them in interpreting the signs of God's loving concern for his children.

3. *The relationship of Scripture and tradition.*[29] Treat-

---

[27] *On the Church*, Art. 66, Abbott, p. 94.

[28] *Ibid.*, Art. 67, Abbott, p. 95.

[29] On the historical issues cf. Hanson, *Tradition in the Early Church*, S.C.M. Press, London, 1962, 288 pp. Among many recent Catholic treatments of the problem, cf. the following: Geiselmann, "Scripture, Tradition, and the Church: An Ecumenical Problem," in Callahan, Oberman and O'Hanlon, eds., *Christianity Divided*, Sheed and Ward, New York, 1961, pp. 39–70, with bibliography on pp. 71–72; Geiselmann, *The Meaning of Tradition*, Herder and Herder, New York, 1966, 123 pp., Tavard, *Holy Writ or Holy Church*, Harper, New York, 1959, 250 pp., Mackey, *The Modern Theology of Tradition*, Herder and Herder, New York, 1963, 219 pp., and Moran, *Scripture and Tradition*, Herder and Herder, New York, 1963, 127 pp., with a full bibliography. The Vatican Council declaration *On Revelation* is in Abbott, *op. cit.*, pp. 107–32. The fullest treatment is Congar, *Tradition and Traditions*, Macmillan, New York, 1967, 536 pp.

From a Protestant perspective cf. Outler, *The Christian Tradition and the*

ments of papacy and Mariology to some degree hinge on how Scripture and tradition are related, since in each case Scripture is used as an authority, but in each case also tradition is employed to complete what cannot be discovered in Scripture alone.

The latter phrase focuses the problem. At the time of the Reformation, the Protestants, feeling that the traditions of the medieval church had corrupted the original Biblical gospel, opted not for Scripture and tradition but for Scripture alone (*sola Scriptura*). The Council of Trent, on the other hand, reacting against the Protestant reaction, strongly affirmed the authority of Scripture *and* tradition, a position later interpreted as asserting that the gospel was found *partly* in Scripture and *partly* in tradition, so that there were "two sources," parallel to one another and partially independent of one another. These were the polemical terms on which Protestantism and Catholicism faced one another for several centuries.

Neither side, however, could finally accept this as a permanent arrangement. Roman Catholicism, despite the setbacks suffered in the "Modernist controversy" of the early twentieth century, has come to terms with a textual-critical understanding of Scripture and a whole new understanding of the centrality and even the "sufficiency" (as Fr. Josef Geiselmann has called it) of Holy Scripture. We have seen how the Vatican Council decisively rejected the "two

---

Unity We Seek, Oxford, New York, 1957, 165 pp., Thurian, Visible Unity and Tradition, Helicon, Baltimore, 1962, 136 pp. Cullmann's essay, "The Tradition" in Cullmann, The Early Church, Westminster, Philadelphia, 1956, pp. 59–99, has been widely commented upon in Catholic circles. Faith and Order reflections on the problem are found in Minear, ed., The Old and the New in the Church, Augsburg, Minneapolis, 1961, the section on "Tradition and Traditions," pp. 12–51, Minear, ed., Faith and Order Findings, Augsburg, Minneapolis, 1963, Faith and Order Paper No. 40, 63 pp., and the report "Scripture, Tradition and Traditions" in Rodger and Vischer, eds., The Fourth World Conference on Faith and Order, Association Press, New York, 1964, pp. 50–61.

sources" theory of revelation,[30] and in the promulgated document *On Divine Revelation* made clear that the basic revelation is Jesus Christ himself—a revelation that is handed on (i.e., "traditioned") through preaching, commitment to writing, and faithful exposition of that writing.

"Hence there exists a close connection and communication between sacred tradition and sacred Scripture. For both of them, flowing from the same divine wellspring, in a certain way merge into a unity and tend toward the same end."[31] Scripture and tradition, then, have a common source, God's action in Jesus Christ, but both are needed for the full explication of the Gospel of Jesus Christ:

"Consequently it is not from sacred Scripture alone that the Church draws her certainty about everything which has been revealed. Therefore both sacred tradition and sacred scripture are to be accepted and venerated with the same sense of devotion and reverence."[32] The two thus "form one sacred deposit of the word of God" who is Jesus Christ.[33]

If, to oversimplify, we may say that Catholicism, having long emphasized tradition, has rediscovered Scripture, we may likewise say that Protestantism, having long emphasized Scripture (and "Scripture alone"), has rediscovered tradition, and that each side has thus moved closer to the other.[34]

In a rather complex statement the 1963 Montreal conference on Faith and Order distinguished between *Tradition* (always with a capital "T") which is the Gospel itself, Christ

---

[30] Cf. Ch. 9 and 10 above.

[31] *On Divine Revelation*, Art. 9, Abbott, p. 117.

[32] *Ibid.*, Art. 9, Abbott, p. 117.

[33] *Ibid.*, Art. 10, Abbott, p. 117. For more extended commentary on the full text of the constitution, cf. Baum, "The Doctrine on Revelation at Vatican II," *The Ecumenist*, January-February 1966, pp. 24–26, "The Dogmatic Constitution on Revelation," *Herder Correspondence*, February 1966, pp. 40–44, and, most fully, Tavard, "Commentary on *De Revelatione*," *Journal of Ecumenical Studies*, Winter 1966, pp. 1–35.

[34] During the 1963 Montreal conference on Faith and Order, it was at one point seriously suggested that the term *sola traditione* be introduced into the report to describe the emerging consensus.

present in the life of the church, *tradition* (lower case "t") which is the process of "handing on" the Gospel, and *traditions* (plural) which can be understood both as (a) the diversity of forms of expression and as (b) confessional traditions such as the Lutheran or Reformed tradition. The basic premise of the report is as follows:

"Our starting-point is that we are all living in a tradition which goes back to our Lord and has its roots in the Old Testament, and we are all indebted to that tradition inasmuch as we have received the revealed truth, the Gospel, through its being transmitted from one generation to another. Thus we can say that we exist as Christians by the Tradition of the Gospel (the *paradosis* of the *kerygma*) testified in Scripture, transmitted in and by the Church through the power of the Holy Spirit. Tradition taken in this sense is actualized in the preaching of the Word, in the administration of the Sacraments and worship, in Christian teaching and theology, and in mission and witness to Christ by the lives of the members of the Church."[35]

The Tradition, thus understood and handed on, is embodied in traditions (in both sense *a* and *b* above), and it is imperative to distinguish between Tradition and traditions. The Tradition in its written form was soon embodied in Holy Scripture, but since Scripture always needs to be interpreted afresh, the crucial question becomes that of the "right" interpretation of Scripture, or, in more formal terms, the search for a "hermeneutical principle."[36] So the question is posed:

"How can we reach an adequate interpretation of the Scriptures, so that the Word of God addresses us and Scrip-

[35] Rodger and Vischer, eds., *op. cit.*, para. 45, pp. 51–52.
[36] The report suggests six criteria for the interpretation of Scripture: (a) Scripture as a whole, (b) the isolation of a central interpretive theme from Scripture such as justification by faith, (c) the individual conscience under the guidance of the Holy Spirit, (d) the discernment of the mind of the church on the matter (Orthodoxy), (e) the discernment of the deposit of faith bequeathed to the church's teaching authority (Roman Catholicism), (f) appeal to creeds and confessional statements. Cf. *op. cit.*, p. 53.

ture is safeguarded from subjective or arbitrary exegesis?"[37]

We need not pursue the Montreal report further to establish the point that Protestant thinking has moved far beyond any conventional view of *sola Scriptura* and has discovered that the problem is not Scripture versus tradition, but rather the proper relationship between the two.

Catholic-Protestant accord has not been reached on this doctrinal question, but accord is closer than it has been for four centuries. Catholic and Protestant scholars, taking the Vatican Council constitution *On Revelation* in one hand and the Montreal report on "Scripture, Tradition and Traditions" in the other,[38] can begin to work together on the problem, and it is possible that illumination may be granted to their corporate efforts where only irritation ensued from their separate ones.

The extension of the dialogue—a foreshadowing

The dialogue as thus far described is an intramural Christian affair. It is appropriate that there should be such give-and-take within the walls. But the contemporary world situation does not permit such dialogue to be an end in itself, nor does the gospel about which the dialogue is presumably talking. Those who confine themselves to this sort of talk can rightly be accused of evading the world outside, and of retreating into a ghetto to deal with private matters.

The Christian community is becoming aware of this danger. Before the council Pope John created the Secretariat for the Promotion of Christian Unity. But during the course of the council two new secretariats were created, the Secretariat for Christianity and the Non-Christian Religions, to enable the church to enter into dialogue with Buddhists, Hindus,

[37] Rodger and Vischer, eds., *op. cit.*, para. 55, p. 54.
[38] Cf. the comment of Max Thurian, present at Montreal and also a Protestant observer at Vatican II, of the high degree of convergence between the two documents (*Herder Correspondence*, February 1966, pp. 43–44).

Mohammedans, and Jews, and the Secretariat for Non-Believers, to foster dialogue with those who are not part of any formal "religion," the particular thrust here being a desire to enter into discussion with Marxists.[39]

In the future, both of these directions of further dialogue must be pursued with as much zeal as the present generation has pursued the intramural dialogue just described, and it is to the beginnings of this wider "dialogue with the world," expressed in action quite as much as word, that we now turn.

[39] The beginnings of this outreach are evidenced in Metz, ed., *Is God Dead?* Concilium series, Vol. 16, Paulist Press, Glen Rock, 1966, 191 pp., the theme of which is described in the preface as "Christian faith confronts contemporary atheism." Avoiding the *cul-de-sac* of the "death-of-God theology," the volume centers its attention on Marx and Freud. From the other side, cf. Garaudy, *From Anathema to Dialogue, A Marxist Challenge to the Christian Churches*, Herder and Herder, New York, 1966, 124 pp. Bibliography on the Marxist-Christian dialogue is contained in *op. cit.*, pp. 3–4.

CHAPTER 16

THE CONSOLIDATION OF COMMON ACTION

[Churches should] act together in all matters except those in which deep differences of conviction compel them to act separately . . .

> Lund report, cited in *The Third World Conference on Faith and Order*, p. 16.

Cooperation among all Christians . . . should be ever increasingly developed.

> Vatican Council decree *On Ecumenism*, Art. 12.

Ecumenical dialogue always runs the danger of becoming ingrown. It can become a precious, if not precocious, activity for those who "like that sort of thing," and it can sometimes isolate Christians from the world rather than immersing them more deeply in it. The danger has been noted from both the Protestant and the Catholic side.

Dr. James I. McCord, president of Princeton Theological Seminary, warns:

"This new Christian community must avoid the danger of becoming another ghetto or sectarian society, thus denying its catholicity. The ecumenical dialogue can advance only when, instead of being a dialogue between two or more ghetto-like ideologies, it is also a dialogue with the modern world. This poses quite a different challenge than merely a dialogue of Christian denominations with one another."[1]

[1] Cited in Bureau of Information, National Catholic Welfare Conference, Washington.

Fr. Avery Dulles, s.j., offers a similar diagnosis:

"Ecumenism has become too exclusively taken up with religious questions—with matters of doctrine and worship. . . . From many quarters therefore one hears the call for a new ecumenism—one less committed to historical theological controversies and more in touch with contemporary secular man; one less turned in upon itself, more open to the world and its concerns. The greatest decisions affecting man's future are being made in the sphere of the secular; and Christianity does not seem to be there."[2]

Fr. Dulles goes on to plead for a "secular" ecumenism that concentrates on the immediate and pressing needs of man, feeling that pragmatic American Christians may be the ones best equipped to initiate it. *America* Magazine likewise notes that the shift from more traditional ecumenical questions to questions of secularity "may well be what is needed to keep ecumenism from turning in upon itself in sterile self-scrutiny."[3]

We can examine this outward thrust of ecumenical activity as it is expressed both through joint Protestant-Catholic *activity in* the world, and through a new *approach to* the world.

Common activity in the world

Many Catholics and Protestants have found that, in the midst of whatever things divide them doctrinally, they share a broad enough base of common civic concern to be able to make common cause on picket lines, at fair-housing commis-

---

[2] From a sermon delivered during the Christian Unity Octave, 1966, cited in *Convergence* (a publication of the Gustave Weigel Society), Vol. I, No. 1, May 1966, pp. 4–5.

[3] "Ecumenism and Secularity," *America*, January 15, 1966, p. 66. Cf. also the important article by van den Heuvel, "Crisis in the Ecumenical Movement," *Christianity and Crisis*, April 4, 1966, pp. 59–63, and "Toward a Secular Understanding of the Ecumenical?" in van den Heuvel, *The Humiliation of the Church*, Westminster Press, Philadelphia, 1966, pp. 92–117.

sion hearings, or in battles for slum clearance. They may disagree, for example, about the dogma of the Assumption of
the Virgin into Heaven, but they do not disagree about the
dogma that all men are made in the image of God and that
differences of race, class, and skin color are thereby rendered
irrelevant—one dogma even Protestants might be willing to
accept as "irreformable." Thus at many points within the
common life of man today Catholics and Protestants already engage in common action. In giving this tangible expression of their faith they are doing nothing more than
taking seriously the convictions voiced both by the World
Council and the Vatican Council, as cited at the beginning
of the present chapter. The Vatican Council decree *On Ecumenism* spells out the matter in gratifying detail:

"Cooperation among all Christians vividly expresses that
bond which already unites them, and it sets in clearer relief
the features of Christ the Servant. Such cooperation, which
has already begun in many countries, should be ever increasingly developed, particularly in regions where a social and
technological evolution is taking place. . . . Christians
should also work together in the use of every possible means
to relieve the afflictions of our times, such as famine and
natural disaster, illiteracy and poverty, lack of housing, and
the unequal distribution of wealth."[4]

It is significant that this theme of common co-operation
also achieved prominence in the decree *On the Missionary
Activity of the Church*. After some introductory words about
the dangers of indifferentism, the decree states of Catholics
and the "separated brethren":

"To the extent that their beliefs are common, they can
make before the nations a common profession of faith in
God and in Jesus Christ. They can collaborate in social and
in technical projects as well as in cultural and religious ones.
. . . This cooperation should be undertaken not only among

---

[4] *On Ecumenism*, Art. 12, Abbott, pp. 354-55.

private persons, but also, according to the judgment of the local Ordinary, among Churches or ecclesial Communities and their enterprises."[5]

But what is true on the "mission field" is now true everywhere in the so-called post-Christian era since the whole world is once again a mission field. If Catholics and Protestants may share common facilities in Tanzania, they must also share them in Kansas City—as they are indeed planning to do in a new building to be used by the United Church of Christ and the Episcopal, Roman Catholic, and Presbyterian churches of that community.[6] If Catholic and Protestant missionaries may produce a joint translation of the New Testament in the Dutch East Indies, it must also be possible for Catholics and Protestants in Britain and America to use the same English translation of the Bible—as they are now able to do thanks to Catholic willingness to authorize the Revised Standard translation (produced by Protestant scholars) for Catholic use.

But such activities, while they represent common ventures for the sake of the world, are only the background for what is becoming an increasing measure of common activity in the world. Out of scores of possible examples, three can illustrate the point.

A symbol—but in retrospect little more than that—of the new degree of shared participation is the experience of 1964 in Selma, Alabama. There, during two crowded, tumultuous, and frightening weeks, 6000 Catholic priests, nuns, Protestant ministers, and Jewish rabbis joined in protests against injustices being inflicted on the Negro citizens of Alabama. In marches, picketing, demonstrations, and a variety of other

[5] *On the Missionary Activity of the Church*, Art. 15, Abbott, pp. 602–3, cf. also Art. 20, Abbott, p. 620.

[6] Cf. *Time* Magazine, July 22, 1966, p. 65, and the *National Catholic Reporter*, July 13, 1966, p. 1. A similar venture is underway in Jerramungap, Australia, with a building to be shared by Anglicans, Roman Catholics, and Presbyterians.

forms of public protest, the American religious community found itself united as almost never before. The interesting thing to those at Selma was that the lines of unity on the civic front did not necessarily coincide with the lines of unity on the theological front. When a Roman Catholic bishop in Alabama told the nuns to leave Selma and go back home "to do God's work," representatives of *all* faiths were aghast. When an Episcopalian bishop in Alabama made virtually the same request of out-of-state Episcopal priests, Catholics and Jews as well as Protestants rallied in their defense. To see an African Methodist Episcopal Zion minister holding hands with a nun and a rabbi as all of them sang "We Shall Overcome" in a Baptist church was to feel closer to the Kingdom of God than is usually the case at an ecumenical conference. Negro minister, nun, and rabbi surely disagreed about many things, but at the point of common action on behalf of the dispossessed, they were *one*.

A similar instance of ecumenical co-operation occurred in California during the 1964 campaign, when a "Proposition 14" was placed on the state ballot by the real estate lobby, which not only proposed to wipe all existing fair-housing legislation off the books but also to make unconstitutional any fair-housing legislation in the future. Save for the thundering silence of the cardinal-archbishop of Los Angeles, the Catholic bishops of California spoke out unequivocally against the proposition, and with virtual unanimity Protestant and Jewish leaders took a similar stand against a measure that proposed to legalize housing discrimination and encourage bigotry. In town after town, priest-minister-rabbi panels spoke against the proposition. Advertisements opposing the proposition were signed by rabbis, priests, ministers, Catholic and Protestant seminarians, Catholic, Protestant, and Jewish lay groups, all making common cause in a signal instance of "secular" ecumenism, perhaps the only occasion in American history where the religious community has been virtually united on a political issue.[7]

More recently, many California clergy have found themselves again joined together on the "secular" front, supporting the striking grape-pickers of the San Joaquin Valley in their attempt (a) to achieve union recognition by the growers in order to bargain collectively, and (b) to gain a minimum wage. Priests, ministers, and rabbis have found themselves on picket lines, organizing food and clothing brigades, lobbying in Sacramento, participating in a 300-mile protest march to the state capitol, going to jail, and in other ways making common cause with the victims of economic injustice in their struggle to achieve human dignity.[8]

Examples could be multiplied of ways in which churchmen are beginning to engage in the struggle for social justice and are finding that from the beginning the venture must be ecumenical. The issues, to be sure, are controversial, and other churchmen often disagree with the very premise that the church should engage in such activity. But it is clear that an important corner has been turned by large segments of the Protestant and Catholic communities, who, when they march together, sometimes feel closer to one another than they do to the uninvolved members of their respective communities back home. Their premise is that they must not simply talk about love from the pulpit, but must incarnate it in the streets, by public alignment with the victims of injustice, whether in Birmingham or Chicago, Jackson or Delano.

This sort of "practical ecumenism" is only in its first stages. Those who deplore it must brace themselves for the fact that there is more to come. Those who participate in it must re-

[7] It is a discouraging commentary on the impact of the *united* religious voices of the state that the proposition carried by over two to one. A later decision of the California Supreme Court, however, ruled that the proposition itself was unconstitutional.

[8] Cf. the forthcoming volume by A. V. Krebs, Jr., *Delano: Beginning of a Revolution*, for the full story of the strike and the church's involvement.

joice that the "thrust into the world" has a kind of irreversible momentum attached to it, and that the ties forged between those who seek to express divine love through the struggle for human justice are deep ties indeed and may form the basis out of which other ties will be forged. If Martin Luther started a revolution in the sixteenth century that drove Catholics and Protestants apart, Martin Luther King has started a revolution in the twentieth century that is drawing them back together again.[9]

A new approach to the world

What are the foundations of this new ecumenical alliance that is emerging? Without attempting to develop a theology of ecumenical involvement—a task to which some of the experts should turn their attention—we can note certain threads emerging out of Catholic and Protestant reflection that are gradually being woven together into a fabric of social involvement.

The *dominant* thread is a new affirmation of the secular order as good in and of itself, since it is the handiwork of the Creator, the scene of the Creator's visitation in Jesus Christ, and the arena of his ongoing, redeeming activity through the Holy Spirit. The goodness of creation, even though creation is marred by man's sinful abuse of it, means that the Christian must affirm, rather than deny or ignore, that which God himself affirmed as "very good." This emphasis is nothing new in Christian thought, but rather the recovery of something old that was long submerged by Christian attacks on the world and the flesh as the abode of the devil. There are

[9] The common flaw in the examples cited above is that they represent primarily clergy activity. This is unfair to the heavy investment of time and risk that many laymen have made, but it is perhaps significant of a failure to take with radical enough seriousness "the priesthood of all believers" that church involvement is still measured basically by the number of clerical collars and nuns' habits in evidence.

dangers, of course, in an over-optimistic world affirmation as a reaction to over-pessimistic world negation, but the ongoing theological debate continues to point these dangers out.[10]

A *second* thread is a rediscovery of the imagery of Christ the Servant, and a recognition that those who call themselves his followers, and belong to an institution they describe as his "body," are themselves committed to embracing the role of servant and must seek to serve the world as he did, including a willingness to suffer alongside him when occasion demands. They recognize that the Gospel offers no assurances of success in this venture, any more than "success" crowned the efforts of the one who was executed on a cross, but that the role of the servant church is the role to which the church is called today.[11]

A *third* thread is a recognition that "Christendom" is no longer a useful or descriptive term, and that Christians live in a world no longer dominated by Christian institutions or ideas. Christians are now a tiny minority and they must accept this status gracefully, rather than bending their efforts toward the reconquest of lost territories. Rather than "making society Christian," their role will be to work through the secular structures of society, entering into alliances with all sorts and conditions of men, with whom they may initially

[10] The pivotal work in this area is Cox, *The Secular City*, Macmillan, New York, 1965, 276 pp., which has reshaped the entire discussion. This book, by a Baptist, has received careful and, on the whole affirmative, attention from the Catholic world. Cf. the comments by Fr. Andrew Greeley, Daniel Callahan, and Michael Novak, in Callahan, ed., *The Secular City Debate*, Macmillan, New York, 1966, Part III, pp. 91–126.

There is an interesting parallel to many of Cox's themes in the essay by Fr. Schillebeeckx, "The Church and Mankind," in Schillebeeckx, ed., *The Church and Mankind*, Concilium series, Vol. I, Paulist Press, Glen Rock, 1964, pp. 69–101. The most authoritative Catholic resource for the new affirmation of the secular is, of course, the Vatican Council constitution, *The Church and the World Today*, discussed below.

[11] For an expansion of this theme, cf. Mudge, *In His Service: The Servant Lord and His Servant People*, Westminster, Philadelphia, 1959, 176 pp., and many of the speeches given at Vatican II, particularly by the South American bishops.

share no more than a revulsion against injustice or a desire to see that children do not starve. They will recognize their minority status as calling for new tactics and will think of themselves as in "diaspora," scattered through the world, and therefore called upon to live out their existence before God in the world.[12]

A *fourth* thread is the recognition that the church is living in a time of revolution that makes vigorous pleas for men's hearts and souls and is willing to employ extreme measures to win the necessary allegiance.[13]

In the process of weaving these and other strands together, Christians will find out many new things about themselves and about their world, but with whatever further insights emerge as the threads are interwoven, we can anticipate a pattern in which the goodness of the secular order will be clearly discernible as the realm in which the Christian must serve, alongside all men of good will, with a holy impatience and a restless urge to better the human situation of all men everywhere.[14]

New Delhi, Rome, and Geneva: a convergence

These insights have gradually been consolidated on a world-wide scale. All of the assemblies of the World Council

[12] The theme of Christians living in "diaspora" has been developed most fully by Karl Rahner, in *The Christian Commitment*, Sheed and Ward, New York, 1963, esp. pp. 3–37. Cf. also Neill, *The Unfinished Task*, Lutterworth, London, 1957, 228 pp., Hans-Reudi Weber, in West and Paton, *The Missionary Church in East and West*, S.C.M. Press, London, 1959, pp. 101–16, and M. Richard Shaull, "The Form of the Church in the Modern Diaspora," in Marty and Peerman, eds., *New Theology No. 2*, Macmillan, New York, 1965, pp. 264–87.

[13] This theme will be more fully developed in comments below about the Geneva 1966 conference.

[14] For further comments on the whole theme of the church's involvement in the world, cf. Gremillion, *The Other Dialogue*, Doubleday, New York, 1965, 308 pp., and Auer, *et al*, *The Christian and the World* (compiled at the Canisianum, Innsbruck), Kenedy, New York, 1965, 229 pp.

have spoken to them, and many are focused in the New Delhi report on "Service."[15]

What is distinctive about "Christian service"? The concern of the Christian for the world springs from his acknowledgment of God's concern for the world and all men in it, so that Christian service "is a response to the God who first loved us." Christians must therefore take on the role of "servants of the Servant-Lord."[16] From this presupposition, the report deals specifically with a number of crucial areas, including rapid technological change (para. 5–28), the responsible society—freedom, order, and power (para. 29–39), racial and ethnic tensions (para. 40–50), the churches' involvement in world affairs and world order (para. 51–65), and the service of the church in a divided world (para. 66–90). An attempt is made throughout the report to relate these diverse areas to the Christian's call to serve in and for the world, under the overarching insight, "The more we are drawn to Christ, the more we are constrained to serve the world."[17]

Certain emphases in the more recent Vatican Council pastoral constitution, *The Church and the World Today*, represent a real breakthrough in Roman Catholic efforts to develop an ecumenism of action.[18] A symbol of the breakthrough is that this is one of two council documents (the other being the declaration on *Religious Freedom*) addressed "not only to the sons of the Church and to all who invoke the name of Christ, but to the whole of humanity."[19] The church is not seeking to carry on an interior monologue *about* the world, but to initiate an exterior dialogue *with* the world. The following are noteworthy emphases in the document:

[15] Cf. 't Hooft, ed., *The New Delhi Report*, pp. 93–115.

[16] *Ibid.*, p. 93.

[17] *Ibid.*, p. 111. Cf. the similar conclusion of Teilhard de Chardin: "In the name of our faith, we have the right and duty to become passionate about the things of the earth" (cited in Auer, *et al*, *op. cit.*, p. vii).

[18] The paragraphs that follow condense part of my analysis of this document in Abbott, ed., *op. cit.*, pp. 309–16.

[19] *The Church and the World Today*, Art. 2, Abbott, p. 200.

1. A positive attitude toward "the world" is in evidence throughout. An earlier draft stated, "We should listen to the voice of God . . . in the voice of the times," and the promulgated version urges the importance "of scrutinizing the signs of the times and of interpreting them in the light of the gospel."[20] To Christians

"nothing genuinely human fails to raise an echo in their hearts. . . . Men are not deterred by the Christian message from building up the world or impelled to neglect the welfare of their fellows. They are, rather, more stringently bound to do these very things."[21]

Such a positive attitude means not only the necessity for Catholics to work together in such a world, but their further obligation to work with all Christians, and indeed with all men of good will everywhere. The periphery of those with whom the Christian is to engage in practical ecumenism is extended to include all mankind, even atheists.[22]

2. The image of the servant church in ministering to such a world is stressed:

"Inspired by no earthly ambition, the Church seeks but a solitary goal: to carry forward the work of Christ Himself under the lead of the befriending Spirit. And Christ entered this world to give witness to the truth, to rescue and not to sit in judgment, to serve and not to be served."[23]

The declaration realistically recognizes that the servant church has not always served the world well and has often

---

[20] *The Church and the World Today*, Art. 4, Abbott, pp. 201–2.

[21] *Ibid.*, Art. 4, 34, Abbott, pp. 200, 233.

[22] Cf. *ibid.*, Art. 21, Abbott, p. 219.

[23] *Ibid.*, Art. 3, Abbott, p. 201. Cf. the even more compelling statement of the theme in Pope Paul's opening allocution at the second session of the council:

"The Church looks at the world with profound understanding, with sincere admiration and with the sincere intention not of dominating it, but of serving it; not of despising it, but of appreciating it; not of condemning it, but of strengthening and saving it." (Cited in Küng, Congar, O'Hanlon, eds., *op. cit.,* p. 234.)

failed to reflect the selflessness of her master. For example, rather than attacking atheists for their disbelief, the document acknowledges that "believers themselves frequently bear some responsibility for this situation."[24] Since atheism often arises in reaction to deficiencies in the "religious, moral or social life" of believers, the latter "have more than a little to do with the birth of atheism."[25]

3. The document also emphasizes the importance of lay activity and involvement in the world. If the Vatican Council did not work through to a full theology of the laity, at least it made some important strides in that direction, and *The Church and the World Today* may give as much leverage for helping the layman "take on his own distinctive role"[26] as any other council document, since it is clear that in many specific and technical areas of modern life the church must first listen to the lay experts before it presumes to have an opinion.

4. Throughout the document, man *qua* man is understood in social rather than individualistic terms. He is not an individual who becomes social; he is a being whose individuality can be understood only in and through his social relations. "This social life," the document insists, "is not something added on to man." For this reason, "Man's social nature makes it evident that the progress of the human person and the advance of society itself hinge on each other."[27] The point has obvious corollaries in the field of "practical ecumenism," for it renders untenable any attempt to describe Christian ethical responsibility in purely individual terms (e.g., "religion and politics don't mix") and underscores the need for corporate human action on a large scale.

5. Part II of the document deals with specifics—marriage and the family, the development of culture, socio-economic

24 *Ibid.*, Art. 19, Abbott, p. 217.
25 *Ibid.*
26 *Ibid.*, Art. 43, Abbott, p. 244.
27 *Ibid.*, Art. 25, Abbott, p. 224.

life, the life of the political community, the fostering of peace, and the promotion of a community of nations. The best emphases of the earlier "social encyclicals" are incorporated into the chapter on "Economic and Social Life," for example, affirming the right of collective bargaining, of unionizing, of striking, and of the need for land reform in underdeveloped areas of the world.

In none of Part II has a last and definitive word been spoken (the section on birth control hedges, pending a decision by a papal commission, and the condemnation of modern war falls short of full condemnation), but a first and basic word has been spoken, and the doors are now open to a higher degree of involvement in the secular order than was previously clear in Catholic teaching. Henceforth, the burden of proof will be on the bishop who wishes to curtail Catholic activity in the secular order, rather than vice versa.

Hard on the heels of Vatican II came the 1966 World Council conference at Geneva on the theme of "Christians in the Technical and Social Revolutions of Our Time."[28] The Geneva conference stands historically in the stream of the "Life and Work" conferences of Stockholm 1925 and Oxford 1937[29] and builds on the intervening World Council assemblies, each of which gave considerable attention to the theme of the church and the world. A number of facts about

---

[28] The following reactions were written shortly after the conclusion of the conference, and before the full reports were available. Four significant preparatory volumes discussed the main themes of the conference: Bennett, ed., *Christian Social Ethics in a Changing World*, 381 pp.; Matthews, ed., *Responsible Government in a Revolutionary Age*, 381 pp.; Munby, ed., *Economic Growth in World Perspective*, 380 pp.; and de Vries, ed., *Man in Community*, 382 pp., all published by Association Press, New York, 1966. The main addresses presented at the conference are printed in *The Ecumenical Review*, October 1966, pp. 417–63. All documents are now available in *The Official Report of the World Conference on Church and Society*, World Council of Churches, Geneva, 1967, 230 pp. Cf. also the report by J. Brooke Moseley, *Christians in the Technical and Social Revolutions of Our Time*, Forward Movement Publications, Cincinnati, 1966, 141 pp.

[29] Cf. further Ch. 2 above for a discussion of these.

the Geneva conference, however, render it particularly significant:

1. The make-up of the conference was unique in World Council history. For example there were many more laymen than professional theologians—the actual head count being 237 to 173, as was surely appropriate in the light of the theme. Furthermore, nearly half of the representatives were from the so-called "developing nations," or "third world," phrases the representatives in question disliked, and this ensured that the conclusions of the conference would not be dominated by Europeans and North Americans, as had been true of previous conferences. (At Oxford 1937, delegates not from Europe or North America were simply lumped together as "other participants.")

2. The conference was more broadly ecumenical than previous ones. Not only were the Russian Orthodox actively represented, but eight officially designated Roman Catholic observers and three "specially invited guests" took an active part in the meetings. Canon Charles Moeller and Lady Jackson (Barbara Ward) both read papers. The caliber of the Catholic participants was exceptionally high, including, in addition to Canon Moeller and Barbara Ward, such experts in the field of "the church and the world today" as Fr. Edward Duff, s.j.,[30] Professor Michael Fogarty, a British economist, Msgr. Joseph Gremillion of Catholic Relief Services, Canon François Houtart of Louvain, and Fr. Thomas Stransky, c.s.p., of the Secretariat for Christian Unity. Since Msgr. Gremillion and Canons Moeller and Houtart had been directly involved in the preparation of the Vatican Council declaration on *The Church and the World Today*, their presence was particularly significant.

3. The conference was able to take for granted that the place of the church is on the cutting edge of the major secular

---

[30] Author of the ecumenically pioneering volume *The Social Thought of the World Council of Churches*, Association Press, New York, 1956, 339 pp.

movements of the contemporary world. Many delegates commented on how refreshing it was not to have to establish the "right" of the church to immerse itself deeply in the movements of the day. While this mood has certainly not made its way down to the so-called grassroots of the constituent member churches of the World Council, it is clear that among all the top responsible leadership the battle for church involvement has been won.

4. The theme of Christian involvement in revolution received its most important airing to date. The conference took seriously the mandate given to it by M. M. Thomas, chairman of the Planning Committee:

"Since the last conference on Church and Society (1937) the world has gone through many revolutions. The most fundamental are those which have resulted from the strides made in nuclear science and technology, and the awakening of new classes, peoples, and races to a sense of dignity and historical mission in the world. These have called in question traditional concepts of social and international justice; and men are building new societies with new techniques upon new moral and spiritual foundations. The Church has to rethink its own understanding of the material and human realities of the contemporary world, and define afresh its own responsibility in relation to them."[31]

For the first time, serious attention was given to the possibility of Christian participation in *violent* revolution, and the conference, while clearly not "advocating violence," made clear that the use of violence in unseating unjust regimes could not be ruled out *a priori*. As a delegate from South America said, "In my country, 200 children die every day of malnutrition. This is a sin of violence, and it will go on until we change the structures of power."[32]

In its treatment of revolution, the conference refrained

---

[31] Cited in the preliminary pamphlet, "World Conference on Church and Society 1966," published by the World Council of Churches, Geneva, 1966.
[32] Cited in Cox, "Geneva 1966," *The Commonweal*, p. 526.

from any attempt to "condemn communism," thus underlining the wisdom of Vatican II in its similar rejection of such proposals. The discussion at Geneva made clear that Christians can live and work within a variety of economic and political regimes, and that there is no basis for assuming that a form of "Christian presence" cannot be practiced under the hammer and sickle. Participation in any form of society, however, must always be "critical participation."

5. The real dichotomy, then, that emerged at Geneva was not between members of the communist and non-communist worlds, but between the inhabitants of what Barbara Ward has termed "the rich nations and the poor nations."[33] The resentment of the latter against the former was openly expressed, and the white delegates in general and the American delegates in particular found themselves subject to a barrage of criticism that shook them to their roots. Harold Fey reported:

"The conference profoundly shocked most Americans, including this reporter. We were not prepared to hear American foreign policy in its entirety, including that in Vietnam, almost universally condemned. We were even less prepared to hear what we call 'foreign aid' characterized as altogether self-serving, often more of a handicap than a help and something which the recipients were planning to do without anyway."[34]

It may be, however, that shock treatment of the kind experienced at Geneva is the only therapy sufficiently drastic to shake America into an awareness of its increasing unpopularity in the community of nations. Robert Theobald went so far as to suggest that unless the privileged nations rapidly face up to the challenges thrust upon them by the conference, it may be that the last real encounter between the rich

[33] Cf. Ward, *The Rich Nations and the Poor Nations*, Norton, New York, 1962, 159 pp.

[34] *The Christian Century*, August 10, 1966, p. 979.

white nations and the poor colored nations has already taken place. White insensitivity must be challenged at every point: "It would be wrong," as one of the reports put it, "for every North American child to have an electric toothbrush before every Latin American child has a daily bottle of milk."

In a closing press conference, Visser 't Hooft mentioned three achievements of the conference: (a) a frank ideological encounter in which Christians with radically different perspectives were nevertheless "able to hold to each other," (b) the "terrific pedagogical experience" of all the participants, and (c) the production of some documents that could have a real impact on the churches as the latter continue to grapple with the theme of "Christians in the Technical and Social Revolutions of Our Time."[35]

The spirit of the conference was epitomized by the comment of Eugene Carson Blake, successor to Visser 't Hooft as general-secretary of the World Council:

"The Church must act, take a stand, and march with those in the society who cannot alone win their battle for justice, freedom and equality. This is a risk. It results always in controversy . . . I am convinced that the putting of one's body in the right place and at the right time is often the only way that a Christian can help his Church to be part of the transformation of society."[36]

The "meaning" of Geneva cannot yet be fully determined, any more than the "meaning" of the Vatican Council can be. But it is already clear that at "Geneva 1966" a dramatic corner was turned in the life of the World Council of Churches, just as was done by Vatican II's constitution on *The Church and the World Today*, and that these two events, as they become assimilated into the life of the contemporary church,

---

[35] Harold Fey commented on the documents that "on the whole they represent a higher quality of thinking on subjects of wider human interest than anything yet published by the World Council." (*The Christian Century*, August 10, 1966, p. 978.)

[36] Blake, "How the Church Contributes to the Transformation of Society," *The Ecumenical Review*, October 1966, pp. 462–63.

both Catholic and Protestant, may do more to thrust Christians into a responsible role in society, and thrust them there *together*, than all the formal dialogue that has taken place over the past decade.

Traffic on a two-way street

But since formal dialogue is one of the things that made possible the ecumenical consensus represented by *The Church and the World Today* and "Geneva 1966," we must emphasize in conclusion that traffic on this street proceeds in both directions. Whether one starts with "dialogue" or with "action," one is led inescapably to the other. If Catholics and Protestants get together to plot strategy on a fair-housing bill, they will sooner or later find themselves discussing the doctrine of man that lies behind such concern—in which case they will be moving from action to dialogue. But if they get together to discuss the theology of the church, they will sooner or later find themselves called upon to implement their theology of the church by giving expression to it in common civic action—in which case they will be moving from dialogue to action. Practically, then, it does not matter too much from which end of the street one starts.[37]

But the story is not yet complete. As Christians confront one another, either in dialogue or in action, they find something else drawing them together and making it imperative that they give common witness. This is their common recognition that efforts at dialogue and action are sustained and empowered by the life of prayer and worship. So the specifics of ecumenical outreach today have not been fully explored until Protestants and Catholics have begun to seek for ways to intensify a life of common worship.

[37] There is a clear analogy in the pre-World Council experience of "Faith and Order" and "Life and Work." Each group discovered that it was led inescapably to an examination of the concerns of the other. Cf. further Ch. 2 above.

CHAPTER 17

THE INTENSIFICATION OF COMMON WORSHIP

> Unless we learn to know one another precisely in the celebration of worship, which nourishes our thought in our everyday life, it will be impossible to discover the values we share in our disagreements.
>
> A letter from the Dutch bishops, issued in 1962.

> Nowhere are the divisions of our churches more clearly evident and painful than at the Lord's Table.
>
> The report on "Unity," in *The New Delhi Report*, p. 120.

The triadic concern of "worship, study, and action" is an old staple of Protestant church life. The order of the first two might occasionally vary, but action always came third. In Protestant-Catholic relations, however, it is worship that always comes third. Dialogue and action involve traffic on a two-way street, as we have seen, but it is usually late in the day before those in the stream of traffic have felt confident enough to broach the subject of common worship. When they have done so, they have usually discovered that the topic was "too controversial" to be pursued.

In recent years, however, both Catholics and Protestants have discovered that those who share a common faith in Christ cannot be content to express that faith solely by talking together or acting together; they must also express it by worshiping together. Sharing so much in other arenas of life, they find themselves unwilling to terminate that sharing at the point where it should be deepest and most real, in their common adoration of the God who is Father of all.

We are thus in a time of transition within the ecumenical situation, moving from a time when common worship was not only discouraged but forbidden, into a time when certain limited expression of common worship is being permitted, and looking toward a situation about which we can only say that those who have experienced a degree of common worship with their separated brethren are not going to be satisfied with less, but are going to demand more.

The lessening of Roman Catholic reluctance

Until very recently in almost all Catholic circles, *communicatio in sacris* (the sharing of things sacred, referring particularly to liturgical sharing) was simply a description of something forbidden in specific terms by canon law, so that the question was not even an open one.[1] The tones used to speak of the possibility of liturgical sharing were tones of horror.[2]

As ecumenical contacts began to develop between Roman Catholics and other Christians, dialogue groups began to form, and (often growing out of them) certain kinds of common action were initiated. But the area of *communicatio in sacris* remained walled off. After occasional groups had begun trying to scale the wall, the Holy Office issued a *monitum*, or warning, on June 5, 1948, reminding Catholics that they could not even participate in inter-confessional discussions without explicit permission from Rome, and that even when such permission was granted it did not extend to include services of common worship.[3] This was a stern dash of cold

[1] The specific canons of prohibition are Canons 1325, para. 3; 1258, para. 1, 2; and 731, para. 2.

[2] Cf. the description by Fr. Abbott in Abbott, ed., *op. cit.*, p. 352.

[3] On events leading to the *monitum*, cf. Swidler, *The Ecumenical Vanguard*, Duquesne University Press, Pittsburgh, 1966, pp. 183–94 and 207–

water in the face of ecumenical contacts that had been developing in postwar Europe, even though it did not represent a new ruling, but was simply a reminder of the relevant provisions of existing canon law.

The *monitum* appeared shortly before the Amsterdam assembly inaugurating the World Council of Churches. Shortly after Amsterdam, and in response to it, an important *Instruction* of the Holy Office was issued.[4] The *Instruction* reiterated the ban on *communicatio in sacris*, but did permit ecumenical gatherings to begin and end with a joint recitation of the Lord's Prayer, or other prayers acceptable to the Roman Catholic Church. This was a modest gain, but a gain nevertheless.

A development on another level has been the regularization of the Christian Unity Octave, a period of eight days of prayer for unity every January. The idea was first developed by two Anglo-Catholics, the Rev. Spencer Jones and the Rev. Thomas Wattson, who worked out a series of corporate prayers for unity. Wattson became a Roman Catholic, and the idea of such prayers commended itself to Pius X, who gave it papal approval in 1909, while Benedict XV made the Octave an official part of the Catholic liturgical year in 1916. The prayers were unambiguously couched in the language of "return"—Catholics were to pray for the return to Rome of the "other sheep" who had gone astray.

It was clear, of course, that the "other sheep" could not participate in such prayers, however eager they might be to pray for Christian unity. In a notable article on "The Psychology of the Prayers of the Octave," Abbé Couturier proposed in 1935 that the Octave be reconceived as a time of the convergence of the prayers of *all* Christian confessions, and

---

15. Latin texts of the *monitum* and the canons under discussion are also available, pp. 273–75.

[4] The *Instruction* was dated December 20, 1949, although it was not publicly issued until March 1, 1950. Attention has been called to the *Instruction* in Ch. 3 above.

that the nature of the prayers be altered so as to be prayers not for "return" but for the unity that Christ wills, through the means that he chooses. On these terms, it became possible for other Christian churches to join in such prayers during the Octave, and what has since come to be called the Week of Prayer for Christian Unity has developed.[5]

The Week of Prayer has been sponsored by the World Council of Churches and each year the Faith and Order Commission distributes special materials so that Protestants, Catholics, and Orthodox can offer similar prayers to God "that all may be one." While the groups originally prayed separately, it gradually became clear that those who pray *for* one another must finally pray *with* one another, so that in recent years joint services of prayer and worship have been held in many parts of the world.[6]

Both the increasing involvement in dialogue groups and wider participation in the Week of Prayer for Christian Unity have spurred interest in the possibility of a wider sharing of common worship. To speak to the problems raised by this new situation, the Dutch bishops issued an important document in 1962 on "The Limits and the Possibilities of Joint Worship of Catholics and Protestants."[7] It seemed clear in 1962 that to take part in "official liturgical celebrations" of another church would be identical with embracing the faith of the church in question. Such action, particularly if communion was involved, was clearly not possible, for it would be acting out a falsehood, e.g., pretending to a degree of unity that did not actually exist. The document, however,

[5] Cf. further on the above, Brown and Weigel, *An American Dialogue*, pp. 124–27.

[6] The increase of involvement in this annual event cannot be directly measured, but the statistical increase in distribution of pamphlets gives some indication. In 1965, 208,000 copies were distributed, while in 1966, a year later, the number was 1,367,000—an increase of over 600 per cent.

[7] A French translation of the text is available in *Documentation Catholique*, May 20, 1962, columns 689–97.

remained open to other kinds of liturgical sharing, and even to the use of one another's religious buildings for such services. In a statement anticipating the mood that later developed in Vatican II, and even going beyond what Vatican II specifically affirmed, the Dutch bishops wrote:

"The development of the ecumenical mentality is bringing into being a new attitude among separated Christians. Alongside a spirit of critical reserve, cultivated in narrow isolation, where the danger of contamination by error played the decisive role, a broader attitude is beginning to be seen, an inclination to evaluate more positively the Christian values which, in varying degrees, are found in the thought and life of our separated Christian brothers, values which are a bond of unity even within our disunity.

"For this reason, the awakening of this ecumenical awareness does not only demand of us the necessary reserve in joint worship between Catholics and Protestants; it also demands the necessary positive appreciation of what unites us despite our separation. . . .

"For ecumenical reasons, therefore, it seems necessary to gain a deeper knowledge of the others in the intimacy of their thought and religious life by attending their official religious services, an attendance inspired by ecumenical love but one which does not go so far as complete participation or unqualified acceptance."[8]

Although the later paragraphs of the document indicated that it would usually be better to meet in buildings not designed for worship, there was recognition that such provision was not always appropriate, and a remarkable openness pervaded the final section of the document:

"Since the ecumenical situation is on the move, it is impossible and undoubtedly would be ill-timed to give specific

[8] As cited in O'Hanlon, "Grass-Roots Ecumenism," *The Catholic World*, April 1964, p. 12. The material in the ellipsis is used as the heading of the present chapter.

regulations which would precisely mark the boundary between the desirable minimum and the maximum which is permissible. Because of the dynamism of the ecumenical spirit it would be impossible to stop at the minimum desirable."[9]

Within this openness, two qualifications were added: (a) "the appearance of complete participation in the official worship of the other Church must be avoided," and (b) "the creation of the appearance of a unity which does not yet exist should be avoided."

Picking up on these themes, the conciliar decree *On Ecumenism* deals with *communicatio in sacris* in carefully guarded terms, but terms that nevertheless register a real advance over the *monitum* of June 5, 1948, and the *Instruction* of December 20, 1949. After recognizing that it is appropriate for Catholics themselves to meet and pray for the unity of the church, the document continues:

"In certain special circumstances, such as in prayer services 'for unity' and during ecumenical gatherings, it is allowable, indeed desirable, that Catholics should join in prayer with their separated brethren. Such prayers in common are certainly a very effective means of petitioning for the grace of unity, and they are a genuine expression of the ties which even now bind Catholics to their separated brethren. 'For where two or three are gathered together in my name, there am I in the midst of them.'" (Mt. 18:20)[10]

Three things are significant about this paragraph: (a) the practice of common worship is *commended* and not simply tolerated—a change in atmosphere that is almost revolutionary; (b) the practice is not to be indiscriminate but is reserved for "special circumstances," those circumstances being ones with an ecumenical subject matter; and (c) two reasons for such action are clearly stated: on the one hand, the practice can move Christians toward greater unity, and on the other

[9] *Ibid.*
[10] Vatican Council decree *On Ecumenism*, Art. 8, Abbott, p. 352.

hand it can give visible expression to the degree of unity they already have.

Having made these affirmations, the decree cites some cautions:

"As for common worship [*communicatio in sacris*] however, it may not be regarded as a means to be used indiscriminately for the restoration of unity among Christians. Such worship depends chiefly on two principles: it should signify the unity of the Church; it should provide a sharing in the means of grace. The fact that it should signify unity [the first principle cited above] generally rules out common worship. Yet the gaining of a needed grace [the second principle] sometimes commends it."[11]

Here we note again the clear reminder that such worship should not pretend to a degree of unity that does not actually exist. The decree also gives a limited measure of freedom to local bishops to make decisions in specific instances (which accounts for the fact that in some areas today there is more sharing in worship than in others), although such decisions are clearly subject to the authority of regional bishops' conferences or the Vatican itself.[12]

"Intercommunion" as a problem within the World Council

The problem confronting the Roman Catholic Church has been a slightly different one from that confronting the World Council of Churches, for, within the latter group, the question of "intercommunion" has been the source of difficulty, as a brief survey can highlight for us.

[11] Vatican Council decree *On Ecumenism*, Art. 8, Abbott, pp. 352–53.

[12] Cf. further on the provisions of the decree, Leeming, *The Vatican Council and Christian Unity*, Harper & Row, New York, 1966, pp. 130–39. Almost as significant as the promulgation of the decree containing the above paragraphs was the conciliar act that occurred toward the end of the council, the joint service of prayer at St. Paul's Outside the Walls, on December 4, 1965, described in Ch. 9 above.

It has been clear from the beginning of Protestant and Orthodox ecumenical discussion that the question of *intercommunion* (i.e., full reciprocity at the communion tables of different churches) is intimately related to the question of *ministry* (i.e., the validity of the ordination of the celebrant at a eucharistic service). If all the churches in the World Council accepted one another's ministries as fully valid, the problem of intercommunion would at least be minimized, although some churches would still demur on the ground that doctrinal understandings of the eucharist, quite apart from the question of ministry, were still too divergent to allow for intercommunion. But certain churches continue to have strong convictions that only certain clergy (usually their own) are properly validated to celebrate the eucharist. Thus the problem of ministry is a key problem, as the Lausanne conference recognized back in 1927:

"By these differences the difficulties of intercommunion have been accentuated to the distress and wounding of faithful souls, while in the mission field, where the Church is fulfilling its primary object to preach the Gospel to every creature, the young Churches find the lack of unity a very serious obstacle to the furtherance of the Gospel. Consequently, the provision of a ministry acknowledged in every part of the Church as possessing the sanction of the whole Church is an urgent need."[13]

The Edinburgh conference on Faith and Order ten years later did little more than reiterate the problem, stating that "We regard sacramental intercommunion as a necessary part of any satisfactory Church unity,"[14] while observing that a custom had arisen at ecumenical gatherings of inviting all who had full status in their own churches to receive communion according to the rite of the inviting church. But later paragraphs made clear that differences about the propriety

[13] Cited in Vischer, ed., *op. cit.*, p. 35.
[14] *Ibid.*, p. 62.

of intercommunion persisted, and that they were usually predicated on differing appraisals of ministry in the various churches. The report of the commission on "Intercommunion" preparatory to the Lund conference also noted that while there were divergences of sacramental doctrine between the various churches,

"When all is said, however, it remains true that the difference of order between the Churches which claim the episcopal succession and other Churches appears to be at the present time the most formidable obstacle in the way of intercommunion."[15]

The fullest discussion took place at the Lund conference in 1952.[16]

The Lund report noted that although the Orthodox did not see a "problem" (since they do not feel that the eucharist can properly be celebrated save by the Orthodox), there was a problem for the rest, a problem that had been intensified by their membership in the World Council. Such membership was a decisive step toward one another that had inescapable implications for their worship and forced them to raise "ever more sharply the question of what justification remains for continuing in division at the Lord's Table."[17] Further facts heightening the urgency of the problem were the new missionary opportunities in Asia and Africa, the stress of persecution of the church, new inter-church agreements, the impatience of youth with the present barriers, and the urgent call of Christ.

Certain agreements were noted: (1) The Table is the Lord's Table, and his children should be able to partake

[15] Baillie and Marsh, eds., *Intercommunion*, Harper, New York, 1952, p. 35.

[16] Cf. the pre-Lund study volume, Baillie and Marsh, eds., *op. cit.*, 406 pp. The report of the commission, a clear spelling out of the problems, is on pp. 15–43. Cf. also Tomkins, ed., *The Third World Conference on Faith and Order*, S.C.M. Press, London, 1953, 380 pp., and Vischer, ed., *op. cit.*, pp. 115–25.

[17] Tomkins, ed., *op. cit.*, pp. 49–50.

thereat as brethren. (2) The church has the responsibility "for the due ordering of the Table," but in this administration "each has a grave responsibility before God, particularly if it withholds the sacrament from any of God's people."[18] (3) Even in the divided churches, the Lord's Supper can be a real means of grace. (4) Certain theological affirmations about the meaning of the sacrament can be made by all:

"This dominical sacrament of Christ's Body and Blood, controlled by the words of institution, with the use of the appointed elements of bread and wine, is: (a) a memorial of Christ's incarnation and earthly ministry, of His death and resurrection; (b) a sacrament in which He is truly present to give Himself to us, uniting us to Himself, to His eternal Sacrifice, and to one another; and (c) eschatologically, an anticipation of our fellowship with Christ in His eternal kingdom."[19]

But, despite such agreements, the basic difference persisted. For although most at Lund felt that there already existed "among the members of the World Council of Churches such a fundamental unity as to justify, or indeed require, joint participation at the Lord's Table,"[20] others, "without questioning the reality of our present unity, believe that fellowship in the Sacrament rightly exists only where there is fuller agreement in doctrine, a mutually acceptable ministry, or organic unity of church life."[21] All, however, with the exception of the Greek Orthodox, agreed that they would not deny the sacrament to members of other churches "in cases of urgent need."

In the light of this basic difference, churches holding different positions were exhorted to examine themselves with a

[18] *Ibid.*, p. 53.
[19] *Ibid.*, pp. 53–54. Cf. the slightly different earlier version in Baillie and Marsh, eds., *op. cit.*, pp. 41–42, which did not include the eschatological emphasis.
[20] *Ibid.*, p. 54.
[21] *Ibid.*, p. 55.

view to rethinking those positions,[22] and the delegates expressed "deep disappointment and concern that there is not a larger measure of agreement among us."[23]

The New Delhi assembly, recognizing that the church's unity involves "breaking the one bread," commented:

"Nowhere are the divisions of our churches more clearly evident and painful than at the Lord's Table. But the Lord's Table is one, not many. In humility the churches must seek that one Table. We would urge the Commission on Faith and Order to continue study and consultation to help us identify and remove those barriers which now keep us from partaking together of the one bread and sharing the one cup."[24]

It went on to ask, however, "whether there are situations, e.g., during unity negotiations, when intercommunion is possible even before full union is achieved."[25] And one new suggestion appeared in the discussion of "eucharistic unity and division":

"Moreover, if we reversed the usual order of discussion and focussed on eucharistic action—what God does and calls us

[22] It was suggested that the churches begin with the challenge laid down by Professor T. F. Torrance in the Lund preparatory volume: "To refuse the Eucharist to those baptized into Christ Jesus and incorporated into His resurrection body amounts either to a denial of the transcendent reality of holy Baptism or to attempted schism within the Body of Christ" (in Baillie and Marsh, eds., *op. cit.*, p. 339, cf. Tomkins, ed., *op. cit.*, p. 56).

[23] Tomkins, ed., *op. cit.*, p. 57. A final section of the report dealt with the problem of "Communion Services at Ecumenical Gatherings," a problem raised since not all present on such occasions acknowledge the validity of one anothers' ministries, and thus not all can communicate together. It was recommended that on such occasions (1) there should always be a united service of preparation for Holy Communion, stressing penitence in the face of division, (2) that there be provision for every member to receive communion somewhere, (3 and 4) that there be "open communion" services for those who could in good conscience attend, and (5) that all be invited to attend particular communion services even if they could not partake. (Cf. Tomkins, ed., *op. cit.*, pp. 57–59.)

[24] 't Hooft, ed., *The New Delhi Report*, p. 120.

[25] *Ibid.*, pp. 124–25.

to do at the Lord's Table—rather than (first of all) on eucharistic administration—i.e. the problem of valid ministry—we might find a clearer way to the heart of an adequate sacramental doctrine."[26]

But all that New Delhi really did was to look back to Lund and forward to Montreal, urging those planning the latter conference to consider the question further.

Montreal did so, but it cannot be reported that it made any fresh headway. Indeed, the report noted "an increase in the number of member churches which have difficulty in accepting intercommunion between the separated churches as a satisfactory concept or procedure," although it also noted "a growing impatience" on the part of many, particularly youth, with traditional approaches to the problem.[27] The report further noted that the churches had not yet taken seriously enough the need for study of differences of eucharistic theology and practice and affirmed that any denial that Christian fellowship must include "table fellowship" could only be viewed as an "ecumenical disaster."[28] It underlined the fact that the views expressed at Lund were "still worthy of attention" and commented that "the sharp difference of conviction indicating two poles within the Council's membership must be recognized."[29]

Leaving matters, therefore, at the same familiar *impasse*, the report made specific recommendations for communion services at ecumenical gatherings similar enough to the Lund proposals to be omitted from consideration here.[30]

To describe these ongoing discussions as inauspicious is an act of generous understatement.[31] In the light of them, it

26 *Ibid.*, p. 128.

27 Rodger and Vischer, eds., *op. cit.*, pp. 76–80, carries the full report.

28 *Ibid.*, p. 77.

29 *Ibid.*, p. 78.

30 *Ibid.*, pp. 79–80.

31 For a refreshingly penetrating attack on the intramural discussions of intercommunion, cf. Hoekendijk, *The Church Inside Out*, Westminster, Phila-

might seem the height of folly to enlarge the intramural problem by considering the further complexity of Roman Catholic-Protestant divisions. Nevertheless, two considerations make it urgent to do so: (a) the existential reality cannot be ignored that Catholics and Protestants in increasing numbers are reaching out toward some commonly shared liturgical experiences, even though at present this stops short of intercommunion, and (b) since intercommunion finally involves the full family of Christians, discussion at any stage that ignores part of that family is unrealistic and evasive.

The new situation—reasons for being drawn closer

It is therefore worth noting some of the reasons why the issue of common worship has become increasingly central to Catholics and Protestants.[32]

1. One reason why the impulse to joint worship has been developing is because both Catholics and Protestants have been engaged in *liturgical reform*, with the result that both groups have been drawn liturgically closer to one another. For Catholics this has meant a "return to the sources," e.g., the liturgies of the early church, in the light of which many portions of the modern mass have been seen to be anachronistic, repetitious, and irrelevant; whereas for the Protes-

---

delphia, 1966, Ch. IX, "Safety Last," pp. 152–70. He points out that many churches seem willing only to allow intercommunion in "abnormal" situations, such as missionary situations, emergencies, and the threshold of death. But Hoekendijk insists that the contemporary church lives in the time of "the abnormalization of the normal," and that what seem to be "unusual" situations are in fact now normal for the Christian church. He thus argues for a much more open-ended and even *ad hoc* approach to the problem.

[32] The issue of *communicatio in sacris* is a very different problem for Roman Catholic and Orthodox, since each acknowledges that the ministry of the other stands in historic episcopal succession. Cf. the Vatican Council decree *On Eastern Catholic Churches* (Abbott, ed., *op. cit.*, pp. 371–88), esp. Art. 24–29 on "Relations with Brethren of Separated Churches," and the decree *On Ecumenism* (Abbott, ed., *op. cit.*, pp. 337–70), esp. Art. 14–18, "The Special Position of the Eastern Churches."

tant it has meant a fresh look at the liturgical practices of the Reformers, which has meant doing what the Reformers did, i.e., examining the liturgies of the early church, in the light of which many portions of contemporary Protestant liturgy have been seen to be anachronistic, repetitious, and irrelevant. If recent Catholic worship had tended to stress sacrament at the expense of the Word, recent Protestant worship had tended to stress Word at the expense of sacrament; what both have discovered, starting from different ends, is that Word and sacrament belong together. Such a principle would be an apt summary both of the liturgical impulse of the Reformers, which Protestants have recently discovered, and of the spirit of the Vatican Council constitution *On the Sacred Liturgy*, which brings to formal fruition the concerns of half a century of Roman Catholic liturgical renewal.

This means that as Protestants and Catholics observe the worship of one another today, they do not find themselves entering upon totally foreign territory. Now that much of the mass is in the vernacular, the Protestant attending mass discovers much that is familiar to him, while the Catholic at a Protestant service is often astonished by its similarity to the basic structure of the mass. The natural impulse in such situations is to join in those portions of the service that are familiar and do not violate one's own beliefs—the offering of prayers, the joining in many responses, the singing of hymns, the recitation of creeds, the hearing of the Word, and other common acts of worship.

2. A second common resource has been *the recovery of a Biblical theology* by both sides. Much of the history of twentieth-century Protestantism has been the history of solid Biblical scholarship, the results of which gradually made themselves apparent in an increasingly "Biblical theology" growing up in Europe and spreading its influence throughout the Protestant world. After the stunning setbacks to Catholic Biblical scholarship sustained early in the twentieth century

by the "modernist crisis" and the papal proscriptions of 1907,[33] the possibility of Biblical study made a slow recovery, formalized by the breakthrough of papal approval in the 1943 encyclical *Divino Afflante Spiritu*,[34] and even more solidly vindicated by the Vatican Council constitution *On Revelation*, which, particularly in Chapter III, gives new assurances of the legitimacy of scholarly investigation of the Biblical texts. But for many years Catholic and Protestant Biblical scholars had made full use of one another's research, and there was an ecumenism of research long before its results began to be felt outside the fraternity of scholars.

The impact of the Bible on worship is too obvious to need elaboration. Scripture and liturgy have from the beginning been interrelated, and no Christian liturgy is explicable apart from the Biblical resources out of which it is drawn. Furthermore, the high place now accorded to Scripture and sermon in reforms of the mass is leading Catholics more deeply into the study of Biblical theology.

3. A third factor drawing Catholics and Protestants liturgically closer has been ongoing reflection about *the nature of the church*. Of particular importance has been the recognition of the sacrament of baptism as the sacrament of initiation, and even ordination, into the Christian fellowship. Baptism can begin to be understood as the sacrament of unity, for if the eucharist is still the sacrament of a unity not yet fully manifested and the reminder of a disunity all too apparent, baptism is the sacrament of a unity already present although not yet fully apprehended. It is a happy fact that the baptismal act of the divided Christian bodies is accepted by the others as valid. Thus if one has been baptized in a Protestant ceremony, he is not normally rebaptized upon entering the Catholic Church, and vice

[33] Cf. Denzinger, *op. cit.*, para. 2001–65a.
[34] *Ibid.*, para. 2292–94.

versa.[35] It is almost universally acknowledged that baptism is not baptism into a denomination but into the Church of Jesus Christ, so that all who have been baptized are in some sense already members of Christ's church, however defective the membership of some may appear to be from a Catholic perspective.

To the degree that this is acknowledged in the practical as well as the theoretical realm, it means that all baptized persons have not only a right, but even a duty, to worship together, not in violation of a rule to be otherwise rigorously applied, but as an expression of a reality not yet fully enough comprehended. Such oneness as they already possess should be given appropriate liturgical expression.

Contemporary expressions of common worship

As a result of these and other factors, various expressions of common worship have been developing. Often this has started with the "observation" of the worship of the other, recognizing with the Dutch bishops that "unless we learn to know one another precisely in the celebration of worship, which nourishes our thought in our everyday life, it will be impossible to discover the values we share in our disagreements."[36] And, as we have seen, fellow Christians who begin to observe one another worshiping discover that observation gradually changes to at least a measure of participation.[37] It is less and less uncommon to find a degree of "official"

[35] The principle is often upset in practice if there is any doubt about the fulfillment of the proper intent on the part of the one originally baptizing. In such a situation the Roman Catholic priest administers "conditional baptism."

[36] From the directive cited earlier in the present chapter.

[37] Almost all of the Protestant "observers" at Vatican II, for example, experienced this transition. Coming initially to watch the mass, many of them gradually began to participate in those portions of the mass that did not violate their own liturgical heritage, and discovered therein a new source of oneness with the council fathers. Cf. further *Observer in Rome*, pp. 43–44.

sharing in such services. Many Protestants have had the experience of reading the epistle lesson in a Catholic mass, while an increasing number of Catholic priests are being permitted by their bishops to preach at Protestant services or otherwise participate in the liturgy.

Degrees of common worship are being experienced on other levels as well. It is significant that the paperback *Living Room Dialogues* not only gives suggestions for Catholic-Protestant discussion, but also includes suggestions for common acts of worship.[38] In many local parishes, joint Catholic-Protestant Bible study has provided the context for prayer and Biblically oriented liturgical acts. In Holland and elsewhere the development of the *agape* meal (a sharing of food and drink having some obvious analogies to the Lord's Supper) has been a means of closer liturgical sharing. The rapid extension of joint services during the Week of Prayer for Christian Unity is another means of deepening the oneness Christians feel toward each other, as is the celebration of hymn festivals in which Catholics and Protestants sing together hymns that are part of their common heritage. (It is no longer the novelty it once was to observe a group of nuns singing "A Mighty Fortress Is Our God," let alone to hear Protestants singing "Father Rivers' Mass.")

Such examples could be multiplied almost endlessly. Each week brings to light new instances of experiences of sharing in worship that serve to deepen an already deepening fellowship between Christians, who find new joy in the unity they share and new sorrow in the fact that the unity they share is not full unity.

The eucharist—sign of unity or disunity?

The unity is *not* full unity. All the examples thus far cited carefully stop short of the place where full unity would normally be expressed, "partaking together of the one bread and

[38] Cf. further Ch. 15 above.

sharing the one cup." There is deep poignancy in this fact for those Catholics and Protestants who have come to discover that they are first of all fellow Christians, and only secondly Protestants or Catholics, and to those who have shared certain levels of common worship, the barriers to fuller sharing become more and more grievous.

The matter is deeply personal and can only properly be stated in personal terms: During the closing weeks of Vatican II, I attended an English-speaking mass each evening, concelebrated by a number of Roman Catholic priests, several of whom were close friends. I participated in about ninety per cent of the service, joining in the hymns, the responses, the prayers, occasionally reading the epistle. When the "peace" was given (an embrace passed in turn from each worshiper to the next, accompanied by the words, "The peace of Christ be with you"), I could both receive and give the peace of Christ. But when it came to the communion itself, I could neither give nor receive the body of Christ.

The incongruity can be described in two sentences. I have never felt closer to my Roman Catholic brethren than at those services. I have never felt more cut off from my Roman Catholic brethren than at those services. There is something terribly wrong about the fact that we can give and receive the peace of Christ but not the body of Christ. And there is a terribly urgent and holy discontent lodged in the hearts of those who have given and received the first and then find that they can neither give nor receive the second.

Is that all that can be said? Must the matter simply be left where it is always left, namely that everyone feels badly and everyone feels penitent and yet nothing happens? An intriguing suggestion has recently been made by Fr. Daniel O'Hanlon, s.j., a Roman Catholic ecumenist (and one of the concelebrants at the mass described above), that might provide the beginnings of a breakthrough.[39]

---

[39] O'Hanlon, "Grass-Roots Ecumenism," The *Catholic World*, April 1964, pp. 8–15.
   Two other articles that clarify the issues involved are Baum, "*Communicatio*

Fr. O'Hanlon acknowledges that "the Catholic psyche has been conditioned to repulse automatically the idea of any *communicatio in sacris*," but goes on to acknowledge that the time always comes when those who have talked together ecumenically feel the need to pray together ecumenically. He then draws on the conciliar constitution *On the Sacred Liturgy* to develop what he calls the principle of *the honest sign*. Liturgical actions must be honest signs, i.e., they must faithfully represent what they claim to represent. For Catholics and Protestants to start visiting one another's altars indiscriminately would not be an honest sign; for it would signify a degree of unity we do not yet have, since many things still divide us. An honest sign would have to reflect both the degree of unity we possess and the degree of disunity that still possesses us.

But does this mean, Fr. O'Hanlon asks, that we must *always* exclude one another from our celebrations of the eucharist? After reiterating that regular communion together would at present be a dishonest sign, he goes on to ask:

"Suppose that, apart from the emergency of war and imminent death [occasions when *communicatio in sacris* has been practiced] but in the equally real emergency situation of a scandalously divided Christianity, other Christians were invited on rare occasions to Communion at a Catholic Mass? Suppose that on the last day of the Church Unity Octave, for instance, those Christians, who could in conscience accept, would be invited to join with Catholics in the banquet of the Lord into whose death and resurrection they have already been baptized? Would not the sad fact of separation be adequately represented by the fact that this was an excep-

---

in Sacris," in Baum, ed., *Ecumenical Theology Today*, Paulist Press, Glen Rock, 1964, pp. 56–64, and Bevenot, "Communicatio in Sacris," in Heenan, ed., *Christian Unity: A Catholic View*, Sheed and Ward, London, 1962, pp. 114–39.

tional event? And would not the yearning for full unity be mightily fostered by such a moving experience?"[40]

In the suggestion Fr. O'Hanlon makes, the important point to note is that *the sign is honest*, since it manifests (by the fact that it occurs at all) the unity we already possess, and also manifests (by the fact that it occurs so infrequently) the disunity we must seek to overcome.

Some Catholics may be surprised by such a suggestion, since it will seem to them to dilute the meaning of the mass and foster a kind of indifferentism. But, as Fr. O'Hanlon replies, if it would be wrong to pretend that all Christian churches are alike, "it would be no less disastrous at this moment of history for the Christian churches to manifest nothing to the world but their scandalous separation."[41]

A Protestant would want to know whether or not the traffic could go both ways. Fr. O'Hanlon, making his suggestion to a Catholic readership, restricts his discussion to the possibility of inviting non-Catholics to receive communion at mass. Most Protestant churches (save those that practice "closed communion") could freely invite Catholics to receive communion with them, since they issue an invitation to all who accept Christ and are members of a Christian church—conditions under which Catholics eminently qualify. The issue of conscience would thus be raised for the Catholic communicant. At present most Catholics would probably feel uneasy about taking such action and would probably be forbidden by their bishops from doing so. However, a number of Catholics have privately remarked that they would personally feel able to receive communion under such circumstances, recognizing that the Protestant service is *not* the mass and that they need impute to it no further meaning than the Protestant celebrant does, but some of them fear that such a move would be open to misunderstanding in both

40 O'Hanlon, *op. cit.*, p. 14.
41 *Ibid.*, p. 14.

the Protestant and Catholic communities, so that they feel extremely cautious about initiating such participation.[42]

Inescapable questions

The goal of the ecumenical movement is unity. Unity is a sham until it includes full sacramental unity. As the theologians continue to wrestle with how the latter can become possible, other Christians must continue to ask the simple, profound, and insistent questions that no Christian, and no church, can be permitted to evade. Such questions were posed with disarming simplicity by a waiter in the small *pensione* near St. Peter's where most of the Protestant and Orthodox observers lived during the sessions of Vatican II. The waiters got to know these observers very well over the four-year period, and toward the end of the council one of them, Gigi, cornered a priest who had been translating for the observers and put to him the following questions:

Gigi: Father, these observers are very good men, aren't they?

Father: Yes.

Gigi: They all believe in God?

Father: Yes.

Gigi: There is only one God?

Father: Yes.

Gigi: So they believe in the same God we believe in?

[42] A new approach to the whole problem of the "validity" of Protestant sacraments and the Protestant ministry may have been initiated by an important article (appearing too late to be incorporated in the main body of the present chapter) by the Dutch Jesuit, Franz Josef van Beeck, s.j., "Towards An Ecumenical Understanding of the Sacraments," *Journal of Ecumenical Studies*, Winter 1966, pp. 57–112. The argument is too detailed and nuanced to be justifiably condensed, but in it Fr. van Beeck makes a persuasive case, from a Catholic perspective, for believing that many Protestant sacramental celebrations fulfill the three crucial conditions of (a) being celebrated in a Church in good faith, (b) reflecting sound doctrine, and (c) celebrated by a minister who is "competent." He then discusses, with due caution, the implications of this fact for *communicatio in sacris*.

Father: Yes.

Gigi: They all believe in Christ?

Father: Yes.

Gigi: There is only one Christ?

Father: Yes.

Gigi: So they believe in the same Christ we believe in?

Father: Yes.

Gigi: They have all been baptized?

Father: Yes.

Gigi: There is only one baptism?

Father: Yes.

Gigi: Then, Father, I do not understand. *Perchè le divisione?* Why the divisions?

APPENDIX I

The Second Vatican Council Decree
On Ecumenism

PAUL, BISHOP, SERVANT OF THE SERVANTS OF GOD
TOGETHER WITH THE FATHERS OF THE SACRED COUNCIL
FOR EVERLASTING MEMORY

INTRODUCTION

1. Promoting the restoration of unity among all Christians is one of the chief concerns of the Second Sacred Ecumenical Synod of the Vatican. The Church established by Christ the Lord is, indeed, one and unique. Yet many Christian communions present themselves to men as the true heritage of Jesus Christ. To be sure, all proclaim themselves to be disciples of the Lord, but their convictions clash and their paths diverge, as though Christ Himself were divided (cf. 1 Cor. 1:13). Without doubt, this discord openly contradicts the will of Christ, provides a stumbling block to the world, and inflicts damage on the most holy cause of proclaiming the good news to every creature.

Nevertheless, the Lord of Ages wisely and patiently follows out the plan of His grace on behalf of us sinners. In recent times He has begun to bestow more generously upon divided Christians remorse over their divisions and a longing for unity.

Everywhere, large numbers have felt the impulse of this grace, and among our separated brethren also there increases from day to day a movement, fostered by the grace of the Holy Spirit, for the restoration of unity among all Christians. Taking part in this movement, which is called ecumenical, are those who invoke the Triune God and confess Jesus as Lord and Savior. They join in not merely as individuals but also as members of the corporate groups in which they have heard the gospel, and which each re-

gards as his Church, and, indeed, God's. And yet, almost everyone, though in different ways, longs that there may be one visible
Church of God, a Church truly universal and sent forth to the
whole world that the world may be converted to the gospel and
so be saved, to the glory of God.

This sacred Synod, therefore, gladly notes all these factors. It
has already declared its teaching on the Church, and now, moved
by a desire for the restoration of unity among all the followers
of Christ, it wishes to set before all Catholics certain helps, pathways, and methods by which they too can respond to this divine
summons and grace.

CHAPTER I

CATHOLIC PRINCIPLES ON ECUMENISM

2. What has revealed the love of God among us is that the
only-begotten Son of God has been sent by the Father into the
world, so that, being made man, the Son might by His redemption of the entire human race give new life to it and unify it
(cf. 1 Jn. 4:9; Col. 1:18–20; Jn. 11:52). Before offering Himself
up as a spotless victim upon the altar of the cross, He prayed to
His Father for those who believe: "That all may be one even as
thou, Father, in me, and I in thee; that they also may be one in
us, that the world may believe that thou hast sent me" (Jn.
17:21). In His Church He instituted the wonderful sacrament
of the Eucharist by which the unity of the Church is both signi-
fied and brought about. He gave His followers a new commandment of mutual love (cf. Jn. 13:34), and promised the Spirit, their
Advocate (cf. Jn. 16:7), who, as Lord and life-giver, would abide
with them forever.

After being lifted up on the cross and glorified, the Lord Jesus
poured forth the Spirit whom He had promised, and through
whom He has called and gathered together, the people of the
New Covenant, who comprise the Church, into a unity of faith,
hope, and charity. For, as the apostle teaches, the Church is:
"one body and one Spirit, even as you were called in one hope of
your calling; one Lord, one faith, one baptism" (Eph. 4:4–5).
For "all you who have been baptized into Christ, have put on

Christ . . . for you are all one in Christ Jesus" (Gal. 3:27–28). It is the Holy Spirit, dwelling in those who believe, pervading and ruling over the entire Church, who brings about that marvelous communion of the faithful and joins them together so intimately in Christ that He is the principle of the Church's unity. By distributing various kinds of spiritual gifts and ministries (cf. 1 Cor. 12:4–11), He enriches the Church of Jesus Christ with different functions "in order to perfect the saints for a work of ministry, for building up the body of Christ" (Eph. 4:12).

In order to establish this holy Church of His everywhere in the world until the end of time, Christ entrusted to the College of the Twelve the task of teaching, ruling and sanctifying (cf. Mt. 28:18–20, in conjunction with Jn. 20:21–23). Among their number He chose Peter. After Peter's profession of faith, He decreed that on him He would build His Church; to Peter He promised the keys of the kingdom of heaven (cf. Mt. 16:19, in conjunction with Mt. 18:18). After Peter's profession of love, Christ entrusted all His sheep to him to be confirmed in faith (cf. Lk. 22:32) and shepherded in perfected unity (cf. Jn. 21:15–17). Meanwhile, Christ Jesus Himself forever remains the chief cornerstone (cf. Eph. 2:20) and shepherd of our souls (cf. 1 Pet. 2:25).[1]

It is through the faithful preaching of the gospel by the apostles and their successors—the bishops with Peter's successor at their head—through their administration of the sacraments, and through their loving exercise of authority, that Jesus Christ wishes His people to increase under the influence of the Holy Spirit. Thereby too, He perfects His people's fellowship in unity: in the confession of one faith, in the common celebration of divine worship, and in the fraternal harmony of the family of God.

The Church, then, God's only flock, like a standard lifted high for the nations to see (cf. Is. 11:10–12), ministers the gospel of peace to all mankind (cf. Eph. 2:17–18, in conjunction with Mk. 16:15), as she makes her pilgrim way in hope toward her goal, the fatherland above (cf. 1 Pet. 1:3–9).

This is the sacred mystery of the unity of the Church, in Christ

---

[1] I Vatican Council, Sess. IV (1870), the constitution "Pastor Aeternus": Coll. Lac. 7, 482a.

and through Christ, with the Holy Spirit energizing a variety of functions. The highest exemplar and source of this mystery is the unity, in the Trinity of Persons, of one God, the Father and the Son in the Holy Spirit.

3. From her very beginnings there arose in this one and only Church of God certain rifts (cf. 1 Cor. 11:18–19, Gal. 1:6–9, 1 Jn. 2:18–19), which the apostle strongly censures as damnable (cf. 1 Cor. 1:11 ff; 11:22). But in subsequent centuries more widespread disagreements appeared and quite large Communities became separated from full communion with the Catholic Church—developments for which, at times, men of both sides were to blame. However, one cannot impute the sin of separation to those who at present are born into these Communities and are instilled therein with Christ's faith. The Catholic Church accepts them with respect and affection as brothers. For men who believe in Christ and have been properly baptized are brought into a certain, though imperfect, communion with the Catholic Church. Undoubtedly, the differences that exist in varying degrees between them and the Catholic Church—whether in doctrine and sometimes in discipline, or concerning the structure of the Church—do indeed create many and sometimes serious obstacles to full ecclesiastical communion. These the ecumenical movement is striving to overcome. Nevertheless, all those justified by faith through baptism are incorporated into Christ.[2] They therefore have a right to be honored by the title of Christian, and are properly regarded as brothers in the Lord by the sons of the Catholic Church.[3]

Moreover some, even very many, of the most significant elements or endowments which together go to build up and give life to the Church herself can exist outside the visible boundaries of the Catholic Church: the written word of God; the life of grace; faith, hope, and charity, along with other interior gifts of the Holy Spirit and visible elements. All of these, which come from Christ and lead back to Him, belong by right to the one Church of Christ.

[2] Cf. Council of Florence, Sess. VIII (1439), the decree "Exultate Deo": Mansi 31. 1055 A.
[3] Cf. St. Augustine, "In Ps. 32," Enarr. II, 29: PL 36, 299.

The brethren divided from us also carry out many of the sacred actions of the Christian religion. Undoubtedly, in many ways that vary according to the condition of each Church or Community, these actions can truly engender a life of grace, and can be rightly described as capable of providing access to the community of salvation.

It follows that these separated Churches[4] and Communities, though we believe they suffer from defects already mentioned, have by no means been deprived of significance and importance in the mystery of salvation. For the Spirit of Christ has not refrained from using them as means of salvation which derive their efficacy from the very fullness of grace and truth entrusted to the Catholic Church.

Nevertheless, our separated brethren, whether considered as individuals or as Communities and Churches, are not blessed with that unity which Jesus Christ wished to bestow on all those whom He has regenerated and vivified into one body and newness of life—that unity which the holy Scriptures and the revered tradition of the Church proclaim. For it is through Christ's Catholic Church alone, which is the all-embracing means of salvation, that the fullness of the means of salvation can be obtained. It was to the apostolic college alone, of which Peter is the head, that we believe our Lord entrusted all the blessings of the New Covenant, in order to establish on earth the one Body of Christ into which all those should be fully incorporated who already belong in any way to God's People. During its pilgrimage on earth, this People, though still in its members liable to sin, is growing in Christ and is being gently guided by God, according to His hidden designs, until it happily arrives at the fullness of eternal glory in the heavenly Jerusalem.

4. Today, in many parts of the world, under the inspiring grace of the Holy Spirit, multiple efforts are being expended through prayer, word, and action to attain that fullness of unity which Jesus Christ desires. This sacred Synod, therefore, exhorts all the

---

[4] Cf. IV Lateran Council (1215) Constitution IV; Manse 22, 990; II Council of Lyons (1274), profession of faith of Michael Palaeologos: Mansi 24, 71E; Council of Florence, Sess. VI (1439), definition "Laetentur caeli": Manse 31, 1026 E.

Catholic faithful to recognize the signs of the times and to participate skillfully in the work of ecumenism.

The "ecumenical movement" means those activities and enterprises which, according to various needs of the Church and opportune occasions, are started and organized for the fostering of unity among Christians. These are: first, every effort to eliminate words, judgments, and actions which do not respond to the condition of separated brethren with truth and fairness and so make mutual relations between them more difficult; then, "dialogue" between competent experts from different Churches and Communities. In their meetings, which are organized in a religious spirit, each explains the teaching of his Communion in greater depth and brings out clearly its distinctive features. Through such dialogue, everyone gains a truer knowledge and more just appreciation of the teaching and religious life of both Communions. In addition, these Communions cooperate more closely in whatever projects a Christian conscience demands for the common good. They also come together for common prayer, where this is permitted. Finally, all are led to examine their own faithfulness to Christ's will for the Church and, wherever necessary, undertake with vigor the task of renewal and reform.

When such actions are carried out by the Catholic faithful with prudence, patience, and the vigilance of their spiritual shepherds, they contribute to the blessings of justice and truth, of concord and collaboration, as well as of the spirit of brotherly love and unity. The result will be that, little by little, as the obstacles to perfect ecclesiastical communion are overcome, all Christians will be gathered, in a common celebration of the Eucharist, into that unity of the one and only Church which Christ bestowed on His Church from the beginning. This unity, we believe, dwells in the Catholic Church as something she can never lose, and we hope that it will continue to increase until the end of time.

However, it is evident that the work of preparing and reconciling those individuals who wish for full Catholic communion is of its nature distinct from ecumenical action. But there is no opposition between the two, since both proceed from the wondrous providence of God.

In ecumenical work, Catholics must assuredly be concerned for their separated brethren, praying for them, keeping them informed about the Church, making the first approaches towards them. But their primary duty is to make an honest and careful appraisal of whatever needs to be renewed and achieved in the Catholic household itself, in order that its life may bear witness more loyally and luminously to the teachings and ordinances which have been handed down from Christ through the apostles.

For although the Catholic Church has been endowed with all divinely revealed truth and with all means of grace, her members fail to live by them with all the fervor they should. As a result, the radiance of the Church's face shines less brightly in the eyes of our separated brethren and of the world at large, and the growth of God's kingdom is retarded. Every Catholic must therefore aim at Christian perfection (cf. Jas. 1:4; Rom. 12:1–2) and, each according to his station, play his part so that the Church, which bears in her own body the humility and dying of Jesus (cf. 2 Cor. 4:10; Phil. 2:5–8), may daily be more purified and renewed, against the day when Christ will present her to Himself in all her glory, without spot or wrinkle (cf. Eph. 5:27).

While preserving unity in essentials, let all members of the Church, according to the office entrusted to each, preserve a proper freedom in the various forms of spiritual life and discipline, in the variety of liturgical rites, and even in the theological elaborations of revealed truth. In all things let charity be exercised. If the faithful are true to this course of action, they will be giving ever richer expression to the authentic catholicity of the Church, and, at the same time, to her apostolicity.

On the other hand, Catholics must joyfully acknowledge and esteem the truly Christian endowments from our common heritage which are to be found among our separated brethren. It is right and salutary to recognize the riches of Christ and virtuous works in the lives of others who are bearing witness to Christ, sometimes even to the shedding of their blood. For God is always wonderful in His works and worthy of admiration.

Nor should we forget that whatever is wrought by the grace of the Holy Spirit in the hearts of our separated brethren can contribute to our own edification. Whatever is truly Christian never conflicts with the genuine interests of the faith; indeed, it can always result in a more ample realization of the very mystery of Christ and the Church.

Nevertheless, the divisions among Christians prevent the Church from effecting the fullness of catholicity proper to her in those of her sons who, though joined to her by baptism, are yet separated from full communion with her. Furthermore, the Church herself finds it more difficult to express in actual life her full catholicity in all its aspects.

This sacred Synod is gratified to note that participation by the Catholic faithful in ecumenical work is growing daily. It commends this work to bishops everywhere in the world for their skillful promotion and prudent guidance.

CHAPTER II

THE PRACTICE OF ECUMENISM

5. Concern for restoring unity pertains to the whole Church, faithful and clergy alike. It extends to everyone, according to the potential of each, whether it be exercised in daily Christian living or in theological and historical studies. This very concern already reveals to some extent the bond of brotherhood existing among all Christians, and it leads toward that full and perfect unity which God lovingly desires.

6. Every renewal of the Church[5] essentially consists in an increase of fidelity to her own calling. Undoubtedly this explains the dynamism of the movement toward unity.

Christ summons the Church, as she goes her pilgrim way, to that continual reformation of which she always has need, insofar as she is an institution of men here on earth. Therefore, if the influence of events or of the times has led to deficiencies in conduct, in Church discipline, or even in the formulation of doctrine (which must be carefully distinguished from the deposit itself of faith), these should be appropriately rectified at the proper moment.

Church renewal therefore has notable ecumenical importance. Already this renewal is taking place in various spheres of the Church's life: the biblical and liturgical movements, the preach-

[5] Cf. V Lateran Council, Sess. XII (1517), constitution "Constituti": Mansi 32, 988 B-C.

ing of the word of God, catechetics, the apostolate of the laity, new forms of religious life and the spirituality of married life, and the Church's social teaching and activity. All these should be considered as favorable pledges and signs of ecumenical progress in the future.

7. There can be no ecumenism worthy of the name without a change of heart. For it is from newness of attitudes (cf. Eph. 4:23), from self-denial and unstinted love, that yearnings for unity take their rise and grow toward maturity. We should therefore pray to the divine Spirit for the grace to be genuinely self-denying, humble, gentle in the service of others, and to have an attitude of brotherly generosity toward them. The Apostle of the Gentiles says: "I, therefore, the prisoner in the Lord, exhort you to walk in a manner worthy of the calling with which you were called, with all humility and meekness, with patience, bearing with one another in love, careful to preserve the unity of the Spirit in the bond of peace" (Eph. 4:1–3). This exhortation applies especially to those who have been raised to sacred orders so that the mission of Christ may be carried on. He came among us "not to be served but to serve" (Mt. 20:28).

St. John has testified: "If we say that we have not sinned, we make him a liar, and his word is not in us" (1 Jn. 1:10). This holds good for sins against unity. Thus, in humble prayer, we beg pardon of God and of our separated brethren, just as we forgive those who trespass against us.

Let all Christ's faithful remember that the more purely they strive to live according to the gospel, the more they are fostering and even practicing Christian unity. For they can achieve depth and ease in strengthening mutual brotherhood to the degree that they enjoy profound communion with the Father, the Word, and the Spirit.

8. This change of heart and holiness of life, along with public and private prayer for the unity of Christians, should be regarded as the soul of the whole ecumenical movement, and can rightly be called "spiritual ecumenism."

Catholics already have a custom of uniting frequently in that prayer for the unity of the Church with which the Savior Himself, on the eve of His death, appealed so fervently to His Father: "That all may be one" (Jn. 17:21).

In certain special circumstances, such as in prayer services "for unity" and during ecumenical gatherings, it is allowable, even desirable, that Catholics should join in prayer with their separated brethren. Such prayers in common are certainly a very effective means of petitioning for the grace of unity, and they are a genuine expression of the ties which even now bind Catholics to their separated brethren. "For where two or three are gathered together for my sake, there am I in the midst of them" (Mt. 18:20).

As for common worship, however, it may not be regarded as a means to be used indiscriminately for the restoration of unity among Christians. Such worship depends chiefly on two principles: it should signify the unity of the Church; it should provide a sharing in the means of grace. The fact that it should signify unity generally rules out common worship. Yet the gaining of a needed grace sometimes commends it.

The practical course to be adopted, after due regard has been given to all the circumstances of time, place and personage, is left to the prudent decision of the local episcopal authority, unless the Bishops' Conference according to its own statutes, or the Holy See, has determined otherwise.

9. We must come to understand the outlook of our separated brethren. Study is absolutely required for this, and should be pursued with fidelity to truth and in a spirit of good will. When they are properly prepared for this study, Catholics need to acquire a more adequate understanding of the distinctive doctrines of our separated brethren, as well as of their own history, spiritual and liturgical life, their religious psychology and cultural background. Of great value for this purpose are meetings between the two sides, especially for discussion of theological problems, where each can deal with the other on an equal footing. Such meetings require that those who take part in them under authoritative guidance be truly competent. From dialogue of this sort will emerge still more clearly what the true posture of the Catholic Church is. In this way, too, we will better understand the attitude of our separated brethren and more aptly present our own belief.

10. Instruction in sacred theology and other branches of knowledge, especially those of a historical nature, must also be pre-

sented from an ecumenical point of view, so that at every point they may more accurately correspond with the facts of the case.

For it is highly important that future bishops and priests should have mastered a theology carefully worked out in this way and not polemically, especially in what concerns the relations of separated brethren with the Catholic Church. For it is upon the formation which priests receive that the necessary instruction and spiritual formation of the faithful and of religious depend so very greatly.

Moreover, Catholics engaged in missionary work, in the same territories as other Christians, ought to know, particularly in these times, the problems and the benefits which affect their apostolate because of the ecumenical movement.

11. The manner and order in which Catholic belief is expressed should in no way become an obstacle to dialogue with our brethren. It is, of course, essential that doctrine be clearly presented in its entirety. Nothing is so foreign to the spirit of ecumenism as a false conciliatory approach which harms the purity of Catholic doctrine and obscures its assured genuine meaning.

At the same time, Catholic beliefs need to be explained more profoundly and precisely, in ways and in terminology which our separated brethren too can really understand.

Furthermore, Catholic theologians engaged in ecumenical dialogue, while standing fast by the teaching of the Church and searching together with separated brethren into the divine mysteries, should act with love for truth, with charity, and with humility. When comparing doctrines, they should remember that in Catholic teaching there exists an order or "hierarchy" of truths, since they vary in their relationship to the foundation of the Christian faith. Thus the way will be opened for this kind of fraternal rivalry to incite all to a deeper realization and a clearer expression of the unfathomable riches of Christ (cf. Eph. 3:8).

12. Before the whole world, let all Christians profess their faith in God, one and three, in the incarnate Son of God, our Redeemer and Lord. United in their efforts, and with mutual respect, let them bear witness to our common hope, which does not play us false. Since in our times cooperation in social matters is very widely practiced, all men without exception are summoned

to united effort. Those who believe in God have a stronger summons, but the strongest claims are laid on Christians, since they have been sealed with the name of Christ.

Cooperation among all Christians vividly expresses that bond which already unites them, and it sets in clearer relief the features of Christ the Servant. Such cooperation, which has already begun in many countries, should be ever increasingly developed, particularly in regions where a social and technical evolution is taking place. It should contribute to a just appreciation of the dignity of the human person, the promotion of the blessings of peace, the application of gospel principles to social life, and the advancement of the arts and sciences in a Christian spirit. Christians should also work together in the use of every possible means to relieve the afflictions of our times, such as famine and natural disasters, illiteracy and poverty, lack of housing, and the unequal distribution of wealth. Through such cooperation, all believers in Christ are able to learn easily how they can understand each other better and esteem each other more, and how the road to the unity of Christians may be made more smooth.

CHAPTER III

CHURCHES AND ECCLESIAL COMMUNITIES SEPARATED FROM THE ROMAN APOSTOLIC SEE

13. We now turn our attention to the two main kinds of rending which have damaged the seamless robe of Christ.

The first divisions occurred in the East, either because of disputes over the dogmatic pronouncements of the Councils of Ephesus and Chalcedon, or later by the breakdown of ecclesiastical communion between the Eastern Patriarchates and the Roman See.

Still other divisions arose in the West more than four centuries afterwards. These stemmed from a series of happenings commonly referred to as the Reformation. As a result, many Communions, national or denominational, were separated from the Roman See. Among those in which some Catholic traditions and institutions continue to exist, the Anglican Communion occupies a special place.

These various divisions, however, differ greatly from one another not only by reason of their source, location, and age, but especially in their view of the nature and importance of issues bearing on belief and Church structure. Therefore, neither minimizing the differences between the various Christian bodies, nor overlooking the bonds which continue to exist among them in spite of divisions, this sacred Synod has decided to propose the following considerations for prudent ecumenical action.

The Special Position of the Eastern Churches

14. For many centuries, the Churches of the East and of the West went their own ways, though a brotherly communion of faith and sacramental life bound them together. If disagreements in belief and discipline arose among them, the Roman See acted by common consent as moderator.

This most sacred Synod gladly reminds all of one highly significant fact among others: in the East there flourish many particular or local Churches; among them the Patriarchal Churches hold first place; and of these, many glory in taking their origins from the apostles themselves. As a result, there prevailed and still prevails among Orientals an eager desire to perpetuate in a communion of faith and charity those family ties which ought to thrive between local Churches, as between sisters. It is equally worthy of note that from their very origins the Churches of the East have had a treasury from which the Church of the West has amply drawn for its liturgy, spiritual tradition, and jurisprudence. Nor must we underestimate the fact that basic dogmas of the Christian faith concerning the Trinity and God's Word made flesh of the Virgin Mary were defined in Ecumenical Councils held in the East. To preserve this faith, these Churches have suffered much, and still do so.

However, the heritage handed down by the apostles was received in different forms and ways, so that from the very beginnings of the Church it has had a varied development in various places, thanks to a similar variety of natural gifts and conditions of life. Added to external causes, and to mutual failures in understanding and charity, all these circumstances set the stage for separations.

Therefore, this sacred Synod urges all, but especially those who plan to devote themselves to the work of restoring the full communion that is desired between the Eastern Churches and the Catholic Church, to give due consideration to these special aspects of the origin and growth of the Churches of the East, and to the character of the relations which obtained between them and the Roman See before the separation, and to form for themselves a correct evaluation of these facts. If these recommendations are carefully carried out, they will make a very great contribution to any proposed dialogues.

15. Everybody also knows with what love the Eastern Christians enact the sacred liturgy, especially the celebration of the Eucharist, which is the source of the Church's life and the pledge of future glory. In this celebration the faithful, united with their bishop and endowed with an outpouring of the Holy Spirit, gain access to God the Father through the Son, the Word made flesh, who suffered and was glorified. And so, made "partakers of the divine nature" (2 Pet. 1:4), they enter into communion with the most holy Trinity. Hence, through the celebration of the Eucharist of the Lord in each of these Churches, the Church of God is built up and grows in stature,[6] while through the rite of concelebration their bond with one another is made manifest.

In this liturgical worship, the Christians of the East pay high tribute, in very beautiful hymns, to Mary ever Virgin, whom the Ecumenical Synod of Ephesus solemnly proclaimed to be God's most holy Mother so that, in accord with the Scriptures, Christ may be truly and properly acknowledged as Son of God and Son of Man. They also give homage to the saints, including Fathers of the Universal Church.

Although these Churches are separated from us, they possess true sacraments, above all—by apostolic succession—the priesthood and the Eucharist, whereby they are still joined to us in a very close relationship. Therefore, given suitable circumstances and the approval of Church authority, some worship in common is not merely possible but is recommended.

Moreover, in the East are to be found the riches of those spiritual traditions to which monasticism gives special expression.

[6] Cf. S. John Chrysostom, "In Ioannem Homilia XLVI," PG 59, 260–62.

From the glorious days of the holy Fathers, there flourished in the East that monastic spirituality which later flowed over into the Western world, and there provided a source from which Latin monastic life took its rise and has often drawn fresh vigor ever since. Therefore Catholics are strongly urged to avail themselves more often of these spiritual riches of the Eastern Fathers, riches which lift up the whole man to the contemplation of divine mysteries.

All should realize that it is of supreme importance to understand, venerate, preserve, and foster the exceedingly rich liturgical and spiritual heritage of the Eastern Churches, in order faithfully to preserve the fullness of Christian tradition, and to bring about reconciliation between Eastern and Western Christians.

16. From the earliest times, moreover, the Eastern Churches followed their own disciplines, sanctioned by the holy Fathers, by synods, even ecumenical Councils. Far from being an obstacle to the Church's unity, such diversity of customs and observances only adds to her comeliness, and contributes greatly to carrying out her mission, as has already been recalled. To remove any shadow of doubt, then, this sacred Synod solemnly declares that the Churches of the East, while keeping in mind the necessary unity of the whole Church, have the power to govern themselves according to their own disciplines, since these are better suited to the temperament of their faithful and better adapted to foster the good of souls. Although it has not always been honored, the strict observance of this traditional principle is among the prerequisites for any restoration of unity.

17. What has already been said about legitimate variety we are pleased to apply to differences in theological expressions of doctrine. In the investigation of revealed truth, East and West have used different methods and approaches in understanding and proclaiming divine things. It is hardly surprising, then, if sometimes one tradition has come nearer than the other to an apt appreciation of certain aspects of revealed mystery, or has expressed them in a clearer manner. As a result, these various theological formulations are often to be considered as complementary rather than conflicting. With regard to the authentic theological traditions of the Orientals, we must recognize that they are admirably rooted in Holy Scripture, fostered and given expression in litur-

gical life, and nourished by the living tradition of the apostles and by the writings of the Fathers and spiritual authors of the East; they are directed toward a right ordering of life, indeed, toward a full contemplation of Christian truth.

While thanking God that many Eastern sons of the Catholic Church, who are preserving this heritage and wish to express it more faithfully and completely in their lives, are already living in full communion with their brethren who follow the tradition of the West, this sacred Synod declares that this entire heritage of spirituality and liturgy, of discipline and theology, in their various traditions, belongs to the full catholic and apostolic character of the Church.

18. After taking all these factors into consideration, this sacred Synod confirms what previous Councils and Roman Pontiffs have proclaimed: in order to restore communion and unity or preserve them, one must "impose no burden beyond what is indispensable" (Acts 15:28). It is the Council's urgent desire that every effort should henceforth be made toward the gradual realization of this goal in the various organizations and living activities of the Church, especially by prayer and by fraternal dialogue on points of doctrine and the more pressing pastoral problems of our time. Similarly, to the pastors and faithful of the Catholic Church, it recommends close relationships with those no longer living in the East but far from their homeland, so that friendly collaboration with them may increase in a spirit of love, without quarrelsome rivalry. If this task is carried on wholeheartedly, this sacred Synod hopes that with the removal of the wall dividing the Eastern and Western Church there may at last be but one dwelling, firmly established on the cornerstone, Christ Jesus, who will make both one.[7]

The Separated Churches and Ecclesial
Communities in the West

19. The Churches and ecclesial Communities which were separated from the Apostolic See of Rome during the very serious

[7] Cf. Council of Florence, Sess. VI (1439), definition "Laetentur caeli": Manse 31, 1026 E.

crisis that began in the West at the end of the Middle Ages, or during later times, are bound to the Catholic Church by a special affinity and close relationship in view of the long span of earlier centuries when the Christian people lived in ecclesiastical communion.

Since in origin, teaching, and spiritual practice, these Churches and ecclesial Communities differ not only from us but also among themselves to a considerable degree, the task of describing them adequately is very difficult; we do not propose to do it here.

Although the ecumenical movement and the desire for reconciliation with the Catholic Church have not yet grown universally strong, it is our hope that the ecumenical spirit and mutual esteem will gradually increase among all men.

At the same time, however, one should recognize that between these Churches and Communities on the one hand, and the Catholic Church on the other, there are very weighty differences not only of a historical, sociological, psychological, and cultural nature, but especially in the interpretation of revealed truth. That ecumenical dialogue may be more easily undertaken, despite these differences, we desire to propose in what follows some considerations which can and ought to serve as a basis and motivation for such dialogue.

20. Our thoughts are concerned first of all with those Christians who openly confess Jesus Christ as God and Lord and as the sole Mediator between God and man unto the glory of the one God, Father, Son, and Holy Spirit. We are indeed aware that among them views are held considerably different from the doctrine of the Catholic Church even concerning Christ, God's Word made flesh, and the work of redemption, and thus concerning the mystery and ministry of the Church and the role of Mary in the work of salvation. But we rejoice to see our separated brethren looking to Christ as the source and center of ecclesiastical communion. Inspired by longing for union with Christ, they feel compelled to search for unity ever more ardently, and to bear witness to their faith among all the peoples of the earth.

21. A love, veneration and near cult of the sacred Scriptures lead our brethren to a constant and expert study of the sacred text. For the gospel "is the power of God unto salvation to everyone who believes, to Jew first and then to Greek" (Rom. 1:16).

Calling upon the Holy Spirit, they seek in these sacred Scriptures God as He speaks to them in Christ, the One whom the prophets foretold, God's Word made flesh for us. In the Scriptures they contemplate the life of Christ, as well as the teachings and the actions of the Divine Master on behalf of men's salvation, in particular the mysteries of His death and resurrection.

But when Christians separated from us affirm the divine authority of the sacred Books, they think differently from us—different ones in different ways—about the relationship between the Scriptures and the Church. In the Church, according to Catholic belief, an authentic teaching office plays a special role in the explanation and proclamation of the written word of God.

Nevertheless, in dialogue itself, the sacred utterances are precious instruments in the mighty hand of God for attaining that unity which the Savior holds out to all men.

22. By the sacrament of baptism, whenever it is properly conferred in the way the Lord determined, and received with the appropriate dispositions of soul, a man becomes truly incorporated into the crucified and glorified Christ and is reborn to a sharing of the divine life, as the apostle says: "For you were buried together with him in Baptism, and in him also rose again through faith in the working of God who raised him from the dead" (Col. 2:12; cf. Rom. 6:4).

Baptism, therefore, constitutes a sacramental bond of unity linking all who have been reborn by means of it. But baptism, of itself, is only a beginning, a point of departure, for it is wholly directed toward the acquiring of fullness of life in Christ. Baptism is thus oriented toward a complete profession of faith, a complete incorporation into the system of salvation such as Christ Himself willed it to be, and finally, toward a complete participation in Eucharistic communion.

The ecclesial Communities separated from us lack that fullness of unity with us which should flow from baptism, and we believe that especially because of the lack of the sacrament of orders they have not preserved the genuine and total reality of the Eucharistic mystery. Nevertheless, when they commemorate the Lord's death and resurrection in the Holy Supper, they profess that it signifies life in communion with Christ and they await His coming in glory. For these reasons, dialogue should be undertaken concerning the true meaning of the Lord's Supper, the other sacraments, and the Church's worship and ministry.

23. The Christian way of life of these brethren is nourished by faith in Christ. It is strengthened by the grace of baptism and the hearing of God's Word. This way of life expresses itself in private prayer, in meditation on the Bible, in Christian family life, and in services of worship offered by Communities assembled to praise God. Furthermore, their worship sometimes displays notable features of an ancient, common liturgy.

The faith by which they believe in Christ bears fruit in praise and thanksgiving for the benefits received from the hands of God. Joined to it are a lively sense of justice and a true neighborly charity. This active faith has produced many organizations for the relief of spiritual and bodily distress, the education of youth, the advancement of humane social conditions, and the promotion of peace throughout the world.

And if in moral matters there are many Christians who do not always understand the gospel in the same way as Catholics, and do not admit the same solutions for the more difficult problems of modern society, nevertheless they share our desire to cling to Christ's word as the source of Christian virtue and to obey the apostolic command: "Whatever you do in word or in work, do all in the name of the Lord Jesus, giving thanks to God the Father through him" (Col. 3:17). Hence, the ecumenical dialogue could start with discussions concerning the application of the gospel to moral questions.

24. So, after this brief exposition of the circumstances within which ecumenical activity has to operate and of the principles by which it should be guided, we confidently look to the future. This most sacred Synod urges the faithful to abstain from any superficiality or imprudent zeal, for these can cause harm to true progress towards unity. Their ecumenical activity must not be other than fully and sincerely Catholic, that is, loyal to the truth we have received from the apostles and the Fathers, and in harmony with the faith which the Catholic Church has always professed, and at the same time tending toward that fullness with which our Lord wants His body to be endowed in the course of time.

This most sacred Synod urgently desires that the initiative of the sons of the Catholic Church, joined with those of the separated brethren, go forward without obstructing the ways of divine Providence and without prejudging the future inspiration of the Holy Spirit. Further, this Synod declares its realization that the holy task of reconciling all Christians in the unity of the one and only Church of Christ transcends human energies and abilities. It therefore places its hope entirely in the prayer of Christ for the Church, in the love of the Father for us, and in the power of the Holy Spirit. "And hope does not disappoint, because the charity of God is poured forth in our hearts by the Holy Spirit who has been given to us" (Rom. 5:5).

Each and every one of the things set forth in this Decree has won the consent of the Fathers. We, too, by the apostolic authority conferred on us by Christ, join with the Venerable Fathers in approving, decreeing, and establishing these things in the Holy Spirit, and we direct that what has thus been enacted in synod be published to God's glory.

Rome, at St. Peter's, November 21, 1964.
I, Paul, Bishop of the Catholic Church

There follow the signatures of the Fathers.

APPENDIX II

An Ecumenical Bibliography

The following book list is intended to be representative rather than complete, and to indicate some of the basic resources for understanding the ecumenical revolution. The list is restricted as far as feasible to books that have ecumenism as their direct subject matter. Books cited in footnotes above are not necessarily included here, so the footnote references form a supplementary topical bibliography.

I. BIBLIOGRAPHICAL RESOURCES

CROW, *The Ecumenical Movement in Bibliographical Outline*, National Council of Churches, New York, 1965, 80 pp.
The indispensable resource and the most up-to-date, although omitting materials relevant to Vatican II. Designed to supplement the following, which are still useful for earlier materials:

BRANDRETH, *Unity and Reunion: A Bibliography*, Adam and Charles Black, London, 1948, 159 pp.

MACY, "An Ecumenical Bibliography," appendix to Brown, *Toward a United Church*, Scribner's, New York, 1946, pp. 234-56.

ROUSE, "General Bibliography," in Rouse and Neill, eds., *A History of the Ecumenical Movement, 1517–1948*, Westminster, Philadelphia, 1948, pp. 747-86.

SENAUD, *Christian Unity, A Bibliography*, World's Committee of Y.M.C.A.'s, Geneva, 1937, 173 pp.

GUILLET, *The Ecumenical Movement: A Bibliography*, Kansas City Ecumenical Library and Research Center, 1964, 35 pp., mimeographed.

The following works have fairly full bibliographical materials:

CAVERT, *On the Road to Christian Unity*, Harper, New York, 1961, pp. 177–87.

GOODALL, *The Ecumenical Movement*, second edition, Oxford, New York, 1964, pp. 193–202.

LEEMING, *The Churches and the Church*, Newman, Westminster, 1960, pp. 312–24.

MACKAY, *Ecumenics*, Prentice-Hall, Englewood Cliffs, 1964, pp. 267–88.

II. THE BASIC ECUMENICAL DOCUMENTS

BELL, ed., *Documents on Christian Unity*, Oxford, New York, 4 volumes, first series 1920–24 (1924), 382 pp.; second series 1924–30 (1930), 225 pp.; third series 1930–48 (1948), 300 pp.; fourth series 1948–57 (1958), 243 pp.
The most comprehensive collection of documents, both Protestant and Catholic, at present available.

BROWN and NOVAK, *Documents of the Ecumenical Movement*, Doubleday, in process of publication.

World Missionary Conference, Edinburgh, 1910, Revell, New York, 1910, 9 volumes.
The full reports of the conference that brought the contemporary ecumenical movement to birth.

A. THE INTERNATIONAL MISSIONARY COUNCIL

The Jerusalem Meeting of the International Missionary Council, March 24–April 8, 1928, International Missionary Council, New York, 1928, 8 volumes.

The International Missionary Council Meeting at Tambaram, Madras, December 12 to 29, 1938, Oxford, New York, 1939, 7 volumes.

RANSON, ed., *Renewal and Advance: A Christian Witness in a Revolutionary World*, Edinburgh House Press, London, 1948, 228 pp.
The report of the 1947 Whitby conference.

GOODALL, ed., *Missions Under the Cross*, Friendship Press, New York, 1953, 264 pp.
The report of the 1952 Willingen conference.

ORCHARD, ed., *The Ghana Assembly of the International Missionary Council*, Friendship Press, New York, 1958, 240 pp.

B. LIFE AND WORK

BELL, ed., *The Stockholm Conference, 1925*, Oxford, London, 1926, 701 pp.
The official report.

The Church, Community and State Series, Allen and Unwin, London, 1937, 7 volumes.
Essays published in preparation for the Oxford conference.

OLDHAM, ed., *Foundations of Ecumenical Social Thought*, Fortress, Philadelphia, 1966, 211 pp.
The official report of the Oxford conference of 1937, reprinted after being long unavailable.

The Official Report of the World Conference on Church and Society, World Council of Churches, Geneva, 1967, 230 pp.

C. FAITH AND ORDER

VISCHER, ed., *A Documentary History of the Faith and Order Movement, 1927–1963*, Bethany, St. Louis, 1963, 246 pp.
The most useful single volume, with generous excerpts from all the Faith and Order conferences through New Delhi with other relevant World Council materials.

BATE, ed., *Faith and Order: Proceedings of the World Conference, Lausanne, August 3–21, 1927*, Doran, New York, 1927, 534 pp.

HODGSON, ed., *The Second World Conference on Faith and Order, held at Edinburgh, August 3–18, 1937*, Macmillan, New York, 1938, 386 pp.

Lund preparatory volumes:
BAILLIE and MARSH, eds., *Intercommunion*, Harper, New York, 1952, 406 pp.

FLEW, ed., *The Nature of the Church*, Harper, New York, 1952, 347 pp.

PEHR, HAYMAN, and MAXWELL, eds., *Ways of Worship*, Harper, New York, 1951, 362 pp.

TOMKINS, ed., *The Third World Conference on Faith and Order, held at Lund, August 15–28, 1952*, SCM Press, London, 1953, 380 pp.

MINEAR, ed., *The Nature of the Unity We Seek*, Bethany, St. Louis, 1958, 304 pp.

The report of the North American conference of Faith and Order, held at Oberlin in 1957.

Montreal preparatory volumes:

BRIDSTON et al, *One Lord One Baptism*, Augsburg, Minneapolis, 1960, 79 pp.

MINEAR et al, *The Old and the New in the Church*, Augsburg, Minneapolis, 1961, 96 pp.

EHRENSTROM and MUELDER, eds., *Institutionalism and Church Unity*, Association Press, New York, 1963, 378 pp.

MINEAR, ed., *Faith and Order Findings*, Augsburg, Minneapolis, 1963, Faith and Order Papers #37–40.

Reports of the commissions to the Montreal conference, on Christ and the Church, Tradition and Traditions, Worship, and Institutionalism.

RODGER and VISCHER, eds., *The Fourth World Conference on Faith and Order, Montreal 1963*, Association Press, New York, 1964, 126 pp.

D. THE WORLD COUNCIL OF CHURCHES

'T HOOFT, ed., *The First Assembly of the World Council of Churches: The Official Report*, Harper, New York, 1949.

Man's Disorder and God's Design: The Amsterdam Assembly Series, Harper, New York, 1949.

Four volumes bound in one, containing papers prepared for Amsterdam as well as the reports of the assembly.

'T HOOFT, ed., *The Evanston Report: The Second Assembly of the World Council of Churches*, Harper, New York, 1955, 360 pp.

'T HOOFT, ed., *The New Delhi Report: The Third Assembly of the World Council of Churches*, Association Press, New York, 1962, 443 pp.

E. ROMAN CATHOLIC DOCUMENTS

ABBOTT, ed., *Documents of Vatican II*, Guild Press, America Press, Association Press, New York, 1966, 794 pp., hardcover edition published by Herder and Herder, New York, 1966.
Includes all the promulgated documents of the council, with Catholic introductions and Protestant and Orthodox commentaries. The most useful and easily available collection.

ALVAREZ, ed., *Documents of the Holy See on Christian Unity*, Graymoor, Garrison, New York, 1961.
Pre-conciliar materials.

BELL, ed., *Documents on Christian Unity*, Oxford, New York, 4 volumes.
Cited above; includes selections from Roman Catholic ecumenical documents from the period 1920–48.

CRONIN et al, *The Encyclicals and Other Messages of John XXIII*, T.P.S. Press, Washington, 1964, 522 pp.
Illustrative of the "breakthrough" provided by Pope John.

KÜNG, CONGAR, and O'HANLON, eds., *Council Speeches of Vatican II*, Paulist Press, Glen Rock, 1964, 288 pp.

LEAHY and MASSIMINI, eds., *Third Session Council Speeches of Vatican II*, Paulist Press, Glen Rock, 1966, 334 pp.
Thus far the only primary source material of speeches made on the council floor. Excellent selections of ecumenical material.

MESSENGER, *Rome and Reunion: A Collection of Papal Pronouncements*, Burns, Oates and Washbourne, London, 1934, 152 pp.

III. INTERPRETIVE HISTORICAL MATERIALS

BAUM, *That They May Be One: A Study of Papal Doctrine (Leo XIII–Pius XII)*, Newman, Westminster, 1958, 181 pp.
An able treatment of the development of ecumenical themes in recent encyclicals.

CAVERT, *On the Road to Christian Unity*, Harper, New York, 1961, 192 pp.

A brief history of modern ecumenism by one of the Protestant ecumenical pioneers.

DUFF, *The Social Thought of the World Council of Churches,* Association Press, New York, 1956, 339 pp.

An ecumenical history of World Council thinking by an American Jesuit. An important resource tool.

GAINES, *The World Council of Churches: A Study of Its Background and History,* Richard R. Smith, Peterborough, 1966, 1302 pp.

An exhaustive treatment with much primary source material not easily available elsewhere.

GOODALL, *The Ecumenical Movement,* second edition, Oxford, New York, 1964, 257 pp.

An interpretive history with useful appendices.

HANAHOE, *Catholic Ecumenism: The Reunion of Christendom in Contemporary Papal Pronouncements,* Catholic University Press, Washington, 1953, 182 pp.

An early treatment of papal ecumenical concern.

HOGG, *Ecumenical Foundations,* Harper, New York, 1952, 466 pp. The basic history of the International Missionary Council.

LATOURETTE, *Christianity in a Revolutionary Age,* Harper, New York, 5 volumes, 1958–62.

A history of Christianity in the nineteenth and twentieth centuries. Particularly useful are Volume 4, *The Twentieth Century in Europe,* and Volume 5, *The World Outside Europe Since 1914.*

LEE, *The Social Sources of Church Unity,* Abingdon, New York, 1960, 238 pp.

A discussion of sociological forces at work drawing churches closer together.

MC NEILL, *Unitive Protestantism,* John Knox Press, Richmond, 1964, 352 pp.

An historical treatment of "unitive" forces at work in Protestantism since the time of the Reformation.

ROUSE and NEILL, eds., *A History of the Ecumenical Movement,* 1517–1948, Westminster, Philadelphia, 1948, 822 pp.

The basic reference work. A supplementary volume bringing the account from 1948 to the present time is in process of completion.

SKOGLUND and NELSON, *Fifty Years of Faith and Order*, Bethany, St. Louis, 1964, 159 pp.

A helpful interpretive guide through the labyrinth of Faith and Order materials.

SWIDLER, *The Ecumenical Vanguard*, Duquesne University Press, Pittsburgh, 1966, 287 pp.

A treatment of the recent contemporary scene, with special attention to the rise of the Una Sancta movement in Germany.

TAVARD, *Two Centuries of Ecumenism: The Search for Unity*, Mentor-Omega, New York, 1962, 192 pp.

An historical and interpretive study of both Catholic and Protestant developments.

VAN DUSEN, *One Great Ground of Hope: Christian Missions and Christian Unity*, Westminster, Philadelphia, 1961, 205 pp.

A treatment of the drawing together of the International Missionary Council and the World Council of Churches.

VILLAIN, *Unity: A History and Some Reflections*, Harvill, London, 1963, 381 pp.

A Roman Catholic treatment of Protestant ecumenism.

IV. REPRESENTATIVE TREATMENTS OF PROTESTANT-CATHOLIC ECUMENISM

ASMUSSEN et al, *The Unfinished Reformation*, Fides, Notre Dame, 1961, 213 pp.

Essays by representatives of the *Sammlung* group of German Lutherans who are eager for reunion with Roman Catholicism.

BAUM, *The Catholic Quest for Christian Unity*, Paulist Press, Glen Rock, 1965, 252 pp., (originally published as *Progress and Perspectives*, Sheed and Ward).

An important contribution by one of the most sensitive Catholic ecumenists.

BAUM, ed., *Ecumenical Theology Today*, Paulist Press, Glen Rock, 1964, 256 pp.

A collection of reprints of short but helpful articles from *The Ecumenist*.

BIANCHI, *John XXIII and American Protestantism*, Corpus Books, Washington, 1967.

A full treatment of the ecumenical impact of Pope John.

BOUYER, *The Spirit and Forms of Protestantism*, Newman, Westminster, 1956, 234 pp.

An early Roman Catholic assessment of Protestantism that is still very useful.

BRIDSTON and WAGGONER, eds., *Unity in Mid-Career*, Macmillan, New York, 1963, 211 pp.

A series of self-critical essays by leading ecumenists.

BROWN and WEIGEL, *An American Dialogue: A Protestant Looks at Catholicism and A Catholic Looks at Protestantism*, Doubleday, New York, 1960, 240 pp.

An early attempt at ecumenical exchange.

CALLAHAN, OBERMAN, and O'HANLON, eds., *Christianity Divided*, Sheed and Ward, New York, 1961, 335 pp.

Still the best single exploration of basic theological issues of division, with a distinguished group of contributors.

The *Concilium* series, a projected 50-volume series dealing with "theology in the age of renewal," published by Paulist Press, Glen Rock, dealing with the major areas, one of which is "Ecumenical Theology." Volumes thus far published in the latter category are:

KÜNG, ed., *The Church and Ecumenism*, Vol. 4, 215 pp.

KÜNG, ed., *Do We Know the Others?* Vol. 14, 180 pp.

CONGAR, *Dialogue Between Christians*, Newman Press, Westminster, 1966, 472 pp.

A collection of writings from one of the most significant of the ecumenical pioneers, covering the years 1935–1964. An important work.

CULLMANN, *A Message to Catholics and Protestants*, Eerdmans, Grand Rapids, 1959, 57 pp.

A plea for offerings for one another's poor during the Week of Prayer for Christian Unity.

KÜNG, *Justification: The Doctrine of Karl Barth and a Catholic Reflection*, Nelson, New York, 1964, 332 pp.

A pioneer work of ecumenical theological construction, indicating the similarities between Barth and the Council of Trent.

KÜNG, *Structures of the Church*, Nelson, New York, 1964, 394 pp.
A thorough examination of basic issues of ecumenical difference written from a Catholic perspective in the light of Protestant questions.

LEEMING, *The Churches and the Church*, Newman, Westminster, 1960, 340 pp.
A pre-conciliar, but still valuable, Catholic treatment of ecumenical theological issues. Helpful appendices.

MARGULL, *Hope in Action: The Church's Task in the World*, Muhlenburg, Philadelphia, 1962, 298 pp.
Exposition and interpretation of World Council materials.

MACKAY, *Ecumenics: The Science of the Church Universal*, Prentice-Hall, Englewood Cliffs, 1964, 294 pp.
A treatment of ecumenical issues from a systematic point of view by one long involved in ecumenical affairs.

MILLER and WRIGHT, eds., *Ecumenical Dialogue at Harvard: The Roman Catholic-Protestant Colloquium*, Belknap Press of Harvard University Press, Cambridge, 1964, 385 pp.
Outstanding essays by outstanding ecumenists both Catholic and Protestant.

NELSON, *Overcoming Christian Divisions*, Association Press, New York, 1962, 126 pp.
A brief and helpful introduction to the whole ecumenical scene.

PELIKAN, *The Riddle of Roman Catholicism*, Abingdon, New York, 1959, 272 pp.
A sympathetic yet critical treatment of Roman Catholicism by an outstanding Lutheran historian.

PELIKAN, *Obedient Rebels*, Harper & Row, New York, 1964, 212 pp.
Historical and contemporary treatment of the relationship of "Protestant principle and Catholic substance."

SKYDSGAARD, *One in Christ*, Muhlenburg, Philadelphia, 1957, 220 pp.
A pioneering work by a pioneering ecumenist that is still useful.

SHEERIN, *Christian Reunion*, Hawthorne, New York, 1966, 272 pp.
An up-to-date account of the American ecumenical scene by a particularly perceptive Roman Catholic ecumenist.

WILLEBRANDS et al, *Problems Before Unity*, Helicon, Baltimore, 1962, 149 pp.

Symposium by Catholic ecumenists for Catholic clergy.

WOLF, ed., *Protestant Churches and Reform Today*, Seabury, New York, 1964, 156 pp.

Protestant response to movements of renewal unleashed by the Vatican Council.

RODGER, ed., *Ecumenical Dialogue in Europe*, John Knox Press, Richmond, 1966, 83 pp.

Instructive essays from a series of French ecumenical meetings.

V. BOOKS DEALING
WITH THE VATICAN COUNCIL

ANDERSON, ed., *Council Daybook*, 3 volumes, National Catholic Welfare Conference, Washington, 1965–66.

Press releases, interviews, and valuable data about each session of the council.

BEA, *The Church and the Jewish People*, Harper, New York, 1966, 171 pp.

A commentary on the council's declaration on the Church and the non-Christian religions, by the man most centrally involved in its evolution.

BERKOUWER, *The Second Vatican Council and the New Catholicism*, Eerdmans, Grand Rapids, 1965, 264 pp.

A solidly theological appraisal of the relation between new currents in Catholicism and their implementation at the council.

BLANSHARD, *Paul Blanshard on Vatican II*, Beacon Press, Boston, 1966, 371 pp.

An appraisal, appreciative on balance, of the achievements of Vatican II by one of Catholicism's most outspoken critics.

BROWN, *Observer in Rome: A Protestant Report on the Vatican Council*, Doubleday, New York, 1964, 271 pp.

Day-by-day report on the second session, from the standpoint of a Protestant observer.

FESQUET, *The Drama of Vatican II: The Ecumenical Council*

June 1962–December 1965, tr. by Bernard Murchland with an American introduction by Michael Novak, Random House, New York, 1967, 864 pp.

A full report on all four sessions by the most consistently well-informed journalist covering Vatican II.

HORTON, *Vatican Diary*, United Church Press, Philadelphia, 4 volumes, 1964–66.

A full Protestant account by the only person to attend every meeting of the council.

JAEGER, *A Stand on Ecumenism*, Kenedy, New York, 1965, 242 pp.

A full history and exposition of the decree *On Ecumenism*.

KAISER, *Pope, Council and World: The Story of Vatican II*, Macmillan, New York, 1963, 250 pp.

Very helpful account of the first session, written at a time when information on the council was hard to get.

KÜNG, *The Council, Reform and Reunion*, Sheed and Ward, New York, 1961, 208 pp.

The most important pre-council volume, still very useful as a picture of creative contemporary Catholic thought.

KÜNG, *The Council in Action*, Sheed and Ward, New York, 1963, 276 pp.

Collected essays on ecumenical themes related to the first session.

KÜNG, *The Changing Church*, Sheed and Ward, London, 1965, 152 pp.

Essays published after the third session.

LINDBECK, ed., *Dialogue on the Way*, Augsburg, Minneapolis, 1965, 270 pp.

The fullest theological assessment of the achievements of the first three sessions, by distinguished Lutheran scholars.

LEEMING, *The Vatican Council and Christian Unity*, Harper, New York, 1966, 333 pp.

An extensive history and exposition of the decree *On Ecumenism*, with valuable appendices.

MAC EOIN, *What Happened at Rome?*, Holt, Rinehart and Winston, New York, 1966, 192 pp.

The best small volume on the council as a whole, by a distinguished Catholic journalist.

MILLER, ed., *Vatican II: An Interfaith Appraisal,* Association Press and University of Notre Dame Press, New York and South Bend, 1966, 656 pp.

The proceedings of a conference held at Notre Dame. Extremely valuable essays on the development of the most important council texts, together with evaluation by Catholic, Protestant, Orthodox, and Jewish participants.

NOVAK, *The Open Church,* Macmillan, New York, 1964, 370 pp.

A book about the progress of the second session that is also a significant statement about contemporary Catholic possibilities.

OUTLER, *Methodist Observer at Vatican II,* Newman Press, Westminster, 1967, 189 pp.

Essays written during the council by the man most likely to write the definitive history of Vatican II.

QUANBECK, ed., *Challenge and Response: A Protestant Perspective of the Vatican Council,* Augsburg, Minneapolis, 1966, 240 pp.

Evaluative essays by Lutheran scholars on the documents promulgated at the fourth session.

RYNNE, *Letters from Vatican City,* Farrar, Straus and Company, New York, 1963, 289 pp.

RYNNE, *The Second Session,* Farrar, Straus and Company, New York, 1964, 390 pp.

RYNNE, *The Third Session,* Farrar, Straus and Giroux, New York, 1965, 399 pp.

RYNNE, *The Fourth Session,* Farrar, Straus and Giroux, New York, 1966, 368 pp.

The four "Rynne" volumes, the pseudonymous production of a group of Roman Catholics, constitute the fullest and most important interpretation of the council. Each volume also contains invaluable appendices.

SERAFIAN, *The Pilgrim Church,* Farrar, Straus and Company, New York, 1964, 281 pp.

A negative assessment of the second session.

SKYDSGAARD, ed., *The Papal Council and the Gospel,* Augsburg, Minneapolis, 1961, 213 pp.

The most important pre-council volume from the Protestant side, produced by a group of Lutheran scholars.

TRACY, *American Bishop at the Vatican Council*, McGraw-Hill, New York, 1966, 242 pp.

An illuminating "bishop's-eye" view of the council.

WENGER, *Vatican Council 2*, Volume I, *The First Session*. Newman Press, Westminster, 1966, 688 pp.

The first of what promises to be the fullest series of conciliar reports. Fr. Wenger's accounts in *La Croix* during the council were basic source material for conciliar interpretation.

YZERMANS, *American Participation in the Second Vatican Council*, Sheed and Ward, New York, 1967.

Primary source material on the contribution of the American bishops to conciliar discussion.

VI. JOURNALS

Cross Currents (103 Van Housten Fields, West Nyack, New York).

A pioneering quarterly containing ecumenical writing of a high order. Many important articles by European theologians have appeared here for the first time in English. Full book-review section in each issue.

The Ecumenist, A Journal for Promoting Christian Unity (Paulist Press, 304 West 58th Street, New York, New York 10019).

A bi-monthly journal, usually about 24 pages, with informative articles by Catholic, Protestant, and Orthodox contributors, and significant excerpts from important ecumenical documents.

Ecumenical Review (150 route de Ferney, 1211 Geneva, 20, Switzerland; can be ordered through the World Council of Churches, 475 Riverside Drive, New York, New York 10027).

The indispensable resource for World Council reports and articles by leading ecumenists. A quarterly review published by the World Council since its formation. Recent years have seen increasing attention to the Protestant-Catholic dialogue.

Faith and Order Trends (National Council of Churches, 475 Riverside Drive, New York, New York 10027).

A brief quarterly, giving news of ecumenical activity, with occasional interpretive articles, developments in the Faith and Order movement, and annotated bibliographical comment. Co-edited by an Episcopalian and a Jesuit.

Herder Correspondence (Herder and Herder, Inc., 232 Madison Avenue, New York, New York 10016).

A monthly magazine produced under Roman Catholic sponsorship, providing otherwise unavailable coverage of world Catholicism, with attention also to non-Catholic Christianity. Coverage of Vatican II and of new movements in the Catholic world has been outstanding.

Journal of Ecumenical Studies (Temple University, Philadelphia, Pennsylvania).

The first scholarly journal to be devoted exclusively to serious ecumenical investigation. A journal appearing three times a year, under Protestant and Catholic joint editorship, with Orthodox and Jewish representation on the editorial board. Contains long scholarly articles on ecumenical subjects, extensive book reviews, and digests of articles from ecumenical journals throughout the world. Indispensable to scholars.

Among journals not dealing exclusively with the ecumenical scene, the following are particularly useful:

Christianity and Crisis
Christian Century
The Commonweal
National Catholic Reporter
Catholic World
Christianity Today

VII. A FEW KEY WORKS
NOT YET AVAILABLE IN ENGLISH

AUBERT, *Le Saint-Siège et l'Union des Églises*, Éditions Universitaires, Brussels, 1947, 160 pp.

Helpful commentary on papal documents up to 1945.

LAMBERT, *Le Problème Oecuménique*, Editions du Centurion, Paris, 1962, 2 volumes.

A sensitive treatment by a Roman Catholic, the more remarkable in that it anticipates many currents of Vatican II.

LITTELL and WALZ, eds., *Weltkirchenlexicon: Handbuch der Okumene,* Kreuz-Verlag, 1960, 1756 pp.

A basic resource reference work.

THILS, *La Théologie Oecuménique,* E. Warny, Louvain, 1960, 83 pp.

Treatment of ecumenical theology as existential confrontation, as a dimension of all theology, and as a special discipline.

THILS, *Histoire Doctrinale du Mouvement Oecuménique,* E. Warny, Louvain, 1955, 260 pp.

A pioneering Catholic interpretation of the development of the World Council of Churches.

Note: books on the Second Vatican Council by Yves Congar, and René Laurentin are in process of being translated from French into English.

INDEX

Abbott, Walter, 10, 189, 245, 266, 300
Abraham, seed of, 249, 257, 262
Acts, Book of, cited, 13–14, 361
Aggiornamento, 155, 162, 179, 187
Agnosticism, 273
America, 82, 233, 307
American Dialogue, An, 49–50, 70, 99, 214, 225, 293, 327
Amsterdam Conference of the World Council of Churches in 1948, 35, 39–40, 53, 88, 116–17, 244, 255–57, 270, 326
Anglican Church of Canada, 142
Anglican-Presbyterian Conversations, The, 145
Anglicans, 44, 47, 89, 139, 144, 197, 283, 309, 357
Anguish of the Jews, The, 247, 271
Antiisms, 48, 89, 253–54
Anti-Semitism, 165, 253–67, 272
Apostles, 113, 262, 297, 347–48, 352, 358–59, 361
Apostles' Creed, 15, 140
Apostolicae Curae, encyclical, 49
Apostolic Roman See, 51, 64, 182
Arab states, 258–61, 264
Assumption of the Virgin into Heaven, 198–99, 298, 308
Athanasian Creed, 15
Atheists, 316–17
Athenagoras, Patriarch, 113
Atomic weapons, 156, 165
Augustine, St., 104
Auschwitz, 252, 269
Authoritarianism, 91, 93, 105, 166, 301, 348
Authority of the Faith, The, 28

Baille, John, 27, 135, 332
Baltimore Catechism, 72
Baptism, sacrament of, 138–40, 196, 206, 284, 334, 338–39, 345, 347, 349, 363–64
Baptist Church, 44, 48, 313
Barth, Karl, 1, 3, 20, 58, 87–88, 98–99, 272, 277, 279
Basis of Religious Liberty, The, 216

Baum, Gregory, 44, 49–50, 52, 64, 77, 81–83, 236, 267–68, 284, 292, 302, 341–42
Bea, Augustin Cardinal, 47, 64–65, 258–59, 264–65, 291
Beliefs, 39, 220, 317
Benedictines, Order of, 57, 90, 161
Berkovits, Eliezer, 251–52
Bible, 266, 309; theology of, 18, 32, 51; interpretation of, 21, 253, 301, 364; study of, 64, 162, 281, 291, 338, 340. *See also* Holy Scripture
Bigotry, 6, 271, 310
Birth control, 186, 284–87, 318
Bishop, office of, 55, 140, 148, 158, 167, 172, 296, 353, 355
Blake, Eugene Carson, 146–47, 290, 322
Blessed Virgin, cult of, 299
B'nai B'rith, 266
Bouyer, Louis, 92–94, 97
Boyer, Charles, 54, 57
Braaten, Carl, 101, 117, 131–33
Brent, Charles, Bishop, 27, 32
Brown, Robert McAfee, 49, 109–10, 146, 225, 236, 327
Buber, Martin, 268, 273
Buddhism, 28, 178, 304

Calvin, John, 22–24, 89, 211–12
Calvin: Theological Treatises, 24
Canterbury, Archbishop of, 34
Cardinal, office of, 59, 160, 165, 172, 231
Catholic Approach to Protestantism, The, 51
Catholic Biblical Society of America, 69
Catholic Church, 19, 52, 155, 282, 302; contemporary activities of, 5–7, 56, 81–82, 96, 103, 165, 176; and Protestantism, 7, 70–71, 82, 249, 270–71, 304, 336; in America, 8, 61; scholarship in, 23, 70, 73, 92, 162, 177–78; opponents of, 24, 52, 227, 234, 243; on ecumenism, 47, 49, 54, 56, 59–60, 78, 156, 198; theologians in, 56, 70,